Magnolia Gardens

Caroline Bridgwood was born in Cheltenham, and studied English at St Edmund Hall, Oxford. After graduating in 1982 she worked in London for three years before becoming a full-time writer. She is the author of two previous novels, *This Wicked Generation* and *The Dew of Heaven*, also available in Pan. Caroline Bridgwood now lives in Oxfordshire.

CAROLINE BRIDGWOOD

Magnolia Gardens

PAN BOOKS
in association with Macmillan

First published 1987 by Macmillan London Ltd
This edition published 1988 by Pan Books Ltd,
Cavaye Place, London SW10 9PG
in association with Macmillan London Ltd
9 8 7 6 5 4 3 2 1
© Caroline Bridgwood 1987
ISBN 0 330 29915 8

Printed in Great Britain by
Richard Clay Ltd, Bungay, Suffolk

In memory of the magnolias of
Locarno; symbols of hope

PART ONE

The First Generation

48 Magnolia Gardens
Frank

I'D ALWAYS DREAMED OF CAMELOT, of having a place all my own. Somewhere with a bit of class; a bit of character. And as soon as I saw Magnolia Gardens I knew at once that was where it should be. That was where I should build us a home, the like of which you never saw. Magnolia Gardens was exactly the sort of place I'd always wanted to live in.

I was born in 1880 in Catford, London.

Not the London that we know now, of course. The London I was born in was all tenement buildings, courts reeking with manure from the costermongers' ponies, barefist fighting, street gambling, large families, and teeming pubs with kids playing on the step while their mothers drank. You've no idea how important booze was in the lives of most of those people.

Not to my parents. Now, they were different. They were what we used to call 'port wine teetotallers'; that is just a small glass of port on a special occasion and nothing more. That was how we could afford a whole house, you see – ten shillings a week, it was – because Father didn't drink away all his wages in beer.

Not that our house was anything special, mind. It was just one of those blackened brick terraces without a garden that faced on to a row of identical houses with a cobbled alley in between. But at least we had the whole house to ourselves – a front parlour for best, a kitchen with a proper range and a scullery, and upstairs two bedrooms. No bathroom of course. We bathed on Saturdays in front of the range in the kitchen, and Mother put up a screen around us so we were decent. There was a privy out at the back – not a proper water-closet but an earth-closet. Mind you, they were very efficient after their own fashion, if you used ashes to damp down the odours as we did. I'll say more about privies later.

You see, a lot of people in Catford in those days were living in one room. Whole families in one or two rooms, because they'd

9

rather spend the money on the booze than on the rent. And half the time they didn't know where their money was coming from next. But my father had a proper job and brought in a regular wage, and my mother worked, so we had a house and a decent sort of life. My father was called Frank – I was named after him, being the first boy – and he had a job on the machines at Collier's, the local boot-black factory. The factory owned most of the property round us, and we rented the house from them. No one owned their own house in those days, you see. You rented it, either from the factory-owners or from the Jews.

Father was a big spare man, handsome in his time, who could look quite dignified when he wore a suit and collar. He was quiet and sober and didn't laugh much – God-fearing, some people call his sort – but that didn't mean to say he had no humour in him. He was good with us children, took time to play with us when we were small. It was just that he took life seriously.

My mother, Ettie, was the one who liked to laugh. She'd throw back her head and laugh and laugh, and Father'd say: 'Oh, Ettie, you're a lovely girl! My Ettie! There's a girl!' (Except it sounded more like 'gel'.)

Us children didn't understand this when we were young, because to us Mother wasn't a girl. How could she be? I suppose life had taken its toll on Mother, but she was still a good-looking woman. I get my high colour from her, and she had sparkling black eyes, just like the jet buttons on her best dress. She'd had seven children, which wasn't so very many in those days, but all of them died except me and Agnes, who's five years younger. Children did die in those days. You just accepted it.

We were the exception in our street, having a whole house to live in. The rest had no respect for that sort of thing, used to call us 'F—ing so-and-so's' and all that lark. People in the street came and went, mind, because if you didn't pay the rent you were always getting moved on. They moved quickly (or 'flitted', we used to call it), usually at night because they owed rent, or had all their windows broken by the neighbours to get them to move on.

People you meet nowadays think the working class are all the same. They're not. Not as it makes much odds to the rest of the world, but there's the rough working class and the respectable working class. The respectable type value education, work regularly, go to church and don't drink. The rest seem to be born old, kids so independent and shrewd it's unnatural. They have to be – there's no one bringing them up while their parents wallow in ignorance and godlessness, pouring their money down their throats.

Agnes and me weren't left to drag ourselves up. Mother made sure of that. Oh, she taught us manners, as far as she could. Put a knife in your mouth, you got a hiding for that.

'Get them arms off the table, Frank!' Slap.

What she really should have said – I know this now – was 'Do you mind taking your arms off the table, please?' but Mother set more store by action than by words.

Mind you, Mother could read, and that was something not many could boast in Catford. When she was a girl her mother was in service as a cook, and the lady of the house had been a good soul who saw to it that young Ettie went to a board school and learned to read. She gave Mother a book, too, the only one we had in the house. *King Arthur and the Knights of the Round Table* it was, and how she loved that book! I was disappointed because it had no pictures. But it was bound in morocco with pages edged in gold. Mother used to run her red chapped fingers over their smooth gold surface when the book was tightly closed. Then she would open it up and read the stories out loud to us, all about Camelot, which we thought was the most wonderful place in all the world.

We didn't have many nice things like that book, but what we did have we treasured. One Saturday, Mother and Father came home all excited. They'd been to a sale at the church hall and they'd bought a ewer, basin and chamber-pot in white china, patterned with big purple irises.

'What's that for?' I asked. 'To p— in?'

I got a slap for that. Mother didn't like what she called my gutter language, things I picked up at school.

'No,' she says, 'it's bedroom china.'

'Well, aren't we going to use it?' says I, thinking of the long cold walk to the earth-closet.

'Of course not; it's far too pretty for that!'

And she put it in the parlour.

The other thing we had was a piano. Mother was musical, she had a lovely voice, and when Father first heard her sing he said: 'Ettie, girl, you sing like an angel, and one day I'm going to buy you a piano, just you see!'

So he put by a few coppers every week and eventually he saved up enough. It took him about ten years, but Father was determined when he took a fit in his head to do something. The piano was secondhand, of course, but that didn't spoil Mother's pleasure when she saw it. She opened those dark eyes wide and clapped her hands to her mouth. Then she let out a sort of sighing gasp.

'Oh, Frank!' she said. That was all she could say: 'Oh, Frank!'

The piano was in the parlour, and Father had put a little round stool in front of it, covered in purple plush. Mother sat down on it, opened the lid and rested her hands ever so gently on the keys. Me and Agnes stood in the doorway of the parlour, just staring. I reckon our eyes must have been out on stalks, just like Mother's.

'Play something, Ettie,' said Father in this low tight voice that we'd never heard before. 'Play something for me.' Then he saw us kids. 'Go on, hop it!'

The door closed in our faces, and then the music began.

Wonderful tunes she could play – and of course she sang, too. We used to have some lovely times after we got the piano. People would come over for Sunday Tea – family mostly, Mother's sisters and their kids. Oh, and there was such a to-do about getting it ready! In the parlour of course. Out came the one Irish-linen tablecloth, and the food was laid out on it: shrimps and winkles, thin bread and butter, sticks of celery and fancy cakes. Mother would have on her best dress with the jet buttons, and the bedroom china would be given a special wash and polish and put back on the whatnot. I used to go and run my fingers over it sometimes. I loved the way it felt smooth and cool under my skin and, most of all, I loved its round curves.

The place looked just so by the time the guests arrived, and then there'd be tea, and then music. The lamps would be lit, and we'd gather round the piano while Mother played 'Bells Across the Meadow'. We all liked that one; it made us think of the countryside and fresh air. Then it would be 'Somewhere a Voice Is Calling', and the ladies got out their handkerchiefs and dabbed daintily at their eyes.

They weren't all serious songs. My favourites were 'When the Old Dun Cow Caught Fire' and 'Knock 'Em in the Old Kent Road'; you know – thumbs in waistcoats or armpits, daft postures and a bit of larking around. It was always 'Oh, come on,

Frank; you show 'em how!' (Frank being me, not Father), because even in those days I was a bit of a show-off, a bit big for my boots, and had a good loud voice. There'd be a glass of port to finish off with, or some of the men had whisky as a chaser. Oh, wonderful evenings they were, with the lamplight sparkling on Mother's jet buttons and showing up the pretty irises on the china.

Believe it or not, it wasn't so unusual for a working-class family to have a piano, but usually it was the first thing to go when things got a bit hard and you ended up in the pawnshop. You never 'popped' your wedding ring, but pianos were fair game; people were always pawning them. There was a pawnshop on the corner two streets down – they were always on a corner so that everyone could see the three brass balls hanging there. In the window there was the usual garish display of jewellery, watches with Albert chains, medals, and above it a sign saying 'UNREDEEMED PLEDGES' in big black letters. I used to like to stop and stare in the window, but Mother would tighten her lips and hurry past, saying: 'There but for the grace of God, Frank Finzel, there but for the grace of God!'

And I used to wonder, if she was desperate, which would she pawn last – the bedroom china, the piano, or *King Arthur and the Knights of the Round Table*?

I suppose it was a good sort of childhood really. We didn't have much, but we had enough and we were happy. We knew where we were, knew what to expect. Not like the kids who came home from school to find the furniture out on the street and their mother half-conscious in the boozer. Mother believed in Values. That was her God, if you like. She used to take in sewing, fancy work, but she always stopped what she was doing when Agnes and I came in from school and got our tea ready. Even when she had a bad chest and had to go to the hospital, she made sure that a neighbour came in to get us off to school and Father off to work and to cook a bit of haddock for his tea. If you were sick, they'd take your washing home with them and do it in their own copper, neighbours would. Most were the rough sort, but there were a few good neighbours in our street. They wore aprons and squabbled in the street, but they'd help out when help was needed.

Agnes and I went to the local elementary school and there was no truant in our family, you can be sure of that. Oh, no, Mother wasn't having that! Some of the kids used to press a bone button into their throat and come in and say: 'Look, miss, I got ring-worm!' And they'd spend months off school that way. Mother tied our hats on with our mufflers and gave us our luncheon-packets wrapped in greased paper and sent us off on our way, and God help you if you bunked off! School was all right. I liked history best; I was interested in other people, curious about them. Still am, I suppose. Maths was a struggle, but I stuck with it until I got the better of those vulgar fractions, denominators, multiples, the lot. That pleased Father, I think. He never said anything, but when Agnes and I did well he got this sort of shiny look in his eyes. And you knew he was pleased then.

They handed out regular canings at school, and then your crime was written down in the Punishment Book and they referred to it if you ever applied to the school for a 'character'. Always getting caned, I was. Didn't matter what I did.

'He hit me first,' I'd say to teacher, 'I hit him after.'

'Oh,' she said, 'I know you, Frank Finzel.'

Weekends were best. There was the Bioscope or the Grand Music Hall or the Saturday markets lit by arc lights and naphtha flares in the winter. Then we'd run home and warm ourselves by the range while we waited for the bathwater to heat. On Saturday we always had a special tea: joint and gravy followed by currant duff or blancmange in the summer. A good meal once a week, that was one of Mother's Values. She was very clever when it came to getting her meat, too. They had no refrigerators in those days, so meat that wasn't sold on the day was chucked out – or sold off cheap. Mother used to send us up to the butcher's at the last minute and get us to ask for 'two penn'orth of block orna-ments'. That's the bits of meat they used to decorate the window-display. You could get decent steak that way.

Sundays weren't quite so good, because it meant church. We walked to the parish church, past the organ-grinder who always played 'Jesu, Lover of My Soul' or 'Rock of Ages' on a Sunday. I suppose he thought he'd get more money that way. All the men were in their best suits and straw boaters, quite a sight. Father looked especially fine with his silver-mounted walking cane. Mother had his picture taken, just like that. Everyone had their set places in church and they stuck to them, even though there were no named pews as such. Everyone in their place, you know – the captain of the Boy's Brigade at the front, with two dea-

14

conesses and the headmistress of the Church Infant School. We were about halfway back. Then after dinner it was Sunday School for us kids, all afternoon, while Father sat in the parlour with a Marcella cigar ('a little luxury at thruppence a time', he used to say) and a copy of *Reynolds News*. I always had this suspicion that Mother used to sing for him at these times, but they never said.

What else was there? Well, there were summer holidays at a boarding house in Ramsgate. Oh, Mother took ages packing the suitcases! Then we took the horse-bus to Clapham Junction and caught a train from there. Even Clapham seemed grand to us then, with the big houses on the Common. Agnes and I loved the beach, and the cockles and mussels and pint jars of shrimps. Father saved carefully for that holiday, just like he saved for the piano, and Mother always used to take us to one side and whisper: 'Don't forget to thank your dad for the lovely holiday; tell him what a smashing time you had, eh?'

Summer was the best time of year. There were horse-brake trips into the country and the fairs on Blackheath. Roundabouts, swingboats, coconut-shies, side-shows. Oh, I love a fair! There were brass-band concerts in the park, with programmes at a penny a go. If you had a programme, you were quite the thing, you know; it looked affluent. And there was just playing in the streets to look forward to in the summer, with it being light. Hopscotch, Knock Down Ginger. Knock Down Ginger was my favourite. That's when you knock on people's doors and run away. Mother went mad at that; it was against her Values. She'd take me to one side and say: 'Frank Finzel, if you do that once more it'll be your father who gives you a hiding, not me!' Slap. Not as it made any difference; we still went on playing it, me and Agnes. I was always leading Agnes off into trouble.

Agnes liked Christmas best; the magic-lantern shows at the Shaftesbury Hall, Borough, and all the carols. I liked Christmas, too, but I've thought about it a lot and I reckon the best thing about my childhood wasn't Christmas. It was the trips to Hyde Park. That's what made the deepest impression on me when I was a child. We used to ride on the top deck of the horse-bus to Hyde Park. We'd see the scarlet-coated guardsmen and the rowing boats on the Serpentine; we'd stroll amongst the well-dressed promenaders. Mother'd be in her best hat, and for a short time we were part of a more colourful life.

The first time I went, I'd never been in the West End before. I couldn't believe it, I really couldn't. Who were these people? They were from another world. Oh, and the houses! The glitter of paint and the brasswork on the doors! It was all so different from Catford; and I could feel, although it was never said, that these people lived by different rules.

'But, Mother,' I said, 'King George said, "We are one great family"!'

'He meant in the eyes of God,' says Mother. 'Here on earth it's different. People are different, see.'

I should add here that at this time the working classes had little time for socialism. We were an apolitical lot. And someone had done some calculations and worked out that sharing out Britain's wealth on a *per capita* basis would make everyone a ha'penny better off.

'What's the point?' we all said. We had no time for ideas like that. But those trips to the West End made me think a bit harder.

It was usually just me and Mother who went. Agnes said the horse-bus made her feel giddy. We'd see the servants opening and closing the doors of those tall elegant houses, and white-gloved hands holding the doors of broughams with coats of arms on the side, and I'd get to thinking about it all. Not that I didn't like what I saw; I did. I've loved shiny things all my life, and my eyeballs were popping out at the sight of those carriages, the craftsmanship, the gleaming curves of the woodwork. Oh, I would have liked one all right!

But I spoke my thoughts out loud to Mother one day. I said: 'Surely these people must be very happy, with so much to enjoy.'

'Oh, no,' she said, and she was shaking her head so that the ripe cherries on her hat trembled. 'Oh, no. Money isn't happiness. I want you to remember that, Frank Finzel. They're not the same thing at all.'

When I was fourteen, two things happened. Father died and I started to work for a living. The one was a direct consequence of the other, as you might imagine.

He died suddenly, just dropped dead one day when he was at the factory. They said it was his heart. They brought him home and put him in the parlour, then they fetched us home from school.

Then it was the funeral. All in black and off to the cemetery in a string of broughams, drawn by horses with high waving black plumes. The neighbours drew their blinds in sympathy until the cortège came back. Then the men had port in the parlour and the women sat upstairs with cups of strong tea and cried. Agnes and I hung around somewhere in between the two, in our uncomfortable black clothes, not quite sure what to do with ourselves.

It was the first funeral I'd been to. I'd been to a wake before, though. Now, there's a story! It was for the husband of a woman who lived down at the end of our street once. They were a rough pair, you know, like I've already described, throwing their money away on beer and beating their kids, but the wife had asked for Mother's help when her old man was first taken sick, and Mother said she felt sorry for her so it seemed the decent thing to go and pay her last respects. So there we were at the wake, with old Albert lying on view in his coffin and everybody acting like he's not there, and drinking, and the children all playing on the floor. Then someone chucks a fag end into the coffin. I must be about seven or so, so I get up and I say: 'Mother, Mother!'

'*What?*' She's annoyed, see.

'That man in the coffin is alight, look.'

'*What!*'

Then suddenly everyone's shouting, 'Old Albert's alight, he's alight, quick!' and they get their jugs of beer and sling it into the coffin!

I shall always remember that. And afterwards Mother said to me: 'It's not going to be like that when your father goes. It's going to be dignified.' And it was.

I was still at school when Father died; and, although Mother said she could manage, that she had a bit put by, I could tell that she was worried about where the money was going to come from to pay the rent. Because the house belonged to Collier's, see, the place where Father had worked. She began talking about moving somewhere smaller, moving near her sister in Bermondsey. So I upped and told her, bold as brass, that I was going to Collier's to tell Mr Partington that I would have Father's old job. Tell, mind you, not ask. Mr Partington was the factory manager and a very important fellow, judging from the size of the wreath he sent to the funeral.

Well, you can imagine there was a hell of a row about that! Mother had her heart set on me finishing at school and maybe even going to college. She insisted that she would manage somehow.

'Oh, Frank!' she said. 'You know an education's important if you're to make something of yourself. That's what we wanted for you and Ag; that's what we always said!'

'Now, Mother,' I say, getting up and putting my arm around her shoulder, nearly as tall as she is, 'I'm still going to make something of myself, you'll see. It'll just have to be in a different fashion, that's all. Now, don't you go worrying, Mother. I'll just go and talk to Partington, that's all.'

You see, I was already acting like the head of the family and telling my mother what to do. Getting a bit big for my boots, I was. So off I went, through those mean streets and through the big iron factory gates with 'S. COLLIER & SONS 1856' in a banner across them, and into Mr Partington's office.

He asked me to sit down, but I stood up until I'd said what I'd come to say. I thought it looked better that way. The truth is that I've never been very tall, though I had a good healthy colour and bright eyes like my mother and I was square and solid-looking. I looked as though I might be a country lad, and that was something people set great store by in those days. The air was so dirty in the city that most people couldn't help but look pale and ill.

'Well,' said Mr Partington after he had heard my tale, 'I must say, Finzel, I admire your spirit! Your father was a good worker, and you look strong and healthy. How old did you say you were?'

'Sixteen, sir,' I lied.

It was customary to lie about your age when you went for a job. Mr Partington probably didn't believe me, but he played along with my game like a good sport. I remember thinking at the time that he seemed a fair man. He was tall with sad eyes and a drooping handlebar moustache.

'I can offer you a position, Finzel,' he said. 'Indeed, I feel it incumbent upon me to do everything I can for your family in view of your father's sad demise. A loyal long-serving employee of the firm. . . .'

I suddenly had this picture of Father working himself to death at those machines and I felt a coldness about my heart. It wasn't fear; I don't know what it was.

'. . . I'm afraid you won't be receiving the same wage that your father earned, though. At least, not until you're trained.'

I grinned at him. 'That don't matter, sir, I'm a quick learner.'

And I was. Within eighteen months of starting at Collier's I was bringing home as much as Father had. Mother still went on a bit about how I ought to be in school, but the rent was being paid and we weren't going short, so in the end she shut up. I even bragged about how I'd put our Agnes through college some day if she wanted. A real cock of the walk I was in those days.

I was one of the youngest working at Collier's but I made more noise than most of the rest put together. 'Fearless Frank Finzel', they used to call me. There were some that used to mouth a bit about me riding for a fall, but on the whole I was pretty popular. I used to entertain them, see. I'd get up on the table and give them a song with a lot of eyeball-rolling and winking, do a bit of a comic turn. Oh, they laughed at that all right! And if ever there was a scrap on you could count on me being in the thick of it. I came home from work with a black eye once, and Mother cried, but she gloried in my boldness really, she did. She used to get this little smile round the corners of her mouth when I told her what went on up there at Collier's.

I might have got myself into real trouble if I hadn't been a favourite of Mr Partington's. He took a special interest in how I was getting on, and some said it was on account of his only son having been killed in some foreign campaign. Anyway, the strangest thing happened when I was about nineteen. Partington came up to me on the shop floor and said: 'I understand that you have quite a singing voice, Finzel.'

'Yes, sir,' I said. 'That's what some people reckon.'

Then he just comes out of the blue and says it: 'Mrs Partington and I are having a little musical soirée. Would you care to join us at home for supper?'

Afterwards, of course, the other men said I shouldn't have gone. In fact a few of them said so beforehand as well, when they heard about this invitation of mine.

'Sounds queer to me!' said one.

'You shouldn't ought to go mixing with the bosses,' said another.

'No good'll come of it! We don't want you fancying yourself any more than you already do!'

Of course, I just said to myself that they were jealous. Mother had her heart set on me going, too. This was getting on in life, as far as she was concerned. She said to be sure and get a good look

19

at all the curtains and carpets and that, so as I could describe it all to her later.

I don't remember much about the Partington house now, except that it was all hung with velvet and little pom-poms and it smelled of mothballs. They had one of those fancy new houses over on Shooters Hill, and my first thought was how Mother would have liked a detached house like that. Refined, she would have called it.

When old Partington had invited me, he'd given the impression that there would be other people there, but there was just me and him and Mrs Partington. Well, I didn't quite know what to make of that.

'This is Frank,' Mr P. said. 'He has a fine singing voice, so I hear, and now he'll have someone to accompany him.'

Mrs P. shook my hand, very formal like. She was his second wife, and from the look of her I'd say quite a bit younger than him. She had a mass of brown hair coiled up in a very fancy style which I tried to take account of for Mother's sake, and merry eyes which had flecks of green in them. Quite plump, she was, but as she sat down at the table her skirt was flicked to one side and I saw a trim ankle and pretty little feet. Of course I'd never met anyone quite like her, a proper lady and all. I couldn't take my eyes off her as we ate, though she was all grave, with her eyes turned down and that. We were in the dining room at this huge table, so shiny I just wanted to run my fingers over it. There were gas-lights on the wall, but the table was lit with candles in these bloomin' great silver candlesticks that could have killed a man if you'd clobbered him with one. So we ate the meal, which was more like tea than supper to my mind, all cold meats and dainty little messes and wine, which I'd never had before and which made me feel sort of dizzy in my head.

Then Mr P. put his napkin on the table and said: 'And now Florence would like to accompany you, if you'd care to sing, Frank.'

We went into the parlour, but he didn't come with us; it was just me and her. Well, before I had time to think about this, I saw the piano. What a piano! It was a grand; long and elegant and silky-looking, with beautiful little candelabra on either side of the music-stand. Oh, Mother would love some of those, I was thinking.

So Mrs P. sat down and started running her fingers over those milk-white keys. Wonderful music, it was, thrilling. Not at all the sort of stuff that poor Mother used to play.

'Do please tell me what that was,' I said, all on my best behaviour.

'Brahms,' she said. 'Rhapsody, Opus Seventy-Nine. Now, what are you going to sing, Mr Finzel?'

'Do please call me Frank.'

'Very well, what are you going to sing, Frank?'

So we did some of those old parlour songs, and I acted it up like hell with all the eye-rolling bit and the tender looks, and she seemed to like that. I sang 'The Rosary' and 'For You Alone', and then it was her turn and I asked her if she knew 'The Dying Poet', which was always one of Mother's favourites. She played it wonderfully, did Mrs P. and I felt quite transported, so I retaliated with 'Somewhere a Voice Is Calling'.

'Oh, Frank, how beautifully you sang that!' She turned to me with those big hazel eyes and fluttered her lashes at me. 'Thank you so much, my dear.' Her hand was on mine, giving it a squeeze, and I noticed that she was breathing so heavily that you could see the lace ruffle on the front of her dress, rising and falling. 'Of course you know that I must give you a kiss now, don't you?'

She stood up, and suddenly she was very close and the room was too warm.

'Look here!' I exclaimed. 'I don't think I know what you mean!'

'Oh,' she said. 'It's merely a custom. It's customary for the accompanist to kiss the soloist in tribute. Didn't you know that?'

I was about to say no, that I didn't know anything at all except that I shouldn't really be there, when she put her arms around me and kissed me. It wasn't difficult for her to reach me, seeing as how I wasn't much taller than her anyway, and she clasped me so hard that I couldn't see anything and I couldn't breathe, and I thought: Hello, what's this, then? – and it dawned on me that it was her tongue and she was snaking it to and fro on my closed lips. I didn't know what to do. I suppose I must have gasped or something, because her tongue came inside of my mouth and I remember thinking: What's this for? I was nineteen, but I was green as grass.

And then the parlour door opened and Mr P. stood there. Yes, just like that, just like in those cheap music-hall comedies or a

Buster Keaton film when the father comes in and he's got his hands on the lovely daughter. He acted the part just like that, too. He went all red under his whiskers and he said: 'Would you mind telling me what's going on, Finzel?'

I got the sack.

Mr Partington said nothing about it that evening, but when I got to Collier's the next day he called me into his office.

'An unpardonable error of judgement on your part, Finzel,' he said. 'I have no option, regrettably, but to let you go.'

I tried to explain that it was nothing to do with my judgement, that his trollop of a wife obviously behaved like a bitch on heat when she heard a young man exercising his vocal chords, but, oh no, he wasn't having that. I suspect she was more than he could manage and he already knew it.

'And I thought you were a fair man!' was all I said, and I walked out.

'Wot's yer game, then, Frank?' the others said as I came out of the office. 'Trying to get in the boss's good books, eh?'

'Trying to get in his old woman's drawers more like!' said someone else, and they all had a good laugh about it.

When I told them I'd lost my job they were angry, but they'd told me, they said, that no good would come of it.

I was angry, too, especially when I saw how Mother cried and took on about it.

'Let me go up there, Frank,' she sobbed. 'Let me go up there, see if I can get him to change his mind.'

'Not bloomin' likely, Mother!' I said. 'Not after the way he's treated me!'

I wasn't so much angry about being out of work as angry because the likes of Mr Partington could decide the fate of the likes of Frank Finzel, just like that. It got me to thinking a lot, and I decided that no one was ever going to have that power again. From now on, I'd be my own boss. I'd have to learn a trade of course, and it didn't take me long to hit on plumbing. It was always me that had to fix the old earth-closet when things went wrong, and unblock the kitchen drain, and I'd got interested in the mechanics of it all.

So for the next year I earned my keep doing odd jobs – selling newspapers and bags of coke, that sort of thing – while I studied at night school at the local institute. Seems to me I didn't enjoy the learning part of it very much when I was at elementary school, but this was different. I couldn't get enough of it. I loved the history. We learned all about the history of plumbing and sanitation. Did you know that the Romans had a goddess of the common sewer? Cloacina, her name was. Mother wouldn't believe me when I told her that. I would have told her more, but she used to put her finger on my lips and say: 'Enough! I don't want no more of that dirty talk in here, Frank Finzel!'

Agnes was all agog, though, and I used to tell her all the things I'd learned, all about washdown-closets and valve-closets. It's a queer thing, you know, that the ancient Minoans had a plumbing system and used pipes to carry water, but it took us until the last hundred years to get around to making water-closets. All those wonderful medical breakthroughs, all that agricultural and industrial machinery – they make the humble WC seem so obvious, don't they? And yet we were all for tipping it into a hole and letting it lie there.

That's exactly the sort of talk that Mother was set against but, as I kept telling her, *sanitas* is Latin for 'health', isn't it? Not about the removal of dirt, that wasn't what I was learning, but about the promotion of health. Good drains mean better health. We learned all about those daring sanitary heroes of Victorian times: George Jennings, Sir Joseph Bazalgette, Edward Johns, John Shanks and the greatest of them all, S. Stevens Hellyer. His *Principles and Practices of Plumbing* was our standard reference work. A good book it is, too: he really knew how to tell a good story. '*A good plumber*', he said, '*should follow the scent like a hound after a fox.*' The scent being the smell from the privy or the bad drains.

Oh, Mother used to pull such a face when I read aloud from Hellyer's book, like she was going to faint.

'Listen, Mother,' I said, 'don't be like that. These men are like social crusaders. Trying to save lives, that's what they're doing!'

'Go on with you!' she said. 'I don't know what's got into you these days, Frank Finzel! It's not like you to be so bloomin' serious!'

'It's because I've had my eyes opened, Mother! Up there at the Institute. In them classes! Night after night! If bad drains are responsible for poor health, then who's to say they're not responsible for people turning to the only medicine they know: spirits and beer!'

She hated excessive drinking so much, did Mother, that I knew I could get her attention this way. 'Now,' I said, 'listen to this awhile.'

And I took out my copy of Hellyer and read in my best voice, only going a bit slow over some of the longer words: *'There are a thousand gates to death! Few are wider, or open more readily than in our own homes, when unlocked by noxious gases or bad air from drains, etc.'*

I looked up at Mother at this point, all glowing with enthusiasm.

She nodded her head up and down like she was considering evidence. 'Well,' she said, 'put like that, yes. I can't disagree with that, can I? What else does he say?'

I went on: *'It is an astonishing thing that while the civilised world use up the resources of their countries in training soldiers and sailors in the art of war, teaching them how to protect life and property from the ravages of war, they do comparatively nothing to teach the people – to teach plumbers, the professions and the trades concerned – how to make healthy homes; that is to save life from the diseases arising from filth and badly drained houses.'*

I slammed the book down on the table.

Mother nodded again. 'Very improving.'

From then on, we read a bit out of Hellyer every night.

After I'd finished at the night school, I set myself up in business.

I'd set a bit of money aside, and I used it to buy a set of tools. I put the word around a bit, took out an advertisement in the local paper, then I had to sit and wait for the work to come in. Of course it was slow at first. People round where we lived didn't have much use for plumbers. They didn't have much that you would have called plumbing, see. After a bit, word got round to the better houses in the area, and then I was busy, rushed right off my feet. It was mostly the same sort of stuff: cleaning grease-traps, mending geysers, putting in air-inlets or new seals.

But I did my bit for reform. I tried to explain the importance of lead soil-pipes and cobweb grating and why the old-fashioned Hopper closets – shaped like buckets, they used to be – were no good for anything but growing rhubarb. To tell the truth, it was the outside of the closet that interested me most, the shape. I loved their smooth curves. I saw all sorts: Trapless Twin-Basin Closets, Ventilating-Pan Closets, Treadle-Action Closets, Pneumatic Closets.

Some beauties, too. I went to the house of a vicar once, and he had a 'Thunder Bowl' in his bathroom. That's a closet with a bloomin' great eye painted in the pan, and when you lift the lid it plays a little tune.

Oh, I would have loved one of those for Mother, but she chose a Beaufort from Chelsea. More refined, she said.

I started off with my plumbing about the beginning of 1902. By 1905 I was doing very nicely but still living at home in Catford with Agnes and Mother. It wasn't like nowadays with young people rushing off to set up home as soon as they can. No, you stopped at home until you were married.

Marriage – oh, that was something we had words about all night, Mother and me!

'What I want to know', she said to me at least once a week, 'is when you're going to start doing a bit of courting!'

Agnes was at the local college by then, training to be a teacher, and she wasn't walking out with no one, neither, being a quiet girl and not what you'd call the marrying kind.

'Oh,' says Mother, 'I don't know! How did I get lumbered with two serious types like you? You used to be such tearaways when you were kids!'

'Look, Mother,' I used to say to her, 'all in good time, eh? I'm too busy for courting now!'

And it was true, too. I had so much work, it seemed to take up all the hours in a day. I decided I would have to get a mate. So I asked around and I found a young lad called Sam. Eight years younger than me, is Sam, so he'd have been around fifteen. He was a street kid, living on his wits since his old man had been in the nick and his old woman had been hitting the bottle. When I first met him, he was holed up in some men's lodging house – a right flea-pit, it was – and he was chesty and underweight, but there was something about him that took my fancy, so I offered him the job. He looked like he could use a decent meal, but it wasn't out of pity that I was taking him on. He's smart and quick, so I reckoned he'd be useful.

Now, Sam's a Cockney, a real one, born in the sound of Bow bells and all that. People from Catford aren't Cockneys, see; that's south-east London, but as far as the East Ender is concerned you're a southerner, practically from the suburbs. I was full of curiosity about what you might call 'the real East End', and young Sam offered to take me up there and show me around.

In fact he told me I ought to spread my catchment area to include it, because around Stepney and Bethnal Green there were a few decent streets of houses which might need the services of a plumber.

He came to me one morning and said there was a family in Bow just moved down to London from Scotland, decent people, and they needed their privy seeing to. Lord knows how Sam came to hear about them; he just picked up odd bits of information all over the place. So off I go with Sam to the East End.

It made me sad, what I saw there.

There were some houses that had a touch of what Mother would have called refinement but, what with all the offices and banks springing up on the edge of the City, it was as if this great rotten tide of humanity was being pushed ever further eastwards. All piling on top of one another, so that tenements spring up, gardens are built on, villas are divided and subdivided into smaller dwellings and there's not a single bloomin' tree or patch of green to be seen. Waxing lyrical I am, I admit it, but standing there and looking at those streets – it affected me. I just stood there with my bag of tools in my hand, and I felt sad.

Then: 'Come on, Sam,' I said. 'Let the dog see the rabbit.'

He led me up some steps and rang the bell. A frowzy slavey answered the door and showed me into a parlour where, to my delight, there was a piano.

'I'll tell the missus you're here.'

The 'missus' turned out to be a young woman, about the same age as myself. My first thought was how different she was from Mother and our Agnes. They were both plump and rounded, but this girl was all angles, and her thin shoulderblades stuck out of her frock, all awkward.

But she had a pretty smile, and she said, 'How do you do? I'm Miss McDowell,' in that lovely lilting Scots accent which I'd hardly ever heard before. Well, you never did in Catford. There weren't even any Irish around then. She led me downstairs to where the water-closet was.

'Oh,' I said, 'a Peacock Blue Poppy, and a fine one, too!' I ran my fingers over its smooth pedestal, stencilled with a really fine tracing of flowers and butterflies.

'The trouble is', she murmured in that low lilting voice, 'it's not . . . emptying properly.'

'Well, let's have a look, then, shall we?' I said, rubbing my hands, very bright and cheerful. She watched me anxiously while I worked. 'Well, it's quite obvious, I'm afraid,' I said. 'You've got an old D-trap down there leading into the soil-pipe, and your dip-pipe – that's the bit that comes down from the bowl – it's all corroded, eaten through. What that means is none of the stuff's getting through!'

'Oh, surely not?' she said, her voice all high and nervous.

I glanced at her, and she was blushing. Of course, I realised that the business of getting rid of the body's waste products embarrassed her deeply. I recalled one of our great sanitary heroes, Daniel Bostel, who watched the reaction of two Victorian ladies faced with a water-closet at the 1851 Exhibition. He said they turned away as if they had been forced to look at a huge and glistening behind. I shall never forget how much that tickled my fancy when I read it: '*a huge and glistening behind*'.

So I leaned back on my heels and explained to Miss McDowell in a kindly tone how it all worked. 'It's really very simple, see. . . .'

I told her how the dip-pipe was made of unsuitable material, and it just needed to be replaced with a similar pipe of drawn lead without a soldered seam. Then I told her how the trap worked, and why in my opinion an 'S' bend was better for the job, drawing pictures in the air with my hands. After a while she seemed to lose her embarrassment and become genuinely fascinated, and why not? Sanitation is a very fascinating subject, as I have already described. But she kept her eyes modestly cast down all the time.

I recommended her to read *Principles and Practices of Plumbing*.

'For Mr Hellyer reminds us', I cried, 'that our own King Edward, when he was Prince of Wales, said that if he were not a prince he would like to be a plumber! And, by the way, I couldn't help noticing that you have a one-and-a-half-inch pipe for your kitchen waste, but really it should be a—'

I got no further, because at this point there was a bloomin' great crash in the hall and Sam appears at the top of the stairs shouting for all he's worth: 'Miss! Miss! You'd better come quick!'

'Oh, no, that'll be Donald!' she said in a low voice, all distressed.

27

She made for the stairs, and I dropped my tools and followed her. A young fellow was being half carried, half dragged through the front door. His lip was split, and his face all bruised and bleeding.

'Oh, no . . . I'll get a cloth,' says Miss McDowell, frowning but looking like she's seen all this before, and worse. She begins to mop at his face, tut-tutting to herself. I'm wondering if he might be her fancy fellow, but when she catches me staring at him she says: 'This is my brother, Donald McDowell. And it's not what you think.'

It turned out that young Donald was one of them new socialists, but people round their way didn't want to know about socialists, so he was regularly beaten up – in parks and tramcars, on the street. That day I met him, he'd been giving a talk at a pro-Boer rally, and the angry crowd had dragged him down from the platform and beaten him cruelly. He was brave, I'll give him that, and determined not to give up.

'Ay, I'm no stranger to pitched battles on collapsing staircases!' he cried, giving me a lopsided grin that revealed most of his front teeth had been bashed in. 'D'you think I might interest you in joining the cause?'

'Oh,' I said, 'Mother would never rest easy in her bed if I started up with all that sort of lark. I'm surprised your mother doesn't feel the same, you being so young.'

'Mother's dead,' he said, his smile disappearing. 'There's just me and Dad and Jeanie who've come down to London.'

Well, I had no desire to join his cause, but I was anxious to talk to him, him being an educated fellow, so I *did* join him for a whisky while I sent Sam off to get the new parts we needed. He moved about their front parlour with self-assurance, and his lean wiry body had a dignity to it, despite the holes torn in his jacket and the trickle of bloody spittle from the corner of his mouth. I was downright shocked when he told me he was only just eighteen. I had him down as ten years older.

It was then that I realised I was in the presence of someone quite extraordinary.

'It's a joke, isn't it?' he said, stretching himself out on the hearthrug. 'Them cursing us socialists when we're trying to educate them about their rights as human beings. They've sunk too low, the people in the East End. That's the problem. Their lives are ruled by an ugly and repulsive philosophy – living for alcohol. The demon drink. . . .'

'Oh, yes,' I said, 'I see that where I come from.'

'And the best they can hope for', he went on, 'is a dull animal contentment, the sort they get from a full belly and an evening pipe with their precious beer, their precious *'arf and 'arf*! Ay, what use have they for socialism?'

'It's poor health,' I said, eager to chip in my bit. 'That's what it is.'

Donald nodded and took a gulp of his whisky, smacking his lips like it was manna from heaven. 'Ah, the drop that warms you, eh? You're right, you know, Frank' – I'd asked him to call me Frank; the Scots are so formal with their Mr This and Mr That – 'they're sunk into their deadly inertia because of all that tarry smoke and sulphuric acid they breathe in the air. What chance do they have? They're sapped mentally, morally and physically before they've even grown up!'

We went on in this fashion for a while, till Sam came back with the parts and I had to get to work again. 'Well,' I said, 'I don't know what you're used to in Edinburgh, but these stories aren't new to me. I've seen the week's wages drunk in a night and the kiddies chucked against the wall until their little bones break!'

'But you say you're a stranger to the East End?' asks Donald.

'That's right.'

'Well, I'll wager you, Frank, I'll wager you that for any poverty you've seen in your neighbourhood, any deprivation, I can show you things ten times worse!'

Of course I never could resist a challenge like that.

'Oh ho!' says I, stepping forward bold as brass and grabbing the hand that he was holding out to me. 'You're on!'

We came back to the McDowells' house about a week later, me and Sam.

I was hoping to catch a look at Miss Jeanie, but she wasn't about, and Donald took us out straight away, out into Stepney. We walked down those wretched streets, the three of us, Donald striding ahead, me hurrying to keep up as he's taller than I am, and young Sam, who's got a queer right leg, shambling along behind.

Oh, the faces we saw! Haunted they were, and the bodies

stunted as if the foul air had stopped them growing. Sometimes you saw a girl who caught your eye because she was pretty (mind, it was sometimes hard to tell through all the muck and filth), but somehow you knew it was never going to last. A weak delicate sort of prettiness that was just going to fade away like it had never happened. And the kids were rooting through garbage, poking about in the mud for rotten potatoes, beans and vegetables.

I wondered what Mother would have had to say if she could have seen the houses. They made the back-to-backs in Catford look like bloomin' palaces! They had no yards, front or behind, and the roofs of those hovels were covered with filth. In some places a couple of feet deep. And all about them was a landscape of fish and meat bones, garbage, mucky rags, old boots, broken crocks. Riding on it they were, those houses, like on the tide of some God-awful sea. And the stink!

Donald must have guessed what I was thinking, because he grinned that sour grin of his. 'Ay!' he said. 'No place like home, eh? And some people can't even afford these. There are piece workers earning one and six a week, and a room – at least, they pass as rooms; pestilential holes, I call 'em – can cost six shillings. Work that one out!'

Well, even young Sam, who had no arithmetic, could see the sums didn't add up. Sam said nothing but, then, he'd been born round there, maybe even lived in one of these places. He'd seen it all before. No wonder he ran down south of the river.

We stopped outside one of the houses.

'There are seven rooms in this abomination,' Donald said. 'Twenty or so people cooking, eating and sleeping in six of them, and the seventh's a sweatshop. You ever seen a sweatshop?'

Sam didn't say anything.

'No,' I say, 'never.'

Donald grins again like a hungry wolf. 'Right!' he says, rubbing his hands. 'There's a lovely treat in store for you.'

The sight of those places just seemed to make him go crazy; he acted like he was demented. You heard him laughing and then you looked in those wild eyes of his and you saw sheer bloody rage.

He led us into the house. To get in we had to climb over a woman who was sitting on the step nursing her baby and we could see her breasts, all naked and scrawny. Just inside the door we fell over an old woman who was sitting in a pool of her own urine, unable to move from her chair. Then into the seventh room. The sweatshop.

It couldn't have measured more than seven feet by eight, and there were five men in there with their work-tables and hardly room to swing a bloomin' rat, though they had rats in plenty, so we heard. These five men were 'sweating' in there, attaching uppers to the soles of shoes. There were no windows, and the air was so thick you could touch it. A lamp burned in the corner, loading up the room with its fumes.

But the worst of it was that they were proud of their thirty bob a week for a fourteen-hour day! Donald called one of them over to talk to us, and it was just pathetic the way he bragged about getting them tacks into the shoes so fast.

'An' you should see us sweat!' he says, his hollow eyes gleaming at us. 'Just running from us! If you could see us, it'd dazzle your eyes – tacks flyin' out of our mouths like from a machine. Look at my mouth!'

He went and showed us his teeth, all worn down from the friction of the metal in his mouth. All coal black and rotten. Horrible. So I said to him then: 'Can't you clean that stuff off them?'

'Oh,' he says, 'I clean my teeth, or else they'd be worse.'

Well, we came out of that place, and we were just sort of silent. Then Sam, who hasn't said a word since we set out, pipes up.

'I can show you a place wot makes that lot look well off,' he says in his funny cracked little Cockney voice.

So we followed him back through the streets a mile or two until we got to Spitalfields Gardens, in the shadow of Christ Church. It's like a park, except you never saw a park like it anywhere on this earth. No flowers, and horrible dingy grass surrounded by sharp spiked fencing. We just stood and stared.

An old woman (well, I think she was old, but she could have been any age) strode past us, a bit rickety on her pins, but sturdy enough in her intention. She had a couple of bulky bundles fore and aft, covered with sacking, which must have contained her wardrobe and feminine possessions, such as they were. Too independent for the poorhouse, that one, I thought. There were benches here and there, and on them some wretched piles of what Donald calls 'humanity', all rags and filth and sores and skin diseases. On one bench there was a baby asleep on the hard seat, with no pillows or covering. But, what seemed worst of all, to my mind – worse than it having no coverings – there was no one appearing to mind it. It just lay there.

As I said, the three of us just stood there looking, and nobody had said a word since we got there.

It was Sam who broke the silence.

'Those women,' he said, 'those women'll sell themselves for thruppence or a loaf of stale bread.'

Well, Donald went on being dragged down from speaking platforms and beaten up, and I kept on going back to the McDowells' house in Bow.

Not as I'd joined the socialist mob, though sometimes I feel like one now when I read in the *Daily Mail* about the goings-on of the 'Bright Young Things'. None of them Bright Young Things has seen a mining village, and how many of them want to? Of course socialism is all very fashionable now, in 1931, but our Donald was thirty years ahead of his time. A remarkable man.

Anyway, to get back to 1905 or thereabouts. I kept an eye on young Donald's business, but it was Jeanie McDowell I really wanted to see. That girl had done something to me, right from the moment when I first set eyes on her. Hard to say what it was really, because she wasn't what we in Catford would call a good-looker. Just like a skinny beanpole she was, with great sad eyes.

Like I said, there was something about her. Donald understood what it was, and he summed it up better than I can. He caught me staring after her one day as she carried the tray of tea out of the room.

He laughed that queer laugh of his. 'Ay,' he says. 'She's lovely, isn't she, our Jeanie? Lovely as only a Celt can be!'

'Yes,' I say, nodding. I was lost for words, which is not like me.

Donald laughs again. 'They know how to bewitch you Southerners, don't they, our Celtic women? It's the contrast between the look of longing in their eyes and the quiet pride in their bearing. You're done for, man!'

It was then that I got into one of my quarrels with him. We were always having them.

'Done for!' I said. 'If that's what it is, it's a wonderful thing to be!' I was drinking Scotch and feeling generous with my advice. 'Let me give you a tip, Donald: never try to understand a woman. Enjoy them, but never try to understand them!'

32

Donald's face darkened. 'I think that's a very dangerous way of thinking,' he said in a cold voice. 'A way of thinking that's held back the human race. We'll never break our chains as a society unless we learn to treat women as equals, with comradeship.'

I opened my mouth to argue, to say that he'd just been banging on about Jeanie's womanly mystique, then thought better of it.

'Well, I may be done for,' I said, 'but if your Jeanie stays here in the East End any longer she'll be done for, too! It doesn't agree with her; anyone can see that!'

Of course at that time I had no knowledge of Jeanie's feelings for me; she was so quiet and dignified like, but I knew she wasn't happy living in Bow. Their father, Mr McDowell, had brought them down to London – not as how he'd had much choice in the matter. He was a schoolteacher, a university-educated man, and I thought the world of him, I did, for his cleverness and his kindness. He reminded me of my own father a bit, being on the serious side. Anyway, he'd been a teacher in a select boys' academy, but they'd thrown him out for his political beliefs and he'd come down to London to find work. He'd found a job in a grammar school in Walthamstow. That was something else Donald and me had a quarrel about.

'Dad's never recovered from the move,' he said to me one day.

I didn't really understand. 'But he's got a good job!' I said. 'And a decent wage coming in. That's more than—'

He laughed in my face. 'You're a real little capitalist at heart, aren't you, Frank? Can't you think further than profit and loss? What about principle? It's the *shame* that's destroyed Dad. The shame.'

There were other more pressing problems for a family like them living in the East End. People like them were slowly being driven out by the greed of the landlords. They rented a whole house, see, for a pound a week, but if the landlord divided that house up into the sort of horrible dwellings you find everywhere else in the East End he could charge six shillings a week for each room; and say he'd got seven rooms – that's two quid or more a week. And with all their savings put by for Donald's college education the McDowells couldn't afford two quid a week, not unless Jeanie went out to work – and what sort of work's she going to find in a place like that?

These were the things that were going through my head in those days, so it wasn't long before I'd decided that Jeanie

McDowell was a damsel in distress and it was up to me to rescue her, just like one of that lot in *King Arthur and the Knights of the Round Table*.

Well, she had other ideas at first, did Jeanie. She was a bit cool towards me to start with, but Fearless Frank Finzel doesn't take no for an answer, and after a bit – but very slowly, mind – we started courting.

Of course Mother was delighted. Jeanie used to come over for tea on Sunday afternoons, and you can be sure she got the whole treatment – the white linen tablecloth, the celery sticks, the glass of port, everything.

Mother never wasted any time letting me know what she thought. 'Oh,' she said after the first time Jeanie came, 'she don't say much, does she?'

'No,' I said, never lost for an answer, 'but what she says is worth hearing.'

Mother was smiling. 'I was going to say, Frank Finzel,' she said, 'that it doesn't matter, since you do enough talking for the pair of you.'

Mother was right; there must have been something in the combination, because in the spring of 1908, after a long courtship, Jeanie McDowell agreed to become Mrs Jeanie Finzel. I had a nice bit of money behind the business, and it had prospects, so we could settle down quite comfortably. I wasn't just an odd-job plumber by then, but running a legitimate business with premises and that. I had an office up Lewisham way, where I did the paperwork and people came in to settle the accounts, and there was a nice cosy flat above the shop with two bedrooms. Mother came over a lot to help us get the place fixed up, and when it was ready we got married.

It was in our parish church in Catford, to please Mother, but we kept it quiet with Jeanie not being a member of the Church of England or anything. Donald was our best man, and he's an atheist.

Well, I gave Jeanie a Chinese carpet for her parlour as a wedding present, and we were very happy, except for one thing. Oh, yes, I'd fixed up everything in our lives just so, but there was this one thing I didn't seem to be able to fix.

I remember coming in late one night after being called out to mend someone's oblique spigot outlet, and I found Jeanie sitting on the edge of our bed, crying. I'd never seen her in tears before.

So, of course, I sit down beside her, taking care not to crease the new sateen eiderdown, and I say: 'Jeanie love, what is it?'

'Oh, Frank?' she says, squeezing my hand tight. 'I do so wish we could have a baby!'

It was four years, and we'd almost given up, and then it happened.

The best thing was seeing the tears of joy in Mother's eyes.

'Oh,' she said, 'I've prayed for this, Frank!'

In November 1912, Amelia Jean Finzel was born, and I doubt there was a couple in the land as pleased to see their firstborn as we were. Jeanie's a year older than me, see, so she was thirty-three by then, and all along she'd been afraid it was her fault because she was too old.

Donald, who was in Oxford studying for his doctorate in political thought, sent flowers and a telegram: 'YOU'D BETTER NOT MAKE US WAIT FOUR YEARS FOR THE NEXT ONE FINZEL.'

Well, we just laughed and sat there staring at this screaming tadpole of a baby who was going to achieve such wonderful things in her life.

'I shouldn't be surprised if she wasn't the first woman prime minister!' I said.

'Oh, Frank,' said Jeanie, blushing. 'You and your nonsense!'

But neither of us could stop staring at her.

Donald's telegram was a bit prophetic in the end. Something seemed to do the trick, because in just under two years we made him an uncle for the second time. And I'm telling the truth when I say I wasn't disappointed not to have a boy. Our second daughter was a quiet pretty baby, quite different from Amelia – Mel for short – who'd grown into a funny-looking little thing with the strangest eyes you've ever seen.

'What shall we call her, Frank?' says Jeanie as she cuddles the new arrival and I sit on the bed like the admiring father. See, to be honest, we'd only really thought of boys' names.

'How about Ethel, after Mother?' I say. 'She'd be awful disappointed if we don't.'

Jeanie pulls a face. 'I don't care for the name much,' she said.

That's my Jeanie all over; she always speaks her mind. In the end we hit on Ethne, which was a North Country name I'd never heard before, but it had a pretty ring to it and it was like enough to Ethel to keep Mother quiet.

Anyway, it was not long after Ethne was born that the Great War came. People were on the move in London, a lot of them shutting up shop and moving out of the city because they were afraid of the zeppelin attacks. It was on account of this that I got hold of a long lease on a house in the north end of Clapham. In a place called Magnolia Gardens.

I'd always rather fancied Clapham, ever since the days when we used to go through it on the bus to catch a train to Ramsgate.

All right, it's not as smart as the West End, but it's got a good, solid, prosperous feel. And Magnolia Gardens is one of the nicest crescents in the area. It leads off from the main road that runs due north, away from Clapham Common. As you turn into it there's a narrow avenue which forms a bottleneck, then another straight bit on the far side, with a dead end. Number 48 is at the far end. And in the middle there's a smashing garden, with trees and that. Our new home was nothing fancy, but what Mother might call 'substantial', detached Victorian with four bedrooms and a decent-sized plot of land around it. When I saw our next-door neighbour's house, there was no doubt in my mind that we were going up in the world. Number 50 looked to me then – being more or less straight from Catford as I was – like the sort of residence a prince wouldn't sniff at. It's a big double-fronted villa built by Thomas Cubitt in 1849 at the same time he built all those grand houses on the Common. When we first moved in I stood there looking at that big enclosed porch and the fancy gas-lamps on either side of the steps. I hadn't met our neighbour yet, but I'd heard he was a fellow by the name of Clifford.

'Oh ho, Mr Clifford?' says I. 'I'm going to be able to afford a place every bit as fine as yours one day – just you see if I can't!'

Of course, I got to see Robert Clifford every day in the end, striding through the Gardens in his posh overcoat with his bowler hat and his brolly, on the way to his chambers – he's a barrister, see. Then later on in an officer's uniform with a lot of scrambled egg on the shoulder when he got some soft job at the War Office. Amazing how quick we came to accept seeing uniforms everywhere. I never went to the Front and I regret that now, in a way. I thought about it, especially in 1917 when poor old Donald goes and gets himself slammed in the nick for being an objector, a 'conchie'. But my doctor said there was something queer about my chest and I wouldn't pass the medical, so that was that; I stopped at home.

Funny, isn't it? I'd never thought of myself as anything other than a perfectly healthy specimen, but all that time my chest had been on the blink. And if it hadn't been for the war I might never have found out.

The war changed everything.

The upper classes all got killed off, so there was more left for the rest of us, the 'little' men. And all through the war I'd been having ideas. I was still reading Stevens Hellyer, and I believed stronger than ever that the water-closet should be like a glorious throne as much as a welcoming wooden seat to sit on. Ever since Mother brought home her chamber-pot with the irises on it and told us it was too good to p— in, I took a fit in me head about sanitary ware being a thing of beauty and not just a necessary evil. I mean, you only have to look at the catalogues some of those early pioneers brought out: beautiful illustrations – what they call illuminations – full of imagination and inventive ideas. I brought home the Twyford one for Mother, and she rated it along with her *King Arthur and the Knights of the Round Table*.

In the old days closets were hand-made and you were at the mercy of the potters, who were slow to agree to making things like a flushing rim inside the bowl. But come 1916 it was mass production, everybody was getting their hand in, and I decided I wanted to have a go. Oh, I'd decided it way back, really, that I wasn't going to go around fixing D-traps for the rest of my life. Besides, I'd always preferred porcelain to pipes.

I had to wait until the end of the war before I could become a fully fledged sanitary engineer. Factory premises were impossible to get in south London then, being all taken up with armament production. But it was all to the good in the end. Because it meant that in 1918 everybody had bathrooms exactly like they'd had before the war, and they didn't want that now the slavey who'd emptied the chamber-pots was getting more money working in a factory. What did all that add up to? It added up to a boom time for sanitary ware that would have had old Stevens Hellyer dancing for joy.

'Oh, Frank,' says Mother, 'you're going to make water-closets? I'm sure I don't know whether to laugh or cry!'

I knew which I was doing all right. I was laughing all the way to my new factory premises in Nine Elms, near the river, where I employed twenty men to start with. I designed the moulds myself, and the patterns I was going to use, and I used the finest china clay.

Not much is generally known about the process of making sanitary ware, so I'll give you the benefit and explain it, just as I explained it all to Mother round about 1920. My designs are made up into a porous mould, and then the clay is liquefied with water and special chemical salts until you get something called 'slip'. Then you pour your slip into the mould, and it absorbs the water leaving the shape you want to be glazed and decorated. Of course, it's not as simple as that, and we made a lot of mistakes at first until we learned how to get exactly the right thickness and shape, and the right strength-to-weight ratio. Oh, we had some laughs in those days! I remember Sam removing a cast and just pointing at the result and saying: 'What in Gawd's name d'yer call that, then?'

Because, you see, what we didn't know at first was how much the thing shrinks during drying and the shape warps. That's why there's a preference for curves; it's easier to make the compensation in the design and get the shape right. Anyhow, we had our failures to begin with, but we got it right damn quick, I can tell you, or we'd have been out of business. We had a few standard designs – 'The Paisley' (named for Jeanie's birthplace), 'The Lancelot' and 'The Columbine' – and we took in special commissions. And it wasn't just WCs, either. We did baths and washstands, too. Churning them out, we were, because they were being snapped up as fast as we could make them.

Not even Mother could have said I hadn't got on in life by 1923, when I'd bought my third factory and could afford to buy her silver candleholders for her piano, and as many books as she could wish for. I felt I had to offer her a home in Magnolia Gardens, though Jeanie was dead set against the idea. Luckily, Mother had no wish to leave Catford, so I just kept on paying for a hansom cab to bring her over for her Sunday tea, and take her back again, and everyone was quite happy with the arrangements.

Sam found rooms in Battersea and kept on with me as my assistant at a handsome salary, and after Donald was finished with his studies I even offered *him* a job. But he just laughed his strange laugh and said: 'Ach, no, I think I'd better stay here in

Oxford and enlighten the masses. Anyway, if the party found out, they'd have my balls off for a capitalist traitor!'

Donald despised money. And when he banged on and on about it I used to remember what Mother said about money not buying happiness, and I'd wonder if she was right. After all, I'd tell myself, I had more money now than I'd ever had, and I was as happy as I'd ever remembered. There had to be a connection.

In 1924 I had my first ever trip abroad. I was thinking of branching into therapeutic sanitary ware – steam-baths and the like. Hydropathic cures had been all the rage in America for years, and I didn't see why we British shouldn't jump on the bandwagon. When my interest became known in the trade I was invited to attend an educational seminar in New York entitled 'A Harmonious Doctrine of Balneatory Hygiene'.

'My little Frank, in America,' sobbed Mother. (She wasn't well at the time, and tended to get a bit weepy.) 'Who would have thought it?'

New York in July was bloomin' hot and horrible. When I wasn't touting for contracts and trying to improve my knowledge of the principles of hygiene I was sitting under a ceiling fan in the fancy hotel and cursing the Prohibition.

But I was curious, see, curious about the New Yorkers and the way they spent their money. So when Bob Kelly, the conference organiser, offered to introduce me to one of his most important clients I jumped at the chance.

'We'll go over to his place, OK?' said Bob.

'His place' was an enormous pile on Park Avenue, and our host turned out to be none other than J. McGarrett Wharton III, one of America's richest men. Bob and I were ushered into a mirrored anteroom which had a bloody great vase in it, made out of green malachite and about eight feet high.

'Blimey, look at that, will you?' I said. 'I could make quite a bath out of a lump of rock like that!'

I was reaching out a finger to touch it when the door opened and this young bloke came in wearing white gloves and gleaming brass buttons on his coat and carrying a tray with champagne and glasses. Well, Bob and I stood around chatting about this and that, but it was a bit like being in a dentist's waiting room and all I could think about was meeting this amazing host of ours.

Finally he appeared. He was a funny-looking bloke: tiny with a shiny bald head and pointed ears. Bit like a pixie. He described the things we saw in this flat deadpan voice, without a scrap of emotion – not even pride. When I made an enthusiastic comment on what I saw, he'd just say 'Oh huh' or 'I guess so'.

But that house! I've never in all my life seen anything to match it. The ballroom was a replica of a room at Versailles, stuffed full of mirrors and red velvet, gilded woodwork and alabaster pillars. The walls were made of solid Caen marble. And the grand hall was modelled on an Italian *palazzo*, rising up to the roof four floors above, supported by marble columns of the same height. Each banister ended in a life-size nude statue of a female slave wearing a tiara of electric lights. Life-size, can you believe it? I got Mr Wharton to switch them on, then off, then on again.

Room after room we went past while our host described their contents in that flat voice of his – mosaic friezes, Gobelin tapestries, Japanese lacquer and books. Books that would have made Mother fall down in a dead faint, books that had never been opened because they were too valuable to be read. I began to feel a bit sick with it all.

But blow me if it doesn't turn out that this isn't Mr Wharton's only home. He takes us into his library and shows us pictures of this other place in Westchester County. He's compiled this enormous leatherbound book of hundreds of photographs and specially commissioned etchings so that people can see what it looks like. And so he can tell them that it took six hundred builders, European sculptors and woodcarvers eighteen months to build.

'The front door weighs seventy tons, you say?' My eyes were popping out of my head. 'Blimey, I wouldn't like to be your doorman. . . . And two hundred people can sit down for dinner at this table? 'Struth! You must have had some right old parties in this house, Mr Wharton!'

'Actually,' said J. McGarrett Wharton III, 'I've never been there.'

Once Bob and I were in the taxi I let out a huge sigh of relief. 'What a miserable old bugger, eh, that Mr Wharton.'

Bob shrugged. 'When you're as rich as that I guess you can afford to be miserable.'

But I was thinking about Mother's ideas on the subject. 'Money isn't the same thing as happiness, Frank Finzel.' She was right. My God, she was right.

If only I could have learned my lesson then!

I've learned from experience that it's always when you're coasting along quietly in life that something happens, like as if God had some mischievous sprites waiting to stick their feet out and trip you up flat on your face.

It was like that in 1925 when I suddenly upped and went to Italy.

New York had given me the taste for travel, and things were going very smoothly then, at the beginning of 1925. My life was very quiet. A bit too quiet for my liking. It made me feel restless, and that's the sort of feeling always gets you into trouble. Like when I was a kid and I was bored, so I'd go out in the streets and play Knock Down Ginger, or I'd go into the larder and pinch a piece of cake – either way, I'd get myself a slap. There I was in 1925, with a new car and able to consider myself well off. Ethne had just joined her sister at the local high school, and the two of them were thick as thieves with their neighbour, a fetching little puss with the queerest name: Loveday. Anyway, they're completely stuck into Magnolia Gardens, and they've been taught to speak nicely at the grammar, and all in all it's as if Catford never existed. Not as I can blame them for that, seeing as how they were only babies when they left it. I try to make sure they want for nothing, and Jeanie says I spoil them. Ethne was always the musical one; she gets it from her grandmother. She used to pick out a tune as soon as she could walk, so I'd started her off with piano lessons to learn to play Brahms and be as good as that lah-de-dah Mrs Partington. Jeanie was spending most of the time down the garden with her vegetables. It seemed that a garden of her own was the thing she'd always wanted since leaving Edinburgh, so she was content, though it wasn't an interest I shared with her, being brought up like I was.

Mother had passed on in 1924, and I missed her a lot, but at least she'd lived just about long enough to see me a rich man. I'd carried out my promise to her to put Agnes through college. She'd trained to be a teacher and she had a job in a girls' school on the south coast and was happily settled down there. It was Mother's greatest disappointment that Agnes wasn't married.

So there we all were, and everything very peaceful, except, like I say, this feeling inside me. There was a fashion for marble washstand-tops then, and after I'd spoken to the tenth customer about the marble shortage and they'd asked me, like they always did, why couldn't I import it from Italy, like the best firms were doing, I said to Sam: 'Right, that's it! I'm off to Italy myself to sort this bloomin' thing out.' It wasn't like it is nowadays when you can just pick up a telephone and ask someone, and I certainly couldn't solve the problem by correspondence since I didn't speak a word of any foreign language, so I decided that it was high time I visited the marble quarries myself.

I made enquiries, and my secretary, Maisie, made up my itinerary. I was to visit the quarries at Pietrasanta and to stay in a *pensione* in the town, but since I'd never been to the place before none of it meant a thing to me. I just packed my bag and took the leap into the unknown – starting with the platform on Victoria Station where the Pullmans leave for the Continent.

I thought Italy was the most wonderful place I'd set foot in in my life.

I suppose I still do. It wasn't just the look of the place, though that was enough to send me giddy, but the sound of it. People bellowing at the tops of their voices. Recordings of that opera fellow, Caruso, floating through open windows. And the smell! The London I knew could be a pretty smelly place, but this was different. It smelled of oil and something very strong, which I now know is garlic.

The town had steep little lanes, and churches round every corner. But it was the colours that knocked me sideways. Houses painted blue and pink and yellow; not like the house-paints you see in a row of boarding houses in Brighton, but thin delicate colours that looked like they had faded and the sun was shining through them. To be honest, my first thought when I saw them was of WCs and baths and whether we could persuade the punters that they'd like them in these colours instead of white. A sort of 'Italian Look'. And the sides of the houses were covered with hanging pots full of flowers and bits of trailing greenery. Jeanie would like those, I thought.

As I say, I was just overcome by it all. I went out to the marble quarries just outside the town, and it was just incredible, like something out of *Alice in Wonderland*, which we used to read to the girls when they were little. I knew if I told the girls about those enormous square hunks of marble being cut away from the hillside with wires, just as if they were bits of cheese – well, they wouldn't believe me. The machine they used to cut with had geared pulleys and weights, and they poured sand into it to use as a cutting edge to slice through the marble. The cut faces formed an amphitheatre with sides two or three hundred feet high, and everything was coated with a white dust so bright it could blind you. After I'd been up there a couple of times and just stood there with my mouth hanging open, I tried to find the foreman, but since I didn't know any Italian and they didn't know any English I didn't get very far. I tried pointing my finger at the top of my head for 'head man', but that was worse than useless. They thought I was complaining because I was balding on top a bit, and they all stood round slapping their thighs and laughing. So I found a fellow who spoke English, a cousin of my landlady's, and he came out there with me to haggle over the price of the marble, but of course the man who made the decisions wasn't around and all we could get out of them was that he'd be back by Easter.

It was the end of February when I arrived in Pietrasanta, and every night for several nights there had been dancing in the streets, and when you woke up you looked out of the window and saw the paved streets covered in streamers and confetti. Imagine seeing that sort of thing in Magnolia Gardens, and Robert Clifford picking his way through them in his bowler! So I asked Mrs Donatelli, the landlady of my *pensione*, what was going on. She spoke quite good English, and she liked to have a bit of a chat as she drank her coffee with a good slug of aniseed liqueur chucked into it.

'*Carnevale*,' she says, grinning at me through her yellow teeth. 'Carnival, you know, Mr Frank. *Carnevale* is – how you say? – meat.' She starts waving her hands around at this point. 'Meat bye bye!'

Anyhow, between the two of us we managed to work out that *carnevale* means 'farewell to flesh', because they're not supposed to eat the stuff during Lent. And Mrs Donatelli said that night was the last night of the carnival – the last *veglione*, she called it – before Lent. Well, there wasn't much for me to do that afternoon, so I went out into the piazza for a bit of fresh air, trying to decide what I should do about this marble business. The sun was shining on the red-tiled roofs, and a cat was chasing the lizards that had come out for a walk like me, and the whole place looked so lovely that I just stood in the centre of the piazza and stared. I was always doing that, just staring, and I reckon the locals must have thought I was stark raving mad, but someone in London told me that all foreigners think we're crazy anyway, so maybe it didn't matter.

There was a group of young people at the other end of the square, just kicking around wasting time, and every so often they pointed at me and laughed. And I wished I could have said to them: 'Look, you don't understand; I've never been in a beautiful place before. We don't have them in London – not what you'd call beautiful like this, with all the colours.' I wanted to tell them that I was finding out what it felt like to fall in love with a place.

Anyway, I never got the chance, because it clouded over all of a sudden, and before I could blink there was thunder and bloomin' great drops of rain pelting down. I went to shelter under an overhanging roof, and the young people rushed off screaming and shouting to take cover.

All except one, that is. There was one girl who kicked off her shoes and ran out laughing into the rain and just stood there, on the spot where I had just been, with her face turned up to the sky and the water pouring down her in rivulets. She was wearing a light cotton frock, and the damp material clung to her and became transparent, revealing her womanly curves. And then the rain stopped, quite sudden, and the clouds began to clear. The girl turned her face up to the sun, with her eyes closed, and the sun glinting on the raindrops that had collected on her lashes.

But that's another story. Believe it or not, the events of that day were what led me to send my daughter Mel halfway across Europe to that place in Switzerland.

Because at that moment I felt my whole world turn upside down.

47 Magnolia Gardens

Magdalena

MY MOTHER WOULD HAVE SNEERED AT MY HOUSE in Magnolia Gardens. It was certainly not what either of us had foreseen for me. But, on the other hand, I was comfortable and I had my freedom. After the things I'd been through, I didn't really want any more than that.

My family were what one might have called 'respectable', but I doubt that the other inhabitants of Magnolia Gardens realised that. My name probably misled them as much as anything. A wicked name. Fast. It made me laugh to think that no such idea would have entered Mama's head as she presided over my christening. But, then, Mama was a self-righteous fool.

I was born in 1885. My father ran a veterinary practice in Devon. His profession carried little prestige in those days, but my mother had money and we lived in a small stone manor-house in the Exe valley. The house stood on a hill and overlooked rolling fields that were golden with barley in the summer. Papa was a big swaggering man with magnificent whiskers, who liked to drink and raise his voice in argument. His face wore an expression of perpetual surprise, as though he couldn't quite believe his good fortune in snaring Mama. So it would have been quite unjust to say that he took his situation for granted, but he exploited it to the full, keeping a stable of horses and riding to hounds. Which proved nothing except that he was a fool, for before long he was living beyond his means and running into debt.

Mama was the daughter of a minor landowner, and the essence of well-bred gentility, modulating her voice to a low and resonant tone, above which it was never raised, even in anger. When I misbehaved I longed for her to lose her temper and snap at me, but she would not. She would lower her eyelids so that her lashes made reproachful shadows on her ivory cheeks, and murmur about 'mortification'. Mama was a handsome woman, and she knew it, though her faultlessly correct manner was enough to foil any accusations of vanity. Her chestnut-red hair was swept up so smoothly that its surface held the light like glass, and her dark eyes were lustrous and thick-lashed. Only the very observant would have noticed – as I had – the stubborn gleam that lurked beneath those demurely lowered lids. Corsetry could hide a multitude of sins in those days, so it is difficult to judge what Mama's figure was really like, but she laced herself in to a hand-span waist, which must have been quite an achievement after five children. She wore her long sleeves very tight with a bell cuff that revealed a generous amount of lace. I used to think they were like flowers, with the lace as the inner petals and Mama's long cool fingers as the stamens of the flower.

I was her fourth child. The eldest was Edgar, born in 1880, then a year later a girl was born. Despite her narrow ways, Mama had a fanciful streak and she called her first daughter Bathsheba. Then came Oswald, and two years later I was born.

I doubt that Mama was much interested in the matter of my baptism, but she had the sense to see that my name would have to be as outlandish as Bathsheba's. People would think it strange, and be sure to comment, if I were dismissed with 'Anne' or 'Mary', so she christened me Magdalena, forgetting that Mary Magdalen was reputed to have done more than just wash the feet of Christ.

Hubert was born when I was five, and when Mama had given up the thought of having more children. He was the only one of my family I ever liked. He grew from an engaging naughty child to a charming reckless young man, only to be killed in the Great War. Pompous Edgar and sly, deceitful Oswald survived; that was to be expected.

The others took it for granted that I would be Papa's favourite because I was the youngest girl. I didn't know whether this was true, since Papa seemed too preoccupied with drinking and horses to be interested in any of us, but he used to swing me up on to his huge knees, tickling my face with his whiskers and calling me 'kitten'. That Bathsheba was Mama's favourite was irrefutable, however. I was a pretty child, but robust and way-ward, and Mama's attempts to instil correct behaviour quickly failed. Bathsheba was also a pretty child, but frail and spineless. The perfect clay for Mama to mould. Papa called me 'kitten', but the epithet would have been more suited to Bathsheba as I remember her. She used to snuggle up to Mama's side with her pale hair in a luminous cloud, her white clothes clean and fluffy. Just like a little white kitten.

Despite Mama, our childhood was not governed by restraint.

The house was surrounded by open countryside, and we ran wild in it. Papa's work meant that we were surrounded by animals, and when I was about eight Papa fenced the paddock next to the house and bought us each a pony. I used to ride alongside the boys with my hair loose, screeching like a Red Indian, while Bathsheba trotted sedately behind on Pandora, who was milk white with a sensitive mouth. We set up a round of jumps with the aid of the groom, constructed from old logs and tea-chests, and soon even Bathsheba was joining in our contests.

In the early years we were educated by a governess, but we all made friends with the village children, particularly Hubert and I, who spent many happy hours roaming around the local farms. Needless to say, Mama did not like this at all, and tried to arrange our social life around the pale, pampered offspring of the local gentry. We were invited to their parties and they to ours. Mama's had been a 'county' family and she had been acquainted with many of our hostesses since her own childhood, so there was no reason why we Stark children should not have been accepted, but Mama's efforts did not have very satisfactory results.

I put this down to the tension between the two different influences in our lives. Mama was very correct and self-conscious in all she did, anxious for us to 'do the right thing' and to do it amongst the right sort of people. Papa, on the other hand, spent his working life associating with the employees of these people: the gamekeepers and the grooms and the tenant farmers. He was never really at home in a drawing room, but he loved to entertain and would perplex – and, I suspect, anger – Mama by bringing his friends home at all hours for a drink and something to eat. Some of these friends, the vicar and the doctor, were respectable, others were not. The less respectable, the later they stayed. The later they stayed, the more they drank and the rowdier they would become.

One of my earliest memories was of sitting at the top of the stairs one night when I should have been upstairs in my bed. There was a shout of laughter from the dining room, and Papa's voice boomed above the rest. Then the dining-room door opened, and Mama came out. Her face was slightly flushed, her lips pinched together. She leaned back against the door and closed her eyes. I saw her raise her hand to them as if to brush away tears. Then I had to creep back into the shadows and slip away, because she came towards the staircase and had probably decided to go up to bed.

Papa had a genuine love of animals, but he was also deeply enmeshed in the sybaritic process of spending Mama's money. I shall never forget the look on Mama's face, or the way Papa laughed, when he spent five guineas on a stuffed bear and gave it pride of place in the entrance-hall. Its mouth was open in a roar, revealing yellowed teeth, and it emitted a faint smell of moth-balls. The bear in the hall became a symbol – a symbol of the fact that Papa didn't take life seriously and was not as cautious with Mama's money as he might have been.

People were prepared to put up with his lackadaisical ways because they needed his services as a vet. Then something happened to change all that, something which affected all our lives for the worse. My life might otherwise have turned out as Mama wanted it to be, and I would not have ended up in Magnolia Gardens.

Another veterinary surgeon moved to the area. He was young, well qualified and ambitious, and he set himself up in open competition with Papa. The results were disastrous. The area simply didn't have the population to keep two practices in business. A hard-working and dedicated man might have succeeded in holding his ground and driving the newcomer away, but Papa did not fit that description. He was a fool. When faced with a choice, people began to remember the occasions when John Stark arrived late with the smell of port on his breath. If the sick animal had subsequently been lost, they were not prepared to be generous. So the new man, Gibbons, was given a chance, and when he was discovered to be not only reliable but also a master of new techniques, people recommended him to their friends. Each time Papa's nose was put out of joint in this way, he consoled himself with a drink, so that when somebody finally did call on his services he had spoiled his chances of redemption with the reek of liquor and the tell-tale tremor of his hands. It was a spiralling situation. It was worse than a spiral; it was a quagmire.

Naturally, losing business meant losing money. I was twelve at the time of Mr Gibbons's arrival in the Exe valley, and considered too young to have the situation explained to me. But from behind closed doors I heard the voices that droned on long into the night, Mama's low and urgent, Papa's loud and undisciplined. I heard the doors slamming. When Oswald came home from school, he told me that Mama had tried to persuade Papa to sell our ponies as an economy, but Papa had refused. Instead he made his own economies. He sent away half of the domestic servants and, when things became even worse and Papa was faced with having to close down the practice altogether, Edgar and Oswald were removed from their public school and sent to the village school instead. I expect Mama found this measure more shaming than the rest, for now her sons were forced to mix with the very rabble she had spent years keeping them away from. She still had money of her own, but most of it was tied up in trust for us when we were older, and she was loath to touch that. Any income of her own went into replacing Papa's income from the practice, and paying for our governess. No doubt she would have been content to let me join the boys at the village school, but it would certainly not do for her precious Bathsheba.

They say that disasters come in threes. The second happened about a year after Mr Gibbons usurped Papa.

Bathsheba was thrown from her pony and broke her neck.

It was as though all the problems that we had had before crystallised and hardened. Mama had met financial and social ruin with her habitual sang-froid, but now the lid of a box had been flipped open to reveal the rottenness beneath.

She did not stand in the drawing room sobbing into a handkerchief and watching through a window as they carried Bathsheba's broken body into the house. She ran through the front door and into the paddock. I was amazed that she even knew how to run. Her smooth hair somehow came free from its restraints, falling about her face, and she was shouting something unintelligible.

I looked on dumbly as she gathered up the dead Bathsheba in her arms and rocked her to and fro with a terrible ferocity. Then she did an extraordinary thing. She dropped Bathsheba's corpse and stumbled over to where the pony, Pandora, had been tethered to the fence, and started to rain blows on its white flanks, slapping it with her bare hands, pummelling it with her fists.

Eventually they led her away, but she had not finished with Pandora yet. By nightfall Bathsheba was laid out, small and white, in her room, and for that reason I was reluctant to stay upstairs alone. I came down to look for Hubert, and as I passed the drawing-room door I heard my parents' voices. I stopped to listen.

'John, you're to go out there and shoot that beast! You can't let it live a moment longer! How could you? After it killed our daughter! I command you to go out there at once and finish the damn thing off!'

Mama was shouting. It was the first and the last time that I ever heard her raise her voice.

'Alice, you must try to compose yourself. There's nothing to be gained—'

'Very well, I shall go out there and shoot it myself!'

There was a silence as Mama took stock of the fact that she did not know how to load a gun.

'I shall get one of the boys to do it!'

'Alice, Alice . . .' Papa sounded anguished. 'You can't blame the animal for what happened. Do try to think rationally, my dear. Bath— We have had that pony for years, and it hasn't misbehaved once. Sensitive mouths need cautious handling. Cautious handling. But I'd warned Bathsheba about that many times. She must have misjudged her timing and set it at the fence too hard. Accidents like that happen all the time!'

Even I could judge that this last comment was foolish in the extreme.

'*All the time*! What do you mean, *all the time*! It only took one accident to kill our precious child! How can you just stand there and look at me like that!'

'But, Alice, I fail to see—'

'I blame Magdalena for this! She rides so recklessly herself, she probably encouraged my poor darling to take that jump!'

I felt my flesh grow cold.

Papa made indignant noises.

'Oh yes, she would! Despite my efforts, she's always been wayward and uncontrollable. If Bathsheba did something dangerous, then it was Magdalena's influence that made her do it! And now my poor baby is dead. . . .'

Papa sounded angry now. 'Blaming Magdalena is even more senseless than blaming a dumb animal. You're obviously completely crazed—'

'It was Magdalena's fault!' Mama broke into wild sobbing. 'Magdalena's fault. *I hate her.*'

I was not sorry that Bathsheba was dead.

I had to pretend to be, but I hadn't really liked her and I could see that eventually her departure might be advantageous to me. Mama eventually regained her composure, and I hoped that she would overcome her resentment and award me a place in her affections fitting to my status as only daughter.

I did not place much value on maternal affection, but I wanted her money. The sum in trust for us was said to be generous and now there was Bathsheba's portion to dispose of as well. I had no inclination whatsoever to go out and earn my living. Mama had described me as 'wild' and 'uncontrollable', but it was a description that only applied to my behaviour in the saddle. Elsewhere I found that I disliked exerting myself and needed to move through life with the maximum of pleasure and the minimum of effort. So I set about being as dutiful and obedient as my independent nature would allow.

After Bathsheba's death, Papa lost all will to try, and abandoned his efforts to survive alongside Mr Gibbons. At the very end of the nineteenth century, when I was fourteen, the house was sold and – though it was too late for it to be considered a victory on Mama's part – so were the ponies and the stuffed bear. We moved to a small farmhouse near Bickleigh, and Mama told the world that Papa had 'retired'. She continued to wear mourning for Bathsheba, compounding the impression that we were a family torn asunder by grief. The governess was dismissed, and I was sent to the local school. I was relieved. Being one of a class of a dozen noisy adolescent girls was much less like hard work than private tuition had been.

It must have been shortly after I left the school, at the age of sixteen, that I realised my attempts to supplant Bathsheba were futile. As far as I could see, my behaviour gave no cause for complaint, but one day Mama summoned me to discuss my future. She was sitting in the window of the parlour, working on a piece of needlepoint. It was stretched tightly on a circular wood frame, and her needle worked fastidiously to and fro on a cluster of moss roses.

'Come in, please. I'd like to talk to you about your future.'

I stood in front of her, watching her silently. She did not look

51

at me, but kept her eyes on the flashing needle.

'Your education is complete now, so you ought to be giving some serious thought to the disposal of the next few years.' She made it sound positively insanitary. 'I have some funds within my reach,' she went on, 'of which no doubt you are already aware.' Cool, formal, proper as ever.

Then: 'It concerns me that since the death of our beloved Bathsheba you may have thought your financial expectations were increased. I'm afraid that's not the case.'

Pause. Lips pursed in concentration over the petal of a mouldering moss rose. 'After giving the matter some consideration, I have decided that your father's unfortunate position necessitates my dividing all the money between the boys. He – your father – will be unable to give them any sort of a start in life, so I feel it incumbent upon me to help them. My duty.'

I waited for her to go on. I sensed that this dry formal speech was only a preliminary to something more unpleasant.

'If I felt that you would be able to take the money and put it to good use, I might consider. . . . However, I'm quite sure that you are incapable of making anything of yourself. Above and beyond what marriage might do, of course.'

Sunlight streamed through the window and illuminated Mama's moving hands. I noticed that the cuff of her silk gown was grubby and slightly frayed.

'I suggest that you think about finding a suitable husband, someone who can offer . . . the security you need. Or some sort of employment suited to your education. The post of governess, perhaps. Although I understand that your French is very poor.'

And that was it. She nodded her head towards the door in dismissal.

Mama had as good as thrown me out of the house. Anyone of a warmer disposition than mine would have hated her. I merely thought she was a foolish woman. She was right about me being unlikely to make anything of myself. But what she couldn't see was that I didn't want to. I just wanted an easy time.

It was shortly after this interview that the third tragedy happened. My father suffered a massive stroke while he was attending to his bees. He died a few hours later.

I can't say that I was prostrate with grief, nor can I claim to have been close to Papa, but I preferred him to anybody except Hubert, and his death affected me. It affected me because it affected the atmosphere in the Bickleigh house. Papa had been ineffectual and a drunk, yet he had managed to exude a positive presence. Without him the house became dead, too. Given Mama's attitude, there seemed little chance of it coming alive again.

That's why I decided to elope.

I doubt that many of the residents of Magnolia Gardens ever realised that I had been married. I'd had a child out of wedlock and, as far as they were concerned, that was that. But I was married. Once. Briefly.

His name was Harry Dando and he was a farm labourer. It might have seemed that I picked him with the express intention of angering Mama, but Mama did not care for me enough to be angered or hurt by anything I did. Besides, Harry Dando was a farm labourer, but a farm labourer with ambition.

We met in May 1902, when I was seventeen. Every May there was a fair on the common, with a maypole and coconut-shies and an Aunt Sally. And a great deal of cider-drinking and sentimentality after the fashion of Thomas Hardy's novels. One evening I was sitting in the parlour turning the pages of a book without reading them, in a torpor of boredom and blankness, when Betsy, our one remaining servant, announced that there was someone at the front door who wished to speak to me. I found a group of girls who had been my classmates at the village school. They were passing our house on the way to the fair, and asked if I would like to join them.

I had been quite popular at school, but they had no reason to do me any favours, so I was pleased that they had thought to include me in their outing. I was also grateful for the opportunity to escape that moribund house, and I did not stop to ask Mama's permission. I paused only long enough to tie up my hair with a red ribbon before setting off for the common with the others.

I shall never forget how I felt as I ran down that steep winding lane, the thundering of my button boots sending up little clouds of dust. I felt an enormous intoxicating surge of liberation. I had escaped, and could not run fast enough to leave behind the stultifying repression of the place that was my home. My heart beat loudly in sympathy with my hurrying footsteps. It was early evening, and the light was fading, but because the day had been clear and warm an impression of sunlight had been left behind and the air was choked with the smell of hawthorn blossom and meadowsweet. Whenever I thought of Devon in the years that followed, I thought of that smell and of running headlong down the lane, crushing the drifting blossom-petals underfoot.

He stood there watching me while I threw cracked wooden balls at the coconut-shy. He had thick curling black hair and a moustache. His eyes, when they looked at me, were burning bright.

'They've started to dance. Would you care to dance with me?' His voice was light and clear, not made indistinct by a West Country burr.

I turned around and looked at the wooden platform where an aged band of musicians had struck up a polka and a few people were lumbering around self-consciously. 'No,' I said. 'No, thank you. I don't want to dance.'

'Some lemonade, then?'

Those eyes were still burning into me; so bright. I consented to follow him to the lemonade-tent. He handed me a cup and bowed in mock deference. As he straightened up, our hands brushed awkwardly and we both smiled. Suddenly I found myself wanting to be much closer to him, to be held by those thick strong arms.

'I've changed my mind,' I said. 'I would like to dance.'

We jostled our way around the crowded dance-floor and he tightened his arms around my shoulderblades possessively. We introduced ourselves and, unable to think of anything else to say, I asked in a fair imitation of my mother: 'And what line of business are you in, Mr Dando?'

'I work up at Morrow's farm,' he said defensively, angrily even. 'Hired help. But it's not going to stay that way, I can tell you. I'm heading to be in the entertainment business. Theatre.'

Before I could even open my mouth to answer, he went on: 'I know about you. I suppose you think you're too fine to associate with farm boys.'

'But I *am* associating with you.' My coolness deflated his aggression instantly. 'And, besides, I hardly think that being the daughter of a bankrupt veterinary gives me the right to be proud.'

He smiled. I noticed the tobacco stains on his teeth for the first time.

It was dark when Harry offered to take me home, but he didn't attempt to take advantage. He merely plucked at the red ribbon that I had tied so carelessly around my hair and asked if he could keep it.

We met frequently after that; almost every day. I would sneak out after supper on the pretext of taking a walk, and by the time I returned Mama had retired to her own room. She must have suspected that I was meeting a lover, but she made no effort to prevent me. She was hoping to hasten the day when I would be off her hands and out of the house.

It would be natural to speculate on what a reasonably well educated young lady and a farmhand found to talk about. The answer is that we didn't talk much. Our meetings very quickly took on the semblance of a ritual. Harry would meet me at the end of the lane near my house, and we would walk together to Morrow Farm where he worked. Sometimes he would borrow a pony and trap and we would travel that way. I liked those evenings best. I still regretted the sale of our horses, and it was good to hear the reassuring sound of hoofs again, even if I could no longer ride. Harry knew of a deserted barn in one of the fields, and this was our destination. We would sit down on a pile of boxes covered with a rug to make it look like a sofa, and Harry would set to work, burying his face in my hair and neck and moaning a little, then kissing me and unbuttoning the front of my dress. The culmination of the ritual was the raising of my skirts and the introduction of his hand inside the leg of my bloomers. After a few damp, desperate caresses he would collapse against me, groaning.

There was little pleasure for me in all this. From the start I enjoyed the sensations that his touch produced, but they led nowhere, and all his grunting and the noise he made seemed ridiculous. But I always allowed him to do as he liked, sensing that life would be simpler and easier if I went along with it. Afterwards we would talk a little, but neither of us had much in our lives worth discussing. I think the moments I enjoyed most in our courtship were not those when I was *with* Harry, but afterwards, when I was alone. When we were together, his proximity was overwhelming; his face so close to mine that his features were blurred. But when I was alone I could savour the thrill of having shared myself with another human being, a moment when someone wanted *me*. I could relish those moments, caress them, gloat over them like a magpie over jewels.

I wouldn't want to give the impression that I had lost my head over Harry Dando. It was just that from the very start he represented a means of escape, and that prospect was very sweet to me then.

Our outings were congenial enough in the summer, but when autumn set in and the barn was dark and damp and increasingly cold they lost their appeal. I began to grow impatient with Harry, then irritated, and finally I decided that I would stop seeing him. But on the evening that I had planned to announce my decision Harry had some news for me.

'I've got a job!' he announced, as we walked down the lane arm in arm. 'A job in London!'

It transpired that Harry had a cousin in London called Jeremiah, and that Jeremiah was some sort of theatrical agent. Harry had written to him, and he had replied with the offer of a job as a stage manager at the Gaiety.

'Well,' I said dryly, 'you've certainly kept this very quiet.'

'I wanted to surprise you. London! Just think, Magda! The West End stage. . . . You'll come with me, of course.'

I laughed. 'You don't think I'm going to stay here in this hole, do you?'

I went with him.

It's not strictly accurate to say that we eloped. We certainly packed our bags and left in an indecent hurry, but I was still a few years short of my twenty-first birthday, and needed my mother's permission before I could marry. The fact that Mama gave her consent without demur speaks volumes for her opinion of me. I was a fitting bride for a farmhand, but Bathsheba would have been restrained behind bars rather than be allowed to suffer the fate of marrying a Harry Dando.

We were married without ceremony in a drab redbrick church in the suburbs of London. I wore my best lawn dress and a hat, and carried a posy of wilted violets. Jeremiah and his sister were our witnesses. They ordered a bottle of champagne for us at a nearby hotel, and that was the extent of the celebration. Not an auspicious start to married life.

I disliked Jeremiah Dando from the start. He was fat and bloated–looking – like a seal – and his dark eyes flickered continually from side to side.

'I don't trust him,' I said to Harry at the end of his first week's employment. 'He's just going to use you.'

'No, he's not. And what happens at the theatre isn't your concern anyhow. . . . Come here and get into bed, will you? Sweet Jesus, it's cold in here! . . . Your concern is the home, woman. . . .'

Home was a drab little terraced house in Battersea. I think I managed to put on a brave face for about five minutes. Then I hated it. The house was mean, cold and uncomfortable. I liked to be comfortable, but I found I lacked the resources to make it so. The streets of south London looked grey and dirty to me, and the women who stood gossiping on street corners stared at me as I walked past. These people prided themselves on their sense of community spirit, but I was not part of their community, and that was that. They took such pride in their homes, yet still managed to appear slatternly. And all around there was evidence of the gross hypocrisy of that age: carriages drawing up in the street and top-hatted gentlemen stepping out of them to visit the mistresses they kept ensconced in anonymous suburban villas, while up and down the street curtains would be twitching discreetly and people thrilling vicariously to this glimpse of illicit love. I suppose I had inherited my father's disregard for class distinction, and I found all this very hard to understand. Why couldn't people just be honest about what they were doing? I saw a lot of what went on because I spent as little time as possible in the house. I spent half my time catching the omnibus to the West End shops to spend hours wandering around and staring at the pretty things I couldn't buy. The other half was spent arguing with Harry.

He usually came home half-drunk in the evenings, but I had expected that. When I questioned him about his job, he was increasingly evasive.

'Oh . . . Jeremiah sent me off to collect some things he needed.'

'But you're a stage manager. What you do is nothing to do with Jeremiah, surely?'

'They don't have the work for me at the moment. I'll be starting on a show in a few weeks. I'm just going to help Jem out for a while.'

The weeks wore on, and it became obvious that Harry was never going to be more than a poorly paid fetcher and carrier for

57

Jeremiah – an errand boy. He was paid about fifteen shillings a week. The house had been rented unfurnished, and I quickly grew tired of sitting on orange-boxes.

'Wouldn't it be better if we just set aside a little money each week so that we can eventually buy a few chairs?' I asked him one night after he and Jeremiah had been soaking themselves in a champagne bar in the Charing Cross Road.

'I'll decide!' he said, lurching across the bed, which was about the only piece of furniture we possessed. '*I'll* decide!'

That was about all he was capable of saying. He reached across and fumbled with my nightdress.

'No, thank you!' I said, and pushed his hand away.

He hit me across the mouth. 'Damn you, you cold bitch!'

Then he passed out. I pushed his heavy drink-sodden body on to the bare floorboards and blew out the candle, covering my head with the pillow to shut out his snores.

I could remember that night clearly for a long time. It was in March 1903, and it was the beginning of the end of our short marriage. It seemed futile to try to persuade Harry that he would be better off without Jeremiah, and to look for a job with better prospects. I was a stranger to hard work and ambition myself, but I could see the sense in not throwing away money and opportunity through drink, the way my father had done. So I persisted in trying to curb his expenditure on drink, and Harry became more abusive, leaving me with quite a collection of bruises. I looked at them, examined them, touched them, and knew that I wanted him to leave.

Eventually he did. He came back to the house earlier than usual and found me sitting in a rocking chair, polishing my nails.

'Where did you get that from?' he demanded.

'What, this?' I held up my little ivory nail-buffer. 'I brought this with me from Devon.'

'Not that. You know damn well what I mean! The chair!'

'Oh, that,' I said, returning to my manicure. 'Yes, someone gave it to me. This morning. Do you know who I mean by Sara Corder? The woman who lives alone on the corner?'

'She's a fishwife! She hangs around on the street, giving men the eye!'

I ignored this interruption. 'She came round this morning to ask if I had any tea to spare. She saw that we didn't have any furniture and offered to lend it to us because she never uses it. Says it makes her giddy.'

Harry had turned white with rage, and he curled back his lip to reveal his stained teeth. 'So that's what you do all day, is it? You get the neighbours in here to stare and cluck and gossip about how poor Mrs Dando doesn't have any money to buy furniture?'

It was my turn to become angry. 'No, that's not what it's like at all, but I almost wish it was! One person, that's all! One person! Sara Corder is the only person who's taken any heed of me at all, and I'm grateful to her! The other women are content just to gossip behind my back! That's what it's like being Mrs Harry bloody Dando, and I'm sick of it!'

He hit me on the side of my face, but it was the last time he ever laid a finger on me. He left the next morning and never came back.

How very obliging of him, I thought a few weeks later when I read Harry's letter asking me to forward his belongings to Jeremiah's address.

The inconvenient thing was that I was pregnant.

Of course I wanted to get rid of the baby as soon as possible; I did not want it, and I knew that I would not love it. The problem was finding the means to do so. I had heard from servants' gossip and some of Harry and Jeremiah's coarser conversations that some doctors were willing to help women out of such a predicament. But you had to pay, and I didn't have any money. I decided it was high time I paid a visit to my elder brother, Edgar.

Edgar was a silly ass, and I had no desire at all to see him, but he was established in London as a manager of his own insurance business in the City, and he was at least in a position to offer me some help. I decided against visiting him at home, since I disliked his sour-faced wife, Frances, even more than I disliked Edgar himself, but chose his office instead as a more appropriate meeting point. I put on my best coat and hat, cursing Harry inwardly when I saw how shabby they had become.

'Well, what a surprise!' said Edgar, and looked as though he meant it. 'And how is married life treating you, Magdalena?'

This question was too fatuous to deserve a reply, and I did not want to become involved in a sordid narrative about my marriage, so I came straight to the point. 'I need to borrow some money.'

Edgar raised his eyebrows and folded his hands across his chest in a ridiculously pompous fashion for a man who was only twenty-four. 'I see. And might I enquire why?'

'I'd rather not say.'

'How much money do you need?'

I had no idea. I groped around wildly and came out with a figure that I hoped would amply cover my expenses.

Edgar raised his eyebrows again. 'That's quite a lot of money. What makes you think I can spare it?'

'If you mean why should you give me any money, there is no reason at all except for the fact that my own inheritance was carved up between you boys. I think that gives you a certain obligation. . . . You know what I'm talking about. Mama's money.'

'Indeed I do, and I think you have a very fair point.' He smiled at me to indicate that he was being fair. 'The money is in a trust administered by Mama, and I'd be very happy to speak to her about it, or perhaps you should approach her yourself.'

I shook my head, smiling slightly. The idea of asking Mama for money to abort my farmboy husband's child was almost enough to make me laugh. 'Can't you lend it to me out of your own funds?'

'Out of my personal expenses? I couldn't possibly do that without consulting Frances.'

Which meant 'no'.

He waited for me to speak. I left without saying thank you.

When I got home I sat in the rocking chair and rocked, and that in turn led me to thinking of the only thing I could do. I asked Sara Corder for her help. As I had guessed, she was familiar with my predicament.

'It's always left to us women, isn't it? In the end we only have one another to rely on, don't we?' She looked me in the eye. 'Is it your husband's?'

Sara was a big untidy woman with red hair. I found it difficult to judge her age, but she looked worn, and gave the impression that she was no stranger to being deserted by men.

'I do know of someone, but. . . .' We were in my house, and she went and sat down in the rocking chair. 'Jesus Christ, I forgot! This bleedin' thing makes me giddy!'

'I don't have any money.'

'That's all right; she won't take money. It's just . . . it's not

60

very nice, that's all. Do you think you can manage it?'

It wasn't very nice, and I wouldn't have managed it at all if Sara hadn't been there to come with me up those vile-smelling back stairs and hold my hand while a greasy old woman shoved her potions down my throat and stuck instruments of torture inside me until all of me burned with pain, or to sit with me at home afterwards while I waited for the bleeding to stop and my strength to return.

When it was all over, I had some thinking to do. I was on my own, with no means of support and a house to pay for. Sara said that I should demand money from Harry to help pay the rent. I didn't hold out much hope of success, but I wrote to Jeremiah anyway, and was informed that Harry had left London to work in a variety theatre on the south coast. I wasn't sure whether or not to believe him, but I could see that I was going to get nowhere by pursuing it. I would have to find a job.

Once again, I turned to Sara Corder.

'Can you cook?' she asked.

I shook my head.

'Can you sew?'

'No.'

'Mind children?'

My face showed distaste.

'Well, you're not much bleedin' good, then, are you?'

I sighed. 'No I suppose not.'

'Look,' Sara said more kindly, easing herself out of the rocking chair, 'I'll see what I can do about it.'

She returned two days later with a smile all over her face. 'I've found you a job! Anyone could do it, and the money's not too bad.'

Her description made me suspicious. 'What is it?'

'A nursing home, up in the West End. Small private place. I know a girl who worked there once, and she says they need someone. A guinea a week.'

'But I'm not a nurse. I don't know anything about nursing! What will I be doing?'

'Oh, you'll just have to help out generally. Fetching and carrying for the patients. Answering the door. They give you a uniform.'

I hesitated.

on, girl. Beggars can't be choosers. . . .'

arted work at the Ivy Lodge Nursing Home in a quiet
al street in Mayfair. At one time I thought of it as the
in the chain of events that had led me to Magnolia
Gardens, but perhaps marrying Harry Dando was the first link.
Or even Bathsheba falling off her wretched pony. The notion of a
'nursing home' changed a great deal in subsequent years, and I
dare say the Ivy Lodge wouldn't really have continued to earn the
title. The time when I worked there was the heyday of the 'rest
cure', and there wasn't much wrong with most of the patients
that common sense couldn't have taken care of.

I didn't exactly dislike the job. I simply had to run up and
down stairs with trays for the patients, exercise their lap-dogs and
stand ready with the smelling salts while the doctor administered
some of the more unpleasant treatments. I had enough money to
pay the rent and buy some bits and pieces for the house, but as
autumn turned into winter and I faced the nightly omnibus ride
to Victoria Station and the bleak train journey to the Common I
began to wonder if I could do better.

I thought about it one night as I walked home through the
shabby dusty streets and the wind blew bus tickets about and
plastered a dirty newspaper, used to wrap butcher's meat, against
my weary legs. Life would be a lot simpler if I could live a little
closer to work, but to do that I would need quite a bit more
money. Then I had an idea. The world of expensive medicine
always had one ear cocked to hear what was going on on the other
side of the Atlantic, and since massage was all the rage in America
the directors of Ivy Lodge had employed a professional masseuse.
Her name was May, and she was a cheerful forthright woman of
about thirty. As we were sitting in the back kitchen together,
enjoying a cup of tea and a few stolen moments to put our feet up,
I said to her: 'May, d'you think I'd be any good as a masseuse?'

She put down her cup in its saucer. 'Let's look at your hands.'

I held them out to her.

'H'm.' She turned them over as though they were pieces of
meat she was considering buying. 'You've got good hands. Good,
strong, well-muscled hands. Padded, but not fleshy in the wrong
way. I wish I had hands like yours.'

'Only, I was thinking, May, you're always saying that you've
got more work than you can cope with here, so perhaps if you
taught me how to do it I could help out with the stuff you've got
no time for.'

May looked at me thoughtfully. 'You'd be expecting to get paid, of course.'

'Of course.'

'All right. I'll teach you. I'll have to clear it with Dr Scott first, but if he agrees you can take on the extra work for five shillings an hour. Agreed?'

'Agreed.'

'Good. Right.' May cleared the tea-cups away and hauled me to my feet. 'The first thing I'm going to do is to teach you some exercises. For the body. You're young and you're healthy, and that's good, but you're also going to need a lot of stamina. It's no good going on when you're tired; you lose your sense of touch and resistance and you may as well not bother. But you don't have to attack the patient, either. The main object of massage is to increase circulation and improve nutrition. You don't need all that gymnastic stuff to do that. In fact it only exhausts the system and burns up tissue. Now, let's look at your hands again. . . . They're a bit rough.'

'It's all the hours I spend in that hell-hole of a sluice, sterilising the instruments!'

'Yes, well, in future you're going to have to wear gloves. And for housework. And get plenty of sleep and a good diet. The masseur's stock-in-trade is not only to be healthy, but also to *look* healthy. It's half suggestion with most of these people. If you can carry the feeling of energy with you when you go to treat a patient, you're sure to be doing good. . . .'

Then May turned me to face her and looked me straight in the eyes. 'I want you to promise me one thing.'

'What?'

'That you won't ever use what I teach you in the wrong way. You know what I'm talking about, don't you?'

I had no idea, but I didn't want her to lose confidence in me. 'Yes,' I said. 'Oh, yes. Don't worry. I shan't use it in the wrong way.'

And so I became a masseuse.

During those months, from the spring of 1904 onwards, I worked harder than I had ever done before, or since. I started with the simple cases – bowels or nervous headaches – and as I progressed and could read the body with my fingers like a map I was entrusted to more difficult work, which was mostly 'spinal'. After a few months my earnings had more than doubled and I was able to leave the house in Battersea for two rooms in Shepherd Market. I was sorry to leave Sara behind, and touched when she let me keep the rocking chair. I didn't like having to work so hard and be on my feet so long, but at least I was making some progress. May was pleased with my work, and the patients liked me and trusted me, particularly the women.

I had always found it easy to gain the trust of other women, perhaps because I was never flighty or giggly or insincere. By this time I had divorced Harry, at his invitation, citing a middle-aged 'lady friend' as co-respondent and using a lawyer recommended by one of the doctors at the home. I went back to calling myself Magdalena Stark, partly because Magdalena Dando had a ridiculous sound to it and partly because I had learned to keep quiet about being divorced. In those days it was still considered a disgrace, particularly amongst the middle classes, and it made other women very wary. Instead of being safely locked inside the bonds of matrimony you were prowling around again, a temptation to the husbands of the married ones and getting in the way of those who haven't yet made the kill. It would have been no use telling them that, having known what marriage was like, I would sooner have swallowed prussic acid than try it again.

Dr Scott, who ran the Ivy Lodge, had a practice in Harley Street and knew a lot of rich pampered women who wanted a masseuse to come to their house. This 'private' work was really May's territory, but one day Dr Scott stopped me in the corridor and asked me if I would be prepared to go to the house of a Mrs Warrender.

'One of those fools with more money than sense, so you can charge a guinea a time. She just needs someone to talk to who'll tell her a risky story from time to time. That's all she wants, and if she's willing to pay a guinea for it somebody may as well profit.'

I asked why May didn't want the work.

'She's too good a masseuse for that sort of rubbish.'

I wasn't offended. I went to Mrs Warrender, and she proved very useful to me. Eventually I built up a whole list of patients who were just like her. Her metabolism was shocking owing to lack of exercise, and to over-eating and over-drinking. Her room stank of spirits, perfume and the powder she covered her body with. I had to dredge her with it before I rubbed her, until she looked like some sort of desiccated coconut bun.

'God, you're a damned witch, you really are!' she would moan as I slapped her, or 'Leave me be, for God's sake, you little vixen!'

But she loved it. She was also very generous about introducing me to her friends. Some women would as soon give away the name of their masseuse as they would the 'little woman' who made copies of designer gowns for them. But, like most people who were too idle to live, Mrs Warrender was very good-natured. She cursed me, but if she lost her temper it was all over in a minute; she simply could not be bothered to remember her grievance.

Mrs Warrender's friends were smart good-time women whose husbands were connected with the Stock Exchange or horse-racing or the theatre. I never cared much for other people's notion of virtue – or, at least, I knew that it had little or nothing to do with sexual morals – but I didn't think much of those women. I soon had my hands full of them: women who spent twenty-three out of twenty-four hours in a day abusing their digestive systems and wearing out their nerves – insomniacs, hysterics and dipsos who wanted to lie with their eyes shut, babbling and whining about their affairs, women who walked about looking taut and smart like Paquin dolls, and who dropped into bags of fat and broken-down muscle as soon as they got their corset and brassière off. For all their money and their leisure, I didn't envy them. They were so unsure of their own tastes that they had to have other people decorate their houses for them and to tell them what to wear, and even then they generally managed to spoil the effect with too many diamonds and expensive rubbish they picked up like jackdaws wherever they went.

I didn't envy them, but I longed to live in comfort without having to break my back for it, so when Mrs Warrender asked me to join her at a private party I accepted on the grounds that I might discover something that would be useful to me. I had become quite a favourite of Mrs Warrender's; she liked to give me presents and show me off to her friends, and I suppose she thought that I was too young to represent competition for the sort of men that she liked to have escort her about.

We met at Mrs Warrender's house first, and then went on to the theatre, where she had reserved four boxes. I had had nothing to wear that would have been at all suitable and had been forced to visit Bond Street and buy a panné velvet dress in midnight blue with a matching coat.

'That looks very becoming, Stark,' said Mrs Warrender graciously as she greeted me, 'and it exactly matches the colour of your eyes. Of course, you don't need any help with your complexion, being so young. And just look at your eyelashes – they're as long as my thumb. Aren't they, everyone?'

She addressed this question to the assembled guests, and the two women looked at me sourly. The men, who included a foxy-looking peer, an actor and a brigadier, looked at me with interest.

We drank several bottles of champagne and then went on to the show, and I'm ashamed to say that I remember very little about it except that the conversation became very loud and very vulgar. Afterwards we all piled into a cab and someone shouted: 'Let's go to Bridie's!' There was a unanimous cry of approval, followed by murmurs of disbelief when I said I didn't know who Bridie was.

'She runs the Dover Hotel,' explained the leery brigadier, who had been stroking my leg for the past ten minutes. 'Surely you've heard of it?'

I had, and I later came to realise that Bridie was one of the *demi-monde*'s best-known figures, riding around the West End in an old-fashioned brougham with a shifty-eyed coachman and a rakish bay. God knows where she had come from. Her 'hotel' was run as a private drinking club and a place for clandestine liaisons, and she claimed to know everyone.

'Ah, hello, Daisy!' she said to Mrs Warrender, whose Christian name was Violet. 'I was just having supper with a few friends. You've arrived at quite the right moment.'

Bridie seemed to have met everyone before, but was very vague about their names, introducing people as 'Lord Thingummy' or 'Dear Little So-and-So'. I had decided that she must have been good-looking once, but now all that remained was a top-knot of frowzy peroxide and a pair of china-blue eyes. I never saw her wear anything other than a mannish suit with a hunting stock at her neck.

We were shown up to an overcrowded sitting room where a fire was blazing fiercely, and a sullen waiter was sent to bring champagne. I was immediately cornered by one of Mrs Warrender's guests, whose name was Olivia Dryfield.

'Violet tells me you're a magician,' she said. She was a petite woman with a very prim appearance, but when I looked closely I saw that her neat features masked one of the most dissolute faces I had ever seen. 'How does it pay you?'

I was taken aback by her frankness. 'Quite well, thank you.'

'Well, when you feel like making some real money, let me know, and I'll put you on to a much more profitable line of country.'

I blinked hard, not sure that I had heard right, but she was staring right at me, as brazen as you please, and pursing that prim little mouth of hers. So *that* was what May had meant when she talked about using massage in the wrong way.

'Of course, Bridie here could be very useful to you. She's got all the customers you could ever need, right here under her roof.'

I disliked Olivia Dryfield intensely, yet afterwards I couldn't stop thinking about what she had said. Did I really want to find a way out of the drudgery of tramping from one spoilt woman to another? Yes, I did. Was I really prepared to go to such immoral lengths? I wasn't sure, but I intended to find out.

I went back to the Dover Hotel the next day.

I had been working late, and it was dark and pouring with rain. I did not get much of a reception from the staff, but I insisted that I was a personal friend of Bridie's and that I had been present at her party the previous night. I gave my name, afraid that it would mean nothing and that Bridie would only remember me as 'Dear Little So-and-So', but eventually someone came back with the message that Bridie wasn't feeling like company owing to a terrible hangover, but she was prepared to offer me a room for the night and see me in the morning. So I signed the register and handed over my damp things to be dried out.

The next morning I was just sitting up in bed and stretching when Bridie walked in. I later discovered that she never knocked before entering her guests' rooms.

'Sorry I couldn't see you last night, m'darling, but I was one over the top.'

'You do remember me, don't you? I came here with Violet Warrender.'

'Of course I do! I never forget a face! You're younger than the rest of that crowd, aren't you? How old are you?'

'Twenty.'

'Twenty? Dear, dear!' Bridie sat down heavily on the edge of the bed and scrutinised me. 'We'd better have a bottle of champagne.'

She rang for the aged waiter. 'A bottle of Pol Roger, you lazy old sod!'

He creaked out of the room, grumbling to himself.

'It's his bunions, poor bastard!' said Bridie gaily. 'Now, what can I do for you?' I had reached for my hairbrush and was starting to pin up my hair. 'That's right, my dear, that's the most important rule of life: never neglect your appearance.'

I considered the stock that had slipped round under her left ear, and the lock of yellow hair that had fallen down, weighted with hairpins. 'I'm a masseuse,' I said. 'I wondered whether you had any clients who needed my services?' I looked her straight in the eye.

'My my! And you're so young! Well, there is old Lord Thingummy. He takes a room upstairs sometimes, and would be glad of a little . . . relaxation. And I have a High Court judge. Perhaps we could discuss terms. . . .'

There was a pounding on the stairs and a hammering on my door.

'Magdalena, lovely Magdalena, open the door or I shall die of grief!'

'Open it yourself!' I shouted.

The door was flung open, and Monty Devereux burst into the room. He was the youngest of my 'clients'; the spoiled twenty-two-year-old son of a wealthy industrialist who was fast developing a taste for life's pleasures. I lit myself a cigarette and appraised him silently as he flung himself into the armchair. His dark hair was sleeked back with brilliantine, and he was faultlessly turned out, as always, from his ivory-topped cane to his hand-tooled pigskin shoes. 'A drink, for the love of God, or I'll disappear in a puff of smoke! You wouldn't *believe* what happened to me on my way up here. This place you live in is an utter madhouse!'

The Dover Hotel had been my home for several years. I had a room of my own, for which I paid Bridie a share of my earnings, and I charged ten guineas an hour, which meant that I only needed to work for a few hours each week to live very comfortably indeed. The rest of the time I was free to sit around and drink champagne and gossip with Bridie and the other permanent residents. There were a handful of us who lived and worked there, and we used to congregate at certain times of the day in a sitting room that was full of oriental knick-knacks and the stuffed heads of wild animals shot by Bridie's father in various corners of the Empire. There were a couple of heavily made-up chorus girls and a young boy with fair hair and sad brown eyes who was at the mercy of various elderly gentlemen who called at the Dover. I suppose he would have been called a catamite.

And what was I? A prostitute, in the eyes of the world, although it didn't really feel that way to me. All I had to do was enjoy a little chit-chat with my clients, then give them a massage which was a preliminary to a certain amount of fondling. The most intimate sort of contact cost extra and not many of them wanted that. They were mostly too old. And they were all very gentlemanly and treated me with a courtesy which other people would no doubt have found inappropriate. I sometimes stopped to wonder what Mama would have thought, but the idea amused rather than shamed me.

'You're a cool customer, you are,' Bridie used to say when she came into my room and watched me get dressed. 'A queer one, that's what you are.'

I would laugh and watch her dispassionately while she played with my rabbit's foot and powder, dabbing it on her face until she looked like an old crumbling meringue. It amused her to try to goad me into losing my temper, but she never succeeded and I think she respected me as a result.

'They got things a bit back to front down there,' said Monty, as I handed him a glass of brandy. 'Thought I was one of *those*.' He trailed his wrist and pursed his lips. 'I suppose I should have given your name, but before I knew what was going on they'd showed me into this room and there was a naked boy on the bed. A *boy!* I ask you!'

I laughed at his indignation.

'That will have been Neville. He caters for that particular speciality.'

My diffidence seemed to threaten Monty's urbane façade as much as what he had seen. 'Good God! My dear Magdalena, he's no more than a child. When I was his age, I was kicking a ball about—'

' — on the playing fields of Eton,' I prompted. 'We all know about you. Poor Neville's fallen on hard times, that's all. Anyway, that's his business.' I looked at the watch I wore pinned to my blouse when I was working. 'You've wasted ten minutes already. Off with your shirt! From the way you're sitting, your spine—'

'Leave me alone with those cruel hands of yours!' Monty made as if to fight me off. 'I don't want all that massage nonsense.'

'That's what you pay me for,' I replied a trifle tartly, turning away from him to light another cigarette. 'And you have precisely forty-five minutes before my next client arrives.'

'Oh, Magdalena, Magdalena, you're a lovely creature. Look at you! Look at the skin on you; it's as soft as a baby's! And eyelashes as long as my arm! . . . Only you smoke too much.'

He snatched the cigarette from my hand and covered my mouth with his own.

I let my thoughts stray back to Monty's embrace several times during the hour allotted to my next client. He was Bridie's High Court judge, Lord Justice Desmond Hallet, one of my 'regulars'. Unlike Monty, he took massage seriously and expected me to be very brisk and businesslike about administering it. Only after I'd slapped and pummelled his plump white body for half an hour did he turn his mind to a more amorous form of contact. But I was barely conscious of his fumbling and groaning as we lay between the sheets, remembering instead the passion that Monty had aroused in me.

'Thank you, my dear,' Lord Hallet said afterwards, polite and courteous as ever. 'I often find that a dish of oysters will do the trick.' He struggled into his long johns, and reached for the garters that kept his socks up. 'Perhaps you would be interested in seeing this, my dear,' he said, reaching into his coat pocket. 'I brought it specially to show you. I thought you might. . . .' He looked bashful as he handed me a small leather wallet. Inside it was a studio portrait of two sturdy young men.

'Oh, these must be your sons, Desmond!' There was genuine pleasure in my voice. Lord Hallet was always talking about his family, and I was touched that he had shown me the photograph.

'Yes, that's right. The latest photograph. M'wife has them done every year.'

'They're fine-looking boys,' I said. I groped around for something to add and chose the wrong thing altogether, given the circumstances.

'They must be very proud of you.'

*   *   *

70

I lived at the Dover Hotel for nearly six years.

I might have stayed there longer if I hadn't visited the doctor one day in 1911 and discovered that I was pregnant.

It was quite a blow. Someone in my line of business ought to have known better. This time, of course, I knew all too well how to get rid of it. In fact I was always being asked myself if I 'knew someone'. But to my surprise I wasn't sure that I *wanted* to get rid of it. I told myself that it was simply the indelible memory of Sara Corder's backstreet abortionist, but there was something else, too. The need for permanence was alien to me, but I was growing a little bored with my situation, and once more I saw the opportunity to move on.

I was meticulously careful about dates, and I quickly reduced the child's paternity to two candidates. Two men. Lord Hallet and Monty Devereux. I sat down and did my sums, and then made my decision. Monty visited me about twice a week and was always more than capable of fathering a child several times over. Lord Hallet's moments of inspiration were rare, and this last one had been an isolated incident. But at exactly the right time. By the law of averages if nothing else, the odds were heavily in favour of Monty Devereux, but I decided to tackle Lord Hallet over the question of the child's paternity. As a mature man of sixty he was in a better position to deal with the problem and to give me what I wanted. I would let Monty off the hook.

'Desmond. . . .'

His Worship was in my bed, balancing a champagne-glass against the matted white hair on his chest. I wondered what he looked like in his robes of office. Without them he looked harmless, almost comical.

'I have something to say to you which may be a shock. Put your champagne-glass down.'

He didn't need to. 'Pregnant?' he said, in the way he might have said 'Guilty?' cocking one bushy eyebrow.

'I'm afraid so, yes.'

'I see. And you think it's me?'

'Yes. It has to be.'

This time he put the champagne-glass down on the night table, his hand trembling slightly. 'My dear Magdalena—'

'Desmond, don't you remember that afternoon when we—'

'Dammit yes! The oysters!' He stroked his moustache. 'That's the last time I'm ever touching the bloody things.' He seemed remarkably calm. 'And I take it you're not going to get rid of it? I assume that's what this is all about.'

'Yes, I—'

'How much do you want?'

I was taken aback. I had expected to take more time getting to the point, and for once I found myself being outdone in sang-froid.

'I want to leave the Dover. I want a decent place to live in, not stylish, but comfortable, and I shall need something to live off. . . . And of course there will be the child's expenses. . . .' I had rehearsed this bit.

'Very well, we shall have to try to find somewhere suitable. I'd rather lease than buy. Easier to be discreet. And an allowance. . . . Paid monthly into a checking account?'

I was completely deflated. I had expected to have to turn a little nasty and remind him how the gutter press would love the story, and the distress it would cause to that worthy doyenne, Lady Hallet. And the two fine sons. . . . It was slightly disappointing to be denied my moment of revenge on his sex, and I found myself wondering, *How many times has he done this before?*

Over the weeks that followed, one of his Lordship's minions conducted a discreet search, and the result was number 47 Magnolia Gardens.

It wasn't what I had had in mind, and I told Desmond as much. I had pictured some pretty little mews house in one of London's more elegant boroughs, or a flat tucked away in a quiet corner of the West End. I had no desire to move south of the Thames again, to some dreary street that would remind me of my brief marriage to Harry Dando. But Desmond persuaded me to go and visit the house, impressing on me that the child was going to need space in which to play when it grew older. I hadn't really thought of it as having needs that differed from my own and I resented its presence in my belly all the way south on the Clapham omnibus.

But when I saw Magnolia Gardens I succumbed to its charm. The house was unimposing and a little shabby, but it was larger than I had anticipated and Desmond had promised that he would allow me a modest sum for furnishings. I stood in the Gardens and scrutinised my new home from all angles, then I returned to the West End and Heal's where I ordered a large white ottoman. I treated myself to tea at Gunter's (pregnancy had increased my appetite) and returned to the Dover Hotel feeling quite pleased with myself.

I sat down in my room and polished my nails for an hour or so. Thanks to the baby, I had nothing more strenuous to do.

My new life of leisure suited me perfectly, and as a result I felt quite warmly disposed towards the coming child.

I moved to Magnolia Gardens just before Christmas in 1911, promising a tearful Bridie that I would come back and visit her as often as possible, and my daughter was born in the spring of 1912. I still couldn't be sure whether the father was Desmond Hallet or Monty Devereux, for the baby looked like no one but herself, though she had inherited Mamma's red-brown hair. To my surprise, I found I rather liked her.

Desmond had allowed sufficient money to pay for a maternity nurse, but after that I was on my own. I dare say my household was not the sort that would have attracted a nanny anyway. Not one who was worth her salt. So I took care of the child myself, and fortunately she was no trouble. Not only was she well behaved, but also her constitution was robust, which was a source of great relief. I realised that I had carried a subconscious fear of producing another Bathsheba.

I called her Loveday. Although I had ridiculed my mother's baroque choice of names, I found that I just couldn't consign my daughter to being plain Mary Stark or Jane Stark or Sarah Stark. As far as I knew, 'Loveday' wasn't even a real name; it just popped into my head and seemed to sound right.

I spent a lot of time during the early months of Loveday's life wheeling her about the Gardens in her pram and thinking about the sort of person I wanted her to be. I decided quite quickly that I didn't care how lazy she was, but I could not tolerate her being a fool.

But maternal contemplation was never quite enough to absorb me, and inevitably I became a little bored. And it was around this time that I met Robert Clifford.

'You should get yourself a man, dear,' said Bridie, patting her yellow frizz of hair and adjusting her stock. 'Whatever happened to young Thingummy?'

Despite my new maternal status, boredom was driving me back across the river at frequent intervals, to sit in Bridie's bedroom and drink champagne.

'You mean Monty? I don't know. . . .'

It had not occurred to me that Monty would be interested in me, given my new circumstances; and, besides, he might take one look at Loveday and start doing his arithmetic.

'I miss Monty,' I said and realised as I said it that it was true. 'But I don't really think it's possible any more. Even if he didn't have to pay.' I smiled ruefully into my glass of Pol Roger.

'It's the baby, isn't it?' asked Bridie. She was no fool.

'Yes.'

'Well, never mind; you're still young and you've got your looks. Never neglect your appearance, that's what I say. Want some more? *Bring us another bottle, you lazy old sod!* I see no reason why you shouldn't have some fun. You should be sitting and drinking champagne with some delicious chap, not with an old bag like me! There must be *someone* down in Thingummy.'

Two men did turn up in Thingummy not long after I moved there. The first was my brother Hubert. He was in London looking for a job, and wanted a place to stay.

I was delighted. 'But how did you find me? I didn't think anyone knew where I was.'

'Mama claimed no knowledge of your whereabouts, but good old Edgar still has your Battersea address. I knocked on a few doors, and a very helpful lady by the name of Sara Corder sent me here.'

Hubert stayed with me for several months and livened the place up a bit, but in 1914 he was one of the first to join up and I never saw him again. I think he lasted about six weeks.

The second person to turn up in Magnolia Gardens was Neville Brownie, the young male prostitute from the Dover Hotel, who moved into one of the flats at number 46. I used to watch him through my sitting-room window as he returned from work in the evenings, wondering why those sad brown eyes seemed so familiar. I think he recognised me as I pushed Loveday's pram around the Gardens, but he looked away furtively each time I tried to acknowledge him, so I abandoned my attempts. He had his invalid father with him and had found an office job in the City, and obviously wished to forget his past. I had no wish to hinder him, so I left him alone.

While I was still dazed and bitter about Hubert's death, Harry contacted me for the first time in years, pestering me for money. He claimed that since I had a fixed income and he was destitute I had an obligation to give him money. I didn't know whether this was true or not but I decided that I ought to find out. I was wheeling the two-year-old Loveday through the Gardens one afternoon when I caught sight of Robert Clifford coming in the opposite direction.

Robert Clifford's professional reputation went before him, and I had learned a little about him from simple observation. At that time he was a young widower, with a son, Edwin, by his first marriage, who was so closeted away behind heavy velvet curtains that I scarcely saw him. I felt sorry for the boy but not for the father, who was making a name for himself through a dazzling career at the Bar, and was engaged to a London socialite called Helena Sarsted.

He was massively tall and broad, with what used to be called an 'athletic' figure. His size reminded me a little of Papa, though he was fairer and more handsome than Papa had been. The gold of his hair shone through the brilliantine. I ran my eye over his clothes. They were of the finest quality, particularly his exquisite cashmere overcoat that looked so soft I longed to sink my fingers into it.

Robert Clifford smiled at me and raised his bowler hat, and I stopped him.

'Mr Clifford, may I congratulate you on your forthcoming marriage? I read the announcement in the newspaper. And may I ask your advice on a legal matter?'

I offered no apology for my impertinence. I had long since lost such scruples. If, indeed, I had ever had them.

'Why, most certainly, Mrs Stark.'

'Miss.'

'Miss.' He smiled. 'It's ridiculous, the way we feel bound to these empty conventions, don't you think?'

He smiled again, an open unpatronising smile, and it was then that I decided I liked him. I liked Robert Clifford very much.

50 Magnolia Gardens

Robert

'GRACIOUS, ROBERT, I don't think I could possibly live here!'
my wife said when she saw the house in Magnolia Gardens. 'It's
so far from town!'

I'm talking about my second wife, you understand. Helena. My
first wife, Lorna, had demurred on the subject of Magnolia
Gardens.

You see, it was not what we, the Cliffords, were used to. My
father's family have been around for hundreds of years, since the
Norman Conquest or thereabouts. William Clifford (or I suppose
it would have been 'de Clyfforde', something like that) was the
first. And my mother's family, the Devignes, were also very
distinguished. They descended from a Huguenot officer in the
army of William III. Down the years both Cliffords and Devignes
have married into baronetcies and the families of peers' younger
sons, so we were well connected, if not exactly aristocratic.

We lived in a house called Hadden Wick, on the border
between Essex and Suffolk. It was rather an unusual arrangement, in that the house belonged to my Great-Uncle Charles. Old
Charles was childless, and Papa was his favourite nephew, so he
made Papa his heir, and he and Mama moved into the house in
1874, the year before I was born. It all worked out rather well,
because Great-Uncle Charles was a keen botanist and he was
abroad most of the time collecting specimens, so Mama and Papa
could look after the house for him and manage the small estate.
And in due course Papa would inherit it, and then I would inherit
it from him, since I was his eldest son.

Hadden Wick is a handsome redbrick Queen Anne house with
all the usual things you'd expect to find in a gentleman's
residence: a large withdrawing room, dining room and billiard
room downstairs, eight or nine bedrooms upstairs, and a rose
garden and lavender walk outside. The three attic bedrooms were

shared by the maids and the cook, and jolly nice they were, too: we were good to our servants. Cook was always known as 'Mrs', whether she was married or not. The kitchens and the scullery were her kingdom; as were the kitchen garden and the apple orchard. The orchard was always my favourite place. It was so beautiful; crammed with blossom in the springtime. The perfect place for taking young ladies courting. They were always enchanted with the blossom.

I was the first child in the family, and I suppose Mama and Papa couldn't help but favour me for that reason. My importance was increased when their second child, Alfred, died in infancy. There then followed my three sisters, Elspeth, Gertrude and Clara, and finally Walter. We were all raised by a nanny, and spent our formative years in the cosy world of the nursery, only going down to see Mama for an hour before bedtime. Nurse was an absolute darling. I adored her. We all did. She made one feel like the most important person in the world.

Naturally I adored Mama, but in a different way. Until we were old enough to spend more time downstairs, we didn't get to know our parents very well, and the nursery was the focus of our existence. The outside world came to us. Cans of hot water carried up by the maids for our baths, and tea brought up on trays. Tea was a hefty meal. And there was a chant we broke into every day at the same time: 'I've – had – two – pieces – of – bread – and – butter – may – I – have – some – cake?' You weren't allowed the cake until you'd eaten the bread and butter. You need rules like that in life, to help you know where you are.

Walter and I addressed Papa as 'sir' once we were old enough to go away to school. He was a good man, in my opinion, always fair and rational. If he was angry, he told one to 'pull oneself together' and one quickly did. Or, if that didn't work and we pushed things too far, he gave us a hiding with his slipper. That always did the trick. Women I've known have sometimes asked if I resented it, and all I can say is that it had rather the opposite effect; it made me think a lot of him. He wouldn't tolerate any nonsense. I admired him even more in retrospect when I had children of my own and discovered just how difficult it is to keep them in line. I suppose our father–son relationship was a distant one, as was typical of that age. That was the way I liked it. I couldn't have tolerated living in a stifling emotional environment the way they do nowadays. Very bad for one, all this confrontation about 'feelings' and 'needs'. If Papa needed to, he would take us on one side and give us one of his Little Talks, in which he was always utterly frank and honest with us, in a careful sort of way. By that I mean he was faithful to the facts without trying to excite any sort of emotion in us.

The first of these was when I was twelve. I was just about to leave home for Rugby, and Papa wanted to give me a Little Talk entitled The More Unpleasant Facts of Life. I remember it clearly; it was August, and the bees were buzzing drowsily in the flowerbeds as we walked the length of the gravelled terrace along the south front of the house. Our feet making rhythmic crunching sounds. Me in my Norfolk jacket, with Papa's hand resting on my shoulder. If some of the things he said appalled me, then I tried hard not to show it. The next Little Talk was far more cheerful: it was about what would happen when he died and the estate was passed on to me. Very reassuring.

Mama was an awfully nice person, gentle and well bred, but with nothing feeble about her. She liked outdoor sports, particularly tennis which she took up in later life. She used to press wild flowers as well, and keep a journal. Not a torrid confessional, but about things she'd spotted in the hedgerows – that sort of thing. Cleanliness, Honesty, Decent Manners, Kindness and Courtesy. Those were Mama's tenets, and she did her best to impress them on her children. There was Godliness, too; but, if anything, that was the one she had the least success with. A very devout woman, Mama.

I look on those days at Hadden Wick as a sort of golden age. We played freely with the farm labourers' children and talked broad Suffolk with as much ease as decent Standard English. There was always plenty for us to do. I liked breeding ferrets, ratting and cricket. We had a pitch in the top meadow, and there were wonderful summer games with local families. All sorts took part – village people as well as gentry. Father and I hunted and shot a little. Point-to-points were a social occasion in those days, not for making money like they are now. And every August there were wonderful holidays in Felixstowe, where we hired a sailing boat.

If there was one blot on the sunny landscape of our childhood, it was Sundays. Sundays were beastly dull. Mama led morning prayers every day of the week before breakfast, which was bad enough, inducing foot-shuffling and suppressed yawns – but on Sundays the torture was intensified. Not only was there church, twice, but one had to learn the collect for the day and repeat it to Mama after lunch. And one wasn't allowed to go out riding, or do any other sort of outdoor activity. One was just supposed to sit and read and contemplate one's navel. I remember every detail of the drawing room at Hadden Wick, simply because of the hours of purgatory there on Sunday afternoons. It was a large oblong-shaped room stuffed with a bewildering muddle of Victorian bric-à-brac. Stuffed animals, things under glass domes. Copies of *Punch* and the *Strand*. At least there was plenty to look at; that was a blessing. I used to sit there, swinging my legs against the chair, counting the teeth on a yellowing stuffed weasel and watching the hands move slowly around the skeleton clock. Willing them to hurry. God, I hated Sundays!

Our pleasant routine was sometimes disrupted by the return of Great-Uncle Charlie from foreign parts. He was a charming old rascal and something of a talker, too. He'd keep Mama and Papa up for hours after dinner with tales of his travels. The Orient, Bengal, Madagascar, Columbia – he'd been everywhere. I'd see Mama's eyelids drooping as she tried to give him her attention. I suppose it's different for the person who's actually been to those places; they can see the scenes as they're describing them. Or maybe Great-Uncle Charlie was just a bit of a bore. I didn't really know him well enough to remember. He was very fond of the girls, I remember that much, giving their curls a playful tug and finding them a humbug in his waistcoat pocket. He always brought us presents. In fact the whole house was full of what we called Charlie's Collections. He brought back crates of ivories, lacquer ware, stuffed parrots, musical instruments. . . . Mama would look worried. 'Goodness, I don't know where we'll put it all,' she'd say. And as soon as Great-Uncle Charlie had gone: 'Into the attic with it!'

In fact, after he'd gone there was a general air of relief all round, despite him being a likeable old fellow. It was as though order returned and everything was safe and predictable. One knew where one was. He'd eventually pop off and leave the place to Father, and Father would pass it on to me.

I started at Rugby in 1888. Being sent away to school represented something of a promotion. The nursery was behind me for good, and when I came home in the holidays I had supper with Mama and Papa while my sisters were still upstairs. That made one feel a hell of a chap.

I had a very cheerful time at school. Up at a quarter to seven and into a cold bath, still drying oneself as one ran to get dressed. A run before breakfast in the winter. Marvellous. And then of course there was all the sport, especially the cricket. At thirteen you can't really see grey; everything's either black or white. One's peers were either rotten or thoroughly good sorts. And, although sport alone didn't make you popular, it did help. You were in the limelight if you were good at it.

It wasn't a class thing, you understand. Most people were out of the top drawer, though there was a policeman's son on a scholarship. He did rather well actually. Became captain of cricket. Certain houses you despised frightfully, and home boarders were looked on with grave suspicion. There were foreigners: a few Indians and one Chinese. But absolutely no colour prejudice. If a person was dark, you'd call him a Nig, but only if you liked him. You wouldn't have said it if you didn't like him.

I breezed through the academic stuff, never had any trouble. We made fun of the masters, but most of them were decent sorts. The Classics master, John Reed, was a good chap He used to speak of feelings 'stirring in the bo*soom*' – always like that – which produced howls of joy every time. He introduced me to the poems of Horace, which I still adore. Nice old boy, Reed, but definitely queer. *And* he was a Liberal. We used to rag him for that.

Apart from lessons and sport there wasn't much really. Sundays were awfully dull; no better than home. All that Greek Testament reading. We used to envy the Jews because they didn't have to go to chapel.

After I had left school, life continued to be both easy and pleasant. I had expected things to get more complicated but I found this wasn't the case: you were still either a cad and a blackguard or a thoroughly good chap. One slipped naturally into the latter category, and life flowed on. It wasn't that I or any of my contemporaries actively pursued excellence. It was just that excellence was there as a natural part of things, as part of the scene. We lived in the best sort of home, ate the best food, danced with the prettiest girls and planned the most brilliant careers. Mine was to be in politics. I had fallen in love with the idea while still at Rugby, fired by our arguments with John Reed.

I went up to Cambridge to read Classics, and in the holidays repaired to Hadden Wick for an endless round of social activities. There was always someone having a house-party, so there were plenty of lively young people around. We'd make up parties for anything – picnics, outings. 'We're going to the theatre. Would you care to join us?' – that sort of thing. I loved musical comedies, and it was fashionable then to develop a low-life taste for the music-halls. Once we even organised a bicycling party, which was great fun. The girls all wore bloomers, and absolutely everyone, without exception, fell off.

In the summer I continued to play cricket in the top meadow, with some success. In my opinion there's no finer sound than that leisurely, polite clapping people make when you stride off the field after a good innings, with the faint rattle of china as tea's served and cucumber sandwiches are passed round.

My best season ever was in 1898, the summer after I'd graduated from Cambridge. I'd just come off the field, bat under my arm, after a respectable fifty when a voice said: 'Do you excel at everything you do, Mr Clifford, or is it only cricket?'

I looked round and, dammit, if there wasn't the prettiest girl I'd ever seen, standing there right beside me. She was tiny and all pink and white as though she'd been made from china, and she had these great thick coils of golden brown hair and the biggest brown eyes.

I just stood there, grinning like the proverbial idiot, not knowing who she was.

Then our neighbour, Lydia Hesketh, rushed forward and introduced us. 'This is Miss Lorna Barkworth, Robert; she's staying with us for the weekend. I've been telling her all about you.'

Upon which Miss Barkworth blushed and lowered her long, thickly curling lashes.

I was bewitched! I thought of nothing else all day. I played as I'd never played before. Oh, I was used to being good at everything and having people think I was one hell of a chap, but this was different. All I wanted was for Lorna Barkworth to think so. No one else.

She was everything I had ever wanted. I was madly in love with her – within five minutes of setting eyes on her. She was pretty and gay and gentle and intelligent. You never saw such a lovely creature. Never.

And the most remarkable thing of all was that she doted on me as I did on her. She made me feel like some sort of god.

There followed many more weekends at the Heskeths' for Lorna, and gradually her family came to know mine and everyone was *au fait* with the shape of things to come. I shall never forget the day I proposed to her. It was in the spring of 1899, about nine months after we first met. Mama and Papa had a house-party, and the Barkworths were among the dozen or so guests. Papa seemed strangely distracted that weekend, and after lunch on Saturday he suddenly announced that he'd got a photographer in, because he wanted to record the occasion. Well, we all thought it was a bit of a caper, and mucked in helping the maids bring the chairs out and line them up on the steps. And then the photographer fellow scurried about and we all sat up stiff and straight and *snap!* – off went the flash. Then we all relaxed and laughed and *snap!* – off it went again; so we had two very different pictures, which I still have to this day.

As everyone drifted inside again, I seized my chance. I beckoned to Lorna, and we slipped off together round the side of the house and into the orchard.

It had never looked so pretty; a mass of pink and white blossom and the grass studded with the first daisies. Lorna bent and picked some and then stood fetchingly beneath the bough of an apple tree, tracing their delicate petals with a fingertip. What a picture she made; her skin as pink and white as the blossom, her gown a delicate blue like the sky. I feasted on her with my eyes for a moment until she blushed self-consciously and looked away.

'Oh, Lorna!' I said, taking her hand, a gesture which she did not resist. 'I'm sorry if I embarrassed you, but I . . . I . . . .'

And there I was, reduced to a stuttering fool. I grabbed her other hand and took the plunge. 'I do so love you, and want you to be mine!'

After that things went very smoothly indeed. We wandered arm in arm through the apple trees, while I described our future together. 'Naturally, we'll live here at Hadden Wick,' I told her. 'Papa will eventually pass its management over to me, and I'll employ a bailiff to keep an eye on things while I pursue a career in politics. And one day I'll hand it down to *our* son!'

This thought prompted Lorna to give a little tremor of excitement, and when she looked at me her big brown eyes were shining.

'Let's go and give the families our good news,' I said. 'Look there's Papa now, waving at us. He can be the first person we tell.'

We hurried towards my Father, hand in hand, bursting with our good fortune.

'Ah, there you are, Robert,' he said. 'I've been looking for you. I'm afraid you and I have to have a Little Talk.'

'But I don't believe it, sir!' I burst out. 'It's preposterous. . . . You never said anything!'

Papa and I were tracing the gravelled path across the south front, marking time with one another. He stared ahead, avoided looking at me.

'I know, and I regret the suddenness with which I have to impart the news, but I've only just been given a full financial statement. Hadden Wick will have to be sold.'

The facts were so absurd that they were almost insulting. While hunting wild orchids in Rhodesia, Great-Uncle Charlie had fallen for some merry widow half his age, had married her only to discover that she was a demon at the gaming tables, and had watched her tip his inheritance – *our* inheritance – down the drain. It was the last thing we'd expected.

'But what will you and Mama do?'

'We're moving to Bournemouth.'

'*Bournemouth?*'

It seemed there was nothing more to be said. 'It's not quite as bad as all that,' said Papa, trying as ever to be fair. 'There'll be quite a bit made from the sale of Charlie's Collections, enough for you and Lorna to get yourselves a decent place to live – even if it isn't quite what you're used to. . . .'

A career in politics was now out of the question, and I was forced to pluck an alternative means of survival out of the air like a rabbit out of a hat. I chose the law, which naturally meant London. And so we went to live in the villa in Magnolia Gardens. It was a pleasant enough house, but the neighbourhood left a lot to be desired. My darling Lorna was very brave about it. 'So many professional men are living south of the river these days,' she said, trying to reassure me. 'It's perfectly respectable.'

* * *

Married life was bliss.

Great-Uncle Charlie or no Great-Uncle Charlie, I still had an awful lot to be thankful for. I absolutely adored Lorna, and our life together was everything I had hoped it would be. My fellow-barristers in chambers used to joke about it when I rushed off home every evening. 'Look at Clifford,' they said, as I threw on my overcoat and grabbed the bundle of briefs I had to look over that evening. 'He can't wait to get back to his household goddess!'

There was soon added incentive to rush home when our son Edwin was born in 1903. I was beside myself with pride and delight, and you never saw a more tender or loving mother than Lorna. But the birth had been a long and agonising ordeal for her and it had left her very weak. She made a feeble attempt at apologising to me, worried that the exemplary wife should be able to produce her offspring without batting an eyelid, and then get on with running the household for her husband.

'It's all right, my darling,' I said, taking her in my arms and kissing her gently on her eyelids. 'I just want you to get as much rest as possible for as long as possible.' And to ensure that this was the case I instructed the maid not to let her mistress lift a finger, and hired a stout Irish nurse to minister to the needs of young Edwin.

Lorna tended to become anxious when I brought my briefs home and worked on them there, since she felt that out of polite-ness she was forced to stay up until I had finished them. Purely out of consideration for her, I started staying at my chambers to do the work. I was only just out of those barren early years in any career at the Bar, and I was desperately keen to make a name for myself, so the hours were unavoidable. I instructed Lorna that if I was not back by eight, then she was to assume that I was working late, and go to bed as soon as she felt tired. This system worked quite well for a while, although it meant that we didn't see very much of one another. Then one evening I was about to leave home early for a change when my fellow barristers restrained me: one of them had just become a father, too, and they were cracking open a bottle of champagne to wet the infant's head. It seemed only polite to stay and keep them company, and then to go with them to a certain hostelry in Soho where one could get a very decent rack of lamb and the waitresses weren't averse to a bit of light-hearted banter. We drank several bottles of claret and had a very jolly time – in fact, I couldn't remember when I'd last had such a jolly time. Then I took a hansom cab home to Magnolia Gardens.

I was rather alarmed to see that there was still a light on in the drawing room. It was a quarter past two in the morning.

'Lorna?' I called, and as I closed the door I realised that I was squiffy. 'Lorna, darling?'

She was waiting for me in the drawing room. And it was then, as I registered the expression on her pretty face, that my life ceased to be easy and pleasant and became very complicated indeed.

'Oh, Robert!' said Lorna, and her brown eyes were brimming with tears. 'Oh Robert, where have you been? I've been so worried! I thought something had happened to you!'

And she flung herself against my chest, sobbing noisily.

I just stood there feeling a damned heel, with the smell of drink still on my breath.

'My darling, I'm so sorry,' I said, and to prove it I carried her up to our bedroom there and then, laying her gently on the bed and hurrying to remove my clothes. It was so long since I had held her in my arms. But after I'd made love to her she sobbed even louder.

'What is it, my love?' I asked. 'If you're angry with me because I came home late, I promise it will never—'

'It's not that. It's just – oh, Robert – I'm so afraid of having another baby. It was so terrible last time, I don't think I could go through that again!'

Lorna miscarried after three months, and it was such a grisly business that I was appalled and kept away from her, out of consideration. It was time for me to get a mistress, I decided, purely for Lorna's sake, so that I would never have cause to inflict such terrible distress on my dear wife again. I took to visiting the music-halls again, and I found a girl at the Gaiety called Ruby, who did a juggling trick with painted wooden balls. Ruby, as well as being the possessor of a very fine pair of legs, was a girl of simple tastes. A bottle of champagne, a good meal and there were no questions asked.

I saw Ruby only when my busy professional life allowed. In the prosperous years before the Great War there was plenty of work for an able barrister, and I could pick and choose the sort of cases I took on. It was natural that I should be attracted to the excitement and glamour of criminal law, and I became something of a specialist in defending lady felons. These women flocked to me, though I'm damned if I knew why, amongst them several widows of ample means and slight morals. There was one particularly fascinating specimen called Edith Birch. Mrs Birch, who dressed in voluptuous black velvet bedecked with jet and diamonds, insisted that her late husband had had an accident with a pair of gardening shears, despite employing half a dozen gardeners. She also insisted on private consultations in her opulent house in Mayfair.

I had just returned from that very house one night, expecting to find my darling Lorna already in bed, when instead I discovered her up and waiting for me. She was lying on the chaise-longue in the drawing room, sipping a glass of champagne. She wore a ruffled lace peignoir I had never seen before that displayed an indecent amount of bosom. Her golden brown curls were piled up loosely in a very fetching manner, and she had a high colour.

I stood there like an idiot, gaping at her.

Lorna stood up and walked slowly towards me, swaying slightly as though she'd had too much to drink. She kissed me resoundingly on the mouth, and then smiled at me, amused at my shocked expression.

Her smile faded. 'Robert, you do still love me, don't you?'

'Of course! You're the only woman in my life!'

'I've been thinking it over and over for months now, and I've decided I can bear to go through with it. I want to have another baby.'

When Lorna discovered, in the spring of 1907, that she was pregnant, we were both delighted. Regrettably I was already very heavily embroiled with the fascinating Mrs Birch, whose case had been postponed pending further evidence from the gardener's boy. I did my best to keep her away, but she was an awfully persistent lady, used to getting her own way.

One warm summer evening she slipped into my chambers in the Middle Temple, just as the shadows were lengthening and the light was beginning to fade.

'My dearest Mr Clifford,' she said, lifting her black veil and fixing me with her brilliant blue eyes. 'It's imperative that I have a consultation with you at once . . . some new evidence . . . it really is *most* urgent!'

'Very well.' I had already stood up and started to tidy away my papers with indecent haste. 'But it will have to take place in a more private location. Confidentiality, you understand. . . .'

She was following me out of my room, walking with quick tripping steps.

'Given the special nature of your case. . . .'

We were hurrying arm in arm down the front steps of my chambers and along King's Bench Walk.

And suddenly there was Lorna.

Standing there, smack in the middle of the pavement staring at us. Her swollen body heaving. I stared back. Mrs Birch had the presence of mind to release my arm and try out one of the innocent smiles she had been practising for the jury.

'Lorna, dearest, we were just—'

'Robert, I—'

We both spoke at once.

Lorna cleared her throat and went on, but her voice was very faint: 'We're due for dinner at the Heskeths'. I forgot to tell you this morning, so I thought I'd come myself, and. . . .'

It was then I noticed how pale she was, grey almost. She seemed to stumble, and clutched at the iron railings as her legs gave way.

'Robert, oh my God, *Robert!*'

I bundled her into a hansom cab and shouted at the driver, swore at him to bloody well get a move on and take us to Harley Street. That was the only place I could think of at the time. Perhaps I should have taken her straight to the local hospital, I don't know.

It was one of the most terrible moments of my life. She was crying out, and in between her cries her face was all screwed up with the effort of holding in the pain. There were brown-red stains of blood on her elegant afternoon dress and on the seat of the cab.

'It's all right, darling, it's all right,' I kept saying to her. But I knew that it wasn't.

I got the cabbie to stop outside the private consulting rooms of a man my family had used for years, and the two of us carried her up the steps and into the waiting room. There had been no way for us to warn them of our arrival, and the sight of Lorna caused much consternation. Everything happened rapidly, uniformed nurses rushing to and fro giving orders, doors opening and closing. Dr Piper was with another patient, so we couldn't even take her into the surgery; they just had to lie her down in an anteroom and draw some screens about her.

And ten minutes later, lying on this makeshift bed, she gave birth to a stillborn child: a daughter.

My beloved Lorna! I adored the girl, I was crazy about her. I spent every spare minute at her bedside while she recovered, filling her room with gardenias, promising her that we'd never be apart.

The gardenias faded and turned brown, and I replaced them with more gardenias as Lorna's convalescence stretched from days into weeks and then months. There were some complications, apparently, an infection in her chest, but I was confident that the medical men could sort it out.

I told Lorna as much. 'Won't be long now, my darling! You just get as much rest as you can!'

I went on telling her that, and telling myself that it *must* be true. And I went on buying the white gardenias.

When she died, I simply couldn't believe it. I'd shut my ears to the doctor's pronouncements, willing them not to be true. I couldn't let it be true; I simply couldn't bear the guilt. I was guilty that I had made her miscarry, and now I felt as though I had killed her. I regret to say that I couldn't bear to be near Edwin, either. Whenever he looked at me it was as though Lorna's big brown eyes were reproaching me.

You see, I really did love Lorna, and without her my world had fallen apart. But the world won't leave a widowed man alone, and very quickly I was sucked into an empty meaningless social round in which spare women of all descriptions were flung, or flung themselves, at me. I didn't want any of them.

For Edwin's sake, I decided, I should marry again, but I would take my own time about it and wait for the great restless tide of grief to ebb. After a year had passed, this showed no signs of happening, so in the meantime I had my baser needs taken care of by a respectable middle-aged lady who lived in Kilburn and kept heavy curtains drawn in her parlour all the time, to keep the dust off her plush velvet sofa.

A depressing existence indeed, and I was much cheered when Lorna's second cousin, Archie Osborne, included me in a house-party that was to take place in Biarritz in August 1912. Biarritz! To me the name alone conjures the leisured world of the well-heeled traveller before the Riviera was made part of their empire. The smell of attar of roses on a hot night and the clicking of ivory counters in a discreet casino. . . .

I liked Archie very much, and I also had a soft spot for his rich wife, Isabel, who was something of a suffragette and actually *smoked* in public, which was virtually unheard of before the war. Isabel had the good sense not to try to pair me off with anyone; but, then, she hadn't reckoned with the determination of Miss Helena Sarsted.

Helena was a wealthy socialite in her early thirties, who had never married. I found this hard to believe at first. She was such a charming and well-read lady, who liked nothing better than to stroll along the palm-fringed esplanade in a shady hat and talk to me about her favourite authors, who also happened to be my favourite authors.

'I cheated,' she admitted later, with her cool smile. 'I sneaked a look in your portmanteau and found out your tastes in reading matter.'

I was surprised at this, since Helena seemed such a proper lady, with immaculate manners, and who expressed horror at women smoking in public.

It also made me feel uneasy. I spent a lot of time with Helena on that holiday, simply because she managed to contrive to be there at my elbow when I was alone. We 'bumped into' one another a lot. If I liked her at all, of which I was not certain, it was because she couldn't have been more different from my dearest Lorna. Cool, controlled, always modishly chic, she glided from one social setting to another.

Yet somehow it was impossible to imagine being alone with her in a bedroom, naked.

'We do get on awfully well together, don't you think?' she asked one afternoon when we had 'bumped into' one another in a bookshop and were strolling back to the villa together. 'Perhaps, when we're back in England . . . you and I might come to an understanding?'

She stopped walking and looked at me from beneath her ivory silk parasol.

'Yes, we might,' I said, thinking it best to agree, since I didn't really know what she meant.

When we reached the villa, we found Archie and Isabel taking tea on the veranda. As we went to join them, Helena took the opportunity to lean rather heavily on my arm. I noticed that she was smiling more broadly than usual and looked excited.

Archie noticed, too. 'What have you two been up to?' he asked. A tactless old duffer at the best of times. He didn't notice Isabel frowning at him. 'You look as though you're keeping a secret.'

'We are!' said Helena.

'Are we?' I asked, not following at all.

'Oh, *men!*' Helena gave a most uncharacteristic schoolgirl simper, and clung on to my arm.

'You mean you two, are . . . ?'

Helena simply nodded, and giggled. I stood there rooted to the spot, unable to say a word.

I have always prided myself on being a gentleman, and therefore it was out of the question to contradict her in public. That would have been tantamount to calling her a liar, or pouring scorn on her feminine charms.

Thank God for Archie's conventional ideas! 'I think we'd better leave our two love-birds alone,' he told Isabel. 'They look as though they have things to discuss.'

As soon as they had gone, Helena's simpering smile disappeared.

'Look at this,' she said, pointing at Isabel's silver cigarette-case. 'Such a disgusting habit, don't you think?' And she tipped all the cigarettes over the edge of the veranda and on to the jacaranda trees below, where they dotted the dark shiny leaves with flecks of white.

'Look here, Helena—'

'You're about to say that you had no intention of proposing to me. But, you know, Robert, if you thought about it, you'd realise that it really would be the best thing for both of us. . . .'

And so I returned to England engaged to Helena Sarsted.

'That boy needs taking in hand. It's time someone was firm with him.'

Helena's arrival in a large motor-car, swathed in furs and with armfuls of presents, had not had the desired effect on Edwin. He shied away from her. And Helena, whose experience of children was limited, decided that she was the one to be firm.

I sighed my agreement. As we were talking, Helena was busy unpacking a crate of her belongings in preparation for the wedding. At first she had insisted that we move from Magnolia Gardens, which she thought beneath her, to somewhere in Knightsbridge or Kensington, but I had resisted. The reason I gave was Edwin's unbalanced state, though I was really doing it to prove that I was still capable of making decisions. But I did not resist her plans for our marriage. I could see its advantages. I needed a wife, but I did not want a replacement for Lorna or a rival for her memory. Helena did not seem to expect me to love her, or even to desire her.

Desire was a different matter entirely.

Having had to fight to stay in Magnolia Gardens, I felt as though I were aware of the place for the first time. I decided I actually quite liked it. I was strolling through it one day on my way to chambers when I bumped into my new neighbour, Miss Stark, wheeling her baby in a perambulator. I smiled at her and raised my hat, and she stopped me to congratulate me on my engagement. Then, with a forwardness that I was unaccustomed to in women, she asked if I could give her some advice.

'And how might I help you, Miss Stark?'

She really was the most charming lady, with a bold eye and the sort of ripe beauty that was favoured in those days. Masses of auburn hair, and the creamiest skin I'd ever seen. While we were talking I glanced into the pram at her daughter. I wasn't much interested in babies, but on this occasion I looked again. You never saw such a perfect little creature. So tiny and so pretty.

It seemed that Miss Stark was having problems with financial demands from her ex-husband, so I promised to see what I could do. I sent a detailed letter from chambers, setting out her exact legal position, but I found that I couldn't stop thinking about the lady and her elfin daughter. On my way back from work one day, I knocked at the door of number 47.

The door opened, and I raised my hat. 'Miss Stark, may I come in?'

'Of course,' she said, but my visit was clearly the last thing she had been expecting. She was dressed in a wrapper, with her hair tied up in a ribbon. And me with my bowler hat and cane.

'I came to enquire whether you had solved your problem satisfactorily?' I sat down on a white ottoman, and it creaked beneath my weight.

'That's very kind of you,' she said. 'Yes. I think so. I've passed on your letter to my ex-husband, so. . . .'

Her daughter was scrambling about on the floor, trying to reach for my trouser leg. I smiled.

'What a pretty little thing she is! What's her name?'

'Loveday.'

'Delightful.' I watched her.

'I think I'd better put her down in the nursery. . . .'

'Do you mind if I come with you?' I asked. It was what we barristers would have called an unpremeditated response.

Miss Stark looked surprised, but she allowed me to follow her into the nursery and together we smiled down at her daughter. Then we went back into the drawing room and I sat down on the white ottoman again.

I was still wearing my coat.

'May I take your coat from you?'

I handed it to her, and she stood there with it held tightly in her arms. Then she buried her face in it, as though she wanted to feel the cashmere against her cheeks and her mouth and her throat. I understood her then, understood that she had something in her that neither Lorna nor Helena had ever had. I stood up and took the coat from her, kissing her very hard on the mouth as I did so. Then I pulled her down on to the ottoman.

We had barely spoken, yet I did not feel that I was in any way insulting her with my behaviour or the possible suggestion that she was 'that sort of woman'. We both knew that it wasn't like that. I had wanted her as soon as I had spoken to her in the Gardens, and she had wanted me, and that was all there was to it.

I went back.

My honeymoon was not long over, but I already knew that, whatever the fabric of my marriage to Helena was to be, it was not to be woven in the bedroom. Helena was a hard, bony, unloving woman. Perhaps I hadn't intended it to happen so soon, but our houses were so close. . . .

I found myself on Miss Stark's doorstep again. 'Oh, hello! I wondered if I might come in for a moment . . .?'

I could tell that she wanted me as desperately as I wanted her, yet she seemed disturbed by something.

'Not *here*, Robert,' she whispered as I pulled her on to the ottoman. 'I'll arrange to meet you somewhere else if you like, but not *here*.' She glanced fearfully in the direction of number 50.

'It's all right. . . .' I stood up and drew the curtains across the window. 'Look,' I said, 'it's simple to shut out the world. We're safe in here. What happens here concerns no one but the two of us.'

It did seem very simple to me – the two houses with two very different women in them. Everything kept tidy, and separate.

'But what about Helena?' she asked.

'Helena?' I repeated, surprised that she would even mention my wife's name. 'Oh, Helena's all right. She's got her entertaining to do, and her charity work and so on. She's all right.' I really couldn't see what all the fuss was about.

But she was persistent. 'And Edwin? Has he come to terms with his mother's death? Does he get on well with his stepmother?'

All these questions. The only way to silence her was to kiss her again.

War had broken out shortly after my marriage, and in 1915 I was drafted temporarily into a job in the War Office. The work was secret, which gave me the perfect alibi for not explaining my late arrival at home every evening after I had stopped off to visit Magdalena.

The war had also brought new neighbours to number 48, the house next to ours, what seemed at first sight to be a very ordinary family called Finzel. The wife was Scottish. The husband looked as though he might be a bank clerk or a shoe salesman. Oh, I'd judged their class all right, a sort of lower middle echelon that Helena considered beneath contempt. But the passage of time was to prove to us that there was nothing ordinary about Mr Frank Finzel. We ate our words, and no mistake.

I was coming back from the War Office one day, dressed in all my military rig, when I caught the fellow admiring our house.

' 'Andsome, ain't it?' he asked.

I replied that I supposed it was. Infected by Helena's prejudice, I had never really thought of it in those terms.

'Ah,' he cried, getting very excited. He went all red in the face; it really was quite extraordinary. 'Just you wait! Just you bloomin' well wait! Magnolia Gardens won't have seen anything-like it!'

And with this cryptic remark he disappeared, giving me a cheery wave as he unlocked the door of number 48.

We had several years in which to ponder his intentions, and then the builders arrived and I realised that he had been referring to the affront to taste that posed as his new house, named Camelot. *Camelot*, for God's sake! It really was the most hideous thing you have ever seen and, as Helena said, King Arthur would rather have died than live in anything so grotesque.

And yet, in a grudging way, one couldn't help but admire Mr Finzel. The expression on his face as he studied my house reminded me in some unaccountable way of the golden age at Hadden Wick, when everything had seemed so simple. A quality of innocence, perhaps. And here was a man who had never sat around and expected excellence to come his way. He went out and grabbed it with both hands.

It was during the war years that Helena suddenly got it into her head that she would like to have a child.

I was surprised. Helena's relationship with Edwin was still an uneasy one, and in addition she was approaching forty – hardly the most obvious material for motherhood.

It was awkward, too. How I hated those awkward months when I would slip down the steps of Magdalena's house and unlock my own front door to find Helena waiting for me in the bedroom. She was waiting, but there was no readiness in her as she sat stiffly against the pillows, her hair immaculately arranged and her face lightly powdered, for all the world like some Chinese goddess. And I would stand in the doorway and look at her and try to smile, feeling trapped into a cycle that had started with my consideration for poor Lorna.

I was relieved when Helena became pregnant and everything could return to normal for a while. Then Magdalena got to know of Helena's pregnancy and told me that she no longer wanted to see me. She said she felt sickened. I could hardly blame her.

I remember I was in my chambers when I received the news of the birth. Although I was doing legal work for the War Office and had the military rank of army major, I still took on one or two civilian cases, and on this occasion I had rushed back from Pall

Mall and changed rapidly from my khaki and into my wig and gown in time to receive my client and her solicitor in my room. I flatter myself that I looked equally dashing in either costume. A barrister's wig and gown seem to excite some women just as military uniforms do; the combination of glamour, mystery and authority.

It was a particularly difficult case of embezzlement, and I was just briefing my client on her rights in the courtroom when the door flew open and my clerk rushed in.

'Mr Clifford! Mr Clifford—'

'What is it, Beekman?' I shot an apologetic glance at my client. 'I told you I wasn't to be disturbed for at least an hour.'

'But, Mr Clifford, the doctor telephoned, sir. It's your lady wife – you've got a little girl!'

I packed him off to hail a cab and excused myself from the consultation amid murmurs of congratulations. I could scarcely contain my excitement as the cab rattled to a halt in Magnolia Gardens and I paid the driver. A girl! I had so wanted it to be a girl. I caught sight of Frank Finzel leaving his house and waved with uncharacteristic exuberance. He came towards me looking somewhat alarmed, as though I might have been stricken with rabies or some other affliction that was known to cause untoward ranting.

'My dear chap,' I said, clasping his hand, 'Helena has just given birth to a daughter!'

He pumped my hand enthusiastically and clapped me on the back. His eyes shone with genuine emotion when he looked up at me (for he was considerably shorter than I) and pronounced: 'A daughter, eh? Well, if I might be so bold as to say, you're a very lucky fellow!'

I pounded up the stairs and found Helena patting a little restorative rice powder on her cheeks, which did not look flushed at all.

I gave her a perfunctory kiss and then looked around wildly. 'Where is she?' I demanded.

Helena laughed.

'Well, you didn't think she'd be in here with me, did you? Nurse has her, of course.'

But she obligingly rang for the nurse, who carried the scented white woollen bundle into the room and placed it proudly in my arms.

I sighed with pleasure and awe as I looked down at the tiny face . . . and then looked again. For instead of a pretty elfin creature I saw a little goblin, thin and angry-looking with a strangely shaped head and straight dark hair sticking up in clumps. I had never imagined this. Helena was a handsome woman, and I had naturally assumed that she would have pretty children. Edwin had been a very good-looking infant.

The disappointment was ghastly, but worse was not knowing what to say to Helena. I groped around, 'Er, well, she's quite. . . .'

Helena, who was looking in a hand-glass, raised an eyebrow at me. 'She's not exactly a beauty, if that's what you're trying to say,' she observed drily. 'But never mind. I understand it's not necessarily an indication of how she'll turn out.'

'Quite.'

'We'll call her Rosanna,' stated Helena, 'if that's all right?'

'Er, yes.' I looked down at my ugly daughter. 'Rosanna.'

I had to go back to Magdalena.

Helena had what she wanted, though she paid precious little attention to Rosanna, and the war was exhausting and depressing us all; two perfectly good reasons for Magdalena and I to try to draw a little comfort from one another once more. I loved being there in her cosy little house with the curtains drawn, no servants to disturb us and Loveday, now growing rapidly, asleep upstairs. Magdalena didn't want her daughter to know of my resumed visits, now that she was old enough to talk and ask questions, so I had to make sure that I arrived after she had been put to bed. But whenever possible I would sneak upstairs and take a peep at her while she lay sleeping, marvelling at her innocence, her innocent femininity. She was such a lovely child.

I returned home from Magdalena's one night, using my own key as I usually did, when the front door was yanked open and I stood there like a damned idiot with my key poised in mid-air. The housemaid stood before me in her best uniform, lace cap and apron, the works. In the background there was a sound of polite laughter and the clinking of glasses.

'Something going on, Rose?'

'Mrs Clifford's dinner-party, sir.'

I looked at my watch. It was half-past nine.

'Oh lord, I'd forgotten all about the damn thing. Here' – I

thrust my hat, overcoat and briefcase into her arms – 'tell Mrs Clifford I'll be with her shortly.'

I set off up the stairs at a brisk run and ran down them five minutes later dressed in white tie and running my hands, still sticky with brilliantine, over my hair. The door of the dining room opened before I had finished smartening myself up, so I had no alternative but to wipe my hands down the backs of my trouser legs and stroll in as though nothing had happened.

'Here's Robert now,' said Helena, holding open the door. Her smile was fixed into place so there was no way of telling what she was thinking. She wore a very elegant gown, I remember, such a dark shade of red that in the candlelight it looked almost black, and long white gloves ringed with diamond bracelets.

'Sorry I'm late, everyone – got held up in chambers!'

'And I expect you wanted to go up to the nursery and say goodnight to little Rosanna,' gushed one of Helena's friends.

'Be glad it wasn't a boy, Robert,' said one of the men. 'That way you don't lose 'em in the trenches.'

Then he remembered I had a son, Edwin, and fell silent. Most people seemed reluctant to discuss Edwin in front of Helena, as though it were tantamount to resurrecting Lorna's ghost.

I was too late for the soup but in time for the fish, and I took my place at the head of the table, opposite Helena, and slipped into the familiar routine of dinner-party conversation. The war had just ended, so there was the usual stuff about the armistice, and who had lost how many brothers, uncles and cousins. This was a topic which obsessed people at that time; many turning it into a sort of competition.

'– of course, my sister lost both her boys; one in '14 and one in '17—'

'Well, poor Lady Lansbury lost three! And her younger brother, too, killed the very same day as her youngest. . . .'

The end of the war had brought about the predictable return of the women's suffrage issue.

'Votes for women? What the deuce next? Votes for *dogs*?'

'Most of those suffragettes are rather vulgar women, and they're all very plain, too – have you noticed . . .?'

One could doze through most of this as long as one interjected the required replies, and my mind was elsewhere as the blaze from the fire and the excellent Château Margaux began to warm me.

'*Robert!*' I was woken after the cheese by Helena's well-modulated shriek. 'Robert, I don't think there's going to be enough port. Would you go and ask Andrews to fetch some more?'

I slipped out with relief, drinking in the cool air that hit my face as I closed the dining-room door behind me.

'I wanted to talk to you.'

Helena had followed me. We stood there at the foot of the stairs, eyeing one another with suspicion.

'How dare you be late for my dinner-party! How *dare* you!'

'I forgot, I was working late, and—'

'Where were you?'

'In chambers, my dear—'

'*Where were you?*'

I stared at her.

'I know exactly where you were, Robert! Number forty-seven Magnolia Gardens!'

I didn't know what to say to her. It had never occurred to me that she knew, or perhaps I didn't care whether she knew or not. Helena's lips were moving, shouting, but at first I didn't hear what she was saying.

'. . . Whatever else I am, I'm not a fool! Do you think I don't see you sneaking in and out of that *whore's* house whenever it suits you? Do you think I'm blind? Well, I'll tell you something, Robert Clifford: I don't care in the least if you bestow your attentions on other women, but I will not have it done right here on my doorstep! I will *not* be made to look a fool, do you understand? And it's going to stop!'

I sighed. 'Very well, Helena, I'll—'

'No, it's going to stop right this minute. Because *I'm* going to stop it!'

And to my utter amazement, while her twenty guests gossiped and laughed in the next room, Helena flung open the front door and ran out into the street. It was a filthy night, I remember, drizzling like hell. I stood there in the porch and watched her disappear, her gloves making little patches of white in the darkness. I tried to imagine how Magdalena would receive her. She was a tough plain-talking woman who would not allow Helena to demean her without giving as good in return. And I thought of her extraordinary sensuality; how I'd never found her match in that department. Then, closing my eyes, I recalled how I'd

touched her that very evening, and pressed my naked body close
to hers. . . .

*Oh, Magda, let me kiss you there, just once, please, just there,
you're so lovely. My lovely Magda. . . .*

'Do you think we might order something to drink?'

I had met Magdalena in a hotel, a rather seedy place she knew
called the Dover. We decided that it was the best compromise in
view of Helena's little outburst.

'Yes, yes, of course, my darling. Champagne?'

She shook her head. 'I don't feel like champagne. Some gin
perhaps.'

I hadn't recognised Magdalena when I saw her in the lobby.
She was dressed in a tight-fitting dark blue suit, with her hair
swept up and a dashing little hat perched on top. There was even
a touch of lipstick on her mouth. Very fast, Helena would have
thought; but, then, that's probably what she would have wanted
Helena to think.

She looked at me as though she was reading my thoughts and
then laughed. 'You look silly.'

I was standing there in the middle of the small hotel bedroom,
still in my overcoat and holding my briefcase. A battered fringed
lampshade dangled from the ceiling, so low that it looked as
though I was wearing a hat. I removed my coat and put it over the
back of a chair, and laid my briefcase carefully on the little
washstand. Then I took Magdalena in my arms. She felt different
with all those clothes on, and I struggled clumsily with all the
hooks and laces and buttons when I tried to remove them. In the
end I had to wait for her to do it herself, by which time I was
lying shivering between the cold smooth sheets. Magdalena
shivered, too, as she slipped in to join me, and for a while we just
lay there feeling cold. With my briefcase on the dresser and her
hat on the bedknob.

Then I found I couldn't do it. I just couldn't do it. I wanted
her, but. . . .

'Darling Magda, I'm so sorry. I assure you this has never
happened before. Perhaps it's just the cold.'

She didn't reply at first, but reached over to the bedside table
and lit herself a cigarette – another 'fast' habit which I rather
admired. 'No,' she said eventually. 'It's this place, isn't it?' She
was always very good at gauging one's mood.

I sighed.

'Is it Helena's fault? Was she beastly to you?'

'She was very polite. Which made it even worse.'

Silence.

'I'm sorry,' she said.

'I'm sorry, too.' I meant it.

We persevered for a while, meeting in hotels, even warmer ones, but it didn't work out. I just wanted to be shut away in Magnolia Gardens with a warm soft Magdalena dressed in her wrapper and little Loveday sleeping innocently upstairs. But it simply wasn't worth defying Helena's edict, not for all the disruption she threatened to cause. So we drifted apart. A new decade began, and then Helena became pregnant with our son Hughie . . . but I still used to look up at Magdalena's window every time I passed number 47. I missed her terribly.

Like many other married couples, Helena and I had come to a civilised agreement. I would play the perfect husband and father as long as I was within a certain radius of our home, and once outside it I could pursue carnal pleasures if I wished. To ratify the treaty, Helena moved into a separate bedroom after Hughie was born.

But the agreement didn't much improve the quality of our life together. We disagreed about everything. Everything, no matter how trivial or insignificant.

The episode with the two little girls, for example. I rarely set eyes on Magdalena; she avoided me as though she was angry – and she had a perfect right to be – but I often caught sight of Loveday on her way to school. She and the older Finzel girl were exactly the same age and apparently inseparable. They made a delightful pair, and when I bumped into them one day in the gardens I raised my hat to them. They giggled, but they were just about of an age to appreciate the gesture, in the awkward stage between girlhood and young womanhood. I noticed they had their best hats and coats on, making a charming sight with their identical tam o'shanters, one a brunette, the other a redhead.

'Going somewhere nice?' I asked.

'Loveday's got to have a wisdom tooth out, so I'm going to have mine done, too,' said Finzel's daughter, Amelia, with an engaging smile.

I commented on this encounter to Helena afterwards.

'You know, Edwin could do worse than to marry one of those two girls,' I mused. 'They're bright as buttons, the pair of them.'

Helena snorted with disbelief and then proceeded to pour scorn on the idea. 'What, a plumber's daughter and the daughter of a —' She found some suitably strong epithet. 'I sometimes think you're losing your reason, Robert. And I can only imagine what Edwin's mother would have thought!'

I thought about Edwin's future a lot. He was away at Cambridge by that time, after an exceptionally moody adolescence when he had wandered around looking unhappy and one had not known what the hell to do about it. He suffered from being a stepchild, an odd one out, and although he was fond of his brother and sister he always seemed quite separate from them, as though he belonged to a different family.

Edwin also suffered badly from religion in his teens, and went through a phase of mooning about in St Luke's Church at the corner of Magnolia Gardens and the Clapham Road. I saw him going in there one day and couldn't resist the temptation to follow him. I stood in the porch and watched him as he walked slowly towards the altar. The light from the stained glass shone on his hair. My son. I couldn't keep back a stab of sentimental pride; he'd grown into such a handsome young chap, strong and straight-limbed, almost as tall as I was. I loved him, but I couldn't look at him without being reminded of how I should have been a better husband to my beloved Lorna. And Edwin seemed to have buried within him all the anger that Lorna should have felt towards me but didn't.

In other words, he had a fierce temper. An undisciplined temper. I had raised my hand to beat him once, and Lorna had intervened.

'No, Robert, don't!'

'Well, I suppose he's a trifle young. . . .'

'No, not ever. I want you to promise me you'll *never* hit him, Robert.'

I reflected that Papa's beltings had never done us any harm but, then, that was in the days when life was simple.

As I watched Edwin, he walked slowly around the transept and the nave, just touching things – the pillars, the candlesticks. I thought: My God, I hope we're not going to have a priest on our hands. I'd never got over my distaste for Sundays.

I coughed, to let him know I was there.

His look was reproachful. 'I was praying.'

I was about to say that in my day one prayed on one's knees, but thought better of it. 'Sorry, old man, carry on.'

I didn't ever discuss Edwin's marriage prospects with Helena again for fear of annoying her. You see, I did try to humour her. I also thought that she should spend more time with her own children but I didn't complain about that, either, despite the fact that Hughie was wild and Rosanna plain unmanageable.

The poverty and unemployment of the twenties provided a rich seam of charitable causes for Helena to champion by giving fund-raising events, and gradually this form of socialising became an obsession, taking over her life. Like most wealthy women she needed a means of justifying her privilege, and since I wouldn't allow her to buy us a grand new house she had either to give it to the poor, or spend it on buying dresses to wear while she raised money for the poor. By the time we turned the corner into the 1930s and the Depression was taking hold, her time was at such a premium that she declared she needed to employ a secretary.

I didn't object; in fact I made a useful suggestion.

'What about one of our neighbours' daughters?' I asked, thinking of Finzel's two girls.

'That's exactly what I thought!' said Helena with some satisfaction. 'In fact I've engaged one of them already. Young Miss Stark.'

I had turned to the window that looked out over the Gardens, and as Helena said those words I experienced the oddest sensation. It was one of those blinding flashes of knowledge one has sometimes for no apparent reason. I knew. I knew that the future of each of those two girls had already been shaped, and there was nothing that Helena, or I, or anyone else could do that would change it.

PART TWO

The Second Generation

48 Magnolia Gardens

Mel

LOVEDAY STARK AND I had lived in Magnolia Gardens all our lives.

That's not strictly true. Loveday had the prior claim since she was born there, and I was nearly two when Father leased number 48. But it certainly felt like the whole of my life.

I suppose I ought to describe Magnolia Gardens. It's almost a character in its own right, though I'm afraid that character might not survive my description.

How can I describe Magnolia Gardens? It was lost in the morass of suburban south London, somewhere indefinable just north of Clapham. Just on the border of respectability. Not like the hurly-burly of the East End where, we're told, each street bursts with communal life, but a province of net-curtain twitching and hypocrisy. The sort of area where businessmen keep their mistresses. So, although I'd like to describe Magnolia Gardens as a lively little place imbued with neighbourly spirit, I'm afraid it wouldn't be true. We knew a little about one another, and I suppose people were friendly enough, but the inhabitants of the Gardens were all very different.

The garden inspiring the name was the oval patch of grass at the centre, with some mature trees, a few straggly borders and a bench or two. The whole thing sealed inside iron railings. I imagine that nowadays one would need a key to unlock the gate, but in the old days it was always open. Not that it was used very much, except as a convenience for the local dogs. I think I sat on a bench once or twice, at a desperate moment when there was nowhere else to go. On the street corner of the Gardens stood St Luke's Church (very 'high'); of which more, much more, later.

Most of the houses were tall, brick and Edwardian with sad little bits of stucco, grouped in twos or threes. There were also a few very substantial villas displaying all the trappings of bourgeois comfort: large gardens, a flight of steps to the front door, elaborate porches, large windows. We lived in the only modern house in the Gardens. The original squat ugly Victorian house was eventually knocked down bit by bit by Father, and new pieces were added in a campaign of aggrandisement that would have put Genghis Khan to shame.

Next door to us, at number 50, lived the Cliffords. Their house was the largest in the Gardens, a square white villa with a flat roof and four storeys, standing alone at the very end of the cul-de-sac. Closer inspection would have borne out the theory that this was the home of a family of quality. Through the window-panes you could glimpse heavy velvet drapes and antique furniture. Robert Clifford was a big barrister. I mean that in both ways. He was a big man; heavy with a handsome boyish face. And he was big in the sense of important. He had taken on a famous murder case once, defending a beautiful widow who wore a veil in the dock, and we had all thought the whole business terribly glamorous. Of course, to be a barrister you had to have private means, and Robert Clifford had 'interests' in the City and knew a lot of influential people. He lived at number 50 with his second wife, Helena. The first had died, leaving one son, Edwin.

The second Mrs Clifford came from a very grand land-owning family and always managed to give the impression that living in Magnolia Gardens was more than a little disappointing. She had given Robert Clifford two more children: Rosanna and Hugh.

The Cliffords' house stood on our right. On *their* right was a pair of semi-detached houses – number 49 and number 47. Ashley Player lived at number 49, a celebrated tenor who had enjoyed considerable national success but never quite broke into the international arena. He was already quite well known when we were children, and we used to watch him being collected in a big black courtesy car. He was a rather insignificant-looking young man – 'pale and interesting' in my mother's terminology, with soft brown hair which he wore rather long in compliance with people's expectations of an 'artist'. The fact that he was well known must have excited our childish imaginations, because later I certainly wouldn't have looked twice if I'd seen a man like that in the street.

Number 47 was the property of Miss Magdalena Stark. What a name to conjure with! It makes her sound like a *fille de joie*, like one of the mistresses I have already mentioned. In a way, she was. I don't think anyone was ever certain of the facts, but it was rumoured that she had been some sort of chorus girl. She certainly didn't pay for the house herself. But I should explain that Magdalena Stark was not a young girl who had been led astray during the first tender blush of youth. She was a middle-aged woman with an illegitimate daughter.

Loveday.

A woman called Magdalena could hardly have had a daughter called Mary or Anne or Jane (a name I particularly dislike). So she called her Loveday. A little too close to 'love-child' for comfort, perhaps. As my exact contemporary, my neighbour and my classmate, Loveday had a special place in my life from the start. What more can I say about her? That I have sometimes had cause to hate her? That I needed her and tried to shut her out, all at once? Loveday was my rival, my enemy, my example and my mentor, and the environment she lived in was as familiar as my own. I always loved going to her house, which seemed to have a rarefied atmosphere. The Stark household consisted only of two women, and the uninspiring and rather neglected exterior of number 47 belied its soft comfortable interior devoted to self-indulgence of the most feminine kind.

Opposite the Starks' house, and on our left, stood a small plain detached villa that had been divided into two flats. One of them was Neville's. Neville Alexander Christie Brownie, to give him his full title. Neville was a rare creature in the Gardens: an ordinary respectable young bachelor, who held down an ordinary respectable job in an office somewhere. He lived with his widowed father, to whom he engagingly referred as 'Mr B.' When I was very young I had thought Neville's blond moustache and sad brown eyes were rather fine, and I had taken special care always to bowl my hoop near his gate rather than anyone else's.

Dear Neville! What a life he had!

By rights the other flat should have been occupied by a tenant as disagreeable as Neville was friendly and generous. But it's only in books that life balances out in such a tidy way. The occupant of the other flat was every bit as delightful as Neville. She was an Irish girl called Rosheen O'Shaughnessy, who worked as a nurse at the local hospital. In many ways she was the most delightful human being I have ever known. All the men were in love with her. Poor Rosheen!

There is a photograph of us all, taken in 1926. By then we were becoming quite rich, and Father had already got into the habit of having expensive portrait photographs taken, the sort that never tell you what the people were really like but impose a sort of uniformity on our impression of an epoch.

Mother was at the centre, sitting on a chair. She was wearing a black crêpe dress. A conventional description would probably go on 'Mother always wore a black crêpe dress', but that was not the case. She always, without exception, wore a silk georgette blouse and a tweed skirt. (I always thought there was something curious and incongruous about tweed in the suburbs.) The sole exception was when she was having her photograph taken, when she would consent to wear a dress. Father was standing behind her with his podgy little hands resting on the back of her chair and his silly little moustache positively bristling with pride. Uncle Donald had agreed to be in the photograph, too, since he was in London at the time. He was standing next to Father, a good head and shoulders taller and looking very much the radical with his burning eyes, hollow cheeks and shoulder-length hair. Ethne and I were on either side of Mother; Ethne dour and serious, and me – well. . . .

I ought to begin a description of myself with my name. Amelia Finzel.

I hated my name. It had never really belonged to me. A-me-li-a. Those pulled-out syllables in the middle sound like a whine. That's why I preferred 'Mel'. It was short, to the point, sexless.

My appearance can be dealt with quickly enough. Medium height and medium build. Hair the colour of cardboard, eyes the colour of sand, and skin like tallow.

Father always said I took after Uncle Donald, but the only resemblance I could find was in the colour of our eyes: a strange yellowish colour. Dear Father! I could never quite decide whether he was an extraordinary man or simply an ordinary man with an obsession. The world is full of people who are fired by an obsession. In the case of Frank Finzel, it was gleaming pristine porcelain. Lavatories, basins and baths with sparkling taps. Outflows and cisterns. It may sound foolish, but he loved them. His origins were lowly (my grandfather had worked in a boot-black factory in Catford), but he was fond of hard work, and by the time we were born he had built up his own plumbing business. He might have carried on being a plumber for ever if it hadn't been for the Great War.

The war changed the way that Father looked at things, but I

suppose he was only one of many in that respect. Society had changed, too, and in Frank Finzel's favour. Wages had risen sharply, and after their war experiences fewer people were prepared to go into domestic service – two factors which combined to put convenience in the home at a premium. They wanted running water now that there was no tweeny to carry hot jugs of it up and down stairs, and they wanted things clean and hygienic now that there wasn't always someone else to do the dirty work. (I'm talking about the fastidious middle classes, you understand. I don't think the upper classes cared very much about things like bathrooms. They were too attached to their chamber-pots.)

Father was mysteriously galvanised into action by this upsurge of concern with ablutions, and he was abetted by the recovery of the stock market, which gave people more money to spend on their homes. He found factory premises and started to manufacture them. Lavatories. And baths, and washstands.

The remarkable thing about Father was the way he rose above his lack of education. He may have been obsessed, but he was never narrow. He never lacked ideas. He had an enquiring mind and he was full of ideas. In 1925 he even went to Italy to visit the marble quarries – an unprecedented step for a man of his background who had never set foot outside London, except to visit the sea-side.

Father became rich. We became rich. We could have had a country house, or even one of the comfortable mansions on the edge of the Common, but Father didn't want to leave Magnolia Gardens.

I think it was Mother who was the more reluctant to move. My mother, Jeanie Finzel, née McDowell. She was the last person you'd imagine being married to a sanitary-ware king. Even when we had become gloriously *nouveaux riches*, beyond the most flagrant of sweltering suburban dreams, she was usually at the bottom of the garden, fiddling about with her runner beans. Mother was a thin shadowy figure; shy and softly spoken. She never said very much, which was precisely why her words were valuable. Sterling watertight pieces of advice uttered with utter conviction. Whenever I was in trouble I would always seek her out amongst the runner beans and ask her what I should do. But she never interfered. As far as I was concerned, that meant she was a good mother. How else could one define it?

Mother and Uncle Donald and their father had moved to London from Edinburgh in 1904. The plumbing in their house in Bow didn't work, and an enterprising young Frank Finzel arrived to fix it. The origin of my being was through a broken lavatory bowl.

As the firstborn I was the object of inflated parental expectation. How disappointed they must have been! But, if that was the case, they were rewarded a hundred times over by Ethne. . . .

I was born in 1912, and my sister Ethne followed in 1914. The celebrated Ethne Finzel. To me she was just Ethne. Dark blonde hair, serious eyes, high forehead. She was the prettier of the two of us, but if you had seen her in the street you wouldn't have been prompted to exclaim: 'What a pretty girl!' She was too unassuming. Because she was very quiet, people always said that Ethne resembled Mother, but she *wasn't* like Mother. Mother had a quiet determination about her. She knew what she wanted. Ethne never seemed to want anything, or to have any strong feelings at all.

As a small child, her sobriety made her a winsome little scrap, and she was always a great favourite of Father's. When he played the pianola, she used to crawl underneath it and press the pedals.

'Oh, our Ethne,' he said, 'by the look of it you're going to play and sing as nicely as your Grandma Ettie!'

The essence of my school career was that I never did as well as expected. I was lazy. I wouldn't push myself. Hence my mediocre results and the oft-quoted phrase, 'Amelia could try harder . . .' I spent long hours staring out of classroom windows. Or, if the mistress in charge was an easy target, I tried to make the other girls laugh. It seemed a fair exchange for me to extract as much fun as possible from the situation in return for the ink-stained grubby pieces of homework that I spent hours labouring over.

On the whole I enjoyed my schooldays, but only with the restless half-hearted enjoyment of someone who is looking forward to better things. We all fancied ourselves as caterpillars about to turn into butterflies. All we would have had to do was don a pair of high heels and perm our hair and we would have walked at once into a new life. Of course it was naïve to think that adult life was so simple, but we *were* right about one thing. The first thing we shed was the hideous uniform. At Stone Hill High School we dressed in navy-blue gymslips; drab and heavy, with the school crest soldered firmly to our left breast. White blouses with Quaker collars and woollen stockings.

At the other end of the street was our rival school, the Sacred Heart Convent. (I was never quite sure *whose* sacred heart it was. Was it Jesus's or Mary's?) For every five of my schooldays, at least three were spent longing to be a pupil at the convent. There was a lovely little statue of the Virgin outside, above the sign, and two bay trees, one on either side of the smartly painted front door.

And the uniforms! If ours represented Anglican restraint, theirs were the epitome of Roman display. Gorgeous cherry-red skirts with box pleats. Floppy neck-ties and swirling red capes, like rich ecclesiastical robes. And the final insult was having to follow a crocodile of convent girls down the street in the summer when they wore white gloves and boaters with *red ribbons*! Whilst we High School girls had to be content with shapeless berets like navy-blue cowpats.

(Or so we saw them at the time. In the forties, when berets became fashionable again and we had all wanted to look like the girl in *Quai des brumes*, we got them out of the drawer, dusted them down and started wearing them again.)

Looking at my old school photographs afterwards, I was struck by how similar we looked, the ghastly uniforms wiping out all traces of individuality. We all used to wear our hair the same way, either scraped back off our foreheads with grips or cut very short in a bob with a pudding-basin fringe (I had the latter).

A closer inspection of the school photograph revealed that there was one very notable exception to that rule. Loveday Stark.

The question of Loveday's appearance ought to be dealt with and then pushed out of the way. She was the living spectre of all my inadequacies. I had always wanted wonderful red-brown hair like Rita Hayworth's and a full scarlet mouth. Loveday Stark had red-brown hair like Rita Hayworth's and a full scarlet mouth. I wanted a creamy white skin like a French film star. Loveday Stark had a creamy white. . . . And so it went on. I had wanted green eyes, too, and my only consolation was that Loveday's were brown.

So there she was in the Stone Hill High School photograph, her hair somehow managing to escape its restraining band and tumble over her shoulders, her pretty mouth pursed slightly in a gesture of self-confidence. Loveday Stark. I sometimes used to think we should swap surnames. Finzel had a tinselly air about it, very appropriate to Loveday. Loveday Finzel. A screen goddess. (Of course it would be pronounced Fin*zell*, with the stress on the last syllable, not plain everyday 'Finzle'.) Mel Stark. Short, harsh, plain. Stark by name and stark by nature. . . .

But we were born Loveday Stark and Mel Finzel – make of that what you will, you Fates! I suppose it was fortunate for Father's business that our names were as they stood. I could hardly imagine people wanting to climb into a Stark bath. Or pee into a Stark lavatory.

Loveday had managed to look passably attractive in her school uniform, which was quite a feat, but think how she would have looked in the gorgeous cherry red of the Sacred Heart! And she could have gone to the convent, too, if she'd wished. Despite her name, Magdalena Stark professed no religion at all, so there was no reason why Loveday couldn't have chosen a convent in preference to a Church of England school. (Or perhaps she would have had to be a baptised Catholic?) But Loveday never shared my obsession with the convent.

'I don't understand you, Mel,' she said to me once. 'What on earth do you want to go there for? The teaching is atrocious, and their exam results are terrible.'

There, again, was the difference between us. Loveday cared about things like exam results. I used to believe that to understand that difference you needed only to look at our mothers. Magdalena was a slut really: my outstanding childhood memory was of her wearing a frilled wrapper in the drawing room *and not changing out of it until noon.*

The other reason for my hankering after the convent was that I was going through my nun phase. I had just read *Villette* for the first time and I was obsessed with nuns. Those lovely mild faces beneath cool white wimples, enveloping black robes. Both benign and slightly sinister. I had recalled the passage at the end of *Villette*, the climax of tension as Lucy Snowe thinks she is about to come face to face with the nun who has been haunting her.

The moment and the nun are come. The crisis and the revelation are passed by. . . .

There was something about that passage that turned my blood cold. 'The moment and the nun. . . .' It sent shivers down my pine, but how I enjoyed them. They were almost as delicious as

112

the shivers I got when Jane Eyre announced: '*Reader, I married him. . . .*'

I started at Stone Hill High School in 1923, and the pattern of my schooldays was quickly established. The school was about a mile away, and there was an omnibus which stopped on the main road just outside St Luke's Church; but for some reason Mother had an aversion to the use of public transport, so we had to walk. Loveday walked with me (though when it was raining she would sometimes desert me and go on the bus; Magdalena did not share my mother's scruples), and in 1925 we were joined by Ethne, bringing the number of hideous blue berets to three and adding a fair pigtail to the brown and the auburn. We made an ill-assorted trio, but I enjoyed our walks to and from school, unless the weather was very bad. I got a sentimental thrill from the sense of silent comradeship and shared purpose.

I was popular at school, without being lionised in any way. I was not popular with the mistresses, however, because of my alternating day-dreaming and disruptive behaviour, which added up to a general lack of concentration on the task in hand. I frequently suffered detention and, while some stony-faced spinster stood over me, I would chew my pencil and stare out of the window and beyond to the portals of the Sacred Heart Convent, sighing for the nuns. The only teacher who didn't disapprove of me (apart from good old Crokey, the English mistress, who liked my essays) was the games mistress, Miss Sykes. I don't remember my athletic prowess being above average, but I was very useful for posting out in distant positions on the hockey and rounders field, where I was content to stand and pretend that I was somewhere else.

Apart from sport, I did very little other than dodge lessons and homework and covet the Sacred Heart boaters during prolonged periods in detention. The school had a flourishing drama department, and I privately fancied myself as a second Sarah Bernhardt, but the best roles were always given to the prettiest girls, so I pretended I wasn't interested.

Predictably, it was Loveday who landed the plum female leads, and I was forced to admit that she was rather good, particularly in Shakespeare. I felt I would never forget her Ophelia. Her red-brown hair rippled over her fragile-looking shoulders, and petals dropped from her fingers.

Loveday and I both matriculated from Stone Hill High in 1930 with only a few mediocre passes in the School Certificate to our names. Mine were mediocre because I was lazy and never tried very hard; hers were mediocre because she was a bit of a plodder and did not possess an academic brain. Neither of us had any idea what we would do with ourselves, and the future was hazy but, to our minds, ripe with possibility.

It was strange walking back on that day in July 1930, across the edge of the Common and past the gloomy building on the busy main road, knowing that it was the last time we would ever walk back from school. I didn't fully appreciate that new freedom, feeling rather melancholy and nostalgic for routine and regimentation. But, then, that was before Father got the idea of the Villa Rosa into his head.

I remember exactly how it started.

It was a few months after I'd left Stone Hill High, and I was in the office of Father's showroom in Nine Elms Lane. He had called me in there to discuss My Future, but before we got started we were interrupted by a client who wanted to see the Italian collection.

It was the Italian collection that had made Father's fortune – not the imported marble, because that was custom-made only, but the coloured sanitary ware. Pink Siena, Florentine Blue and Tuscan Gold. Father was one of the first people to introduce coloured glazes, and it seemed that people couldn't buy enough of the stuff. He also worked very hard at making sure people bought it. In fact, ever since that trip to Italy he'd behaved as though he was driven, working harder than ever before and somehow being more *serious* about the whole thing. I often wondered why. It wasn't as if we were exactly poor beforehand.

I stood in the doorway of the office and watched him do his act with the customer. She was a very grand old thing called Lady Batten, done up in furs and wearing a dreadful lorgnette, and I could hear her complaining about the prices of the Italian collection. Father always used to say that the upper classes were a lot more picky than one might expect.

'Oh dear, I don't know,' she said, pulling a face as though she was in pain. 'They're really *frightfully* dear.'

'Well, madam, there's two reasons for that.' Father was never without a ready answer. 'One is that we only use the finest china clay. If you use cheap fire-clay, it chips and cracks and then it lets in the water. And you don't want that, do you, madam?'

'No, I suppose not,' said Lady Batten, drawing out the words as though she was yawning.

'And the other reason is the colours. Our unique process for dyeing the glaze is very, very tricky. But no other supplier uses it.'

That did the trick. No one can resist one-upmanship, not even the aristocracy. She chose the Florentine Blue, and Father brought her into the office to take down the order. I was duly introduced.

'Madam,' said Father as he took out the ledger, 'I wonder if I might ask your advice about something. Seeing as how you're a special client. . . .'

'Very well.' Lady Batten raised her eyebrow at him.

'It's Amelia here. She's just left school and I wanted to do something for her – something special if you like. The money's no use to me in the end—'

'You mean, have her finished orf?' I was scrutinised through the lorgnette with an expression that implied that such a project would be rather futile.

'That's exactly what I mean,' said Father, and while I looked on in astonishment they embarked on a conversation about fish-knives and etiquette which ended with Lady Batten recommending some dreadful establishment called the Villa Rosa in Château d'Oex, where her niece had been a pupil.

The worst thing was seeing Father apparently abandon all the things he had always believed in. Advancing on one's own merits and not by whom one knew or how nice one's manners. All he seemed concerned with was being seen to spend a lot of money on his family. It was not about what *we* wanted. He'd just arranged some very expensive piano tuition for Ethne that she neither wanted nor needed, on the grounds that 'You'll be welcome anywhere if you can play a bit of a tune'. It had been like this ever since Italy.

'But, Father,' I pleaded, 'Loveday and I have just enrolled at stenography school. We were going to do it together!'

'When you get back from Switzerland you can do what you like, I promise. I just want you to do this, my pet. For me. So no one can say I don't treat you right.'

'No,' I said. 'Absolutely not. I'm not going.'

Damn-hell-bloody-fuck-bugger. . . .

I closed my eyes and said all the swearwords I could think of, to make me feel better. Then I said them in reverse order.

I was thinking of the wretched finishing school, and how much I hated it. And I hadn't even arrived there yet. I was sitting in a first-class rail compartment between Paris and Dijon. The seat was deep and comfortable, but the antimacassar on the back of it had a greasy look to it, and I didn't like to lean against it if I could help it. 'The greasy French', Uncle Donald had called them, but he had laughed as he said it, and I laughed, too, when I remembered it. I tried to sit forward as much as I could and look at the scenery. It was early autumn, and the fields and trees were golden, all except for the straight avenues of plane trees. They were dusty green. It all looked very strange to me, and very exciting.

It wasn't that I didn't want to travel. I desperately wanted to see Europe. It was just the finishing-off bit that I objected to. Not only did Father make his money from lavatories and baths but once upon a time he'd also been a plumber. I knew that the other girls would find this funny, I just *knew* it, but I could hardly explain that to Father, could I? Sanitary ware was his life, he looked on his WCs as though they were Sèvres or Limoges masterpieces, and he didn't see anything at all funny in what he did. 'A man obsessed', Uncle Donald called him. Besides, I didn't want to hurt Father. I found him comic at times but always felt guilty when I did. I loved him; I even respected him.

But I still couldn't understand why he wanted me to finish up like one of those horse-faced débutantes.

Loveday had pointed out a photograph of Queen Charlotte's Ball in 'Londoner's Log' in the *Daily Express*.

'Look, Mel, this is what you're going to be like when you get back from finishing school!'

She was being spiteful, and we both knew it, but I still managed to laugh when she showed me the photograph, and Loveday joined in. The débutantes were penned together like cattle, and their facial expressions were a unanimous blank. A corsage grew up each bodice like fungus, and their badly applied cosmetics made them look like music-hall queens.

'Oh, how ghastly!' I said, when I had regained my composure. 'I'm not going to look like that, not ever! I'm going to come back a mature and glamorous young woman, and I'm going to have a whole wardrobe of Parisian clothes. Father's promised me loads of money to spend!'

'I knew he'd end up bribing you,' said Loveday sagely.

I was not sick till after we passed Margate, and deep was the pleasure I drank in with the sea-breeze; divine the delight I drew from the heaving channel-waves, from the sea-birds on their ridges, from the white sails on their dark distance, from the quiet, yet beclouded sky, overhanging all. In my reverie, methought I saw the continent of Europe, like a wide dream-land, far away. . . .

There was a knock on the door of my compartment. It was the dining-car attendant bringing in a tray of tea, so I put my book down for a while.

I had chosen my favourite novel, Charlotte Brontë's *Villette*, for the journey. It seemed very appropriate given that the opening chapters describe Lucy Snowe's journey across the Channel to visit Europe for the first time.

I sighed with pleasure as I sipped my tea and let my eye follow row after row of dusty plane trees and cultivated vines. Europe *was* a dream-land, from what I had seen of it so far. Loveday would have laughed me to scorn if she had heard me say that, or if she had been able to read my thoughts. 'An incurable romantic', she would have called me, or, if it was one of her less charitable moments, 'a romantic bloody fool'.

We once had an argument about *Villette* along the same lines. When we were about fourteen our English mistress, Miss Croker (her unfortunate name attracted all the predictable epithets), set an essay in which we had to pretend that we were the heroine of romantic fiction. Most of the girls chose Juliet, or Cathy Earnshaw from *Wuthering Heights* or Richardson's Clarissa. I chose ugly insignificant Lucy Snowe because she seemed the most interesting and the least romantic of the lot. Loveday disagreed.

'If you read the book carefully—'

'I have,' I said. 'I know it by heart.'

'If you read the book carefully, even though Lucy's ugly and insignificant no one can ignore her. Can they?'

'It's worse than that,' I said. 'The other characters only let her exist according to their perceptions of her. Lucy Snowe doesn't really exist.'

'Rubbish! They just recognise that she's an enigma. There's nothing more romantic than an enigma.'

She's just jealous, I had thought. She's just jealous because I'm better at English than she is, and because I've written a better essay. I could always tell when Loveday was jealous. A brisk bossy note crept into her voice. I could hear it when I went across to her house to say goodbye before leaving for the Villa Rosa.

'Well, that's that, then,' she said. 'It looks as though I'm off to the Southam Road Stenography School all by myself.'

Loveday was sitting on the ottoman in the front parlour of number 47, with her feet on a footstool, painting her fingernails with a bottle of her mother's varnish. She waved the brush around delicately, then reached over to the wireless and switched it on. The voice of Richard Tauber filled the room, sentimental, teutonic, full-bloodedly romantic, singing 'You Are My Heart's Delight'. 'I'm disappointed that you won't be doing the typing course with me, but it can't be helped.'

'I don't *want* to go, Loveday.'

'Well, you know what they say – learning to muck in and do things we dislike is what growing up's all about.'

I stared in awe at Loveday's vermilion‚toenails. Everything about her was so delicate and feminine. 'I'll be coming back here afterwards,' I ventured tentatively.

Loveday slammed the pot of varnish down on the table and turned to me with a radiant smile that masked her own bitterness. 'Why come back? Take my advice and stay away while you've got the chance, and a father to support you.'

That was always the difference between us, you see. Loveday was always obsessed, from a very early age, with doing well and 'getting on'. Push, push, push – that was Loveday. Look for opportunities and grab them. Whereas I was always quite happy just to let things go on around me. The inside of my head was where life happened. That way reality stopped where I wanted it to and fantasy took over. I was like the heroine of a book, like Lucy Snowe, and I was also the author, writing scenes in which the heroine is always set off to advantage. I didn't want reality.

You see, I never believed you could change things in the real world. I believed that the things that happen to us are already planned and settled by Fate, Fortune, Destiny – call it what you will. And that leaves little chance of a happy ending. Loveday, on the other hand, being a supremely rational creature, believed that we are all in charge of our own destiny. That it's up to us.

And yet it was me who was off to Paris and Loveday who was staying behind, me who had a wealthy father and Loveday who had no father at all. She didn't even know who he was. As I watched Loveday take up the brush and start on her fingernails the irony and injustice of the situation made me so uncomfortable that I mumbled a hasty 'goodbye' and beat my retreat. It was dusk as I walked across to number 48 where we lived, and Magnolia Gardens looked beautiful and rather mysterious under its delicate covering of the first autumn leaves. This is what I'm leaving, I thought, and this is what poor Loveday wants so desperately to escape. She thought that the answer to all her problems and all her dreams – to everything in fact – lay beyond Magnolia Gardens.

'*Montreux! Montreux!*'

Father Turnbull, the plump rosy little priest from St Luke's, was standing in the middle of Magnolia Gardens preaching from a soap-box, and Rosheen O'Shaughnessy was sweeping up piles of damp leaves at his feet, when the station announcer's voice interrupted my dream.

I sat up, shaking myself and repressing a shiver of horror at the memory of those dark, damp, clinging leaves. Then I glanced out of the window and saw the guard about to blow his whistle and only just remembered in time that I was supposed to be changing trains here. I had a dreadful scramble with my hat-boxes and cases, and had to be rescued by a sympathetic Swiss guard.

As I stood on the platform waiting for the tiny toylike train that would shunt me up the mountainside to Château d'Oex, I imagined myself as a sort of Anna Karenina figure standing alone by the side of the track. . . . I would be wearing a long sable coat and a fur hat from which only my brilliant glittering eyes would be visible. . . .

'Are you going to the Villa Rosa by any chance?'

The voice was sharp, the vowels so proper it was difficult to decipher them. I turned and stared at my travelling companion. She had a sharp foxy face, sandy hair and a good complexion. Her tall slim body was draped with a pomegranate-red velvet wrap-coat trimmed with fox, and Loveday would have been able to confirm that her hat was made by Reboux.

'Yes. Yes, I am. I've never been there before,' I said ineffectually. She looked me up and down, and, since I wasn't Anna Karenina but a very ordinary-looking girl in a pale-green tweed suit with a piqué collar and a hat of Normandie straw, she decided I was of no interest and wandered down the platform whence she had come without saying another word.

That was all the confirmation I needed that I was going to hate the Villa Rosa, so I didn't allow my spirits to be lifted by the sight of the painfully pretty mountain villages, like chocolate-box illustrations, or by the sight of the Villa Rosa itself, a large white chalet whose outline stood out clearly against the dark blue sky. I disliked the building on sight. The small windows with their ridiculous shutters and boxes of geraniums made me feel gross and uncomfortable, as though I was being forced to live in a doll's house.

I was shown into my room by Madame and introduced to my room-mates. There was Juliana, the foxy girl from Montreux station who pretended she had never seen me before, a girl called Cecily who had freckles, and an Italian girl called Angelina. Cecily asked me a few questions about my family then immediately fell silent. Angelina looked about the nicest of the lot but was obviously painfully shy.

I attempted to make conversation with Cecily. 'I understand that the school sometimes arranges trips to Paris.' I had always longed to visit Paris, and the glimpses I had had when I had changed trains in the night from the Gare du Nord to Gare de Lyon had been frustratingly brief.

'Oh, yes,' said Cecily. She added obscurely: 'But not everyone goes on them. You have to be picked.'

Her look implied that I was unlikely to be one of the lucky few. My heart sank like a stone as I sat down on the edge of my bed, and I felt an overwhelming urge to cry. I remembered Loveday's pronouncements on growing up, and told myself I was being ridiculous. Loveday wouldn't have cried.

My first day at the Villa Rosa was a nightmare.

The routine had been patiently explained to us new girls, but of course information undiluted by experience never sinks in, so I found myself forgetting whether French conversation came before flower-arranging, and whether 'luncheon' was at twelve or at one. It was all so humiliating. I was nearly nineteen years old and I was going through something I'd last experienced in the

Mixed Infants when I couldn't find the peg to hang my shoe-bag on. Several times I had to blink back angry tears, and I cursed Father for a callous insensitive tyrant.

The worst lesson was 'Etiquette'. We were all shepherded into the tastefully decorated pink and green dining room, where we were to have a practical demonstration in five-course place-setting. The table was already set; we looked closely at it, then the pink linen cloth was cleared and we each had to start from scratch, setting our own place. I was so flustered that I didn't even notice that the knives were different sizes.

'Perhaps Mam'selle Finzel likes to eat 'er tournedos with a dessert-knife?' quizzed Madame, a sarcastic little brute of a woman with black hair fiercely parted in the middle. The other girls sniggered, and none louder than the foxy Juliana.

Over luncheon the conversation was entirely devoted to pre-finishing school education. Several of the girls had been at a place called St Mary's, which they referred to in a series of boring anecdotes. The Italian girl, Angelina, caught my eye.

'Did you go to a boarding school?' she asked. She was so shy that she seemed incapable of raising her voice above a whisper. Thinking that she was confiding some secret, the other girls fell silent.

'No,' I said. 'I didn't go to boarding school,' I added boldly. 'Not everybody in England does, you know. Only a very small percentage.' This last statement was bound to inflame the likes of Juliana.

'Oh, do tell us,' she drawled, right on cue. 'Did you have a governess at home, then, Ameelyah?'

There was an expectant silence. I looked at Juliana defiantly. With slow deliberate movements I picked up my napkin and wiped my mouth with it, leaving a smear of gravy on the pink linen. I would have liked to blow my nose in it to show Juliana what a dirty little guttersnipe I was, but the idea offended even my sense of propriety. The others waited. You could have heard a pin drop.

'No, Juliana' – I gave her my sweetest smile – 'I went to a grammar school in Clapham.'

Locking horns over the luncheon-table with Juliana Digsby-Roe brought a feeling of heady triumph. But the triumph was short-lived. It was replaced rapidly by gloom when I realised that

Juliana was going to make things harder than ever for me. If only I didn't have to share a room with her! There were some single bedrooms at the Villa Rosa, and I felt that life there would have been almost tolerable if I had had a private sanctum to which I could retreat. But the system by which they were allotted seemed to rely on a mysterious order of privilege. I was used to having my own room, and had never realised before I arrived in Switzerland how important privacy was.

After lunch I complained of stomach pains and took myself off upstairs to the bedroom. I just wanted the luxury of being alone for an hour.

Besides, there was something I had to do.

I sat down on the edge of my bed and rummaged around in the locker until I found what I was looking for. It was a sealed envelope, given to me by our neighbour Neville Brownie on the day before I left England. I had gone round to visit him in his flat to say goodbye, and after several cups of tea, as I stood up to leave, he had pressed the envelope into my hand and given me a chaste brotherly kiss. Looking at the drab brown envelope I felt uneasy, almost nervous. I already knew, or feared I knew, what it contained. Inside the envelope there was a photograph and a brief letter in a childish hand: *'Dear Mel, Just wishing you all the best for your trip, not that you need luck, you'll knock the spots off all of them. I wanted you to have the enclosed, I'm sure you'll understand and take good care of it for me. Yours ever, Neville Alexander Christie Brownie.'*

The battered photograph slid out and fell on to the floor. I picked it up, and as I sat staring at the face of Rosheen O'Shaughnessy, her strawberry-blonde hair curling in tendrils around her smiling eyes, I was eleven years old again, and back in Magnolia Gardens.

'How's my favourite girl?'

I was bowling my hoop along the pavement in front of Neville's front gate. He had just come back from work, and carried the evening paper and a rolled-up umbrella. I smiled shyly at him and made my hoop do an extra-special turn, encircling his ankles.

'Aren't you the clever one, then, doing that? How on earth d'you get it to stay up straight like that? If I do it – see' – he demonstrated – 'it just falls flat on the floor.'

I wasn't really watching what he was doing, so great was my pleasure at discovering that I was Neville's favourite.

Soon afterwards I was at Loveday's house and I overheard Magdalena and Rosheen O'Shaughnessy gossiping about my beloved Neville.

'. . . I knew a bit about the sort of thing he did for a living before . . . you know. . . .'

'Yes,' said Rosheen. 'Imagine! All those terrible men.' (She pronounced it 'tarrible' with her pretty Irish accent.) 'Poor Neville! Still, he's very respectable now, isn't he, and managing quite nicely. Oh, Magda, sure I know I shouldn't say it, but really you can't help but respect him in a way. . . .'

Magdalena sighed in agreement as she replaced her tea-cup.

I was intrigued by this conversation, and kept turning it over in my mind. Who were the 'terrible men'? What had they done to Neville? I confided in Loveday, and the next time Neville invited me in for tea she came with me.

Tea was always brewed by Mr Brownie, a big hairy bear of a man, who shuffled around in leather slippers and wore a perpetual grin on his face. He acted as a sort of housekeeper while Neville was out at work earning the money to support them both. He can't have been much older than sixty, but because his health was poor he seemed much older.

'No, no, no, you sit down, Mr B.,' Neville remonstrated as we all took our seats at the kitchen table and Mr Brownie shuffled around us pouring tea. 'Let *me* wait on *you*. Mel, fetch the sugar-tongs for Mr B., would you?'

Mr Brownie beamed, and we all smiled, too. There was something very affecting about their regard for one another.

I toyed with my stale Shrewsbury biscuit. 'Neville, did you ever have other jobs before you had this one . . .?'

'What did you do?' asked Loveday. Directness was both her most appealing characteristic and her greatest shortcoming.

Neville blushed slightly and fingered his blond moustache, but his tone of voice was jovial. 'Now, then, I don't want to bore you young ladies with details like that. Do I, Mr B.? Like a lot of people nowadays, I've done several jobs, including fighting for king and country.'

This reply was profoundly unsatisfactory and thus succeeded in firing our nasty little minds. 'Do you think he was in prison?' Loveday wondered.

123

'Perhaps he was a deserter,' I suggested. 'Or a conchie like Uncle Donald. *He* went to prison in the war because he didn't want to fight.'

We tackled Rosheen on the subject when we next took tea with her. She used to ask us in sometimes when she returned from her shift at the hospital with the bands of her nurse's cape forming a cross on her ample bosom and her lovely hair tucked beneath its cap. I realised later that she must have been dog-tired when she returned from her duties, but she never showed it, answering our fatuous questions with supreme patience. I loved having tea with Rosheen as much as I loved having tea with Neville and Mr Brownie. I loved the way her uniform crackled as she bustled about the room; it was infinitely comforting. I loved sitting cross-legged on the hearth in front of the gas-fire in her cramped little sitting room. I loved the lily-of-the-valley scent she wore, and I loved to watch her remove her starched white cap (which was almost as hideous as our navy berets) and pull the pins from her lovely hair one by one, shaking it down her back with an exclamation of 'That's better. . . .'

We asked Rosheen about Neville.

She smiled cautiously as she skewered a crumpet with the toasting fork. 'Neville? Oh, well, now, I'm thinking he's done all sorts of odd jobs in his time. Some of them were . . . menial, so that's why he doesn't want to talk about it.' She added gravely: 'He's had his invalid father to support, so perhaps he hasn't been able to pick and choose as you or I would. Oh, but it's been a tarrible worry for him. Poor Neville!'

'Poor Neville!' we echoed loyally.

'So be good girls and don't go blathering about it now? We don't want him to think we're interfering, do we?'

We shook our heads.

Ah, Rosheen, lovely Rosheen! If I couldn't have had hair like Loveday's, I would have happily settled for Rosheen's instead. It was thick and soft and the most wonderful shade of reddish blonde. There was no trace of classical beauty, but her smile was dazzling. For a young woman her bearing was very motherly, yet I can't think of a man who didn't adore her. Suitors flocked round her, calling on a Sunday afternoon in their best suits, clutching bunches of flowers wrapped in waxed paper. ('Fools rosheen. . . ,' I had quipped to Loveday once.)

As we left her flat that day after discussing Neville, something occurred to me that I had never thought of before. 'I wish Rosheen would marry Neville!' I burst out.

Loveday raised an eyebrow in that cool way of hers. 'Perhaps she will.'

'I hope she does, because if Mr Brownie dies Neville'll be all alone, and I couldn't bear the thought of him being lonely!'

I got my wish. Over the next few years the number of suitors bringing flowers to Rosheen's door dwindled, and in the spring of 1926, a year after Father had returned from Italy, Neville and Rosheen announced their engagement. They were thirty-three and twenty-seven respectively, and everyone was delighted. No one more so than Loveday and myself, who were to be brides-maids at the November wedding.

'You girls must get on over here and have your dresses fitted! Don't leave it any longer now, or I'll be walking up the aisle all on my own and looking a right idiot and all!'

We said we would, but that summer there were so many things to distract us. I was spending more and more time in number 47 with Loveday, seduced by the soft feminine aura of the place. It smelled of face powder and hair lacquer. There was the smell of gin, too, fragrant with junipers, as Magdalena slipped a spoonful of it into her tea (I thought this was horribly quaint at the time, and I still do). The wallpaper was striped with pink and cream, hung with sentimental oils in oval Victorian frames, and the drawing room was dominated by a large and rather grubby otto-man heaped with lace cushions.

It was on this ottoman that Magdalena spent most of her wak-ing hours, plump and tawdry, resplendent in her old-fashioned wrapper. She never got up to make tea for us. Loveday would disappear into the kitchen and make it, while I sat and watched Magdalena paint her nails with coloured lacquer.

I was fascinated. Not just by the nail polish, which Mother would never have *dreamed* of wearing, but by everything about Loveday's mother. I found myself wondering then, as I did at intervals throughout my life, what it was like to be Loveday. What was the connection between this idle, sensual, self-absorbed woman with her harsh rasping voice, and all the things that made up Loveday? I knew nothing whatsoever about Loveday's father; Magdalena had refused to discuss it until Loveday was older, so I had no means of judging who she resembled. She may have inherited some of her beauty from her mother, but Magdalena had grown so plump it was hard to tell. Her face was puffy and dead-looking, and she had her auburn hair 'touched up'. One day I called round to find Magdalena about to go out on a business call, to her lawyer or someone like that. She was corseted beneath a trim navy-blue suit, and her hair was piled up beneath a neat little hat. I was amazed. She looked just like anyone else's mother. Strangely, she seemed almost embarrassed to be caught looking like that, pursing her lips and shutting her handbag with a loud 'snap'.

When I came for tea, Loveday and I were usually ignored while Magdalena carried on obstinately with whatever she was doing. But when she got talking she was a good raconteuse, telling us stories about London in the old days in her low husky voice. Loveday's attitude to her mother was one of feigned indifference, as though there was no connection between the two of them, and sometimes she called Magdalena by the most frightful names. But these criticisms were only the surface of a bedrock of defensiveness, and she would not tolerate anyone else criticising the infamous Magdalena Stark.

Magdalena was so lazy that I doubt it was her influence that prompted Loveday to try to earn some extra pocket-money in her spare time. Nevertheless, I was thumbing through one of Mother's magazines in that summer of 1926 when I came across a photograph of Loveday modelling for the girls' sizes of a lingerie pattern. Most of the models were a little shamefaced, as if they hoped that nobody they knew would come upon them posing for lingerie patterns. Only Loveday wore an air of detachment; seraphic or perhaps a little smug, as though she was thinking of the money they were going to pay her.

'Why don't you girls come over for tea some day, like you used to in the old days?' asked Rosheen. 'I never see anything of you at all just now.'

We had been for our fitting of the bridesmaid dresses, but we still found very little time for Rosheen, who wanted a sympathetic audience to listen to the ups and downs of the wedding arrangements. There were so many other things to do that summer. There were Loveday's money-making ventures, and there was the cinema. We had developed a passion for moving pictures and spent all our spare time and money at the Majestic in

Clapham High Street. Father's recent spurt of generosity provided funds to cover the cost of the best seats for Loveday and myself. I kept meaning to drop in on Rosheen, but then the annual trip to Eastbourne got in the way. We spent the month of August each year staying with my father's sister Agnes, who taught at a girls' school near Eastbourne. She lived in a tall narrow house that looked over the sea. It had a lovely bay window with a view over the cliffs and a window-seat built into it. I would curl up in this window-seat when it was raining and look at the books that Aunt Agnes had bought for us. She bought a lot of things like that for us, including our first party-dresses (Mother never cared enough about clothes to bother), because she didn't have any children of her own to buy things for. I found this dreadfully sad. I liked Aunt Agnes very much and I couldn't understand why no one wanted to marry her; she had such a nice kind face and she was always so cheerful. Did some people actually prefer to be on their own?

It was a problem, and since Loveday wasn't around when we were on holiday I posed the question to Ethne as we kicked our way through the shallow waves with our skirts tucked into our knickers.

Ethne just said: 'I don't know.'

I should have expected this. Ethne was devoid of opinions on any subject. The only thing I disliked about staying with Aunt Agnes was the fact that I had to share a room with Ethne. She caught frequent colds and kept me awake at night with her sniffing and sneezing.

But, apart from that, I was always happy at Eastbourne. I loved the feeling of the damp grey sand oozing between my toes and the glasses of shrimps that Ethne and I would devour while Mother and Father walked arm in arm down the esplanade with a look of perfect contentment. I returned fit and sun-tanned and resolving to be a good neighbour and call and see Rosheen more often.

But somehow I never got round to it.

'Have either of you two seen Rosheen?'

It was a Saturday morning two weeks before the wedding when Neville stopped Loveday and me on our way out of the Gardens. We shook our heads. He looked anxious. 'Only, it's very strange; she was supposed to get back from her duty at the hospital late last night and she's not home yet.'

'Perhaps you should ask at the hospital,' Loveday suggested; and, eager to be helpful, I said: 'You can go and use our telephone; I'm sure Mother will let you.'

There wasn't really much else we could say and, besides, we had some pressing business of our own. We had recently discovered the adolescent joys of smoking, and we were on our way to find a quiet spot where we could sample some of Magdalena Stark's latest Turkish blend. My mother, naturally, would *never* have smoked.

The ideal situation presented itself to us as we walked up the main road towards the Common. There was a narrow alley leading from the pavement, no more than ten feet wide and with high wooden fences on either side. A sharp right-angle bend ensured that we would be able to puff away without being seen, completely alone apart from a small flock of starlings who were jostling one another to peck at a piece of bread. We leaned against the fence, and Loveday groped around in her coat pocket for the precious burden. We would have liked to keep our cigarettes in a slim silver holder that would open and close with an elegant 'click', but we didn't have one, so we used an empty toothpowder-tin instead. The first cigarette was always shared, passed to and fro to give us a chance to accustom ourselves to the sharp smoke in our lungs.

Loveday took a tentative drag. Then she frowned. 'What's that?' she asked, pointing with the toe of her shoe. The alley was covered with leaves, darkened by the rain that had fallen during the night. They had drifted into heaps along the edge of the fence, but one pile was much larger than the others. I focused my eyes on it, and it acquired ominous angles. Loveday bent forward and poked it. The toothpowder-tin slid from her grasp and rattled on the ground.

Something peculiar had happened to Loveday. She retained her self-control, but her face went a funny grey colour and her hand moved involuntarily to her chest. 'It's—'

'It's a body!' My over-active imagination was at work.

'No!' Loveday was shaking her head violently. She seemed to be having difficulty speaking. 'No. Mel, it's—'

She moved to stop me, but I was already pushing back the damp leaves. I had to force myself to do it, shaking with a mixture of fear and ghoulish curiosity.

128

Then I saw what Loveday had seen, and it was only too terrifyingly clear what she had been trying to tell me.

Oh dear God, no. . . . Oh God, please. . . . Say this isn't happening. . . . Let me . . . let me just close my eyes and pretend I didn't see it. . . .

The sky seemed to close in, and the ground moved beneath my feet with a sickening whirling sensation. As I stumbled the starlings took fright and beat their wings, wheeling above my head and crying their sharp, ugly cry.

At first I had an impression of light, of something shining. A uniform badge depicting an angel of mercy, glinting in the watery sunlight. A lock of bright strawberry-blonde hair. And then flesh, glistening with rain, and blood — dark, coagulated and sticky-looking. Lots of it. Dark blackened blood and shining white gristle where her throat had been cut.

Glistening rain, glistening flesh, glistening blood. . . . Life's blood. . . .

I needed desperately to get away, but in my terror my limbs were uncontrolled. I stumbled, falling towards the body, the wet leaves clinging to my hands and wrists. The dampness and the leaves were everywhere, and I couldn't shake them off. . . .

And then Loveday was there, grabbing my elbow and pulling me away, holding me with small firm hands while I vomited down the palings of the fence, tasting sour bile and the salt of my tears all at once.

'Mel. . . . Come on, Mel. . . . We've got to tell someone . . . now.'

'No! . . . No, we can't go, we just can't. . . .' My own voice sounded strange to my ears, the garbled jibbering of an idiot. 'We shouldn't leave her here . . . alone. . . .'

Loveday was shaking me by the shoulders. 'She *dead*. She's dead, Mel, *don't you understand*?' Loveday's hands were trembling now as they gripped my shoulders, her face white, with staring eyes, like. . . .

I wanted to look back to be sure I hadn't imagined the horror of it, but Loveday was pulling me along, forcing me to run. I glanced back over my shoulder. I still felt that it was somehow wrong to leave her.

We ran and ran. My legs were shaking so much that it was a great effort to move them, like running through cement, like trying to run in a dream. And all the time I was aware of a terrible hollowness, as though the world were coming to an end, because nothing good or nice would ever happen again after this day. We ran until we came to the corner of Magnolia Gardens and there we found Mr Clifford's son, Edwin, who had come home from college that summer. He was carrying a bag of golf-clubs.

I don't know how we found the words to tell him, but somehow we did. By now I was calm enough to feel miserably conscious of my vomit-streaked dress, and avoided looking at his face, but I remember his knuckles tightening around the golf-bag.

'Oh, Jesus Christ in heaven, no!' He sounded angry, as though Jesus was to blame. 'Oh God, no. . . . Are you *sure*?' But he could see that we were. 'You'd better come into the house.'

He led us into number 50, that big grand house neither of us had entered before.

'Father! *Father!*' He flung open the door of the study, and there was Robert Clifford with a sherry-decanter in his hand and the firelight glinting on his brilliantined hair. Sophisticated, worldly, handsome. But I was aware of the contrast between what we saw and what we knew, and I thought: This is too ugly. . . .

'Edwin! What can I do for you, boy?' Then he saw our faces and he stopped smiling.

'Father, they've. . . .' He lowered his voice as though it would save us from further distress. *'They've found a corpse in the alley. It's Rosheen O'Shaughnessy.'*

Robert motioned for us to sit down on the sofa, and for a long moment the incongruous foursome stared at one another in silence: two little girls, a father and his son.

I went back to the alley alone a few days later, after the funeral.

I still don't know why, but I had a compulsion to go and visit the place where she had died. I stood there and stared at the spot where the pile of leaves had been.

'Rosheen,' I said out loud. 'Rosheen?' Was she there?

And then I cried. I cried and cried until the roof of my mouth ached. Poor Rosheen, I was thinking, but I was crying for myself as much as for her.

God forgive us for the things we have done, and for those we have left undone. . . .

For the things we have left undone. . . . I had promised time and time again that I would pop in and see Rosheen, as I used to in the old days, and I hadn't bothered. I hadn't got round to it. For months afterwards I walked round with the burden of that guilt on my shoulders, as though I had committed a hideous crime. 'You weren't to know,' said Loveday unhelpfully. 'Anyway, you're the one who believes in Fate. You couldn't have changed anything.'

I couldn't have changed anything; that was exactly why I grieved, for months, years even. And it had all been for nothing. She had been attacked by a thief who was never caught, slaughtered for the theft of a handbag containing seven shillings and sixpence and a list of hymns to be sung at her wedding. I don't know if Loveday suffered the same devastation, the same terrible realisation that real life was too ugly and should be avoided at all costs. If she did, she kept it well hidden, along with all her other feelings. I certainly never got over seeing Rosheen's mutilated body; her beauty desecrated, her sweetness gone. Even after I had stopped crying every time I thought of Rosheen, I went on having dreadful nightmares about damp clinging leaves. If I was lucky, I woke up before I saw her.

Rosheen's death had opened up the mysterious portals of the Clifford household to Loveday and me. But it was really through Ethne that I came to know the Cliffords better.

From the beginning of her life, Ethne was terribly musical. She could pick out tunes by ear, using the thumb and two fingers of her right hand, even before she started school. Father replaced the pianola with a real piano and bought Ethne a copy of *Smallwood's Piano Tutor*. He had inherited an enthusiasm for music from our grandmother, and he supervised her progress diligently.

Eventually the sound of piano music from number 48 reached the ears of the Cliffords, and one day they sent one of the maids round to ask if Ethne would consider accompanying Miss Rosanna, who had recently taken up the cello.

I was furious. I pretended that I was furious because Mrs Clifford had sent a servant instead of coming herself, but really I was furious that Ethne had gained an entrée into the Clifford household and I had not. Rosanna Clifford was a very strange girl, even then. She was a little younger than Ethne; thin and scrawny with closely cropped hair and big eyes. She kept a pet rat, which was her only companion apart from her governess.

Mrs Clifford had virtually disowned her, unable to cope with her 'oddness'.

Of course, I didn't know all of this on my first encounter with Rosanna. It was an evening in the autumn of 1927, a year after Rosheen's death. Ethne was very late for supper, and since it had already grown dark and Mother was anxious I volunteered to go next door to the Cliffords' and see if Ethne was there with Rosanna.

She wasn't. (I later discovered that she had taken to sneaking over to number 49 to accompany the singer, Ashley Player. The foolish girl had developed the most monstrous crush on him.) Rosanna invited me upstairs to the nursery to see her pet rat. After I had made the appropriate gestures of admiration and handed the wretched little creature back to its owner, I made for the door, but Rosanna closed it and leaned against it, blocking my way.

'You can't go yet; you've only just got here!'

'I'm afraid—'

'I like you.' There was a sly look in her eyes which quite belied her twelve years, and alarmed me, though I did not really know why. I explained that my family were waiting to eat supper and couldn't start without me.

'All right, I'll let you go.' Rosanna flashed me another look with those scheming adult eyes. 'But only if you promise to come back and see me tomorrow. I'll show you my books.'

I agreed with extreme reluctance, and when I passed Edwin on the stairs and saw the curious look he gave me I wondered why on earth I had allowed myself to be bullied by a skinny scrap of a twelve-year-old girl.

I tried to persuade Ethne to accompany me when I went, but she was busy with her piano practice, and Loveday refused to contemplate the idea, so I went alone. I told myself that I was only going to see her books. It's true that I did love books and she certainly had a very fine collection: all the children's classics bound in hand-tooled morocco. But I was also profoundly curious about Rosanna Clifford.

We looked at the books together, and I was forced to acknowledge that she was very well read, and very quick for her age. In fact I quite enjoyed her company, but only when she wasn't looking at me with those big knowing eyes. This time she didn't try to prevent me from leaving, but she said that her governess,

Miss Markham, had asked if I would be prepared to come round on a regular basis to supervise her reading. I promised that I would return the next day with my answer.

I didn't know what to do. I couldn't honestly say that I liked Rosanna, but she had said that her parents would pay me, and my presence in the house as her unofficial tutor would put paid to Ethne's advantage over me. I decided to ask Mother's advice.

I found her at the bottom of the garden, wearing a pair of galoshes and an old coat of Father's over her tweed skirt and georgette blouse. She was pulling up the first leeks of the season. I watched her fingers working deftly, parting the dark wet soil in exactly the right place and releasing the sharp tangy scent of the leeks. I told her about Rosanna's offer, and she continued to work while she thought about it.

'I think you should do it,' she said after a while. 'It'll do you no harm to think about someone other than yourself for a change.' Her Scots accent had all but disappeared, but her quiet voice still had a pleasant lilt to it. She put down her trowel and smiled up at me. 'And you say that you'll be earning some money of your own? That's good. Not that Father wouldn't be prepared to help if it was extra money you were after.' This was true. Father was always very generous when it came to handing out pocket-money. 'But you make sure that it doesn't interfere with your own school work.'

I decided I wasn't going to do it. Lurking within me was the normal desire to do good without personal inconvenience, but Rosanna would be an inconvenience. She would be too demanding and, although I was curious about the Cliffords and the goings-on in their grand gloomy house, I did not want to be trapped into spending more time there than I intended.

She was upset when I told her; so upset that she ran into her large silk-draped bedroom and flung herself down on her bed, crying. It was a poignant sight in that chilly formal room: the high satin-covered bed and the neglected-looking child with her rumpled skirt and holey stockings bagging on her legs. How sad, I thought. She must be dreadfully lonely for this to matter so much to her.

I sat down next to her on the bed and patted her hand. 'Come on, Rosanna, it's not because I don't *like* you,' I fibbed. 'It's just that I have a lot of school work of my own, and I don't want to risk doing badly in my exams.' I couldn't help thinking that it would be much better for Rosanna if her hatchet-faced mother would send her away to a decent school rather than shutting her in with a governess and allowing her to keep vermin.

She sat up, sniffing. 'You mean you like me?'

'Of course I do!' I said, with a lot more enthusiasm than I felt.

'And you'll come and visit me and Attila sometimes?' Attila was her disgusting rat.

'I'll try!' I was anxious not to commit myself.

'Oh, Amelia, I think you're the nicest person in the world!' She pressed very close to me and wound her skinny little arms around my neck. 'I'm going to kiss you!'

She did, but not on the cheek. She kissed me full on the mouth. I recoiled, still feeling the imprint of her mouth on mine, warm and dry and tasting faintly of liquorice. I stood up hastily and stumbled to the door.

I should make it clear that I didn't think Rosanna had harmed or compromised me in any way. It wasn't *what* she did. After all, I was at a girls' high school where it was commonplace for the juniors to have a 'pash' for an older girl, and it seemed conceivable that this admiration should include the desire to kiss the other person. No, it wasn't what she did, but the *way* she did it. It seemed absurd in view of her extreme youth, but when she looked at me with those big eyes I saw it.

She knew exactly what she was doing.

I can't express it any better than that. And, although I was certainly not a willing participant, the incident with Rosanna marked a turning point in my sensuality. It was as if her knowledge infected me, so that things I'd been only vaguely aware of rushed sharply into focus.

I bumped into Edwin Clifford on the way out. This time he stopped to talk to me, though I had no wish to strike up a conversation. I could still feel Rosanna's mouth on mine, and I just wanted to get out of that frightful house as quickly as possible and plunge my face into a basin of water.

And there was another reason for wanting to rush past him. It was the first time we had spoken since Rosheen's death, and I couldn't help but remember our encounter on that terrible day. I knew that he would be thinking about Rosheen, too, so I avoided looking at his fair handsome face and stared instead at his correspondent's shoes. Altogether too smart for a theology graduate, I decided.

'I'm glad I saw you,' he said. 'I wanted to ask you how poor Neville is managing these days. I hear his father died recently. Another terrible blow for him. . . .'

'Yes,' I nodded, and then came out with the only rejoinder I could think of: 'Poor Neville!'

'I make believe she's still alive.'

I was in Neville's house the day before I left for the Villa Rosa, the day he gave me the photograph. Neville moved his biscuit round and round his plate, staring into his cup of tea as though he wished it were a lake that could drown him. The agony was written plainly in his limpid brown eyes, all the more affecting because his face had never lost its cherubic innocent look. I didn't know what to say, so I reached out tentatively and covered his hand with mine.

'Do you think it's wrong . . . I don't know . . . to fantasise like that?'

I shook my head. 'No,' I said. 'I think it's quite natural to do that.'

Had he asked me the same question several years later, I would have been more vociferous in my support. Never underestimate the potency of fantasy, I would have said. I would have told him that I had come to be quite at home in that world. The only place where you could control the outcome, where things were *complete*. The only place where the sexes were kind to one another. Where you never woke up with a pimple on your chin. Ah, my fantasies had been kind to me!

'I used to do it before I even met Rosheen, in the old days,' Neville went on. 'You know, when things were hard, or life just seemed too sordid . . . too ugly. . . .'

I wondered if he was referring to his war experiences.

'I used to dream up this world where I was happily married and everything was . . . normal. When it actually happened I couldn't believe it – Rosheen agreeing to be my wife!' He buried his head in his hands as though he were trying to shut out the last trace of light. 'And now that it's not going to come true I have to go back to the fantasising, only this time I have to pretend she's still alive. It wasn't so bad when Father was here – it helped me keep a sense of reality – but now there's only me here. . . .' Neville looked round the room and sighed. 'I conjure up scenes of married life, the ones I was going to have, the ones I thought of as my right. I imagine she's standing there, by the cooker, and she's making me some of her soda bread and I've just got in from work and I go and put my arms round her waist and bury my face . . . in her hair. . . .'

Neville turned away from me and broke into wild sobbing. I had never heard a man cry like that before.

I moved to comfort him, but he stood up and went to the dresser, fumbling in the drawer for something. 'Look. Look at this.' He held up a small brown fragment of material. 'You know what this is? It's her wedding dress. On the day . . . when Mr Clifford came to tell me, I got that bloody dress out of her wardrobe and I threw it right into the fire and watched it burn. Then I found myself thinking that she loved that dress and she wouldn't have wanted me to destroy it. So I tried to pull it out, but this was all I could rescue.' I handled the fragment reverently. The ivory silk, the same material that our bridesmaid dresses had been made from, was just visible beneath the angry scorchmarks.

'Come on now,' said Neville, putting his hand on my shoulder. 'I'm sorry. I'm sorry; I shouldn't have showed it to you. I didn't want to upset you.'

'I don't want to go to bloody Switzerland, Neville!' I burst out. 'I just don't want to go.'

He crouched down beside me and grasped my hands in his. 'You'll be all right, girl, don't you worry. You'll show them. If there is happiness to be found in this world, it won't come to you. You've just got to get out there and grab it.'

A sentiment with which Loveday would have wholeheartedly agreed. I couldn't bring myself to tell him that he'd got the wrong girl.

'Where's everyone going for their holidays next summer?'

It was a grey rainy day towards the end of term; our daily walk from the Villa Rosa into the village had been cancelled. Instead we had been sent upstairs to tidy our rooms. Juliana Digsby-Roe had thrown herself on to her bed and was flicking through a magazine. She waited for the others to answer her question.

'I expect it'll be the Riviera,' sighed Cecily.

'Well, whatever you do, don't go to the Hotel Carlton. It's become awfully *nouveau*. ' Juliana tossed a meaningful glance in my direction. 'You know the sort of thing – all Schiaparelli beachwear and jewellery loading them from head to foot. How about you, Angelina?'

'The Lido, I suppose.'

'Ah, but Venice is becoming awfully chic, you know. Look, they've even got a picture in here.' Juliana held up the magazine and displayed a photograph of several minor princesses and Russian ballerinas basking on the Lido sands in backless bathing suits. 'They're already running articles on "Plage Society" and what to wear "à la plage". I fancy one of these fearfully elegant pyjama suits.'

'Let's have a look! Oh, yes – with the jaunty little sailor hat!'

I wasn't included in this discussion. It had been that way since I was caught with Rosheen's photograph and they had demanded to know why I was crying over a picture of a girl. I had told them, with as much dignity as I possessed, that her throat had been cut, but that just made them look on me as very strange indeed.

'Are you going to the show tonight, Ameelyah?' asked Juliana casually.

I should have realised from the simple fact that she had addressed me that there was something afoot. But I didn't – or at least not until I was sitting in the auditorium that evening. It was customary for the pupils to put on a humorous revue at the end of the Christmas term, but as it had been directed by Juliana and her cronies I had declined to become involved. As the lights dimmed and the curtain lifted it quickly became obvious that the title, 'A Finished Product', referred to the luckless heroine who was being transported to a finishing school in the Alps. Poor thing, I thought, gritting my teeth. I felt the same way. . . .

A cold sensation crept down my spine. What exactly were they up to?

It became sickeningly clear. The revue had been inspired by George Bernard Shaw's *Pygmalion*, with the addition of songs and slapstick, and as soon as I saw Juliana in the lead role I knew what was about to happen. She shuffled on to the stage in a threadbare cotton dress, her hair tied up in pigtails, her cheeks grotesquely rouged with circles of red.

And as she stood in the spotlight the rest of the cast began the first song.

> *She's only a poor plumber's daughter.*
> *Who don't behave better than she oughter.* . . .

It doesn't even scan, I thought witheringly, clenching my fists against my sides. I was determined to sit it out, but then Juliana began her first speech and that was the final straw. She came out with what she imagined was a stream of Cockney, and amongst the 'gorblimeys' dropped a nonchalant mention of a grammar school in 'sarf London'.

I left the auditorium.

I was so angry that I was almost crying, the whole of my inside seemingly twisting with rage. But I was not going to cry. Juliana's performance had given me the final incentive I needed to do something I'd been contemplating for a long time. I took my suitcase from under my bed and began to pack it.

There were footsteps on the stairs, and Cecily came in.

'Mel, what on *earth* are you doing?' she asked, but her surprise was not genuine and I could see from her eyes that she was as guilty as the others.

'I'm leaving,' I said coldly, picking up my case.

She blocked my path. 'Mel, don't be an ass. Where will you go? You can't; you'll get into frightful trouble.'

'*You bloody hypocrite!*' I pulled myself up to my full height. 'You're worried about what Madame might say when she finds out why I've gone. Do you really think I'd believe you cared what happened to me?'

'But, Mel—'

'And if you think I'd stay here just so Juliana Digsby-Roe and her tribe don't get into trouble you're even more of a bloody fool than I thought! Now get out of my way!' I pushed her roughly aside.

'What will you do for money?' Cecily called plaintively as I hurried down the stairs.

'I've got plenty,' I shouted. 'It's one of the advantages of being a jumped-up *nouveau riche* plumber's daughter!'

Cecily was right about one thing: if they caught me on my way out of the school at nine o'clock in the evening, I'd be in a great deal of trouble. I slid down the drive, pressing myself close to the shadow of the wall and turning to look back at the Villa Rosa, with lights blazing cheerfully from every window. In my mind's eye I saw myself as Jane Eyre, fleeing the malign influences at Thornfield Hall, or Lucy Snowe stumbling dazed into the darkened streets of Villette. . . .

I reached the station in time to catch the last train to

Montreux. I received a few suspicious looks from the stationmaster as I sat alone on the platform bench, and I pulled my collar up and the brim of my hat down to hide my face from his gaze. I decided that it would look better if I was occupied, so I pulled a notebook and a pencil out of my handbag. It also occurred to me that I ought to tell someone, at least *one* person in the world, where I was going to be. The obvious candidate was Loveday.

As I tore a page from my notebook I remembered what she had said about getting on with things you don't like being part of growing up. She was sure to think running away was very childish, and it would be impossible to explain in a letter why Juliana and the others had driven me to take this step. I would have to minimise the running-away element and be bright and breezy about the whole thing.

'Dear Loveday, I decided it was time to explore Europe a little, so I'm taking off by myself for a few days. I bet you you'll never guess where! I'm going to Paris. . . .'

47 Magnolia Gardens

Loveday

THE CLIFFORDS WERE THE SORT OF PEOPLE who didn't
seem to enjoy being rich.

Their house had a terrible atmosphere; desiccated and dead,
filled with chiming clocks. But I was drawn to it, and had been
ever since the terrible day of Rosheen's death. Mel and I were
shown into the study and made to sit down on a big leather sofa
that creaked and squeaked as we sank into it – the sort of noises
that would have made us giggle if there hadn't been such a
terrible, terrible thing happening to us. Edwin Clifford stood in
front of us explaining what the police would want to know, and
Mel sat there staring at his feet. But I was looking up at him and
thinking about the way his hair curled behind his ears.

I looked him straight in the face, and he blushed.

'Edwin's coming back tomorrow.'

It was my first day of work at the Cliffords', and Rosanna
pounced on me as I came in through the front door.

'Edwin's coming back tomorrow. He's been staying with
friends in the country – *don't you know*. Are *you* glad he's coming
back?'

'I'm sure I don't know. It doesn't concern me.'

'But it's the prodigal son's return! The prodigal son's returning, and we're *all* supposed to be glad, aren't we? *Everyone*.'

She jumped on to the lower stair and did a pirouette, turning to
face me with a flourish.

I didn't know quite what to make of Rosanna, but one thing
seemed certain: she was a very strange child indeed. I say 'child',
although by then she was about sixteen. She was a strong little
figure, narrow-hipped and wide-shouldered, her flanks as wiry
and thin as a greyhound and no bust at all. Her eyebrows were
too thick and wide for beauty, and she had a large square brow,
but there was a kind of splendour about her, the splendour of the
grotesque.

She lunged forward at me in a dueller's pose, her hand holding an imaginary sword. 'Have at ye, Miss Stark!'

She laughed coarsely. I stared.

'It's all right; I'm just playing at pirates. Well, *actually* I'm supposed to be Horatio Nelson. That's what this is for.'

'I did wonder. . . .'

Rosanna was dressed in a tailcoat pinned with medals and a shabby tricorn hat.

'I'm only playing at dressing up!' she said defensively. 'Where's the harm in that? *Everyone* plays at dressing up!'

'You're too old for dressing up!' I snapped. 'Now, will you please tell me where I can find your mother?'

Her eyes followed me as I walked to the morning room, and I had the distinct sensation that her eccentric behaviour was just a ploy. Whom she was trying to fool, and why, remained unclear.

I found it remarkable that Rosanna was the offspring of a woman like Helena Clifford. Helena reminded me of a Chinese mandarin: when she spoke she never moved her head, as if she was afraid of cracking the white-powdered veneer of her features. Her eyes glittered like a snake's. But she was elegant, and I envied her couturier clothes and her smart costume jewellery.

'Ah, Loveday, there you are!' She was sitting at the desk in front of a big picture-window. A critical survey of my working suit, grey and sober, seemed to meet with her approval, for she gave a brief nod and said: 'Well, then, shall we press on?'

It seemed I was to meet her in the morning room each day to receive a list of her social engagements for the day. Once I was armed with this, any enquiries that might arise in her absence could be referred to me. Then there was a second list of people to be telephoned and letters to be written. A typewriter had been set up in the study for this purpose.

I didn't expect any of this to be too demanding, nor did I foresee it filling a whole day. I said as much to Mrs Clifford, and she looked annoyed.

'Yes – well, in that case I may prevail on you to deal with domestic problems as well, any queries the servants might have. And then there's Rosanna. She can be a little high-spirited. . . .'

'*High-spirited*? Are you sure that's the right word, Mrs Clifford? At this moment she happens to be dressed as Horatio Nelson.'

Icy glare. 'There's no need to be pert, Loveday! You're a bright girl – bright enough to know your place.' The implication was clear. As the illegitimate daughter of the local scarlet woman I should be grateful for any chance that was offered to me.

I bit back my reply. *My place*, I almost said, *is the only thing I don't know, you stupid woman! I wish I did!*

'Anything I can do?'

I looked up from my typewriter to find Robert Clifford in the doorway of the study. He approached the desk with his arms folded behind his back in a respectful gesture. 'Just checking, you know. Just seeing if there was anything I could do for you. Anything you want?'

This was ridiculous of course, since he was the employer and I the employee. But such inverted deference was no doubt considered part of that blatant old-world charm.

I decided to test him out. 'There's Rosanna,' I said baldly. 'I'm worried about Rosanna. Is she still being taught by a governess?'

A shadow passed across his face, but the charm didn't falter for a moment. 'Ah, yes, our Rosanna. Zanna, we call her – pet name, you know. Yes, *une vraie petite Amazone*, eh? Wants to learn to fence now, pestering me for lessons. It'll be a horse next, you'll see!'

He hadn't answered my question. Perhaps he thought that dazzling professional smile was answer enough. I imagined him bestowing it on mysteriously veiled widows in the witness-box. 'Actually, there is something *you* can do for *me*,' he went on. 'A *tiny* little thing. I'm taking my wife to the theatre tonight. I wondered if you might telephone the box office. It's that Noël Coward thing – what's the name . . .?'

'*Cavalcade?*' I suggested.

'That's it. You've seen it?'

'No. I don't get much opportunity to go to the theatre.'

'You ought to. You'd enjoy it.'

With whom, I thought crossly, *and how am I supposed to pay for it*? Of course, he *would* choose something like *Cavalcade*. Mother had seen it and dismissed it as 'sentimental nonsense', but I could imagine that overblown romantic patriotism was exactly what Robert Clifford liked. 'Our English heritage . . . the tradition of Empire . . . the pageant of history. . . . '

There was a loud crash from the hall and a shriek of laughter.

'What the—' Then Robert's face relaxed. 'That'll be Hughie, I expect. I tend to forget they come home in the holidays. Throwing firecrackers again, I'll be bound.'

He flung the study door open. 'Hughie! Hugh! Come in here at once, sir!' He dragged the thirteen-year-old Hugh into the room, boxing with him playfully. I saw a bright mischievous face with sparkling eyes beneath a mop of curly hair. 'Come here, you young scoundrel, you! Firecrackers again, is it? Scaring the maids?' Robert seemed delighted at the idea. '*And where are your manners?* Hughie, this is Miss Loveday Stark. Say "How do you do, Miss Stark".'

Hughie didn't even look at me, but struggled from his father's grasp and ran from the room shouting '*How-do-you-do-Miss-Loveday-Stark!*' at the top of his voice.

'I hear that Edwin's coming back today,' I said to Mrs Clifford as I brought her a tray of tea. I poured very carefully. Helena Clifford was the sort of person who cared whether the tea or the milk went in first.

'Yes, this evening. He's been staying with friends in the West Country. We shall meet his train. Perhaps you'd better write that down, Loveday.'

'And how was the show last night?' I asked, after I had made a note of a dressmaker's appointment and a charity committee meeting.

'Oh, splendid! Yes, it ended with the cast drinking a toast to king and country. We were all on our feet. Of course, these things do one good,' she added obscurely.

As I reached the door she said: 'Oh, Loveday, I wonder whether I might ask you one more thing . . . tonight . . . of course, one doesn't like to impose . . . Robert and I should like to go and meet Edwin, only there's Rosanna. She's a little *unsettled* at the moment, and I don't like to leave her here with the servants. . . . I wonder, would you . . .?'

I could see that I *was* going to be imposed on if I wasn't careful. 'I should be glad to stay here this evening,' I said in my firmest voice. 'I will take some time off this afternoon, in lieu.'

'But the typing. . . .'

Helena Clifford took one look at my face and saw that she had better not argue.

*   *   *

'How's my favourite girl, then?'

I bumped into Neville Brownie as I was leaving the Cliffords', and his greeting took me back immediately to my childhood, to the days when Neville was happy and would swing me up in his arms or chuck me under the chin and say:'How's my favourite girl, then?'

I replied this time as I used to then.

'I bet you say that to all the girls,' I quipped. 'And I bet the more foolish ones believe you!'

'Going somewhere? Like a cuppa?'

'Why not?'

I didn't really have any plans for the afternoon. I had taken the time off as a matter of principle, to prove that I wasn't Helena Clifford's skivvy. And it was quite a while since I had visited Neville.

I sat at the kitchen table with him and let him ramble on about Rosheen and about Mr B. I looked on my visits to Neville as a sort of social work. He didn't seem to have any family or even any close friends. Mel and I were closer to him than anyone since Rosheen's death. We were all he had.

With pride and pleasure, Neville had displayed a picture-postcard from Mel in Paris, showing Notre-Dame, and she was on my mind as I walked to number 47.

Still in Paris. . . . What the hell's she up to?

It occurred to me then how much I was missing Mel. Her gusts of laughter, her stubbornness, her whimsical ideas, her blind romanticism. She came so vividly alive in my mind that I almost expected her to rush into the room in a flurry of 'dreadfullys' and 'horriblys'. I wasn't surprised, therefore, when the doorbell rang and I found Mel's sister, Ethne, there on my doorstep.

'Loveday – may I come in, please?'

'Yes, of course.' Mother was lying on the white ottoman, 'resting', so I led Ethne into the morning room.

'So, how are all your family? Do tell me their news.' My enquiry sounded very formal but, then, I was always slightly at a loss with Ethne Finzel. She was so quiet and yet she was not shy and therefore couldn't be coaxed out of herself. There was a strength there. 'How's your father's business these days? Still providing plumbing for the international set?'

Ethne gave me a wry smile. 'I'm afraid so, yes. The latest order is from Mr Chips Channon in Belgrave Square. Apparently he and Mrs Emerald Cunard require portable bathtubs for their safari in Kenya.'

'I'm sure the redoubtable Uncle Donald had something to say about that!'

Again that grave little smile. 'Indeed yes! A contravention of his left-wing principles. Father's defence is that Donald's ivory tower in Oxford is as removed from the real world as the life of the rich and fashionable. Maybe he's right. I don't know. . . .'

'And you, Ethne? What have you been up to since you left school? Still studying the piano?'

'I'm still learning. Yes. And soon I shall start teaching children.' She spoke without enthusiasm, her eyes riveted on the wireless that stood on the sideboard as though that were all she was thinking of. 'Do you mind if I . . .?'

She leaned forward and turned the knob. A concert was being broadcast, and a woman's voice, a rich contralto, filled the room. '*O death, how bitter*. . . .'

I looked at Ethne. She looked as Joan of Arc must have looked when she received her visitation; her cheeks pale but her eyes alive with joy.

Ethne. Ethne's voice.

I had gone round to the Finzels' house one summer evening to persuade Mel to collaborate on our maths homework. We were both notoriously stupid when it came to algebra. The back door of the kitchen was open, and through it I could see Mel with her mother at the bottom of the garden. They were picking raspberries and putting them in a colander. The evening sun glinted on Mel's dark hair, bringing out its strange brassy lights. The house was very quiet.

Then I heard it.

From behind the closed parlour door came a few hesitant piano notes. Ethne's playing, I thought. Nothing unusual about that. Then she began to sing. I stood there like a stone and listened. Her voice was sweet and full, soaring like a bird's. Could this be Ethne? Ethne, who had joined the school choir only to be told: 'Sing softly; your voice is husky.' I was mystified.

A few days later I saw Ethne with her music-case, opening the gate to Ashley Player's garden. I quickened my pace so that I could intercept her. 'Is Mr Player teaching you?' I asked. 'Is that it? Is he teaching you to sing?' I was abrupt, accusing almost.

Poor Ethne blushed. 'No – no – I – it's for his accompaniment only. I accompany him while he sings, rehearses.'

'But you'd like to sing, wouldn't you?' I was afraid that my directness, which Mel chided me for, would frighten her off, but she smiled and said with quiet dignity: 'I would like to be a singer, yes. But I'm not good enough.'

'But I heard you!' I remembered that sweet sound and became quite excited at the memory. 'Ethne, *I heard you*, and you were wonderful, you were *good*!'

My enthusiasm seemed to have brought quite a change in Ethne. She seemed eager to confide, she who had rarely uttered more than a sentence in my hearing. 'You thought so? Well, I don't know; I don't think I am really, only . . . I do so want to sing, to sing *well*. . . . I asked Mr Player if he'd teach me to sing, but he just laughed. I don't think he knew I was serious. He said . . . he said that I could acquire the technique but my voice has no outstanding quality. Oh, but, Loveday, I do so want to, even after he's said that! Do you think—?'

'Do it!' I said. 'Ethne, you must! Just think, if you succeed, you can get away from this place!'

She looked doubtful, and I realised that she could hardly be expected to share my dissatisfaction with Magnolia Gardens. Then she said a strange thing.

'You won't tell Mel, will you? About me wanting to sing. I . . . she'd laugh, I think.'

'If she did, it would be because she was jealous. But I won't tell her. I promise I won't mention it to anyone if *you* promise me something.'

'Of course.'

'That you won't give up. That you'll go on trying.'

'Are you still singing?'

Ethne leaned forward and switched off the wireless as abruptly as she had switched it on.

'I came here to talk about Mel.'

'Is there some problem?' I asked, though it was obvious there was.

'We . . . yes, there's a problem . . . yes. We've had a letter from the Villa Rosa saying she's left the school. Run away. . . . They contacted the local police, but then one of the girls – she's an Italian girl apparently – she had a telephone call from Mel to

146

say that she was all right, she was safe, but she wasn't coming back.' Ethne's blue-grey eyes wore a look of mute appeal. 'I . . . Mother . . . they wanted me to come and ask if you know. Know where she is.'

I told her I'd had a letter from Paris.

'. . . but surely she told you that? I assumed you had friends there,' I said, knowing damn well they didn't. Friends in Paris – Jeanie Finzel with her shabby tweed skirt and gardening galoshes?

Ethne was reaching into her pocket. 'This is the last letter we had from her, but it was written nearly two months ago. It just says how she feels cut off from everything that's going on over here, and describes her attempts to keep up. . . .' She handed me the letter.

'. . . *Switzerland is hardly the real world. We're not expected to read newspapers or take an interest in politics (no wonder Uncle Donald disapproves of the place so terribly!). Safe, bourgeois little Switzerland is all agog at our unemployment troubles and the wage reductions. Their newspapers made much of the naval mutiny at Invergordon last month when the poor ratings refused to sail (good for them!). Did the British press try to hush it up? Over here they made it sound no less than a revolution! I expect Uncle Donald had plenty to say about it anyway. He wrote me the sweetest letter from Oxford. . . .*'

I gave the letter back to Ethne. 'I see what you mean. . . . Look, Ethne, I don't know where she's staying. I really mean that. She started her letter to me on the train journey to Paris, and there was no address. But I'm *sure* she's all right.'

Ethne looked doubtful. 'Loveday, what should we do? Father doesn't . . . he's so *worried*, you know.'

'I can imagine.' I stood up and walked to the window, trying to collect my thoughts. The chief of which was still envy. *Lucky Mel, holed up in Paris. The theatre, the galleries, the fashions. . . .*

'I wouldn't think it's a good idea to tell the school you don't know where she is. If I were you, I'd fob them off with a story about how she's had to get away for reasons of health, and she'll return soon. . . . H'm. Doesn't sound too convincing, does it? They'll probably demand she leaves the school anyway.'

This seemed an unsatisfactory note on which to end but, when I promised to tell the Finzels as soon as I heard something from Mel, Ethne went home looking much relieved.

After she had gone I reflected on my role as confidante and supplier of good advice. It was so easy to give. I didn't mind how many people made demands, or how often. I could still give to them. It was taking I found difficult. My own needs were the cause of so much uncertainty, so much insecurity. To say 'I want' seemed to require an 'I am'.

And I didn't know who I was.

'What's a Daddy Rabbit?'

Myself aged four, sitting on the floor with my picture-book. Pictures printed on cloth pages.

'Tell me . . . *Mummy . . . tell me!*' My already high-pitched voice becoming insistent and demanding. 'Mummy . . . look in the book . . . *look!* . . . "Mummy Rabbit, Baby Rabbit, *Daddy* Rabbit." What's a Daddy Rabbit, Mummy, what's a—?'

I shuffled across the carpet on my backside, book in hand, and tugged at Mother's hem. A wreath of cigarette smoke floated somewhere above my head, and impatient fingers ground a stub in an ashtray.

'*Mummy – what's – a – Daddy – Rabbit!*'

As I grew older my tactics grew more subtle, but no more successful. My paternity was the bottom line in every argument. If I was accused of being difficult or disagreeable, it was 'Well, tell me who my father is, then!' If I needed to be cajoled into doing something, my response was 'Only if you'll tell me who my father is . . .'.

The answer was always 'When you're older'.

So I started creating my own fathers. One day he might be a member of the royal family. The next, a leading politician. Or a Russian émigré. Or a Hollywood star. My father could be anyone I wanted him to be.

The Cliffords had just engaged a paragon of a kitchenmaid. Or so I was informed by Rosanna, when I went back to number 50 to resume my duties that evening.

'She's called Jessie and she's lovely!' sighed Rosanna, swinging from the newel post at the end of the banister.

I stared at her in exasperation and disbelief. She sounded like a child, but she was a young woman, and with such knowing eyes. And I quickly discovered that it was to be my job to drag her away from the kitchens and the poor harassed Jessie.

'Just come and meet her!' pleaded Rosanna.

I followed her into the scullery where the object of her passion was scrubbing potatoes with her sleeves rolled up. She was a country girl, plump and rounded with sparkling dark eyes.

'Jessie – would you like a chocolate drop? Or a bull's-eye?' Jessie took one without hesitation, popped it in her mouth and continued with her work, unabashed by Rosanna's piercing stare.

'Rosanna, Jessie has plenty to do. I think you and I ought to leave her to get on with it, don't you?'

Edwin Clifford had been away for three months, and the fatted calf was duly being killed. Helena had ordered a particularly elaborate dinner to be prepared, though I had the distinct impression that she was doing it because she felt she ought to, rather than out of any feeling of joy at her stepson's return.

I persuaded Rosanna to come into the drawing room with me. She fidgeted incessantly, wandering around the room, picking things up, putting them down again.

'We could play cards,' I suggested. 'Or there's the wireless. There may be a dance-band—'

'I don't like dancing,' said Rosanna. 'I want to hear about you. I never went to school, you know, don't you? I had a smelly old governess. I want to know what it was like at *your* school.'

I plunged into my new role as storyteller, but it was not possible to tell Rosanna everything. There were some things that I preferred to forget.

'Loveday Stark is a filthy bastard!'
Stone Hill High School, 14 January 1925. One of The Worst Days of My Life.

We were hanging around in the corridor at break-time, the usual crowd; me, Mel, Theresa, Win, Molly H. . . . Then Margaret Collins walked past. She was a big girl, fat and bad-tempered (which was the cause and which the effect?), with bad breath. There were sniggers from our little group: '. . . won't you just look at the size of that behind!'

Mel, always the clown, imitated her waddling walk, and I laughed louder than anyone else. Margaret Collins pretended not to hear.

After our divinity lesson I walked back to School House alone, as I'd left something in the cloakroom. I saw Margaret Collins coming out of the sixth-form room. Then I realised she was following me.

I had too much pride to quicken my pace, so I just tossed my hair and pretended I didn't care. Inwardly I was panicking. She was twice the size of me.

Into the cloakrooms, full of thumping, grinding copper pipes, the smell of sweaty socks and cheap pulpy soap. Her footsteps behind me, her asthmatic breathing.

'Oh, little Miss Loveday! With the lah-de-dah name! Queen of the third form! We *are* pretty, *aren't* we?'

(I'd taken my brush out of my satchel and started brushing my hair in front of the mirror.)

'Well, *I know all about you*, Loveday Stark, so you needn't go round putting on airs. Quite the little beauty queen! *Sweetheart* of the school! Well, I know that your mother's a whore and you don't even know who your father is.'

She yanked me around to face her by my hair, pressing me backwards hard so that the cold porcelain of the basin dug into my back. 'Admit it. Admit you're nothing but a filthy bastard!'

I just stared at her. But she was twice my weight, and she used her strength to crush me hard against the basin. 'Go on – admit it.' She leaned against me so that I could hardly breathe, and so that her sour breath was in my face. 'I'm not going to let you go until I hear you say it. Go on – I'm a filthy—'

'*I'm a filthy bastard!*'

Margaret Collins laughed in my face and slammed out of the cloakroom.

I started crying. I ran out into the playground and cried my eyes out. Behind the bike-sheds, near the dusty chalked-out squares where we played hopscotch. No one had ever made me cry before, and I vowed then that nobody was ever going to do it again.

I don't care what I do to people, or how much I hurt them, but no one's going to make me care about being a bastard ever again.

Then I dried my eyes and went back into the form room, and didn't mention Margaret Collins to anyone. Until we were walking back from school, when I told Mel how ugly I thought Margaret was, and how hateful.

'Oh, I *agree*,' she said fervently. 'Terribly ugly! Ugly horrible freckles and dreadful *bad breath*!'

'*Oh!* It's Jessie . . .!'

Rosanna's attention wandered from the tales of my schooldays

150

when Jessie came into the drawing room with a tray of cocoa and biscuits.

'Thank you, Jessie! Jessie, why don't you stay in here for a while, by the fire? There's no need to go back to the kitchen just yet, is there? Loveday's telling the most fabulous stories about her school—'

'Rosanna, don't be ridiculous!' I made up my mind then and there that I wasn't going to tolerate any more of Rosanna's infantile nonsense. It had been clear from our discussion of the academic aspects of school that she had an able and perceptive brain. 'For God's sake, let Jessie get on with her work!' My voice was sharp. 'It's almost eight o'clock; they'll be back soon. And your mother will expect everything to be ready.'

A relieved Jessie disappeared, and I, too, felt that I would be glad when my vigil was over and I could get away from Rosanna. She wandered over to the window and pulled back the heavy velvet curtain. 'No sign of them yet. . . .' There was a whirring and a clicking and a distant rumbling as all the clocks in the house rolled into action and began to strike eight.

'I had a rat once . . .,' said Rosanna dreamily. 'He was called Attila. Did *you* ever have any pets, Loveday?'

'No. My mother never really cared for animals. Except for horses. She used to ride once, a long time ago. . . .'

'Oh, I *do* so long for a horse, Loveday! I've ridden at the livery stables. I'm no end of a heroine when it comes to riding.'

I could well believe it. The lean sinewy body would look better astride a horse than anywhere else.

'I'm working on Daddy at the moment. I can get him to buy me one, I'm sure of it!' For a moment that adult knowing look came into Rosanna's eyes. 'So what *did* you use to do in your spare time, then? If you had no animals.'

'Went to the pictures. Played games. We used to play a game called "Knock Down Ginger". . . .'

'I bet I can make you run!' said Mel.

'I bet you can't!' I replied.

We were about eight or nine and, bored with our hoops and our spinning tops, we were roaming Magnolia Gardens looking for mischief. Mel ran up to the nearest house, knocked loudly on the front door and ran round the corner. I had to run, too. I found Mel leaning against a wall, helpless with laughter.

'I told you I could make you run!'

Her next victim was Father Turnbull, rector of St Luke's Church, who lived at number 26. His housekeeper stuck her head out of the front door while Mel and I crouched behind the privet hedge, stuffing our handkerchiefs in our mouths.

'Oh, I could go on playing this game for ever!' said Mel.

I tired of it more quickly, however. 'Come on, let's find something else to play.'

'We could go and have tea at my house. Uncle Donald's come to stay!'

Donald McDowell was in his early thirties at that time. Although Mel talked about him incessantly, I had never met him before. He was sitting in the best parlour at number 48, surrounded by Frank Finzel's collection of tasteless bric-à-brac, balancing a glass of Scotch in one hand and a cherry bun in the other. Everyone else was drinking tea. As we came into the room Mr Finzel was saying something that made Donald laugh, and a delicious shiver of awe and curiosity ran down my spine. His laugh was the eeriest sound I had ever heard.

'Donald, this is Loveday Stark, Mel's friend,' said Jeanie Finzel in her quiet voice.

'Well, come here, then, lass. Let me take a look at you!'

I approached with trepidation. By nature I was a precocious self-assured child, but in front of this man I felt very shy indeed. I had never seen a man who wasn't wearing a collar and tie, but Donald McDowell wore his shirt unbuttoned at the neck and his waistcoat open. His legs were long and ungainly and seemed to take up a lot of space in the small parlour.

'Well, come on now, eh? Stop staring at your boots and give us a wee look at you!' His wild eyes flashed with impatience, and he slammed his empty glass down on the hearthstone.

I looked up.

'Oh, but she's a lovely wee woman, isn't she, our Miss Loveday? Look at that hair!' He reached out a finger and touched one of the fine waving curls that were held back by my blue Alice band. 'I wouldn't be at all surprised if there was some Celt in you. Is your daddy Scottish? Or Irish maybe?'

Jeanie Finzel leaned forward and whispered something in Donald's ear.

'Her mother's not married?' he said loudly, and Jeanie blushed. 'Well, good for her! Marriage puts a woman in chains.

152

It's a way of keeping her down, making her subservient. Don't you ever go debasing yourself by offering yourself as some man's wife, Miss Loveday, as his *chattel*!'

'Hush now, Donald! She's only a child!'

But Donald just laughed, baring his teeth.

Frank Finzel was bouncing on his heels, looking at his watch. 'Get a move on, Donald, or we'll be late for your bloomin' meeting, or whatever it is you're dragging me off to.'

Mel asked if we could go, too, to wherever their destination was, but it transpired that the outing was to a political rally in the East End. Workers were gathering to protest at the closure of a factory, and Donald was to give a speech.

'Not suitable for little girlies, my pet.' Frank gave Mel a consolatory kiss on the top of her head.

'Oh, I don't know – why not?' said the irrepressible Donald. 'We ought to take them with us and show them some of our old haunts. Show them a bit of the real world, eh?'

They were terrible, the things we saw that day.

We went to Bow first to have tea at the house of Donald's father, Mel's grandfather. He was a thin timid man, who reminded me of his daughter Jeanie rather than of Donald, who seemed more and more like a character from a story-book. Like Captain Hook from *Peter Pan*, I decided. We left the house in Bow and walked through the streets to the hall where the meeting was to be held. Mel and I stared, our eyes wide with horror. It was like walking through a foreign country, a nightmare landscape cluttered with broken bottles and dead dogs, staring children and the thick overpowering smell of rotting fish guts.

Donald McDowell saw my mouth pucker. 'You don't like it much, eh? Don't like looking at all the infernal *dirtiness*.' He rolled his tongue around the word, savouring it. 'Well, these people have to look at it every day of their lives, so don't you go feeling sorry for yourself now!'

But he held my hand when the crowds of children pressed too close.

There were no chairs in the hall where the rally was being held, and it filled rapidly. The sour smell of greasy clothes and unwashed bodies became unbearable. We stood near the back, and Mel and I each clung tightly to one of Frank's hands. I would have liked him to hold me up so that I could see Donald walk to the platform. As it was, I could only hear his voice ringing out, clear and vivid, over the crowd.

'. . . "a fit country for heroes to live in", that's what Lloyd George promised us! And, with the upper classes slaughtered in droves in the war, we – you and I, brothers – we could have been forgiven for thinking that there would be more to go around. More for all of us. But we've a different war on our hands now, brothers. It's called class war. . . . The miners strike for more pay and they're starved into submission. And what of those high-sounding promises, you ask, the ones that Lloyd George made to this so-called *proud nation*? How is it that now, in the summer of 1921, we find that two million of our brothers are unemployed? While the stock-market prices soar and the rich get richer. What is that, if not class oppression. . . ?'

There were angry murmurs from the crowd, and several men started to shuffle and stamp their feet.

'Get on with it!'

'Bloody middle-class hypocrite!'

'Irrelevant!'

The noises grew louder, and missiles began to fly through the air: tomatoes, eggs, rotten vegetables.

'You can throw all you like, brothers, but that doesn't change the facts!' Donald pressed on, struggling to raise his voice above the jeers. 'Look at the Church of England, that so-called democratic institution. A cesspit of corruption and privilege. . . .'

No, you mustn't throw things at him! I wanted to shout. I felt fiercely proud of him at that moment, proud enough to want to be openly associated with him. For a few crazy minutes I even wished that he could be my father and I could be his little girl, like Mel was Frank's.

But when I opened my mouth no sound came out. The commotion had reached the back of the hall by now, and Mel and I found ourselves being jostled roughly from side to side.

'This is no place for you kiddies,' said Frank Finzel, tightening his grip on our hands. 'Come on, we're going to hop it! I'll take you up the West End on the omnibus and buy you tea at Fortnum's.'

Frank Finzel's generosity was legendary.

It was thanks to Mel's unlimited supply of pocket-money that we were able to see every film ever shown at the Majestic cinema in Clapham High Street. Moving pictures became a devouring passion, an obsession.

"This is the home for heroes, and this loving darkness a fur you can afford. . . ."

Mel murmured the words of Cecil Day Lewis's poem as we queued for tickets; the most expensive ones, of course. 'Come on, into the dream-house,' she ordered once she clutched the precious tickets in her gloved hand.

My own fixation was more straightforward. I simply wanted to emulate the film stars and become rich and famous. Every week I bought the tuppenny *Picture Show* magazine, and I stuck the pull-out souvenir picture of Ronald Colman in *Lost Horizon* underneath the lid of my desk.

Greta Garbo was our greatest idol. In the summer holiday of 1928 we went to see her in *Love*, the film based on Tolstoy's *Anna Karenina*.

'Dreadfully sad,' said Mel, brushing away a tear, as we emerged from the auditorium.

Years later I could remember little about the film (except for Garbo's strange glittering eyes), but I had a clear recollection of the conversation that followed it. The three of us (Ethne was with us on this occasion) went to the ingloriously named Copper Kettle across the road and ordered a pot of tea and a round of toasted tea-cakes.

'Just imagine!' said Mel. 'Just imagine dying for love! And being someone's secret mistress! Would *you* do it, Loveday?' She bit deeply into her tea-cake.

'I might,' I said, taking a sip of tea and trying to look worldly, 'if that was what I wanted.' I tended to act a lot surer of these things than the others, so that no one would guess that inside I was uncertain of everything.

'How about you, Ethne?'

'I don't know.'

In those heady days we cared nothing for the General Strike or Ramsay MacDonald's electoral victory, for rising unemployment or the Wall Street Crash. The real world that we aspired to was the one we saw on the cinema screens, where sultry girls in sequined head-dresses had plenty of 'It'.

'You're so lucky . . .,' Mel would sigh to me. 'At least you

155

could become a film star if you wanted, and no one would laugh!'

*VEN-YUSA keeps the Skin Clear and Velvety. . . . Study your
complexion as well as your frocks.*

I had picked up a pot of the latest face cream and was standing
in front of the mirror, plastering it on my skin. Mel was watching
me.

'This stuff promises miracles,' I muttered.

'Oh, Loveday, it's not fair; you don't *need* that stuff. *Your*
skin's perfect already! In fact you win hands down when it comes
to looks, so I don't know why you bother standing in front of that
mirror so much!' She sounded exceptionally sulky.

'Come here, Mel.' I made her stand in front of the mirror with
me, so that our two reflected faces looked back at us. Next to
Mel, my features looked very sharp and defined, my brows very
dark and finely shaped, my chin very pointed. Hers were more of
a blur. And against my reddish hair that fell in rippling waves
Mel's straight brown locks, with their brassy lights, looked drab.
I decided it was best to gloss over her odd yellowy-coloured eyes
and her teeth, which were slightly gapped. But when she smiled
the lines of her face and the curve of her jaw were greatly
improved, and she had long sweeping lashes that made shadows
on her cheeks. I pointed this out to her.

'You know, you're really very striking.'

She looked at me as though I'd just told her that God was a
woman.

'I don't believe you,' she said.

Mel was always uselessly comparing her looks to mine and
complaining about the difference.

'Looks! What are looks?' (*At least you've got a father*, I would
think, but never say out loud.)

'They get you good parts in school plays!' complained Mel.

She was right about that. Juliet, Cordelia, Rosalind, Ophelia –
I had played them all. I used to tell myself that it was because I
could *act*.

The drama master, Mr Carnie, was certainly quick to praise
my dramatic powers. He was a small grubby-looking man with a
goatee beard, who always wore a buttonhole in the lapel of his
velvet jacket. A few weeks before the school production of
Hamlet, in which I was to play Ophelia, he bounded up to me in
the corridor.

'A *rehearsal* . . . a rehearsal, I think, Miss Stark, is needed?'
Mr Carnie had a curious way of stringing together his sentences,
ending with a question. 'After afternoon classes, I think, perhaps
five o'clock would be a suitable time?'

This put paid to my plans to walk back from school with Mel,
and she grumbled about it. As I prepared to leave our final lesson
she said: 'Why don't I come and watch the rehearsal? Then we
can still walk back together.'

The assembly-hall where rehearsals were held was silent and
unlit.

'Oh, Loveday, *honestly*, I thought you said—'

'Wait here.'

Mel stood at the back of the hall while I groped my way down
the aisle to where the stage had been set up. Suddenly the stage
lights went on and Mr Carnie's slight figure was silhouetted, his
pointed beard like some grotesque parody of a satyr.

'Where are all the others?' I asked.

'We should rehearse principal parts *alone*, better that way,
better for the *concentration*, wouldn't you say?' He failed to notice
Mel standing in the shadows at the back of the hall. 'Now, Act
Four, Scene Five, could we start with?'

I opened my script and found the place.

'O heat, dry up my brains! tears seven times salt burn out the
sense—'

'Stop! No, no, no, Miss Stark. Watch me!' Mr Carnie minced
across the stage, tossing back imaginary hair. He forced his voice
an octave higher, and lisped: 'O heavens, is it possible a young
maid's wits should be mortal as an old man's life?'

At the back of the hall I could just make out Mel's quaking
figure convulsed with silent laughter.

'You see, Miss Stark?' To my relief he lapsed into his normal
voice again. '*Feeling* your way into the part, that's what must be
achieved here. *Think* what it is that poor Ophelia has suffered.
Suffered at the hands of Hamlet.' Mr Carnie came closer, so close
that I could hear his asthmatic breathing. He put his arms around
my waist. 'Imagine I am your lover and I have held you close!'

He demonstrated by pressing me against his wheezing chest.
His hands felt damp through my school blouse and he was
salivating slightly. 'Then, I have *rejected* you!' He thrust me
violently away and held me at arm's length. 'Now, how is it that
you're feeling? *Concentrate!*'

I would have been alarmed, had it not been for Mel's reassuring presence at the back of the hall. As it was, the knowledge that we would laugh about this afterwards encouraged me to play up to Mr Carnie as much as possible.

'Oh, yes, I see. Yes, that does help. . . .' I proceeded to give a wildly melodramatic performance, with much wringing of hands and eyeball-rolling.

'There's rosemary, that's for remembrance, pray you love remember.' I snatched the carnation from Mr Carnie's buttonhole and used its petals to strew my way across the stage.

At the end of my speech he clapped his hand to his brow and sank on to one knee.

'Truly beatific . . . a new Bernhardt . . ." he wheezed.

Mel was laughing so much that she could hardly walk home.

'Imagine that I am your lover and I have held you close . . .,' she groaned. 'The divine Miss Loveday Bernhardt, I kiss your feet!'

Then she stopped her cavorting and looked me in the eye. 'You know, Loveday, you really *were* rather good.'

'. . . so what with trying to pass exams and acting in school plays, I didn't have time for much else,' I told Rosanna.

'So why are you doing *this*?' she demanded. 'Why don't you become an actress? Much more fun! You could dress up as a pirate, or a musketeer!' She picked up the poker and lunged across the room.

There was the sound of a car drawing up outside. I walked over to the window and looked out. 'I think they're here.'

They burst into the drawing room, and it seemed as though they were all laughing and talking at once.

'*Such* excitement! Edwin's to be a priest!'

'Well, it's not quite as simple as all that. I—'

Rosanna bounded up to her half-brother and flung her arms round him. 'Will you be a canon, or a bishop in a tall hat? I think those hats are *splendid*!'

'Hello, Zanna.' Edwin planted a kiss on her forehead. He was the only member of the Clifford family I had ever seen display affection towards the repugnant Rosanna.

'Oh, but we're being very rude! Loveday my dear, this is Edwin. Edwin, this is Loveday Stark, without whom we simply couldn't manage – could we, Robert?'

Wincing at Mrs Clifford's patently insincere description, I extended my hand and received the briefest of shakes.

'Now, if you'll excuse me, I'd better take myself off and see what's happening in the kitchen. . . .' Helena Clifford wafted out of the room in a cloud of ermine and French perfume.

Robert muttered something about fetching his best malt whisky, and Rosanna ran off to plague Jessie. Edwin and I were left alone.

I had found it surprising that he had chosen to study at a theological college, and I found it even harder to imagine him as a priest, except perhaps wearing some grand embroidered robes. He was very tall, like his father, but more finely made with dark deepset eyes and a noble sloping brow. While Robert Clifford was large and bulky, Edwin was as graceful as it is possible for a man to be without seeming effeminate. He crossed the room in three single strides and stood in front of the drinks-tray, taking all his weight on one of his long shapely legs in the manner of Michelangelo's David.

'You'll join me in a drink?' He spoke without looking at me, and I felt my hackles rise at this display of arrogance. *A priest indeed. . . .*

'No, thank you. I should be getting home.'

'You must let me walk you, then.'

Doesn't he even remember who I am?

'I live next door but one,' I said coldly. 'I think I can manage on my own.'

He turned to face me. 'Yes, I know.' His voice was lowered. 'But even on a short journey . . . in the dark . . . it's not always safe. . . .'

And then we were both forced to remember Rosheen O'Shaughnessy, lying dead under a pile of leaves. That day was the last time we had met. A fact so glaringly, oppressively obvious that I felt bound to mention it. But Edwin got there first.

'I think that both of us would like to forget the last time we were together under this roof. Let us hope that now. . . .' He spoke stiffly, formally, as though he were making a speech. But then he smiled, as though he had caught himself being pompous. He raised his glass. 'To a more auspicious beginning!'

I walked to the front door, and Edwin strode ahead of me and held it open deftly. 'Perhaps we'll see you in church on Sunday?' he enquired.

'I don't believe in God.'

His face fell.

'And, before you ask why, I've got a question for you. If your

159

God is so fair, why did he allow someone to murder Rosheen?'
'Sanctimonious prig!' I muttered as I walked down the Gardens.
But, even as I said it, I couldn't resist turning back to look over
my shoulder, just in case he was watching me.

'Don't you follow me around, and don't always be staring!'

A harassed Jessie was scolding Rosanna when I arrived at
number 50 the next morning.

'But, Jessie, I could help you! I could carry the coal-scuttle for
you! I'm stronger than you are – look.'

'Come on, Zanna, don't be a pest!' Edwin's tall graceful figure
appeared at the top of the stairs. 'I'm just going off to the garage
to take a look at a couple of cars. If you go and tidy yourself up,
you can come with me.'

Rosanna disappeared, and Edwin strolled towards me with a
formal 'Good morning, Miss Stark'.

'Loveday will do,' I said, in a tone that was undoubtedly pert.

He smiled at me. 'Father tells me you're very good at handling
Rosanna. I – we – are very grateful to you.'

'Well, if you can persuade her to wear a skirt when she goes out
with you, it will be a step in the right direction.'

Edwin appeared to share his family's reluctance to discuss
Rosanna's stranger habits. Their attitude was more than mere
laissez-faire. 'If you see something you don't like, pretend it's not
happening' summed it up better. 'She has too much time on her
hands, that's the trouble,' he said. 'Now that she's no longer
having lessons. She needs something to do.'

'That would seem to be a good start!' I picked up Mrs Clifford's letters from the salver on the hall table and walked briskly
into the study.

Edwin followed me. 'There are a couple of books . . . I'd like
to dig them out . . . if you don't mind, that is. . . .'

'Of course not, if you don't mind my getting on with this. I've
a lot to do.' I sat down at my typewriter and began to open the
letters.

'It must be wonderful to be busy. I shall have to try to fill some
of my time with reading worthy tomes. . . .' He reached for a
volume of Cardinal Newman's essays, muttering to himself:
'Now, are this lot his *Catholic* phase or his *Protestant* phase
. . .damned if I can remember. . . .'

'Or buying new cars?' I suggested. 'When exactly is it that you
get word from on high? When does God issue the contract?'

The smile was forced, chilling. 'It's a very great step; one doesn't take it lightly. I won't just be taking on a job; it's a whole way of life. The Christian life.'

'Oh? I'd always imagined it was a nice soft career for the sons of the well-to-do. You know, the Army, the Church—'

'Unless, like me, you happen to believe that adoration of God and the corruption of society are opposed!' Edwin looked troubled suddenly, as though the thought alone had caused an internal struggle.

'Oh, I see—'

'No,' he said coldly. 'I'm afraid you don't see at all. I don't think you understand.' And he strode from the study.

There was a gentle tap at the open door of the study. 'May I?' Robert Clifford's massive frame filled the doorway. 'Mind if I come in?' His expression was so polite it bordered on grovelling.

It's your own house, you foolish man. . . .

'Of course. I was just finishing this last letter. Well, it's a list actually, guests for a garden-party. . . .'

'And then I should think it's time you went home, young lady! It's almost six.' As he spoke, the deafening chorus of chiming clocks began, from distant parts of the house. 'Annoying, aren't they?' Robert frowned at a striking carriage-clock on the fireplace. He then proceeded to wander around the room, humming to himself, edging ever nearer to my desk. He stood a couple of feet away, with his hands clasped behind his back, watching me.

'You don't mind if I watch you doing that, do you? Only it fascinates me. Fearfully clever the way you girls learn to press the right keys without even looking. Difficult, is it?'

'Very.' I frowned at the keyboard.

Robert strolled over to the bookshelves. 'Rosanna been causing you any trouble? The *enfant terrible*. . . .' He appeared to be speaking to himself rather than to me, and he was walking towards the door again. 'Just had an idea . . . won't be a jiffy.'

He returned carrying a bottle of champagne and a couple of glasses. 'Well, why not; eh? You've worked jolly hard today. You deserve a drink. . . .' He eased the cork from the bottle with careless expertise. 'I presumed . . . I hope you like champagne . . . most people do.'

'I'm sorry, Mr Clifford; it's very kind, but I really can't. I ought to be getting back.'

'Oh. . . .' His face fell. 'Do forgive me. I'm sorry. I wouldn't dream of holding you up . . . but. . . .' He looked around the room. 'Here, the evening paper's finished with. Why not take it with you?' He seemed so eager to impress his courtesy on me in some way that I accepted, just as I accepted his holding my shabby coat for me while I put my arms in the sleeves. It was a relief to close the front door behind me and go home.

'Is that the evening paper?' asked my mother needlessly. She was lying on the ottoman with a book in one hand and a cigarette in the other.

'I thought I might see what's showing at the Majestic.'

'It's the job columns you ought to be looking at. . . .'

I made myself a pot of tea and sat down to read the paper. An advertisement on the back page leaped out at me: 'YOUNG ENGLISH ACTRESS REQUIRED FOR MAX TORRANCE PRODUCTION, "THE JAZZ BABY". EXPERIENCE DESIRABLE, BUT NOT ESSENTIAL. APPLY: SHAFTESBURY THEATRE, LONDON, W.'

I laughed at the idea at first. But then Rosanna's words came back to me. 'Why are you doing *this*? Why don't you become an actress?'

I took out my notebook and copied down the telephone number.

'. . . Oh, Loveday, if only you could see Paris by night. That's my favourite time here. I go out and just wander around, looking at it all. The Seine under the stars, the narrow streets jutting off at curious angles into the darkness, the multiple bridges with their mysterious arches – I feel I could never get tired of it! And the mansard roofs have little round "ox-eyes" that seem to be winking at you!

'In the day there's not much to do, so I just read or go and sit at a street café. The Sélect and the American Bar are the ones where most of the foreigners congregate. I wish I had the nerve to be more adventurous. I'm sure there's another side to Paris, and I long to see it. There's a lot of sitting around in bars here, and couples sit together or stroll around being far more openly demonstrative than we're used to. No wonder the English think that Continental life revolves around sex (in a manner that their nannies would not approve of!). . . .'

I read Mel's letter through to the end, but there was no mention of the Villa Rosa or her plans for Christmas, which was fast approaching. Nor was there an address.

But I had other things on my mind that day. I had to persuade Mrs Clifford to let me go and audition to become a jazz baby. I went to find her in the morning room. The door was open, and I could see Robert Clifford's over-sized shadow on the Chinese carpet.

'I'm sorry, Robert, but that really won't do!' Helena's voice was high and brittle.

'But, my darling, I—'

'You *know* what we agreed. That sort of arrangment was to be left to me. The running of the house is my affair. You might at least allow me that, if nothing else!' Her words were barbed with a meaning that I did not understand, but which Robert surely would.

'My dear, I didn't think you'd mind if—'

'Robert, I *will* not be taken for granted!'

I cleared my throat. Helena's powdered face tightened into a smile. 'Ah, Loveday. . . . Robert, *we will have a discussion about this later.*'

I didn't rate my chances of getting time off very highly, particularly if I told the truth about where I was going. I told her I needed to go to the dentist.

'Well, of course, my dear. These things have to be done, after all. . . .'

She smiled, but Mrs Helena Clifford didn't fool me. Oh, she had perfect manners and affected a fashionable languor, but beneath it all there was a dreadful suppressed energy. And she seemed to be angry with me, as if her politeness was a poor substitute for the sarcasm she would have liked to unleash.

At lunchtime I took the opportunity to call on the Finzels and give them news of Mel, as I had promised to do. Ethne opened the door, looking exceptionally dowdy. Her hair was scraped back from her large forehead, and she was wearing a tweed skirt that looked as though it might have been handed down from her mother.

'Mother's in the garden,' she said, when I told her about the letter. 'Would you mind awfully going and telling her about it? She has worried so. . . .'

As I walked out to the kitchen door Ethne followed me and caught me by the arm. 'Loveday . . . I. . . .' She blushed and looked embarrassed. 'I took your advice . . . what we talked about the other day.'

I looked blank momentarily. She pointed at her throat as if to jog my memory. 'My voice. I'm enrolled for lessons now, with Herbert Wilkins at the Cathedral School.' She added, 'He's quite famous,' as if I might think she had gone to a total charlatan.

'I'm very pleased to hear it.'

'And, Loveday, I'm to be entered for the South London Music Festival. In the contralto class.'

I squeezed her hand. 'Well done!'

'I wanted to thank you.'

'That's all right. As long as I can take the credit for being the person who discovered the famous Ethne Finzel. . . .'

Only Mrs Finzel could be in the garden in this weather, I thought, pulling my coat around me more tightly. She was raking up the last of the dead leaves from the lawn, her skinny legs looking vulnerable in a pair of huge galoshes. It was difficult to believe that she was married to the king of the sanitary-ware boom.

'I've heard from Mel,' I said. 'I've had a letter. She's still in Paris and having a fine old time from the sound of it.'

She gave me her gentle smile. 'Oh, that's good, isn't it?'

'I'm afraid she didn't give me her address. I've brought her letter along, in case you didn't believe me. . . . You might have thought I was trying to protect her. Here.' I offered the crumpled envelope.

Jeanie Finzel looked aghast. 'Oh, no, lass, of course I won't read your letter. You love Mel as we do.'

I had never thought of my relationship with Mel in those terms, but when she said it I could see that it was true.

'I don't think we should worry too much. She's rented a room somewhere, and she seems to be able to take care of herself. Anyway' – I smiled at the memory of the schoolgirl Mel eating two helpings of spotted dick – 'I expect she'll be back for Christmas. Catch old Greedy Guts missing out on the plum pudding!'

'Ay, she always had a hearty appetite.' With that, Jeanie returned to raking leaves. She had never been given to saying much.

I didn't blame her. Whenever she gave Mel a piece of advice, Mel always went and did completely the opposite.

'Can I offer you a lift?'

'God's representative on wheels, eh!'

As I set off to my audition in the West End, Edwin Clifford

came to a halt at the kerb in what I assumed was the result of his trip to the garage.

I settled myself in the seat next to him. 'And when you're the Archbishop of Canterbury I'll tell everyone that you drove around with a showgirl in a yellow sports-car with' – I took hasty stock of the vehicle I was riding in – 'with a leather hood and fancy wheels.'

'A showgirl?'

I explained about the audition, and only then did a faint smile creep over Edwin's lips. 'I didn't *think* girls got so dressed up just to run errands.'

I was wearing my best dress; a draped grey jersey cut on the bias that moulded to my figure. I had told Mother I was going to see about alternative employment, and she had lent me her best fox-fur tippet.

Edwin's car roared into the West End, and I gasped with delight at the glitter of the plate-glass windows with their elegant loot on display.

'Oh, Edwin, do stop the car! Look! Look!'

'What is it?' Edwin narrowly avoided hitting a parked car.

'That dress, there! The one that's sort of sculpted, with the spangled evening jacket over it. It must be a Vionnet . . . or a Lanvin!'

'Do you care about clothes?' He might have used the same tone to say 'Do you smoke opium?'

'Oh, passionately! But I can never afford anything really decent. Not *yet*, anyway.'

'But when you're the new Gertrude Lawrence. . . .'

The car drew up outside the Shaftesbury Theatre. Edwin handed me out with a brief smile. 'Good luck! I expect to hear all about it later.'

'Oh, Edwin,' I shouted after him as the car pulled away, 'as far as your stepmother's concerned *I'm at the dentist*. . . .'

'. . . though I wouldn't like to involve a man of God in telling fibs,' I muttered through the roar of the engine.

As soon as I saw the crowd of girls, I knew it had been a bad idea.

We were herded into a tiny dressing room and ordered to change. I had brought nothing with me, but some of the girls were putting on satin shorts and tap-shoes with the resigned air of those who have done the same thing many times before. After a long wait we were ushered through the wings and on to the stage, where we stood in a line blinking in the fierce spotlights. There was a pianist at the back of the stage and two men at the front of the auditorium. One of them I recognised from photographs as Max Torrance, the American producer. He was hugely fat, with lavishly brilliantined hair and spats. The other, a thin irritable-looking man who would have seemed more at home in a bank than in a theatre, introduced himself as Bob Cotton, the director. He came up on to the stage, making fussy movements with a clipboard and a pencil, and proceeded to inspect the assembled row of hopefuls, who looked very pale and bedraggled under the bright light. He ran his eye from hair down to feet as though grading livestock, sniffing unhappily at what he saw.

'You,' he said, pointing his pencil at a small fluffy blonde in pink satin shorts. 'And you.' His pencil came to rest a few inches from my left nostril. 'The rest of you can go.'

Still reeling with surprise, and wondering whether I wouldn't rather have been dismissed with the failures, I stood in the wings while the blonde girl auditioned. She sang 'Love for Sale' very badly, and followed it with a recitation of a whimsical verse in a lisping voice. She was despatched with a peremptory 'We'll let you know' from Bob Cotton. Max Torrance didn't even look at her.

'Next!'

I walked very slowly into the spotlight, remembering Mr Carnie's advice on compelling your audience to look at you. Max Torrance raised his head at last and chewed his lip thoughtfully. 'OK, you can go ahead.'

Since I hadn't prepared anything, naïvely thinking there would be a script to read from, I had no choice but to fall back on Shakespeare. I recited Ophelia's mad scene from memory, treading a wary mid-line between monotony and melodrama. There was silence after I'd finished.

'Sing something, please, Miss – er.'

'Stark.'

'Miss Stark,' barked Bob Cotton.

Again I was unprepared, so I launched into the first thing that came into my head: 'Rock of Ages'. My performance would not have done credit to Ethne Finzel, but it was at least more tuneful than 'Love for Sale'.

'OK. Give us some high kicks, honey!'

'I'm sorry. . . .'

'You know, kick! Like, get your legs up in the goddam air!'

I looked down at the clinging folds of my calf-length dress. 'I'm afraid I'm not really dressed for it.'

Max Torrance gave an ostentatious sigh. 'Bob. . . .'

Bob Cotton looked up from his clipboard. 'Mr Torrance would like you to show us your legs, please.'

He met with my most glacial stare.

'Your legs, please, Miss Stark. We haven't got all day. . . .'

I raised the hem to knee level.

'A little higher, please.'

I revealed a few inches more.

Bob Cotton's face remained expressionless. He scribbled something down on his clipboard. 'OK, that's all, thank you.'

I arranged my fox fur round my shoulders and walked to the front of the stage.

'Well?' I raised one eyebrow in Max Torrance's direction. He advanced towards me, the brilliantined surface of his hair shining like jet, his fat hands folded across his belly.

'I'd like to know what you thought, Mr Torrance,' I persisted. '*Thought?*'

'Yes, I mean was I any *good*?'

'Sure you were good! C'mere, honey.' I walked down the steps of the stage. Torrance pressed a plump hand on my shoulder. 'I'll tell you what, you were the best we've seen. The best.'

'Well, does that mean I've got the part?'

'Leave it with me. I'll see what I can do, OK?' He winked.

I went back to Magnolia Gardens feeling rather pleased with myself – a pleasure that was only marred by not seeing Edwin for the rest of the day. I wanted to tell him how well I had done.

'What do you mean, Mr Torrance isn't there?' I hissed into the receiver, glancing at the door to make sure that Helena Clifford wasn't in earshot. 'He told me to telephone this morning.'

Mr Torrance, the voice informed me, was in a meeting with his 'financial people'.

'Well, then, may I please speak to Mr Cotton?'

'Mr Cotton isn't here, either.'

'But how am I supposed to . . .? Oh, never mind!' I sent the receiver crashing into its cradle.

Helena appeared, her face lavishly powdered, her bracelets tinkling. 'Loveday my dear, I've found the sample of silk that Mrs Jay needs to match with the buttons. Will you telephone her and tell her I'll have it dropped round?'

'Why don't I take it there myself?' I said, my mind doing some hasty calculations. Helena's dressmaker was in Burlington Street, only a short walk from the Shaftesbury Theatre. That would give me an opportunity to speak to Max Torrance personally.

Hugging my coat around me tightly to keep out the damp December wind, I hurried across Piccadilly Circus and towards Shaftesbury Avenue. A small band of unemployed ex-servicemen were shuffling along the kerb in the opposite direction, playing cornets and holding out a cloth cap to collect money. I stopped to give them some coins before running up the street to the stage-door entrance.

There was no one in sight except a young lad perched on a stool who appeared to be acting as doorman. He had a box of matches in his hand and was engaged in striking one after the other and then blowing them out.

'Excuse me . . . I'm here to see Mr Torrance.'

'Mr Torrance ain't here. He's just gone out to lunch.' He returned to striking matches.

'I was wondering . . . I came here to audition yesterday . . . for *The Jazz Baby* . . . and Mr Torrance said—'

'If it's the part you're after, he's given it to some other girl. *She* was here yesterday an' all. Little blonde one.'

'*Her?* He gave *her* the part?'

'She had a friend, see.'

'I'm sorry, I don't—'

The boy looked up. 'That's what they say in the business, see; you know, they talk about "having a friend" when someone. . . .' He put the matches down and explained patiently, as if I was a child.

'She hung around, the other girl, after it was all over . . . wanted to talk to Mr T. They went out to dinner together, then he asked me to get him a cab and she went back to his place with him. . . . It was *late*, if you see what I mean. Then this morning she comes in here with him and he gives her the part. . . .'

I returned to Magnolia Gardens in a state of shock. For I realised that I had already built up a scene in my own mind, had done what I scorned Mel for doing and created a fantasy in which

168

I was the new star of the West End stage, in which *The Jazz Baby* was a great success and I went on to other successes, to money, to fame, to escape. . . .

It was like receiving a bucket of cold water in the face. I had taken part in a sordid charade and I was left with *this*, with being at the beck and call of a spoilt unhappy family, with being little more than a *servant*.

My habitual defence was to appear not to care. Nevertheless, I snapped at Rosanna when I came into the study and found her loafing around dressed as Horatio Nelson.

'For goodness' sake, grow up, Rosanna! *How* old are you? Eleven? Twelve?'

To my dismay she burst into tears. 'You're just as bad! You're just as bad as . . . as all the rest of them!'

'Rosanna—'

But she had fled. I followed her upstairs and found her sobbing in her room.

'Oh, Loveday. . . .'

I sat on the edge of her bed and waited for the anguished sobs to subside. She turned her tear-stained face towards me. 'Do you think I *could* be a man? Supposing I wished and prayed very hard. . . .'

I had watched Rosanna play the eccentric so many times, watched a performance calculated to anger and estrange her family, but this was different. The pain in her eyes was real.

'One day soon you'll be wanting nothing but pretty frocks and make-up.' To compensate for my lack of conviction I reached out and tousled Rosanna's short hair. Her surprise was pitiful. None of her family ever touched her.

'Oh, Loveday, I do love you *awfully*.'

Rosanna's troubles had at least succeeded in distracting me from my own disappointment, but as soon as I saw Edwin standing in the hall I relived it again, for I knew I would have to explain.

'What bad luck,' he said, adding more gently: 'I *am* sorry to hear that. Still, I'm sure there will be other opportunities.'

I shrugged.

'Look, I've plenty of time on my hands at the moment – why don't I take you out for a drink somewhere this evening, cheer you up?'

'I'm sure your stepmother will *love* that.'

'What she thinks isn't important,' Edwin said firmly. 'Anyway, it's up to you. I'll have the car out at the front around six. . . .'

He drove me out of London on the Brighton Road, to one of the new 'roadhouses', peopled by beefy young men with three-litre sports-cars and plus-fours. We settled ourselves on high stools at the mock-Tudor saloon bar and ordered daiquiris, agreeing that such brash newness was fun once in a while. But despite his fresh healthy complexion, despite his youth, Edwin's sombre beauty looked out of place in the roadhouse. He didn't laugh raucously like the other young men, or joke with his companion, but kept his eyes on his drink as though he were trying to read some message in the cloudy liquid. The words 'through a glass darkly' floated, unbidden, into my mind. He spoke at last, just when his silence was beginning to unnerve me.

'I'm sorry I was abrupt with you the other day, when we were discussing the Church. . . . I rather flew off the handle.'

'No, I'm sorry. Trying to score points like that. It was cheap.'

Edwin continued to stare into his glass. 'I've had a lot to think about these last few days . . . a lot of decisions to make. I'm afraid it's made me snap at the slightest provocation.'

'Did you . . . did something happen to you when you were away?'

He looked up and smiled for the first time, but there was a burning light in those dark deepset eyes. 'Yes . . . oh, yes, it did. My friend . . . she . . . or, rather, her father is a bishop. I had the opportunity to see the life of the ecclesiastical hierarchy at first hand . . . and I know without doubt that I was terribly attracted to what I saw. . . .'

'But for the wrong reasons?' I suggested.

'Yes, exactly. How am I to know that it's not love of power I'm driven by, rather than love of God? I *must* know! I *have* to be sure. And yet. . . .' He appealed to me again with his dark eyes. 'That begs another question, doesn't it?'

'Does it?'

'Yes, of course. I'm forced to ask this: even if my motives *are* pure, even if they *are* good, how can any of us ever hope to fathom the mysteries of God's universe – mysteries so profound – how can we *presume* . . .?'

There was a roar of laughter from behind us, a clinking of glasses. I found that I simply had no answer for Edwin, so we sat in silence for a while.

'Have I done something wrong?' I asked eventually.

'No, no. Oh, goodness me, no. I'm often silent because I can think of nothing to say. Words are so often wasted, don't you think?'

I thought that was how priests earned their living, with empty words. I bit back my spontaneous reply. Edwin was curiously unsatisfying to argue with. Instead I asked: 'So what sort of sermons do you think you'd give, if you became a priest?'

He thought for a moment. 'I'd have no tricks . . . no inflation of words . . . nothing artificial. But how to appeal to the head *and* the heart, that would be the hardest thing. As it is elsewhere in life. . . .'

I nodded, staring at the silkiness of his brown hair as it curled behind his ears, at the almost girlish perfection of his skin, with its fine shading of stubble. I accepted another drink, but found myself quite unable to make conversation. It was *I* who had completely lost all self-composure, despite Edwin's unorthodox presence in the roadhouse and the incongruity between our surroundings and the subjects he chose to discuss. He had the certainty of his faith, and before that I was nothing. Before I had time to assess this newfound helplessness, the manager stepped up behind a microphone.

'And now, ladies and gentlemen . . . with that big-band sound . . . a warm welcome, please, for Ralph Jarrett and his orchestra. . . .'

It was Edwin who suggested that we dance; I just allowed myself to be pressed against his strong graceful body and guided around the room, almost cowering in the shadows cast by his shining presence. Edwin Clifford might have been inept in the art of conversation but he danced like a god. We danced until I was seeing all his professed humility as a strength, until I believed that my own godlessness reduced me to a debased level before him. This sensation of weakness, of passivity, of feminine frailty, was new to me and quite delicious. I wallowed in it. And was I in love – I, Loveday Stark, who had always assessed life with sense rather than with feeling? No, I was not. But I was learning for the first time to admit need. To feel desire.

Oh, I knew what I wanted. I wanted Edwin.

'Jesus-Mary-Mother-of-God!'

The Cliffords' Irish cook came screaming from the kitchen as the peaceful afternoon was shattered by a deafening crash. I

171

looked out of the study window into the garden. Rosanna was standing at the bottom of the lawn with a brick in her hand, which was presumably about to follow another brick through the gaping hole in the window of the potting shed.

'What the bloody hell—?'

I ran out into the garden, pursued by the hysterical cook.

'Jesus, she just threw the brick at the window, shouting and screaming like the devil himself was in her!'

Rosanna herself offered no explanation of her behaviour. Only when Jessie and a red-faced gardener's boy emerged from the potting shed did it become clear what had happened. Rosanna's rage had been fired by the sight of her precious Jessie in the arms of her sweetheart.

'*She was kissing him!*' shouted Rosanna. Her face had turned a sickly grey colour and she was shaking.

The rest of the family and half of the staff seemed to have joined in the commotion.

'Rosanna's a cuckoo, Rosanna's a cuckoo!' chanted Hughie, skipping round his sister in circles. He picked up a brick and swung it through the air like a cricket bat. I snatched it from his hand.

'That's enough, Hugh!' I said sharply. 'Go back into the house with Cook and perhaps she'll find you some biscuits. Jessie, you'd better clear up this broken glass and see that a new pane's put in.' It seemed the easiest thing in the world to take charge of the situation while the others all stood around helplessly. 'I think Rosanna would like to be by herself for a while.'

Helena's white-powdered face was tight with anger, and for a moment I thought she might strike her daughter. But she restrained herself, flinching and moving aside when Rosanna rushed past her and into the house.

Helena came into the study at five o'clock to check the letters that I had typed, and from the way she lingered over the task I could tell there was something she wanted to say.

'Loveday my dear, that foolish girl Rosanna has locked herself in her room. I wonder whether. . . .'

I duly gained admittance to Rosanna's bedroom and managed to calm the sobs that racked her body, but as soon as I tried to set foot near the door she began to scream hysterically: '*Loveday, don't go, Loveday! Please don't leave me here!*' Promising that I would return, I went to find Helena. She needed me, and she was now going to be forced to admit it. I couldn't help a little *frisson* of triumph as I saw her working to control her anger behind the impassive mask. Her smile was so brittle that she looked grotesque, like a middle-aged geisha girl.

'Loveday, you know how I hate to impose, but you can see the predicament we're in. . . .' She waved her hands, and her bracelets rattled. 'Could I possibly ask you to stay here tonight?'

'They're using you,' Mother said sourly when I went back to number 47 to collect my night things. She lit herself a cigarette and poured a generous measure of gin. 'I told you they would.'

But I couldn't help feeling rather proud of my position of importance in the Clifford household. They needed me. And that need was now reciprocal. They had something *I* needed. Edwin was considering taking holy orders, but he hadn't reached his decision yet. I intended to help him decide. All he had to do in return was offer me a way out of Magnolia Gardens.

I knew that what I was about to do was wrong by most people's standards.

I knew it, yet that knowledge only increased my excitement. I had pulled a thin robe over my lace nightgown, and brushed my hair until it fell around my shoulders in a shining cascade. Then I closed the door of the Cliffords' guestroom behind me and walked down the passage. I made no overt efforts to be quiet. After all, if anyone saw me, I had the perfect alibi. I could simply say that I was going to check on Rosanna.

I opened his door so carefully that at first he didn't hear me. He was sitting on the edge of his bed, a thin stream of moonlight outlining his fine figure, which seemed to be hunched forward as if he was in pain. Then it dawned on me.

He's praying.

I stepped out of the shadows and put my hand on his shoulder. He flinched visibly with surprise. 'You . . . why are you here?'

'I'm the answer to your prayers.' I smiled down at him and reached out to caress his fine sloping brow. His skin was miraculously soft to the touch.

'Loveday, I don't think I—'

'Sssh!'

I raised my finger to my lips, and as he opened his mouth to protest it seemed right to silence him by pressing my own mouth over his.

Then I drew back, and a silence hung between us. It occurred to me that I didn't know how to take the lead. I had no actual experience of sex; all my factual knowledge had been gleaned from a copy of Marie Stopes's *Married Love* that Mel and I had once found in Mother's bedroom. But facts alone were not enough in this situation. I had to give Edwin the impression that I knew what I was doing, for if my inexperience showed for a moment he would not go on, I was sure of it. I felt I was balancing on a knife-edge from which I might topple at any moment. The sense of danger was intoxicating. And how much did Edwin know? I wondered. Surely a great deal more than me. A man of his imposing beauty. There must have been plenty of women.

He made no move to touch me, so I ran my fingers over his forearms, inside the open neck of his nightshirt and over his long muscled thighs. Then, trying not to flinch or seem awkward in any way, I reached beneath his nightshirt and touched his hardened penis, closing my fingers round it possessively. Then my own nightgown was tossed to the floor and I stood naked before him, blocking the moonlight and making shadows on his face.

'Loveday, we shouldn't—' He was staring, mesmerised, at my breasts.

'You want me, don't you?'

In reply he groaned and leaned towards me, touching my breasts with his mouth like a blind hungry newborn child. 'You *are* beautiful . . .,' he muttered, as though he were trying to convince himself.

We toppled backwards on to the bed, and his body covered mine, seeming to crush the life out of me with its weight. It was too late to turn back now; I knew he must enter me, but I was afraid. Not afraid of the pain, but afraid I would show it and he would be able to tell.

It came and went quickly, a hot fierce stabbing, and I clenched all my muscles hard to keep them from giving me away, turning my face to one side so that he shouldn't see how I grimaced. I bit my lower lip so hard that I could taste blood. Blood. I still didn't know if I would bleed or not. I just prayed hard that he wouldn't notice.

I could not hold out. I arched my back and kicked despite myself, wriggling away from the pain, but I had the presence of mind to make the movements look deliberate. Edwin rolled on to his back and I straddled him, pretending that this was what I had intended.

'It's better this way,' I whispered, crossing my fingers behind my back.

And as I used my weight to control the pace of his wild thrusting I smiled to myself. One day perhaps I would tell Edwin the truth, but for the moment the secret burned inside me like a wonderful flame. I had succeeded.

'*Oh. . . .*' He cried out so fiercely that I was afraid we would be overheard. '*I love you. . . .*' But his eyes were shut, and he addressed the air. His voice took on a harsh edge, and he shuddered violently, reaching out with his arms. I thought at first that he was trying to fold me in an embrace as his pleasure reached a climax, and I moved towards him. Then I realised with horror that he was pushing me away.

'*No . . . no, Loveday, I can't. I can't. . . .*'

The next day Edwin had gone.

I had expected him to avoid me, but not to disappear altogether.

'So many difficult decisions for him to make . . .,' murmured Helena. She gave a meaningful glance in the direction of the first-floor landing, and for a moment my heart leaped to my throat. 'This business with Zanna. It appears to have upset him. He's driven down to Somerset again to stay with friends. *Good* friends.'

He returned three days later. I was in the drawing room with Helena, taking down a letter in my notebook while the parlour-maid in her frilled cap and apron poured out the tea, taking care to put the milk in the cups first, just as Helena liked it. The drawing-room door opened abruptly and Edwin walked in, followed by a tall young woman with a mass of heavy ash-blonde hair coiled on the nape of her neck.

My fiancée.'

I smiled. I smiled, but it was an enormous effort and an effort that cost me great pain. I had been so blind, so deliberately blind, ignoring the signs. *Friends in the country . . . decisions to be*

'*Helena – Loveday – I'd like you to meet Jane Everingham.*
made. . . . I should have seen what was coming.

What would Mel have made of my predicament? I used the irrelevant and academic question as a lifeline, a rock to cling to throughout that ghastly afternoon when Robert Clifford opened bottle after bottle of champagne, pressing me to join in the celebrations, through all the discussions of wedding dates and honeymoons and whether the ceremony would take place in Wells Cathedral or in the private chapel at the palace where Jane's bishop father lived . . . her father . . . her powerful, influential father. . . .

I had never felt more of a nobody.

I thought of Mel as I walked through the Gardens after work. I knew that I would never be able to tell her about my affair with Edwin. I would never tell her that I had been disregarded in the end, since I was really little more than a servant. My pride – or was it my shame? – was too great. But all the same I wished she was there.

She had been away too long.

Everything had turned out nicely as far as the Cliffords were concerned.

Robert had solved the problem of Rosanna by buying her the horse she had always wanted. It was kept in livery stables near the Common, and she now spent happy hours swaggering around in corduroy breeches and gaiters, with a cast-iron excuse for dressing in trousers that even Helena Clifford could not refute. She called the horse Jessie. Its namesake had been sacked and replaced by a thin sour-faced woman who became the object of a campaign of sabotage by Rosanna.

Robert Clifford still had some doubts about the wisdom of Edwin's vocation, and he had successfully persuaded him to take more time to consider his future. He was to spend the months before his marriage travelling on the Continent. I suspected that Robert intended him to sample a few final worldly pleasures well out of sight of the pious Miss Everingham.

I stood on the steps of number 50 and watched with Rosanna as Edwin climbed into the taxi that was to take him to the station And as it pulled away I made a silent vow.

That I would never give myself to a man again unless he had given something to me first.

50 Magnolia Gardens

Edwin

'YOU DO WANT ME, don't you?'

She stood before me with the moonlight playing over the waves of her red-brown hair, her sharp delicate features blurred by shadow.

When she was first introduced I had thought Father said her name was 'Lovely'. Loveday. Lovely. And she *was* lovely. A beauty as light as air, exquisitely pretty, undeniably feminine – but with an impenetrable hardness about her, the hardness of self-possession and pride.

And, yes, I did want her. My body wanted her as a balm for my uncomfortable conscience. She seemed to hover above me, bearing down on me from above like an angel and I abandoned myself to her, swept along on a fast-moving tide, then ascending a hill, upwards, ever upwards until . . . I was drenched by a rush of pleasure I'd never felt before.

'*I love you . . . I love you. . . .*'

But I didn't know to whom I was speaking. And as the pleasure subsided and drained out of me I knew that the word 'love' was a travesty. Already, after only seconds, I regretted what I had done; I had betrayed myself, and in doing so I had given Loveday the proof she sought that I was merely hypocritical flesh and blood, with the weakness and appetites of other men.

As soon as I rose the next morning, I knew that I must go back to Wells again, to see Jane Everingham. The trip was to be a penance, an atonement for any attraction I might have felt for Loveday. Before I left I felt I ought to apologise to her, to make some explanation of the past few days, which I had spent drifting in a state of spiritual self-indulgence. But the right words refused to come. When I remembered her standing over me, glowing in the moonlight, it became impossible to see myself as an apostate.

After all, who had been deflowering whom?

'I doubt you have any notion of what it feels like to be a woman.'

Jane, standing by the window overlooking the ornamental gardens of the moated bishop's palace, while I mumbled ineffectually about 'respect' and 'partnership' and 'sharing life's joys and woes'. Jane with her quiet countrywoman's clothes, her cool smile, her firm voice and her philanthropic energy.

She was to be my wife, yet it wasn't Jane I was thinking of as I sped across France on the Continental Pullman. I was escaping them all: Jane, Loveday, my family. I was escaping myself, too – the doubting, fearful, tempted Edwin that I had become – and my doing so naturally brought time full circle and filled my thoughts with the distant past, a past that became vividly alive again.

It had been Father's idea that I go away for a few months before the wedding, even though the Christmas season was approaching.

'This church business, Edwin . . .,' he had said, handing me a glass of malt whisky with a smile, employing the usual brash charm to disguise the hollow fact that we didn't really have a relationship at all.

'I'm all for the wedding, you know . . . Helena and I; well, we're very pleased. But taking holy orders . . . you've thought it through, I hope.'

'Of course,' I said, returning his smile with one that was polite rather than warm. 'I've thought of little else for several years. My decision to go to St Godric's and study theology should have prepared you for that.'

'Of course, of course, dear boy, but consider. . . .' Father made an expansive movement with his hand, eliciting the sympathies of an invisible jury. 'You're still a young man. Still only twenty-seven—'

'Twenty-eight.'

Father raised his eyebrows at me as though I were guilty of celebrating a birthday in secret. 'You're still only twenty-eight. I had hoped that you would wait at least until you were thirty before making this decision. After all, to . . . er . . . "walk with God" – shall we say? – it's not the profession it was, say, fifty years ago. It's harder than ever. Takes courage. And I can't help but be aware that Bishop Everingham . . . that you may have been influenced by the profession of your future father-in-law. My duty—'

'Father, the decision is made.'

And not by me, I wanted to say. *It is the will of God*. But I remembered Loveday's touch, and my mouth turned dry.

'Well. . . .' He held his glass up to the light and smiled at the patterns it made on the cut-glass surface. 'Well . . . if your mind is truly made up, it is not my place to try to dissuade you. I would, however, like you to look on this trip abroad as a gift from me. An early wedding present if you like. See Paris . . . the Riviera . . . Rome . . . do it in style. . . .' He pulled out his cheque-book with a flourish and wrote a cheque for an excessively large sum. 'Don't deny yourself a few little pleasures . . . a few treats. . . .' He gave me a meaningful look, bringing a blush to my face that made me resent him even more. 'This may be your last chance to *enjoy* yourself.' He pressed the cheque into my hand.

I checked into the Hôtel Crillon in Paris and tipped the bellboy generously with Father's money. Looking from the window of my spacious room to the elegant eighteenth-century courtyard below, I thought of all the things I would have liked Father to give me, and I was transported back to the days of my childhood.

My early childhood was fashioned by my mother's illness.

She was there in the early years of my life, always behind a closed bedroom door. It was either '*Ssshh!* Master Edwin, your mother's sleeping!' or else she was sitting up in bed propped against a mountain of lace-edged pillows, clothed in a gauzy peignoir. I would reach on tiptoe to grasp the doorknob and hang from it, letting my weight push the door open so that I could look past it and see her.

'Now, Master Edwin,' Nursie would admonish, 'your mamma doesn't want you in there disturbing her. She needs to get her rest, bless her soul.' And she would cross herself fervently.

But Mother thought differently. 'Edwy, oh, Edwy darling, come to Mother. Come here, my pet!'

I approached shyly.

'Climb up on to the bed, dearest. Let Mother see you, see what a big boy you've grown into.'

And her thin arms would do their best to lift up my sturdy little body as she kissed and fondled me. Her embrace was feeble, but her gaze was steady and she seemed to caress me with her velvety-brown eyes, eyes which Nursie said were exactly like my own. I didn't see the shadows beneath them; I only noticed the flower she had pinned in her soft brown hair and the scent of gardenias.

'Mother' – I pawed at her arms, clung round her neck – 'Mother, when will you be better? When will you come and play with my train set?'

'Soon dearest, soon.' She pressed her fragrant cheek against mine. 'Do you remember about the little baby I told you about, my precious? The little baby who was going to be your own dear little brother or sister, only he or she died before they had a chance to grow big enough to be born? Well, after that happened, Mother was very tired, and she needs lots of lovely rest before she gets well enough to play with you again. Dearest Edwy!'

She didn't mention the shadow they had found on her lung after she had miscarried, or the wasting disease that was wearing her away before our eyes. And always Father was hovering near the bedroom door, his face pale and his hands clenched together as though he suffered pricks of guilt like a physical pain. For he could do nothing to save her.

'Nursie, what's that noise?'

'There's no noise, lambkin. I don't hear any.'

'Listen – that funny noise.'

It was the middle of the night, but below the floor where the nursery was situated doors were being opened and closed and people were talking in hushed voices.

'There's no noise, my poppet. Come to Nursie. Climb into Nursie's bed, and she'll give you a cuddle.'

But I slithered free from Nursie's fat embrace and ran out of the nursery and down the stairs.

I saw my father leaning against the closed bedroom door, screwing up his hands and making that noise I had never heard before: the sound of a grown man crying.

'No . . . Lorna . . . oh, Christ, no . . . Lorna . . .!'

I walked up to him and touched his arm, staring up at his face, silently beseeching him to stop.

He looked at me as though he had just seen a ghost.

My mother died in 1908, when I was five years old.

The house became a terrible void; dark, as though her loving presence had been its only source of light, silent except for the ticking and the chiming of the clocks. There were seventeen of them. I counted them on the day of the funeral when my black-clad aunts told me to 'run along'. Father, who had always been a distant figure constantly busy at his chambers, virtually disappeared. The management of my grief was left to Nursie.

Nursie was a stout middle-aged Irish woman from County Galway, and a devout Roman Catholic. Her solution to the problem of my mother's absence was reassuringly simple to my five-year-old mind. Mother was quite nearby, 'up there' in heaven, and could be reached through prayer.

'Ave Maria, gratia plena – on your knees, Master Edwin, hands together nicely, that's it. . . .' We knelt before Nursie's makeshift shrine: a small table covered with a lace cloth on which were arranged a sepia photograph of my mother, several lighted tapers and a wooden crucifix. On the wall above the table was a picture, painted on wood, of a rather severe-looking Virgin Mary. 'Where was I now . . .?'

Nursie straightened her wire-rimmed spectacles. 'Hail, Mary, full of grace . . . Dominus tecum: benedicta tu in mulieribus. . . . The Lord is with thee: blessed art thou amongst women . . . et benedictus—'

'Can you see her yet? Can you see Mother?' I was not yet old enough to understand the difference between prayer and clairvoyance.

'She's up there in heaven, my lamb, at the side of the Blessed Virgin Mary and surrounded by the host of angels.'

I didn't much care for the idea of the Blessed Virgin Mary, who sounded autocratic and forbidding, but I thought the angels sounded nice. I wanted one of my very own. She would be wearing a long soft garment like a nightgown and would wrap me up warmly in a gardenia-scented embrace.

Over the next few years, encouraged by Nursie's prayer sessions, piety and mother-love entwined themselves in my being, the uplifting of the soul grew to be identified with feminine mystique and a cult of angels. I loved the sights and sounds of religion, the candles flickering before the image of my mother's face, making me feel that she was still with me. And I loved the sound of the words, so mysterious in Latin, so soothing in English.

'Say "Star of the Sea", please, Nursie,' I would beg. 'It's my favourite.'

181

And Nursie, relishing her role as high priestess and confessor, would chant: 'Ave Maris stella, dei mater alma. . . . Hail, star of the sea, gentle Mother of God. . . .'

Gentle Mother. . . .

Then Father met a young woman called Helena Sarsted, who took one look at the shrine in the nursery and told Father that Nursie was 'subverting' me and turning me into a Roman Catholic, which was a sin and a disgrace. And Nursie, my dear kind Nursie, was made to pack her bags and return to Parknasilla in County Galway.

'Come here, Edwin. Come and sit next to me.'

Helena Sarsted was sitting on the drawing-room sofa, her ankles crossed to reveal silk stockings beneath her fashionable hobble skirt.

I shook my head and edged away.

'What an odd little boy you are!'

I stared at her.

'Oh well, you know what happens to ill-mannered children, don't you? They are sent to their rooms.'

I fled only too gladly, but Helena wanted to please my father by making an effort with me, so she persisted. She came up to the nursery where I had flung myself on the bed, sobbing, at the sight of my dismantled shrine.

'What's all this about, then?' she asked, attempting to put her arms round me. No doubt she meant to be kind, but her embrace was stiff, as though even her soul was corseted. I decided to confide.

'I haven't got Nursie here to do the prayers, so I can't know if Mother's still with the angels in heaven. I can't talk to her.'

Helena, who clearly didn't understand, muttered something under her breath about 'popish nonsense' before fixing me with her smile again. 'Never mind, dear, I've brought you some lovely presents. They're downstairs in the hall if you'd like to go and look at them. And you shall have me for company instead of your old nurse. Aren't you pleased about that?'

I looked up at her fearfully through my sniffs. Nursie had impressed on me that I must always tell the truth. 'No. I'm afraid I'd rather have Nursie, thank you.'

She went on smiling, but her eyes flashed. 'Well, if that's all you have to say, you'd better keep quiet.'

I did. It was Helena who impressed on me the peril of words, and gave me my fear of smalltalk. And before long it had become obvious that she was there to stay. The house began to fill with things that she had bought, and Mother's possessions were gradually tidied away to make room for them. Photographs of Helena by Lenare appeared on every table, and pride of place was given to her portrait sketched by Helleu. It was about the time of the portrait being hung that I stopped having lessons with a tutor and was sent away to preparatory school, which was only tolerable because my size allowed me a certain amount of respect from the other boys. I sang in the chapel choir, my greatest pleasure, and since singing was considered 'soft' I compensated by learning to box.

It soon became apparent that I was to spend my holidays away from home, too.

'Hullo, old chap.'

Father had found his way to my room. I was mildly surprised that he knew where it was. He extended his hand and patted me on the shoulder, then moved away again quickly. Since his courtship of Helena had begun, his attitude towards me had been one of apologetic restraint, as though he were sorry that he was defiling Mother's memory by forcing a stepmother on me. I was puzzled, but when I remembered how he had cried the night Mother died, I couldn't feel angry.

'Now, Edwin, about the summer hols. . . . You don't want to be hanging around here, do you, old chap? The wedding preparations are going to be awfully dull. So you're going off to Sandwell to stay with your Uncle Tom and your Aunt Iris and all your cousins. You'd like that, wouldn't you?'

I was tired of being told what I should or shouldn't want. I broke my habitual silence. 'I'd much rather stay here and play cricket with you. We could play in the garden.'

I knew that Father still kept a very fine cricket-bat, used in his university days. It was behind the door in the boxroom. I used to creep in there to fondle it, holding it up to my face to inhale the sour-sweet linseed oil, running my fingers up and down its silky surface. And I used to dream of how we would play with it together.

'Come on, you don't want to be playing cricket with an old duffer like me! You'll get a much better game at Sandwell. There'll be nearly enough of you to make up a team!'

'I'm not going.'

'Now, now, old chap, that's—'

'I'm not going. I'm going to stay here in Magnolia Gardens and play cricket with you, and with your bat. You're my father.'

'Edwin, the arrangements are all made. Helena will be very upset—'

'I'm not going!' I shouted and ran from the room.

They knocked on the door, they cajoled and pleaded, they hammered on the door, but I would not open it without eliciting a promise that I didn't have to go away for the summer. The bursting, surging of anger against my breastbone was new to me, making me feel tingly and light-headed. I was alarmed by the way these feelings were impossible to stop once you gave in to them, but I was also thoroughly enjoying my bad behaviour. And I was about to learn that anger could only be suffused and deflated by being brought to an ugly climax. *There was no turning back*.

In the end Helena sent for the gardener's boy to break down the door. She stood there on the threshold, not a hair out of place. Father towered behind her.

'Edwin, old man . . .,' he began.

'Let's have an end to this nonsense,' Helena cut in. 'Edwin, I simply won't tolerate this sort of attitude. You're going to Sandwell if I have to put you on that train myself! Do you understand?'

I did not understand. All I knew was that fury was leaping and raging inside me, just like the fires of hell that Nursie had once described.

The fire. . . . It was a cool evening, and fires had been lit in the bedrooms. Before the door had been forced open I had amused myself by playing with the poker, holding it in the flames until it glowed red hot. I snatched it up now and advanced towards Helena, threatening her with it, my teeth bared, snarling like a small Beelzebub. . . .

Helena gasped and clutched at her throat. Father leaped forward with a cry of 'Have you lost your wits, boy?' and knocked the poker from my hand. He raised his own hand, and it hovered before my face for a few seconds before he lowered it again. I discovered years later that he had promised Mother he would never strike me. But he was certainly angry enough to do so, and perhaps it would have been better for both of us if he'd never made that promise.

They left me alone to reflect on my sins. As Helena pulled the splintered door to behind her I heard her say: 'I always suspected that boy had a wicked temper, Robert. I shall expect you to *do* something about it.'

And Father had laughed. 'Don't worry, my dear, he'll have it crushed out of him at Sandwell.'

My cousins were barbarians, which was strange because they seemed quite intelligent.

I spent the summer of 1914, the last summer of peacetime, at the home of my mother's elder brother, Tom Barkworth. He lived at Sandwell Manor, a rambling and commodious Jacobean house in the Windrush valley, and had filled the house with his nine children, mostly boys, and with a host of dogs, goats, chickens and sheep. My cousins were boisterous and outdoorsy in the extreme, experts in animal husbandry and preferring to be out with gun and rod than continuing the education that my vague bookish Aunt Iris had planned for them. She employed a Belgian tutor for the boys, a Monsieur Bargas, and on the day I arrived he was giving them a scripture lesson.

'. . . so zat is why St Christopher 'as his name. Because he bore the infant Christ across ze raging river. You see, *Christo* from "Christ" and *ferre* which we all know is ze Latin verb "to bear".'

Aunt Iris had brought me up to the schoolroom to introduce me to my cousins. 'But, *monsieur*,' said Maurice, the loudest and the untidiest of the boys, 'Monsieur, we don't understand, do we, boys?'

The other boys shook their heads in unison.

'We don't understand how St Christopher did it.'

'Well . . . he picked up the Christ child, who was only tiny, remember—'

'Show us, monsieur! You'll have to show us how he did it!'

And Aunt Iris and I watched in astonishment as the boys made the good-natured Monsieur Bargas re-enact the bearing of Christ by taking each of them on his own back in turn and fording an imaginary river. Since they were all twice his size, it made a bizarre sight.

My Barkworth cousins created endless entertainment for themselves by teasing and picking on one another. They were delighted at my arrival for the simple reason that I provided them with a fresh target.

'Edmund's a prig! Edmund's a prig!' chanted Louisa, the most obnoxious of the girls, when she had discovered my tendency to be tongue-tied.

'Edmund's a pig! Edmund's a pig!' shouted Daisy, the youngest, who did not quite understand.

'No, no, you're both wrong!' Maurice advanced towards me with a grin on his face. 'I know what we'll call you, Edwin. We'll call you "the Priggish Pig" – "PP" for short.'

So 'PP' I became for the rest of the holidays.

It wasn't all bad. There were the games of cricket that Father had promised; and he had lent me his bat, which was responsible for some fleeting popularity on my part when the others wanted to use it. And there was a tree-house.

I loved the tree-house. It was on a hill at the edge of a scrubby copse, and from it you could look down on Sandwell, on the sleepy cornfields and the River Windrush snaking through them, reflecting the sky like a piece of blue satin ribbon. It had been built years ago, and the boys were blasé about its attractions, but I was quite happy to go up there alone and read, or simply sit and dream.

Then came 3 August, the day war was declared. The children went on playing French cricket in the garden while Uncle Tom and Aunt Iris talked in hushed voices. Long after they had heard the news Uncle Tom paced up and down, muttering to himself, unable to relax. The German aggression was a personal insult which he had a duty to revenge. He did so by taking an axe and in a frenzy of nerves hacking up the tree-house.

'It's time you boys started to grow up,' he said over dinner. 'Today of all days. That's why I did it – show you it's time to grow up. Besides, you'd outgrown the ruddy thing.'

None of my cousins seemed perturbed by this destructive act and continued to munch on their mutton chops, dribbling gravy down their chins and licking their fingers. But I, who had watched the demolition of the tree-house from a hiding place and cried by myself, felt my lower jaw trembling.

'And what's the matter with you, Edwin?' barked Uncle Tom. 'Sentimental little ass!'

My cousins all roared with laughter at Uncle Tom's insult, and none loader than Nicholas, or Nico. He was closest to me in age and rivalry, the most intelligent of the brothers, with sharp all-seeing eyes and a quick smile. The next morning I came down stairs to find him standing on the lawn, taking practice swings with my precious cricket-bat. I strolled towards him with my hands in my pockets, but despite my nonchalant pose I felt a familiar surging and burning under my breastbone.

'Hey, you know you're supposed to ask my permission before you use that bat. It belongs to my father.'

'It belongs to my father.' Nico did an unflattering impersonation, and then laughed. 'No, we don't. We've decided we don't have to ask your permission any more because you're a sentimental little ass. Father said so, and sentimental little asses don't have their permission asked. In fact that's what we've decided to call you. You're not "PP" any more, you're "Sentimental Little—"'

I swung back my fist and hit him squarely across his face. A stream of blood trickled from his nose and splashed on to his white cricket-shirt. Nico cried out in surprise and pain, but he wasted no time in dropping the bat and grappling with me, trying to pull me on to the ground. But, although we were the same age, I was much taller than he was, and with my boxing experience behind me it didn't take me long to get the better of him. And I was spurred on by anger.

'Pax! Pax! All right, you win!'

I stopped thumping Nico, and he wiped the blood from his face. 'We won't call you "PP" any more, either. Is it a deal?'

I held out my hand, and he shook it. We both lingered over the ritual, slowed down by a sense of disbelief. It was hard to tell who was more horrified at the discovery of impulses I could not control. But from then on Nico made sure there was no more teasing and a sort of grudging affection grew up between us, the nearest thing to friendship I had ever known.

My adolescence, which largely coincided with the post-war years, imposed a new loneliness. And, as its uncomfortable longings and unfamiliar desires burgeoned within me, the role of religion in my life developed accordingly. It moved from its association with succour and mother-love to the warmer emotions. It became synonymous with passion.

When I was at a loose end during the school holidays, which was frequently, I would walk to the end of the Gardens, to St Luke's Church. I spent hours there; praying, thinking, or simply walking around, touching things. Once I walked up to the altar and touched the golden chalice and the sacramental cross. Father Turnbull came in from the vestry and disturbed me. I thought he would be angry, but he was a benign man, with no trace of the ascetic in his nature, and he took me to the back of the church and unlocked a huge chest which housed its very special treasures, used on feast days. I think he was glad that someone was taking an interest.

St Luke's was an unremarkable example of nineteenth-century ecclesiastical architecture, but it did have a painting that was of special interest. It was an oil painting, some ten feet square, specially commissioned from a lesser-known member of the Pre-Raphaelite school. Father Turnbull explained its allegory to me. The young man with stricken eyes who knelt on the ground and had his hands bound by chains was the Sinner. He represented mankind, all of us. The other figure in the painting was the Angel of the Lord, hovering above him and trying to get him to turn his eyes in the direction of heaven. For only if he accepted God's love would the Sinner be free.

I was fascinated by the painting and spent much of my time in the church staring at it. It was not, however, from any worthy motive, such as the recognition of my own sins, or a resolution to turn to the Lord.

I was in love with the angel.

In classical literature angels are always men, but this painter had chosen to depict a woman, wisely exploiting all the seductive and beguiling qualities of the weaker sex. She had thick dark hair which fanned out around her face in a cloud. Her large eyes, so bright that they glittered, stared beseechingly from her pale face; a face whose expression was at once unbearably sweet and unbearably sad. She wore a soft, light garment that clung to the contours of her body, and all of her was oppressed by the weight of her heavy white wings, the wings that Nursie had described to me. The wings that had borne Mother up to heaven.

And as I stared at the Angel of the Lord I felt a shameful tingle in my loins and a quickening of the breath, and all I wanted was for an angel, my own angel, to descend from heaven and envelop me with her gift of love.

The decision to go to St Godric's Theological College was a simple one. By the time I was nineteen I had spent years wanting to do nothing more than immerse myself in examination of the divine. And I had no desire at all to go on living in Magnolia Gardens with my father's guilty distance, Helena's coolness and the infantile tantrums of Rosanna and Hughie.

The college was in Cambridge and, although it was not a part of the university, it was set in a leafy street in the heart of the city, near enough to the magnificent chapel of King's College for me to be able to walk to evensong. Studying at a theological college made it acceptable at last for me to pursue a solitary life, and this was a great relief; I spent hours sitting at my desk, staring out at creeper-covered walls and pondering questions which were of little interest to the troubled world outside. What happens to the Church when the people cease to believe that the Bible is true history and that miracles happened? Do the forms set by the Church enhance or stifle our prayer? Which is better, to receive too much, or to receive too little?

But I didn't pass the three years as a total recluse. I still spent holidays at Sandwell with my Barkworth cousins, and since Nico was reading French at Queens' College I saw him and his friends during term time, too. These were the only occasions on which I had any female company.

One baking-hot day in June, Nico thundered up my staircase at St Godric's and insisted that I join him for a punting party.

'Come on, absolutely *no* excuses tolerated. Let's take these' – he picked up my copy of Newman's essays and hurled it out of the window – 'and chuck them into the jolly old quad where they belong. Dust to dust. . . .' He rubbed his hands together with glee, still an incorrigible Barkworth barbarian. 'Now, come along, Edwin, chop, chop. All work and no playmate, makes PP a dull dog.'

And I was dragged without further ado to the banks of the River Cam, where a group of Nico's boisterous friends, equipped with gramophone, picnic-hamper, parasols and gin, were squabbling like overgrown children about how the company was to be divided between the three punts.

'. . .No, I *shan't* go without Bunny! If I'm not in the same punt as Bunny, I shall simply *die*! Expire!'

Not being part of the group, my position was simple. I stepped alone into the first punt.

'Well, that settles it for me! I shall have your cousin, Nico – and, what's more, I shall have him all to myself. Edwin *the Divine*!'

They all laughed at this witticism, since my study of theology was a source of endless amusement and curiosity. And, clutching a bottle of gin to her fashionably flat bosom, one of the girls clambered into the punt and pushed us off from the bank.

I was so taken aback that we had floated several yards before I had a chance to take stock of the situation. My companion was Sibella D'Aubny, one of the bright, hard little flappers from Newnham. Before long she was very drunk.

'Come on, Edwin, shove up, there's a love! I want to sit beside you.' She squeezed on to the seat beside me and promptly dropped the punt-pole that she had been holding in one hand while she drank gin with the other.

'Whoops! There it goes! Never mind, I dare say we shall get to Grantchester under our own steam, if we're clever about it.'

Sibella fluttered her sooty eyelashes at me. She wore a lot of make-up, and her lacquered black hair was cut in a short geometric bob, aping the screen goddesses of the day.

'Now I've got you all to myself I simply must probe your mysteries!' She pressed her hand into mine. 'Did you know that you have the reputation of being cold? Does that surprise you?'

I shook my head.

'Well, why won't you ever talk to us? Nico's forever telling us what a good sort you are. "Oh, Edwin's a good chap, fearfully intelligent" – that sort of thing – so, why so silent?'

I avoided her intent gaze, staring instead at the green brilliance of the boughs that overhung the river and the patterns made by the sun glinting on the water. 'The reason I'm so silent, as you put it, is because I've had cause to realise how dangerous words are, and how poor in expressing our feelings. . . . Words prevent us from putting across the reality of our feelings.'

'How mysterious! How *deliciously* mysterious!' Sibella hiccuped. 'And I suppose you realise that you have a reputation for being the most beautiful man in Cambridge? Have you *any* idea how beautiful you are?'

I felt myself blushing.

'And I'm afraid, *divine* Edwin, the combination of utter beauty and mysterious silence is devastating to us women. May I?'

She leaned towards me and planted a greedy, gin-soaked kiss in my neck.

'Sibella. . . .'

She sat up.

'Oh my God, you're not . . . are you?'

'No.'

'Well, what do you want, then?'

I couldn't look at her, but there was no hesitation in my reply. 'Love. Romantic love.'

'Then, you're a fool. And I may as well try to retrieve that punt-pole.'

In 1925 I completed my preliminary degree in theology and returned to Magnolia Gardens.

I spent several months trying out my newly acquired skills on the golf-course while Father alternately cajoled and bullied me towards a career in the City or at the Bar. Eventually, when I could stand no more, I escaped to the Continent and spent several months visiting the cathedrals of France and the churches of Italy, searching their frescoes and wall-hangings for an angel who would entrance me as the angel in St Luke's had done. I found none, but I did enjoy a certain peace of mind in those hallowed places that was more persuasive than any of Father's arguments, and in 1927 I returned to St Godric's to embark on the postgraduate study that would prepare me for ordainment as a priest.

Nico Barkworth had long since left Cambridge, and without his interruptions and noisy demands I enjoyed a more peaceful few years. From time to time I would be courted by a like-minded female graduate and we would enjoy chaste walks along the river-bank, but I never demanded more than a hand to hold and an occasional kiss and, intimidated perhaps by my aloofness, none of them offered more.

In the summer of 1931 I completed my preparation for holy orders and was invited to a ritual dinner by the principal of St Godric's. This dinner was part farewell and part a chance to confirm and seal one's career through discussion with senior clerics. A sort of ecclesiastical recruitment drive.

I found myself sitting next to the Right Reverend Dr Alfred Everingham, Bishop of Bath and Wells. He was a distinguished-looking man in his late fifties who reminded me of a grey dog. Not a greyhound or a similar aristocratic breed, but an intelligent terrier with a square head and short wiry silver hair. We conversed politely about my family for a while, and then, fixing me with his alert watchful gaze, he asked: 'And when are you to take orders, Edwin?'

I knew my reply would sound foolish and weak in the extreme. 'I have no firm arrangement yet, my lord . . . there is no date set.'

'And might I enquire why?'

'I. . . .' I gazed around the room for inspiration but found none, except the decanter of vintage port that was being passed in front of me. I poured myself a glass. 'I'm afraid I don't seem to be quite ready. Not ready for the final step.'

'You wish to devote yourself to God?' The bishop's tone was kindly. He held his own glass of port up to the chandelier and watched the light make the crystal sparkle.

'Yes, I do, of course, but—'

'But the call of the outside world is hindering you, holding you back?'

'Yes.'

The bishop smiled a mysterious smile. 'Ah, but such doubts are the most natural thing in the world. Jesus himself spent his troubled last hours in Gethsemane, asking himself the very same question. Whether he was strong enough to do God's will.' He smiled again. 'I would not dare to suggest, my dear Edwin, that you have not examined your conscience often, and fully. However, I can invite you to be my guest at the palace in Wells, where I will show you how you can be of the world and still serve God. Will you do that, Edwin?'

Swayed by the port and general amiability of the evening, I agreed, but thought no more about the bishop's offer until I received a letter from him some weeks later.

                                        The Palace, Wells,
                                        7 September 1931
My dear Edwin,
I am prompted to take up my pen and write to you, as today my personal chaplain departs for his native town of Rotherham to tend to his terminally sick mother. He is much in my prayers, but I am without my familiar right-hand man! Perhaps you would like to come and stay at the palace for a while, for the dual purpose of assisting me with diocesal duties and continuing our discussion of your future in the Church? I await your reply.

                                        Your assured friend,
                                        ALFRED EVERINGHAM

I replied at once, promising to be in Wells within a week.

'Now, dear friends, pray silence a moment! I would like you all to meet our guest, Mr Edwin Clifford.'

It was my first evening at the palace, and the bishop had arranged a small dinner-party in my honour. I was so overwhelmed by the grandeur of the palace – a massive turreted edifice of grey stone, rising above a moat, and filled with a warren-like system of corridors and grand reception rooms – that I had scarcely taken in the names of the people who were being introduced to me. They were sitting around a fire banked high in a massive stone grate, surrounded by vast portraits of scarlet-robed priests.

'This is Canon John Peters and his wife, Phyllis; and this is my archdeacon, Dr Carol Godwin, and Mrs Godwin. . . .'

I shook hands with two pinched elderly men and their desiccated wives.

'And here we have Councillor Cyril Hatton-Jones and his wife, Blanche. Councillor Hatton-Jones is a pillar of our business community and possibly our next mayor!'

Councillor Hatton-Jones made the appropriate noises of self-effacing denial, but he looked very pleased with himself as he thrust his large hands into the small pockets of his satin waistcoat. He was a sleek, over-fed man with a high complexion, and his wife was smart and handsome; the elegant effect of her rose crêpe gown marred by the harsh peroxide of her permed curls. She wore huge diamond clips at her décolletage and on her ears. They were an incongruous pair at this very ecclesiastical gathering.

'And last – but naturally not least – my beloved daughter, Jane.'

Dr Everingham was a widower, and his domestic needs were looked after by his thirty-year-old spinster daughter. Jane Everingham was tall and handsome and had a natural dignity. When we rose to go into the dining room I noticed that she swept forcefully ahead of the other ladies, despite being their junior. Clearly she was determined – and that determination boarded on arrogance – to assume the full privileges of her rank as bishop's daughter.

The dining room was magnificent by candlelight. Its ruby-red walls were hung with still lifes in rich dark oils, all fruit and dead game, and the thick white cloth was laid with Venetian glass and gold plate that might have been centuries old. Cyril Hatton-Jones picked up a gold spoon and examined it minutely, trying to read the hallmark.

'Benedice nos domine, et haec tua dona. . . .'

After a stately Latin grace we sat down to lobster soup, and I was instantly sucked into conversation by Blanche Hatton-Jones, who was on my left, and Jane Everingham, who was opposite me. Or, more accurately, Blanche made shallow, prattling noises while Jane responded with a series of words and smiles. I plucked up my courage and asked Blanche how long she had lived in Wells.

'Only a year, darling, since I've been married to Cyril. Before that I lived in Bath – *such* a lovely town, you know – and that's where we met. It was at a dinner-dance in the pump room, in aid of some charity – can't remember the name of it but, anyway, they put on a marvellous do. And there was Cyril; he just walked in the door and just sort of stood there *oozing* with charm, so I thought—'

'And do you have children, Mrs Hatton-Jones?'

'Darling, I'm forty if I'm a day! Simply not possible – but bless you for asking. The utter charm of you – don't you agree, Jane? Jane's giving me ever so cross looks because she thinks a lady oughtn't to discuss being infertile at dinner. Well, some women just *are*, aren't they? And how they *suffer*. When I knew I couldn't have Cyril's child, that it was too late, I cried for *weeks*—'

'And we're all very sorry, Blanche, but we can hardly expect Mr Clifford to contribute to the conversation. He's a single man. You're not being very polite.'

It was amazing to see the younger woman dealing with the ghastly Blanche so calmly and yet so firmly, stamping out her emotional excesses.

'Jane's being perfectly horrid to me, isn't she?' Blanche turned to me in appeal, the diamonds on her earlobes sending out dazzling shards of light. 'Tell her how horrid she's being!'

I blushed.

'*Tell her!* Or I shall think you're on her side!' Looking at the tablecloth to hide my embarrassment from my hostess and avoid being blinded by Blanche's diamonds, I said: 'Mrs Hatton-Jones thinks—'

'Oh, but we love Jane, we absolutely *love* her! And she loves us – don't you, darling? – even if she is being horrid. But, then, if you're a natural bonde' – she wagged an accusing finger at Jane's abundant ash-blonde hair – 'you can get away with being naughty! You can get away with anything, even with being a perfect crosspatch. Which you *are*, Jane darling. . . .'

I struggled to include myself in the discussion of prayer and worship at the other end of the table, but this time it was Cyril Hatton-Jones who trapped me. 'What d'you think of all this, then?' He waved his fork, complete with the venison steak he had just speared, at the carved wooden ceiling. 'Not a bad old place to live, is it, the palace!'

I agreed.

'So d'you fancy being a bishop, then? Done up in a fancy apron and a shovel hat like old Alfred here?' He used his fork to indicate Dr Everingham, who was drinking claret with relish.

'I can't deny that it would be a wonderful life, but—'

'Seduced by the archiepiscopal splendour, eh? Well, Alfred told me you were thinking of joining the firm, so to speak. We were discussing it on the golf-course the other day. "Cyril," he said—'

'Dr Everingham plays golf?' I couldn't help a sinking disappointment at the thought of the learned man in golfing tweeds.

Cyril laughed, his mouth full of meat. 'Oh, good Lord, yes! A man of parts, is our right reverend brother!'

The man of parts was conducting a debate from the top of the table, and I was determined to make an impression on it.

'. . . I should like to see a return to a state of reverence in worship,' Dr Godwin was saying.

He was encountering strong opposition from Canon Peters, who took a low-church, almost congregational stance. 'Dangerous nonsense! And those who follow such practices are mere ritualists. External show should be treated with suspicion—'

'I'm afraid I must disagree, John,' said Dr Everingham quietly, smiling his mysterious little smile. 'For all that we should treat the gilt-gingerbread men with caution—'

'Oh, jolly good, my lord,' wheezed the archdeacon, Dr Godwin, an enthusiastic supporter of his bishop. '*Gilt-gingerbread men.* Yes, very clever. Perhaps you could include that in a sermon this week—'

Jane, who nad been following the discussion closely, interrupted him. Her low voice somehow managed to cut through the talk. 'Father has preached nine sermons already this week,' she said with the same firmness she had used on Blanche. 'Twenty-three this month. Too much for the strength of anyone. He shouldn't do too many.'

'Oh, no, of course not, Miss Everingham, I do quite agree. I only meant . . . I thought . . . perhaps I could use the phrase in one of my own sermons. With his lordship's gracious permission. . . .'

'Of course, of course,' said Dr Everingham, his authority establishing itself once more. 'But I would like to suggest, gentlemen, that, though we must suspect external show, external order is necessary. Edwin, what are your thoughts on the matter?'

'I would like to put the case. . . .' I raised my voice, and hush fell round the table. 'I would like to put the case for the beauty of holiness.' I received a disapproving frown from Canon Peters, but I went on boldly. 'I believe that worship must move our emotions. How else can God hope to enter our hearts?'

There was a second's silence. Then Blanche dropped her spoon into her peach melba and began to applaud. 'I thought that was utterly *wonderful*! He's really very good, isn't he, everyone?'

Blessed are the meek: for they shall inherit the earth. . . . Blessed are the merciful: for they shall obtain mercy. . . .

I pondered these words as we knelt in prayer at Holy Communion in the cathedral the next morning, bathed in thundering organ music. I watched Jane Everingham. She was dressed in fine expensive tweed, and her pale hair was swept up in a chignon. Discreet but lustrous pearls shimmered in the pale light from the lofty windows. She arranged her feet neatly behind her hassock and bent her head in a meek attitude. But there was steel beneath the meekness.

Dr Everingham stayed behind at the cathedral to attend Sung Eucharist, so I had nothing to occupy me on my return to the palace. I wandered aimlessly from room to room, until I came across Jane. She was sitting in a turreted window holding a pen. There was a small leather-bound book on her lap.

'This is my Journal of Mercies,' she explained. 'Given to me by one of the elderly ladies in Father's congregation. I use it to record daily the mercy shown to me. Rather a quaint idea, but a useful discipline, don't you think?' Her laugh was high and self-conscious.

I couldn't think of a suitable rejoinder, so I just nodded.

'I think Father was quite pleased to see you get the better of Canon Peters last night. He is something of a purist.'

'But you didn't enter the discussion yourself, Miss Everingham. May I enquire—?'

She closed her Journal of Mercies with a pitying smile. 'I have no time for such hair-splitting, Mr Clifford. That's not what the Church is for.' She pointed to a pile of papers at her feet. 'Every week I have to sit on countless boards and committees. *That* is my concern, and if I dare say it. . . .' She gave a proud toss of the head. 'That is God's concern, too.'

'But surely loving God—'

'Loving God is caring for the flock.'

It was clear that in matters of religion Jane Everingham tended towards an interest in organising the parish. Her father made constant reference to her good works.

'Of course, my dear Jane gives up much of her time to come here and visit the sick,' he told me, when he took me to see the work of Cantor's Hospital, a charitable institution in the cathedral close. 'This place was founded in the eighteenth century by a local philanthropist named William Cantor as a home for incurables. Well, the word "incurable" has gone out of fashion now, but it is still we who are William Cantor's heirs. These people need our care.'

I followed the bishop through white wards with barred windows and narrow iron bedsteads, past drooling or shouting mental patients, past scenes that were horrific or simply depressing.

'Now, before we leave we must have a word with my friend Charlie.'

We stopped at the bed of an inmate whose limbs were most hideously twisted and deformed. His face was a complete blank, devoid of expression.

'Hello, Charlie. How are you, my friend?' A most wonderful softness came over the bishop's terrier-like features as he patted Charlie's twisted hand. He was rewarded with a grunt and something approaching a smile.

'He's blind,' explained the bishop as we walked on. 'God has been kind to him and prevented him from seeing his own deformities. Indeed, how much kinder God is to us than we are to ourselves.'

From anyone else this judgement would have sounded grossly naïve or dismissive. Poor twisted Charlie – the recipient of God's kindness? Yet when this good man pronounced that this was so I could believe that it was true; I could *see* God's mercy for myself on the face of the blind man. Alfred Everingham's conviction became my conviction.

As we emerged from the quaint cobbled Vicar's Close on to the cathedral green, he said simply: 'Shall we pray?'

We went into the lady chapel and I knelt before him as he read the words of the creed from the Book of Common Prayer. From some echoing stone vault came the exquisitely sweet sound of choirboys singing the Magnificat. The harmonies of the music moved me, describing a glory that cannot be described in words. Even the bishop's praying moved me, as though I was realising for the first time how beautiful, how apposite and how intelligible the Prayer Book was. He read with simple dignity and decorum, the tracery of the stained-glass windows splashing regal colours on his plain black cassock. And when I looked up at him and saw the utter conviction of his face I envied him as I had never envied before.

'My dear Edwin, I feel our discussion of your vocation is long overdue. Perhaps you would come to my study after we have dined this evening?'

I had been in Wells for two months, content to play my part as the bishop's shadow with no thought to the future. They had been happy months. For the first time I felt that I fitted into my surroundings, that I was no longer a solitary or a man apart. And during this time I had struck up a close friendship with Jane Everingham. We shared long country walks by day and games of chess in the evening, and these quickly became a pleasant habit. Ours was not a warm friendship, for Jane Everingham was not a woman who inspired warmth, but I respected her. She was sensible and reliable and unselfish, and we had intellectual tastes in common, though she made no attempt to mask her disapproval of my mystical leanings.

'My chaplain is due to return to Wells shortly,' said Dr Everingham when I had made my excuses to Jane and joined him in his study. 'That is why I wished to speak to you now. It is my greatest hope' – he smiled to himself – 'that your time here has helped you to a decision to take holy orders?'

The hope was written there plainly in his eyes, and I could not let him down.

'Yes, it has. I wish to be ordained.'

'My dear Edwin! I *am* delighted! Champagne would be somewhat profane, perhaps . . . but you might care for some brandy? Now, tell me your plans. What sort of work do you have in mind?'

I blushed. 'I had hoped I might be able to find something like the work I've been doing here – bishop's chaplain – it has suited me well, I think. . . .'

Dr Everingham sighed. 'Indeed it has. What a pity that the post here is already filled.'

'Or I suppose I may become a curate in some country parish, and eventually—'

'You do realise, Edwin, that I carry some influence in these matters? As a bishop I have many incumbencies within my see that are disposed at my own discretion. I could get you your own church, if I felt that you were ready for the responsibility. You are nearly thirty . . . though regrettably being single is something of a disadvantage. . . .' He sighed again and picked up a heavy leather-bound book from the bookshelf. He thumbed the pages as though he were reading it, but I could tell from his eyes that he was not. 'Time moves on for me, too. In ten years from now I shall be an old man. I must confess that I worry about dear Jane. She works so hard – you've seen how hard she works, have you not? – and so unselfishly. I fear my failing health will be yet another burden on her one day. I should have liked to delegate many of her duties to a housekeeper, set her free to enjoy herself, find a man to love, bear children. But she insisted that as my only child her place was with me. I tell her it's still not too late for her. But I mustn't burden you with all this; you have decisions enough to make. Perhaps you would think about my offer, and remember that I can help you.'

I returned to Magnolia Gardens in a state of shock. Dr Everingham had discussed first my career and then Jane. He had made no overt connection between the two subjects, yet it was abundantly clear that I was being offered a deal. I would be given a desirable job within the Church . . . if I married Jane. I could not despise him for this move, prompted as it was by his hopes for his daughter, and for me; two people he cared about. But I found myself wondering uncomfortably whether he had gleaned this sharp business sense from Councillor Hatton-Jones as they strolled together towards the eighteenth green.

It was Loveday Stark who drove me into the arms of Jane Everingham. Had she known this, I think Loveday would hardly have been flattered.

She was there in Magnolia Gardens when I returned from Somerset, working as my stepmother's secretary. I spent several days gripped by mounting anger towards her, and told myself that her flippancy and overconfidence were the cause. It was only when she came into my room in her nightgown that I acknowledged the true reason for my anger. I wanted to touch her. Worse, I wanted to make love to her.

At first my brain was gripped by one ridiculous fear – that she would somehow be able to tell that I had never had intercourse before, and would laugh at me. Then fear gave way to a pleasure so intense that I thought I was feeling love. I thought that my angel had at last descended.

Looking at the painting in St Luke's in the cold light of the next day, I knew, and could not pretend, that Loveday Stark bore no resemblance to my angel. I was wavering on a threshold between sacred and profane love, and it was a place where I could not exist with any contentment. I would have to go in either one direction or the other.

I went straight back to Wells.

I did not warn the bishop of my imminent arrival, but when I went to the cathedral to find him (leaving my suitcases in the vestry) he did not seem surprised to see me.

'My lord,' I said, 'I don't know how to say this . . . I hardly know what you will think or if you will forgive . . . but . . . I wish somehow to make a confession as they do in the Roman Catholic faith, a confession of my sins. I hope you don't think I want to convert or to defy the Church, but—'

'My dear Edwin, I understand. You must believe that. You are troubled and you wish to confide. But you also know that it is not within my scope, as it were, to hear a confession. . . .' He smiled. 'After all, we have no confessional, no box. But I am empowered to offer you absolution for your sins, if that is what you wish.'

As I knelt before him I murmured: 'I'm afraid, you see. I'm afraid I'm too weak in the flesh. . . .'

When he had finished the prayer, I was asked to rise. 'Now, Edwin, I have something to ask of you. You had a decision to make. Have you made it? Is that why you are here?'

I nodded.

'Go to Jane, then. Go to her. She has been waiting.' He smiled to himself. 'And you may go in peace.'

I stared at the bishop. Could he really be suggesting that by marrying a 'good' woman I would have permanent absolution from God? No one but a fool could believe it was that simple. But as the sun blazed through the cathedral windows and crowned him with a circle of light, as the sweet voices of the unseen choir soared around us, it was possible to believe.

I found Jane with her Journal of Mercies, sitting in the turreted window. She kept her back to me as I spoke, and both of us watched the ravens on the lawn below, strutting between the borders of the ornamental garden, hiding in grotesque shadows cast by the topiary: trees carved into birds, a horse's head, the ace of spades. . . .

When I had finished my speech, Jane turned to me. 'I'm glad you didn't mention love, Edwin. That was very sensible of you. It's not love that counts in a marriage but suitability. . . .'

'You mean compatibility.'

'Not compatibility,' she corrected me. 'Suitability. You are to be a clergyman. I am a clergyman's daughter. It is a very suitable match. I will make you the best possible wife.'

My recollections of early childhood, when my mother was alive, carried both nostalgia and an aura of tenderness. And as I sat in my room at the Hôtel Crillon in Paris and thought about the events that had led to my engagement I could see that my life had come full circle. Now I was about to marry and have children of my own.

Yet there was something missing.

I left the hotel and strolled across the Pont de la Concorde to the Left Bank. It was eight o'clock, and by the time I reached the streets of Montparnasse where I was headed, Parisians were braving the cold to stroll beneath a pallid moon and the air was filled with rich smells of cooking from restaurants. It was still a little early for the artists and intellectuals who thronged the cafés of the Boulevard Montparnasse, so I was able to sit at a pavement table outside Le Sélect and sip my Cognac in peace. I had still not quite recovered from the long train journey, and a general air of unreality was soon accentuated by a light-headedness from the Cognac. Was I only *imagining* that I knew the girl who was sitting alone at the corner table, or had I really seen her before? She glanced at me, then looked down intently at her plate with a mixture of embarrassment and irritation. So she *was* who I thought she was. And she had recognised me, too, so there was nothing for it but to go and be polite, even though we would both have preferred our anonymity.

'It's Amelia Finzel, isn't it?'

'Mel.'

'Yes, Mel, sorry. Edwin Clifford, d'you remember . . .?'

'Yes, I know. Would you like to sit down?'

There was an awkward silence.

'What a surprise to—'

'I had no idea you were—'

We both spoke at once, then laughed self-consciously.

'Are you going to have something to eat?' she asked. 'These cakes are really dreadfully good. I have an absolute weakness for this sort of thing. If I stay in Paris much longer, I shall be fat as a pig!' She ordered another cake while I made the required polite enquiry about how long she had been in Paris. She had been at a school in Switzerland, she explained, but was spending the holidays in Paris.

'But surely you're not here by yourself?'

'Oh, yes.' She licked whipped cream from her fingers with relish. 'All by myself. I'm renting a little studio in the Jewish Quarter, in the rue des Rosiers.'

I could not conceal my surprise at this unconventional arrangement. 'But your parents . . . surely they worry about you being in a foreign city alone?'

'Travel improves the mind,' she said airily. 'My father would be the first person to confirm it.'

I couldn't help feeling she was avoiding my question, but the waiter arrived bearing a plate of gâteaux, and she was distracted again. 'Goodness, look at that strawberry one! You don't mind if I tuck in, do you? I know it's terribly rude, but I'm *so* hungry. This is all I eat – cakes – because I don't understand the menus.'

There was nothing for me to do but sit and watch her eat, but she didn't seem to mind my silence or expect me to talk. She had a hearty appetite and ate with gusto, and I was acutely aware as I watched her that I had never really looked at her properly before. When her pale face was in repose it was plain, almost pudgy, but when she smiled her cheekbones were accentuated and her whole face somehow lifted and transformed. Her thick brown hair grew back untidily from her forehead, and she ran her hands through it constantly when she talked, making it stand on end. Her dress and coat were unpressed, adding to a general air of scruffiness. Apart from her smile the only feature that redeemed her from complete ordinariness was her strange feral eyes which moved through a myriad shades of expression as she talked.

When she had finished the last *mille-feuille* we made smalltalk again, this time about Paris and its attractions. I explained that I had been in Paris before, and had already seen most of the famous sights: the Louvre, the Eiffel Tower, the Bastille, Notre-Dame. . . .

'Oh, I haven't bothered with any of that,' she said. 'Full of crowds and tourists. I hate crowds. I spend most of the day asleep and look around Paris by night. That's when it's most alive.'

I must have looked appalled, because she laughed a loud delighted laugh. 'You must think I'm quite mad! But it's fascinating, really. Haven't you ever wondered what goes on *inside* Paris, behind the walls, behind the façades?'

I admitted that I had.

'Well, there's a much better chance of finding out at night, isn't there? Why don't you come with me tonight? I bet you anything you like that, if you do, there'll be no going back. You'll be converted to my style of tourism.'

We set out towards the Jardin du Luxembourg but found it locked. After Mel had rattled the iron gates impatiently she agreed to content herself with a view of the park from the Boulevard St-Michel as we walked towards the Sorbonne.

'This is wonderful, isn't it?' I said as we stood alone on its steps and admired its magnificent domed Jesuit-style church. 'I can quite see why you prefer to avoid the crowds.'

But Mel still wasn't satisfied. 'We're not high enough,' she complained. 'The best way to see Paris is from above.'

We continued towards St-Séverin. Mel stopped suddenly and pointed to a seventh-storey attic window in a decaying house opposite the church.

'There! Look, Edwin, up there! The *perfect* viewpoint.'

'But we don't know who lives there. We can't—'

'Of course we can! Oh, do come, Edwin! Don't be a spoil-sport!' She looked up at me, pleading with her eyes.

I followed her.

We climbed the seven flights of stairs, which were lit only by two lamps, and Mel hammered on the door at the top. It opened, and there stood the ghostly figures of an old man and an old woman dressed in nightgowns, their faces lit by the faint reflection from the pink sky of Paris outside.

'If you please, we would like to see Paris from your window,' said Mel in her best schoolgirl French. The old people stared straight at us, their faces blank. The man spoke. 'Yes – you may look if you wish. We don't know what it's like. We're both blind.'

It was breathtaking. Paris was ageless, formless, a maze of dark indefinable shapes in a milk-white mist. I could just discern the Hôtel Dieu, the Tour St-Jacques, the Quartier Latin, the Sorbonne. . . .

Mel gasped with delight. I turned to smile at her, but she could not see me. She was looking far ahead in the distance. 'Don't you think,' she whispered, 'at times like this when you see something completely beautiful and wonderful . . . don't you think that you could be someone else if you wanted to? A sort of heroic version of yourself. Have you ever felt like that?'

'Yes,' I agreed. 'You glimpse the sort of strength that seems out of reach when you're on the ground.'

'Perhaps it's because we're nearer to heaven.'

I was silent, thinking of Nursie and her sort of heaven which was just 'up there'.

'Edwin, why don't we try to get nearer to heaven still? Why don't we climb to the top of Notre-Dame?'

At first it seemed impossible.

'Non, c'est défendu,' said an irate concierge, implacable in the face of Mel's pleading. But by now I was so infected with her desire to climb to the heavens that I added my voice to hers, together with a five-hundred-franc bribe, which spoke much louder than our pleas. We were grudgingly given the key on condition that we returned it within an hour and told no one.

The climb was arduous, and we were both out of breath when we reached the first platform after two hundred steps.

'We can see the city from here. . . .'

'No, no, we must go to the very top!' Mel insisted.

There were another 378 steps, but what we saw was worth each painful leg-aching inch. Paris stretched before us like a luminous carpet. Behind the cathedral's spire the Seine glittered like a curving sword.

Mel was shivering, but whether from the cold or from excitement I couldn't tell. 'Oh, Edwin . . .,' she said. 'This *must* be the nearest to heaven anyone's ever been!' I could not reply, overwhelmed by the grandeur of our isolation. As I moved nearer the parapet, anxious to get still closer to the sky, my foot brushed against something soft. I bent down, and beneath my fingers I felt feathers. A dead pigeon, still warm.

The next afternoon found me sitting outside Le Sélect, hoping I might see Mel. I'd even chosen the same table, as though it would somehow increase the chance of her being there.

We had parted the night before without making any arrangement to meet. The view from Notre-Dame had been so magical that we stayed long past our allotted hour and walked back through the streets in the small hours, the only people about except for the half-dressed girl who stood in a doorway murmuring the same words of invitation that her predecessors had used for centuries. For a while the charm of nocturnal Paris was ruined by a foul stench as the Ancient Guild of Cesspool Cleaners went about their nightly work of emptying the old sewers. But Mel insisted that we watch them for a while, so we followed them like mourners at some bizarre funeral. The macabre wagons, drawn by white horses, advanced in a lugubrious column through the narrow streets of the Jewish Quarter, a process as noisy as it was smelly, with the creak of the wheels and the clatter of iron-shod hoofs on cobblestones.

'I wish my father could see this,' said Mel, as two black-clad workmen lifted off a heavy cesspit-cover. 'He'd find it fascinating.' She kept her voice level, but there was a mischievous smile playing around the corners of her eyes as she said: 'The disposal of sewage is his bread and butter, after all. It sounds strange put like that, doesn't it?'

I longed to tell her that I, too, was about to embark on a strange and solitary profession, but with the smell of excrement in the air and the guttural cries of the workmen the moment didn't seem quite right.

As we neared the rue des Rosiers, Mel said suddenly: 'I'm not really on holiday, you know. I lied to you. I ran away.'

She stood facing me, one hand thrust in the pocket of her tweed coat, the other running restlessly through her hair. She looked so vulnerable that when I replied it was with a gentleness that I truly felt.

'I thought there might be something like that.'

'They do have holidays at the Villa Rosa, only they're very short and most of the girls don't go all the way to England and back again . . . they organise trips for us. . . . Oh God, Edwin, I did hate it there! Those girls . . . they didn't understand me, and I had nothing to say to them. . . . You do see why I left, don't you?'

I was about to tell her that I saw only too well, but before I had a chance to reply she stood on tiptoe to give me a swift kiss on the cheek and disappeared, as if she was afraid I would see where she lived and report her whereabouts to someone.

'Do you want to see Paris by night again?'

She was there by my elbow suddenly, ordering a *citron pressé* and a plate of gâteaux and taking her place opposite me as though it was the most natural thing in the world that I should be waiting for her.

'What are you intending to show me this time?'

'Aha, you're hooked! I told you you would be! My landlady tells me there's a fair tonight, but it probably won't get interesting until much later on.'

At my suggestion we filled the intervening time with a trip to Montmartre, saving our legs and taking a taxi, which Mel thought was the height of luxury, lolling about on the back seat like a child who has never ridden in a car before. 'I don't know how long my money's going to last me,' she explained, 'so I have to be very careful how I spend it. Shanks's pony every time!'

She was delighted with the church of Sacré Coeur. 'The *sacred heart*,' she breathed. 'I always wondered whose heart it was, but it doesn't really matter; it sounds so beautiful. . . .'

There was a service going on, and we stood at the back and listened to the singing for a while; unfamiliar tunes and the heady smell of incense. I had always imagined a Roman mass would be tawdry, but instead it was grand and rather awe-inspiring, the huge interior in darkness apart from the glow of hundreds of small tapers, flickering as the singing moved the musty air. And I felt a thrill of joy when I recognised the words 'Ave maris stella'.

' "Hail, star of the sea," ' whispered Mel. 'Edwin, aren't those the most *beautiful* words?'

I told her about Nursie and the shrine to my mother, and how I had always been secretly attracted to popery.

'How funny – so have I!'

And she told me that as a child she had longed to attend the Sacred Heart Convent in Clapham and be 'at the mercy' (as she put it) of the nuns. It seemed a fitting moment to reveal that I was about to take holy orders. We were descending the steep white steps of the church, and she stopped and looked at me with something bordering on dismay. 'You must be very brave. If it were me, I don't know whether I'd have enough to offer.'

I stared back at her, uncomprehending.

'You know, to offer God.'

I didn't speak for a long time after that.

'Have I said something wrong? You look . . . you seem angry.'

'No, no.' I gave her hand a brotherly squeeze. 'You've made me think, that's all.'

The truth of it was that this young girl, some ten years younger than myself, had seen more clearly than I, and that made me deeply ashamed. For I had only ever defined religion in terms of what it offered me: Mother Church giving me comfort, warmth, security. But what did I have to offer her? And I found myself thinking of Jane and our conversation about loving God.

'What is loving God?' I said to Mel, posing the same question I had put to Jane.

She thought for a while, chewing her lower lip. 'It's a mystical experience . . . an emotional experience . . . like seeing a blinding light.'

She had answered as I would have answered, but for some reason this made me feel depressed.

The street fair in the Place d'Italie lifted our spirits.

'Oh, I love a fair, don't you?' exclaimed Mel, half-running in her excitement so I had to hurry to keep up. I didn't tell her that I had never been to a fair before. She sniffed the air, inhaling the odours of vanilla powder and fried potatoes. 'It has its own smell – a really *French* smell!'

It had its own sounds, too, the din of roller coasters, the lament of wild animals in cages, voices announcing shows through megaphones, and the crash of the dodgem cars.

We went on the dodgems first, Mel insisting that she would drive and me reaching across her to take the steering wheel and avoid the dangers she never saw coming. Then I tried my hand at the hoop-la and won a yellow silk rose, which I presented to a delighted Mel. And we went together to the palm-reader, Mel clutching my sleeve in a state of nervous excitement.

The crystal ball was disappointingly small, and despite the exotic Japanese screens the fortune-teller looked like a housewife with her hair neatly parted and a clean white collar on her spotted dress. She used a magnifying glass to examine both our palms before pronouncing: 'Vous allez rentrer à Paris.' She did not make it clear to which of us she was referring.

We strolled past a raised stage populated by girls in diaphanous pyjamas. A hoarse-voiced woman was shouting through a megaphone.

'Messieurs. We have here tonight for your enjoyment the Naked Idylls: Lesbos, the Naked Libertines, Diana the Huntress and many more. Sensual, passionate, exciting! If you like flesh, if you like lovely bodies, if you like sex, you've got to see this!'

I felt a burning flush rise to my cheeks. The woman had spotted me, standing head and shoulders above the rest of the crowd. 'Ah, venez, monsieur . . . *vous* . . . le beau monsieur, le *grand* monsieur!' She laughed coarsely.

I had scarcely dared look at Mel, but I was so desperate to get away that I reached for her arm to hurry her along. The crowd of swarthy Frenchmen who had sprung up around us jeered and made suggestive gestures. They began to jostle Mel, and one of them reached out and plucked at her coat.

I felt a surge of uncontrollable anger exploding inside me like a volley of fireworks.

'*Leave her alone!*' I shouted, hurling myself at the man who had touched her. I grasped him by the collar and held my fist under his nose. He backed off, shaking his head.

Mel was standing alone, white-faced with shock. I put my arms round her and hugged her tightly.

'It's all right,' I murmured. 'It's all right. . . .'

When I found Mel outside Le Sélect the next day, she was writing a letter.

'I'm writing to Loveday,' she said. 'Loveday Stark. You remember her, don't you?'

'Yes,' I said.

'I haven't told her that I've seen you, in case they pester you to find out where I am. You don't mind, do you?'

I was weak with relief. 'Not at all.' I sat down opposite her and broke the news that I was about to leave Paris. 'I'm afraid I'm expected by friends of my father's who live near Lake Como. My reservation on the sleeper has already been made. So tonight is my last night.'

'You deserter! You dreadful coward! I thought you were just starting to develop a taste for *la vie bohème*!'

She tucked into her cream cake cheerfully enough, but her expressive eyes betrayed her disappointment. 'In that case we shall have to do something very special indeed tonight. Leave it to me to arrange it. Just meet me here . . . latish . . . say, ten o'clock.'

Mel was already sitting outside the café when I arrived, sipping a calvados. At first I scarcely recognised her, for she looked about ten years older. She was dressed in a narrow clinging black dress and there were diamanté clips in her hair. Had she made a special effort for my sake, I would have been touched, but Mel was not alone. There was a dark young man sitting at the table with her.

'This is Yves,' she said, 'my landlady's son. He's going to be our guide tonight for our special mystery tour!'

I asked her to explain, and she did so with an excited gleam in her eye. 'D'you remember how we talked about wanting to see the "other" Paris? Well, Yves has promised to show us Paris at its least cosmopolitan and its most alive! The *real* Paris! I've asked him to show us everything: the bars, the nightclubs, the opium dens where the mobsters and the addicts go . . . the' – she hesitated over this next word – 'bordellos. Everything! Are you game?'

I felt I ought to say something about these scenes being unsuited to my intended profession, but I found I could not. Indeed, I found I was smiling. Her enthusiasm, her ingenuous romanticism were completely infectious. 'You win. You've roused my curiosity.'

Yves commandeered taxis, for which I was to pay. The first stop was quite tame – a *bal-musette*, a sort of bar-cum-dance-hall, full of girls with satin blouses and spit curls coiled and flattened on their temples, smoking and drinking with a sultry boredom. We had a few drinks ourselves and danced the java to the music of a mock South American band. Then Yves snapped his fingers for another taxi and moved us on.

The next port of call was Le Monocle Club.

'It's only for men,' hissed Mel as we descended the steps.

'No, no, you are wrong – ees only for women, *les dames*!' laughed Yves.

And we saw that the men in suits were really women, dressed as men. They were an uncomfortable reminder of my half-sister Rosanna's strange games, and I was not sorry when the '*patron*' – a woman in a tail-coat – politely moved us on.

Our taxi took us next to the summit of the hill behind the Panthéon, to the dance-hall of the Montagne St-Geneviève. At first sight the place looked ordinary enough: an open-air dance-floor and a four-man band, couples sipping brightly coloured drinks. . . .

Yet another optical illusion. Men were dancing with men, some of them wearing women's clothes, holding one another's thick calloused hands like timid children. Mel insisted that we stay for at least one drink, and sat staring at the dancers with ill-concealed fascination.

'Does this sort of thing go on in England?' she demanded.

Our final port of call took us back into the heart of the city. The taxi pulled up outside 4 rue de Hanovre, near the Opéra.

'Voici la vraie vie Parisienne . . . la maison d'illusion!' said a triumphant Yves.

'A house of illusion?' said Mel. 'Is that some sort of cabaret?'

'It's one of your bordellos,' I told her, the tension making me suddenly irritable. 'A whorehouse, in fact.'

Mel peered doubtfully down the steep steps. 'Well, shall we go in, then?'

'Are you *sure* you want to?' I asked. 'After all . . . the things we might see . . . I feel responsible. . . .'

But she was already halfway down the steps.

It was like a descent into hell. We fought our way through a suffocating haze of smoke, so dense that the end of the room was invisible. There was a long line of men at one end and at the other a line of naked girls. Some of them wore half-open satin kimonos. Yves explained that they were worn to hide scars. There was an overwhelming combination of smells: of tobacco, garlic, hair oil, anise and jasmine. Every so often a man would move forward and choose one of the girls, and she would loll all over him while he kissed her neck and ears, rubbed her naked buttocks and sucked at her nipples. . . .

Mel had turned very white at the sight of this abjection of love. 'Can we go now, Edwin, please . . .?'

As we stumbled up the stairway again she said, almost in tears: 'Oh, Edwin . . . I had no idea it could be like that . . . I never thought . . . I'm so sorry!'

My only reply was to slip my arm round her shoulders, but I longed to tell her that everything was tainted if you looked hard enough. Bishops who play golf and mimic the tactics of their businessmen acquaintances. . . .

'You would like to go somewhere else?' asked Yves.

'No, thank you,' I said. '*Ça suffit*. That's enough.'

I told Mel that I had something to say to her before I left Paris.

Over the few days we had spent together, I had developed a warm brotherly affection towards her and had come to assume that role. I did not wish to leave her alone in Paris after I had gone.

'I want you to go back to your school,' I told her. 'Please. I feel responsible—'

'But, Edwin. . . .'

'Yes, I know you've told me the reasons for your hating it, but I've been thinking. Suppose I speak to the headmistress on the telephone and persuade her to let you have a single room? And I'll tell her that your French is much improved—'

'She probably won't take me back.'

'I think I can cope with any misunderstandings and bring some influence to bear. Is she a Catholic?'

'Yes.'

'There you are, then. I'll tell her I'm a priest. Catholics always do what priests tell them.'

'Edwin, that's dreadfully cynical!' said Mel, but she laughed just the same. 'I rather like the idea of you putting the fear of God into Madame. It'll be rather like having my own personal confessor. They'll think I'm rather grand!'

'So we're agreed? You'll go back?'

She sighed and pulled a face. 'I suppose so. I think I've seen enough here.'

'And your money won't last for ever,' I reminded her as I paid the bill at Le Sélect for the last time. 'You'd either have to go back to Switzerland, or back to London in disgrace. Much better to return at the end of the summer, fully fledged and finished off.'

Mel waited quietly in my room at the Crillon while I made the necessary phone-calls to the Villa Rosa. Then she allowed me to escort her to the Gare de Lyon, still maintaining a subdued silence.

I felt a terrible pang as I saw her on to her train and waved goodbye to her: a solitary figure in a rather grubby coat, struggling with an unruly pile of cases and hatboxes.

Later that night I boarded the train to Lake Como, but as I closed my eyes and listened to the rhythmic clatter of the wheels I was not thinking about Italy. Instead my mind was crowded with vivid and colourful images: the fairground, the steeple of Notre-Dame, the Cesspool Cleaners' creaking wagon, the satin-clad whores and Mel's strange wild eyes, aglow with excitement at it all. I found I could not think of God, either, or Jane, and for the rest of my Continental tour until I returned to the safe world I had created for myself in England I found both my vocation and my marital intentions curiously undermined by my glimpse of *la vie bohème*.

For Mel had not only shown me the 'real' Paris. She had also unwittingly shown me myself.

48 Magnolia Gardens

Mel

I RETURNED FROM SWITZERLAND in the summer of 1932 to find that Loveday had grown up.

From external appearances, I had, too, but the problem was I felt exactly the same inside. When we were at Stone Hill High our great golden goal – being Grown Up – seemed impossibly far away. Now, after a brief in-between stage at the Villa Rosa, I had arrived. I was an adult.

Mother obviously thought so. I put my suitcases down in my room and surveyed the changes. All my sentimental knick-knacks were gone: the ugly placard made from sea-shells and bearing the message 'GREETINGS FROM EASTBOURNE', the cherished photographs of matinée idols, the long-suffering teddy bear. . . .

'I thought you wouldn't be wanting any of that stuff any more,' explained Mother. 'So I tidied it away. I've put new curtains in, and there are new covers on the chairs. . . .' She watched me anxiously, waiting for my reaction.

'It looks very smart.' I appraised the chintz loose covers, the glazed cotton curtains with their stiff-looking overblown roses. 'I expect it'll take me a while to get used to . . . such a smart room.'

'Well. . . .' Mother straightened her tweed skirt. 'You're a smart young lady now.'

After she had gone I moved restlessly round the room, touching the spaces where my childhood treasures had lain and remembering the oft-quoted New Testament verse: *When I was a child, I spoke as a child, I understood as a child; but when I became a man I put away childish things.* . . .

I opened my suitcase, took out the yellow silk rose that Edwin had won at the fair in Paris and propped it against the dressing-table mirror.

Coming home was strange and uncomfortable for all sorts of reasons. The awe with which my family treated me was one. Of course, they were delighted to see me.

'Let's have a look at you, then, girl,' said Father when I went down for tea, bouncing up and down in his excitement. 'She looks bloomin' marvellous, doesn't she, Jeanie? Ethne?' But he seemed reticent when it came to kissing me, perhaps because my high heels forced him to stand on tiptoe to reach my cheek. And he frowned at my hair, which had been shorn into a fashionable 'gamine' cut. I kept forgetting it was short and reaching up to run my hand through it, only to find there was nothing there.

'Why don't you sit down over here?' He showed me to an armchair as though I was a guest.

'Mel's showing us up, isn't she, with her lovely clothes?' said Mother as she poured the tea. 'Isn't she, Ethne?'

Ethne surveyed my slim pale linen skirt, my cream silk stockings, my lipstick in a fetching shade named 'Rose Tendre'. 'Mmm.'

I blushed, feeling guilty of a misdemeanour.

Throughout the meal I was watched closely, as though my new sophistication might at any time be responsible for unorthodox or unprecedented behaviour. At no time were my defection from the Villa Rosa and my three weeks in Paris discussed, making the episode even more unreal in my mind. Yet it was only this active protest that had made the rest of my time at the Villa Rosa bearable. When it was known that I had been in Paris *with a man*, I had become something of a heroine. Especially since I was now granted a room of my own, as though my worldly experiences made me contagious, dangerous. . . .

In order to endure my remaining six months at the finishing school, I had prepared to fall back on my old tricks. I had muddled through adolescence as a kaleidoscope of different personalities, a figment of my own imagination. What and who I was depended largely on what I happened to be reading. I would cope with ostracism, I decided, by seeing myself as Jane Eyre, plain and dowdy but steadfast in spirit. Thus I would be able to stand the cruelty of the Reeds – in this case, the hateful Juliana and her friends – and in the end show myself to be superior to them.

But it turned out that I was able to be myself after all. The fact that I was different was a *coup de grâce* after I returned from Paris, and I only had to tell how I had bribed my way to the top of Notre-Dame and visited a brothel, in order to press home my full advantage. It became desirable to be seen talking to me, and everyone was eager to find some way of professing friendship. Cecily showed me how to make the most of my face by using cosmetics. Juliana grudgingly suggested that I would look better with my hair short, and gave me the name of a salon in Montreux. And in the Easter holidays Angelina invited me to join her family in the exclusive German resort of Baden. We stayed in a sumptuous hotel, dined in the grandest restaurants and whiled away our evenings in the Casino, watching the Conte Belaforte, Angelina's father, losing his money at the gaming tables. The contessa, a plump effusive woman, took me with her to the *salons de couture* and helped me spend my dress allowance.

With the result that, rather despite the Villa Rosa's efforts than because of them, I was 'finished off'. Father had got what he wanted. Watching him eat his tea in the best parlour of number 48 Magnolia Gardens, he didn't seem entirely happy about it. He looked rather like the little boy in the fairy tale who is granted a wish by the old crone, only to find that it isn't what he wants after all. Father had lavished a large amount of money on a very spurious form of education, and for his pains his beloved daughter had been replaced by a smart elegant stranger, someone who seemed to bear no relation to him or his lifestyle.

We strayed on to the safe topic of neighbourhood gossip. Father Turnbull was retiring, and the incumbency of St Luke's would be vacant. Edwin Clifford had just been married at Wells Cathedral and was now honeymooning in Scotland. And Loveday had left her job at the Cliffords' and had moved out of the Gardens. She had a flat of her own, 'somewhere in the West End'. Mother made it sound like Outer Mongolia.

'And tell her your news, Ethne love,' said Father, giving her a prod. 'Tell her about your singing, girl.'

Ethne looked reluctant to speak.

'She won a prize in a singing competition!' said Father, bursting with pride.

'Music festival,' Mother corrected him.

Ethne blushed furiously.

I was at a loss. 'Really? How nice.' It sounded mean, so I added: 'You must tell me more about it later.' I stood up. 'Now, if you'll excuse me' – I found myself rising to their expectations and behaving very formally – 'I'd like to go over to number forty-seven and ask Magdalena Stark for Loveday's new address.'

* * *

215

'The colour of the walls is . . . er . . . nice.'

I was sitting in Loveday's flat the next day, wondering what to say in the presence of someone who so obviously wanted to be treated as Grown Up.

'Isn't it?' said Loveday brightly, curling up on the sofa with her feet tucked underneath her. 'Oh, darling, but you should have seen it before the decorators got to work – an absolute *dump*!'

I looked round the room, trying to imagine it as a dump, but all I could see was a perfect setting for Loveday's exotic looks: silk hangings, rich Persian carpets, brocade pouffes and cushions, bowls of pot-pourri and jars of incense. And walls the colour of fresh blood.

'I told them I wanted it to be à la Lady Ottoline Morrell.'

'Oh,' I murmured, wondering who 'they' were. I was also wondering how on earth Loveday could afford a flat like this. It only had one bedroom but it was very spacious and so comfortable as to be almost luxurious. It was also situated in a very prestigious block of apartments opposite Hyde Park. Surely she couldn't afford to rent it on her salary as a receptionist and 'manageress' at a very exclusive couture house in Mayfair?

'Why on earth didn't you become a mannequin?' I asked.

'Oh, I thought of that, don't worry. But they told me I'm not tall enough. Too utterly sick-making, isn't it?'

'How about acting? You were so good at it. . . .'

Loveday just pulled a face as she lit a cigarette. I was surprised to see her smoking after her years of vehemently condemning her mother's habit, but then I realised that she wasn't really smoking properly, just using the long ivory holder as a prop to wave around. I looked at her curled up on the sofa, so little and pretty with her red-brown hair still worn long, rippling from a complicated series of tortoiseshell clips and combs. She wore a simple black dress that would have looked severe on anyone else, but on her looked extravagantly chic. Without going anywhere near Paris, Loveday had somehow contrived to make herself look like a Parisienne. I smiled at the irony of this.

'You're looking nice, Mel,' said Loveday in a tone which suggested she wasn't sure whether to be surprised or dismissive. 'Though your eyes would look better if you used a little mascara, darling. Accentuate your long lashes. . . .'

As I squatted awkwardly on my pouffe, I was not at all sure whether I liked this Loveday. She talked in a curious upper-class slang which was about ten years out of date. I had the distinct impression that she was playing a part and that in doing so she had lost touch with reality. But the Loveday I *knew* was always supremely realistic, practical and down to earth.

I decided that she had camouflaged herself to fit in with her new surroundings. Hyde Park, where she now lived, was chic and Bohemian, and Loveday had to be at one with her habitat. There must be no trace of Magnolia Gardens; shabby, unpretentious, even provincial in contrast.

'How much are they paying you at Dulong's?' I asked. She had already told me that the hours were 'flexible', which explained her presence at home in the middle of the afternoon.

'Oh, enough to cover one's needs.'

'Yes, but, Loveday, how—'

'That suit really is divine, Mel. Tell me, is this one of the things you bought in Baden?'

We fell to discussing my Continental trip again.

'I saw Edwin Clifford in Paris,' I said.

'Oh, really?'

'Yes, we did some sight-seeing together and he was really dreadfully—'

'Yes, well, now he's safely off on his honeymoon,' said Loveday obscurely. 'And you, Mel? How about you? Are you going to try to find a job?'

'Well . . . I don't really know . . . I mean, I haven't—'

'Well, for goodness' sake don't content yourself with sitting around and waiting for some man to marry you!' The tone was brisk, and I had a glimpse of the old Loveday, using bossiness to hide her own disappointment. 'That's all I ask. . . .'

The telephone rang, and Loveday went into the hall to answer it. She spoke in a low voice as though she didn't want to be overheard, but I caught the odd sentence.

'You can't come here now. . . . Because I've got someone here, that's why. . . . No, of course it's not like that. Don't be so silly, darling. . . . Look, come over in about an hour, all right?'

Loveday sat down on the sofa again and put another cigarette in the ivory holder, but she seemed distracted. After a few minutes she jumped up and said: 'I'm sorry, Mel, – d'you mind awfully? – I shall have to go out now.'

I struggled up off the pouffe, mumbling about it being time I went anyway, and wondering why I couldn't pluck up the courage to say: *But I heard you on the phone just now telling someone else to come over here.*

'Oh, and drop in on Neville some time, won't you, Mel? He's so down in the dumps these days, I can't do anything with him. He's been counting the days till your return. . . . Promise now, there's an angel. . . .'

I promised, but as I was ejected from Loveday's flat and left to find a taxi in the pouring rain my thoughts were far from angelic.

'Neville?'

It was late in the evening, after dinner, and I had wandered out into the Gardens for some fresh air. There on the pavement was a slight figure, shadowy in the fading light.

'Neville? Is that you?'

Then as I moved closer I realised that it was not Neville, but Rosanna Clifford. I stepped back into the shadow of the privet hedge. I still got a lurching feeling in the pit of my stomach when I thought about the way she kissed me years ago, and I didn't want her to see me.

It was not surprising that I had mistaken Rosanna for a man. Her hair was cropped short over her large skull, and she was dressed in a man's suit. The thin silvery evening light illuminated her face as she half walked, half ran down the pavement, and I could see that it was thrust forward with a strange eager look, her eyes half closed, as if she was galloping into the wind. She appeared to be muttering or chanting to herself.

I decided that I would drop in on Neville, so once Rosanna was out of sight I went to number 46. He was already there on the front steps as I arrived, locking the front door.

'Neville, hello! It's me, I'm back!'

But, far from seeming delighted to see me, he looked annoyed. 'I was just going out. . . .'

That much was obvious. 'Oh. . . .' I couldn't think what to say; I was so disappointed that he wasn't overjoyed to see me.

'Why don't you come over another time? Evenings aren't a good time at the moment.'

'Oh, Neville, have you got a new lady friend?' I was rather pleased with the idea, but he looked so disturbed at the suggestion that he had replaced Rosheen that I said quickly: 'Well, why don't I at least walk as far as the main road with you?'

'No need for that. . . .' And, straightening his tie, he hurried down the steps and vanished from sight.

Neville was by no means the only person acting strangely that summer. Father was oddly agitated and restless, and from his reserved attitude to me it was clear that the results of my finishing-school education were more than a disappointment to him. It was as though he had failed in some way. Then he suddenly announced that he was going to Italy, to look at some marble samples.

Mother made no complaint, but she went very quiet whenever the proposed trip was mentioned.

'I think I'd like Donald here for a bit, when you're away,' she announced to Father one evening.

'What on earth for? You managed all right by yourself last time I was away, didn't you?'

There was a tense silence. Mother's face clouded slightly.

'Well, didn't you?'

'I'd just like Donald to be here, that's all.'

'For Christ's sake, lass, put that mendacious fascist propaganda-sheet down! I can't bear to see you soil your hands with it!'

Uncle Donald had caught me reading the *Daily Express*. The débutantes still looked out from the 'Londoner's Log' with their smooth, fair, guileless faces, just as they had done in the days when Loveday and I had pored over it, but I sensed that things were changing for my generation. It was becoming politically sensitive, rejecting the ideals of England, Home and Glory. I tried to convince Uncle Donald that I, too, scorned the old sort of flag-waving jingoism, but even to my ears my argument sounded weak, for what was I but the leisured daughter of a businessman, dressed in my smart Continental wardrobe? Uncle Donald simply gave me a pitying smile and called me a 'drawing-room pink'.

It was through him that I became aware of suffering for the first time. So far I had only known my own suffering, which had largely been of my own making, but through my talks with Uncle Donald, the 'family conscience', I caught disturbing vivid glimpses of the real meaning of poverty, hunger, cold, cruelty. He turned my attention away from the gossip columns and towards the stories of hardship cases – a whole family living in one room, children dying of cold in the winter, old people who couldn't afford sugar in their tea.

'No sugar in their tea? Now, in 1932? Surely not!'

Loveday made exclamations of disbelief at this story when I took Uncle Donald to have tea in her flat. I had been rather worried about bringing these two polar opposites together, expecting sparks to fly, but despite Loveday's being rigged out in the trappings of sophistication, wearing them like a heavy disguise, the two of them got on terribly well. Loveday declared that she thought Uncle Donald 'a perfect pet', while Donald seemed as mesmerised by Loveday as he had been when she was a child and he had exclaimed over her hair and called her 'our little Miss Loveday'. He tried to needle her about living a life of the senses and being politically apathetic, but Loveday, curled up on her sofa like a pretty little cat, just laughed.

'And what about you?' she asked in that dreadfully direct way she had. 'I don't see you living in hardship. I believe you have nice comfortable rooms in your ivory tower at Oxford and, what's more, a college *servant* to wait on you. I find that utterly shocking, Mr McDowell.'

'I can assure you that when I see what's going on in the world I feel far from comfortable—'

'Yes, that's the trouble, isn't it?' said Loveday sweetly, sipping on her Martini. 'Being materially in one world and spiritually in another must be a very uncomfortable business. After all, you're under threat from all sides.'

'Meaning?' Donald raised his eyebrows.

'Meaning that the working class despise you and see you as part of the haunting danger of the *bourgeoisie*, while the fascists . . . well, I should imagine they'd like to do all sorts of nasty things to you.'

I was afraid that Uncle Donald would get angry at this point, and was about to interject some pacifying remark, but he seemed amused by Loveday's cattiness and laughed loudly. Looking at him in the dim sultry light of Loveday's sitting room, I decided that he grew more attractive as he got older. He was over forty, but the silver streaks in his hair only served to accentuate his wild vulpine looks.

Afterwards, as Uncle Donald and I walked along Park Lane to catch a bus back to Clapham – a democratic form of transport that I was prepared to suffer despite my high heels – I confided my suspicions about Loveday's new lifestyle.

'A flat like that must be dreadfully expensive, must cost the earth. You don't suppose—?'

'Someone's keeping her, of course!' pronounced Donald, and then laughed aloud at the look on my face. 'So, she's someone's mistress. What's so wrong with that? At least she's got her independence and can leave whenever she likes, which is more than can be said of married women.'

'Yes, but what if—?'

'I admire the lassie, and I'll tell you this: I'd rather see her like that than spending a lifetime being trained to be kind to servants and animals and then sitting around waiting for the right husband.'

This last remark was a jibe at my finishing-school education. But I was thinking about Loveday and our childhood conversations about sacrificing all for love. Was that what Loveday was doing? If so, why didn't she confide in me as she had done in the past? It was worrying but, then, so was my own reluctance to ask her about her life. I decided to look for an opportunity to have it out with her.

One morning, while Father was away in Italy, I went to his office in Nine Elms.

He had asked me if I would look over some French Customs dockets for him, and I was making a conscious effort not to be lazy and leave the task until the last minute, as I always had done at school. Besides, there was very little for me to do at home, and I was uncomfortably aware of the views of Loveday and Uncle Donald on women who sat around and waited for a man to come and put an end to their restlessness.

I also rather enjoyed being in Father's office and sitting at his big desk, which had three telephones; a touch of the Hollywood movie mogul. Evidence of Father's exuberant personality was everywhere: over-large studio portraits of myself and Ethne beaming at him from elaborate photo-frames, his framed plumber's diploma hung proudly on the wall, heaps of books by Victorian sanitary reformers including a leather-bound copy of his favourite, *Principles and Practices of Plumbing*. The desk overflowed with piles of sketches and diagrams in Father's bold hand, and sitting squarely on top of them was his prized possession, a hideous brass paperweight: a statuette of King Arthur astride his horse. I picked it up and stroked it, feeling Father's brash uncompromising presence in the room, and acutely aware of how much I missed him.

The door opened, and Sam, father's assistant, stuck his head round the door. 'You all right there, Miss Finzel?'

Sam had known us since we were babies, but he still preferred to address us formally, and treat us as 'the boss's daughters'. When I was small I was a little afraid of him; he dragged his leg as he walked, and his chest made dreadful wheezing noises. If Father had left me alone in a room and I heard Sam approaching with his distinctive 'shuffle-shuffle', I found a place to hide from him. Now I felt rather ashamed of this aversion, for Sam was quite harmless and completely devoted to our family, not having one of his own. He had always been there in Nine Elms, and it was impossible to imagine the place without him.

'Like yer new hair, Miss Finzel,' he said, nodding towards my smart shorn locks. 'You really look the business. Grown-up and that.'

'Thank you, Sam,' I said, reflecting that adulthood seemed to be judged entirely by one's appearance, everyone assuming that I would now think, feel and behave differently.

'Can I get you anything? A nice cuppa?'

'A cup of tea would be lovely – yes, please, Sam.'

A few minutes later the door opened again. 'Put the tea down over here, will you, Sam?' I said, not looking up from my French dictionary. The cup of tea didn't materialise. I looked up.

'Father! What on earth—?'

'Hello, girl.'

'But we weren't expecting you back for weeks yet. What on earth are you doing back here?'

I stood up to embrace him, and then recoiled in alarm. 'My God, what's happened to you? Your eye. . . .'

Father was sporting a black eye, only it was still at the red and purple stage, and there was fresh blood on his face where the skin had been broken.

'Who did that to you? Here, you'd better come and sit down in this chair. . . .' I gave up my place at his desk, and he sank down wearily, as though his body was stiff and aching. 'Did you get into a fight with some hot-blooded Italian?'

'No. Donald did it.'

'*Donald? Uncle* Donald? But why, what – was he drunk?'

'I've just been home now. I said one or two things to Donald that he didn't like, so he thumped me.'

'You mean, about politics?'

Father shook his head and sighed, closing his eyes. When he opened them again he looked directly at me and said: 'I'm going to tell you the story I just told to Donald, only I want you to promise me that *you* won't bloomin' well thump me.'

I nodded. Sam came in with a tray of tea and two cups. I dropped two sugar lumps into Father's, handed it to him and said: 'Go on.'

'D'you ever get like you feel . . .? No, you wouldn't, I suppose, being so young. Let me put it another way. I put my nose to the grindstone and work pretty hard, and most of the time I'm happy doing just that . . . it's just that sometimes I feel fed up with it all and I have to get away. It's like when you came back from Switzerland; I looked at you and I thought: Well, she looks really smashing, our Mel. You can be proud of yourself, Frank Finzel; you done a good job there! But somehow it wasn't enough, and I just felt, well—'

'Disillusioned?' I suggested.

'Yes, if you like. Anyway, I tried to explain all this to Donald, and I told him that I went back to Italy because last time I went there, there was this girl and I—'

'Girl?' I felt a horrible numbness around my heart. 'You mean—?' I stared at him, then: 'Go on, Father. Tell me what happened in Italy.'

'It was raining,' he said. 'And I just stood there staring. And the next thing I know there's a voice in my ear and she's standing right next to me.'

He laughed. 'I can even remember what she said to me. "You are lost?" she says. Her voice is queer, all low and husky. "Oh, no," I say. "Not lost. I am not lost. I am staying at the Pensione Donatelli." '

Father smiled at me. 'You know how it is with these foreigners. You speak very slowly and clearly so they understand.'

I nodded.

'Anyhow, she just laughed at me. She's got these big teeth, see, big and white. Anyhow, I was worried about her catching cold in her wet dress, so we ended up in the local café together, drinking espresso and chasing it down with grappa. Blimey, I can remember every little detail. Picture of Jesus on the wall. Someone had put pale primroses all round it to decorate it. And the water

223

dropping down from her dress and making puddles on the floor. . . .'

Father sat down at his desk, staring straight past me at the wall and toying with the brass King Arthur.

'Her name was Mariella Giovanetti, and she was twenty-five. Shiny black hair. Lips like red cherries. Plump like the best fruit. . . . She told me all about herself. Her people were *con-tadini* – tenant farmers. She was raised on a farm outside Cortona, but at eighteen she ran off and became a bar girl. Met a lot of American travellers passing through the town – that's how she'd learned the language.'

'So what happened?' I asked. As if I didn't already know.

'She said there was a *veglione* – a dance – in her village that night. A masked ball. So I met her in the piazza at nine and got a ride out to the village with some friends of hers who had an old car. I was worrying about whether the car would make it up those hills, but the others didn't seem to care; they just sat there eating nuts and chucking the shells out of the window. And every so often Mariella would give my hand a squeeze and I'd forget all about the bloomin' car.

'The dance was in this great big barn that had been emptied and dusted and that, and everyone was arriving, the women with their best hats on and the men with laundered shirts and faces red from work in the fields. And then it began. The musicians were up on this makeshift stage, looking all solemn, and suddenly they struck up a polka and Mariella grabbed me and we were off.'

Father smiled. 'Very fetching she was, in a dark red dress with a lace collar and a flower in her dark hair, and she didn't seem to want anyone else to dance with me, so I was torn between pressing up close and taking in everything that was going on around me.

'Oh, I'll never forget that night, girl. They were dancing the tango, and I'd never seen it before in my life, nothing like it. You remember you went to see Rudolph Valentino doing it at the Majestic once? All that head-jerking and bending backwards. No wonder they call it a dance for lovers. Anyhow, I didn't have a cat in hell's chance of doing it, so Mariella went off to tango with one of her young cousins. I couldn't take my eyes off her.'

I was staring at Father, spellbound. He, in turn, seemed scarcely aware that I was there.

'Then the door's flung open and a great crowd of masked

figures moves in, in fancy dress. Oh ho, I think, here come our masqueraders. And then the band struck up a different tune, and they started dancing a fast dance – *minuetto*, they call it – and with their faces all blanked out with veils they looked really sinister. Then they grabbed people from around the floor, and the music got faster and faster, and before I knew it I was whirling round and round with them and Mariella's dress was just a blur of red. And then the village clock struck midnight, and it's just like *Cinderella*: the music stops and the masqueraders disappear.

'So we had a rest then, a bit of a breather, and some refreshment. There were tables laid out with little cakes and spicy sausages and dark wine – you know, the kind that gives you a bloomin' awful headache – but before we had time to get much down us more revellers came in and the music struck up again and we went on dancing, getting wilder and wilder.

'It was four o'clock before people started going home, and then there was just me and Mariella standing there in the empty barn. "We sleep here tonight, OK?" she says. Turns out our lift's gone home two hours earlier. "What, here?" I says. The floor's all covered with streamers and confetti, see. Anyway, it turns out she means in the hayloft. So we went up there and . . . and then. . . .'

Father was still staring straight ahead, oblivious of me.

'Suddenly she's straddling my chest and planting kisses all over my face. And then, you know, she did a queer thing. She unbuttons the front of her dress and shows me . . . well, shows me her whatnots. Sort of lifts them in her hands and squeezes them. In the moonlight, they . . . I don't know . . . they looked funny . . . kind of greyish white like the marble I'd seen in the quarries. And then she starts unbuttoning my trousers.'

I was profoundly shocked.

I felt strangely dizzy, and my fingers started tingling. I wondered if Father had lost his mind, talking like this. Then he glanced at me and seemed suddenly to remember who he was talking to.

He looked as shocked as I was. 'I'm sorry, I've gone too far.'

A deep blush spread over his face. He was no prude, but neither he nor Mother ever talked directly about the facts of life. About sex. I stared at him, feeling curiously light-headed, as though his features were ones that I had seen in a photograph somewhere, belonging to someone else and not to my father – *my* father, naked in bed with a *girl*, his silly moustache touching her and his bald patch bobbing up and down. I remembered the naked girls being pawed in the underground clubs of Paris, and I must confess I felt slightly sick.

'I'm sorry,' he said again.

'That's all right,' I said, still reeling. 'There's no one else for you to tell. Except Donald, and look what he gave you for your pains.'

Father gripped the edge of the desk, suddenly desperate. 'I do want you to understand, girl, I do. I want *somebody* to understand. Something happens to you in Italy. I don't know what it is, but I know that if you're not careful you end up never coming back.

'Lord knows what Mariella can have seen in *me*. A short stoutish fellow of about forty-five, beginning to go a bit thin on top.'

'Were you in love with her?' I had to ask.

He shook his head. 'Lust, I suppose you'd call it. It was a sort of fizzy feeling like I had champagne bubbles in my blood. Of course it was all physical. . . .'

He suddenly started talking very fast, as if he was desperate to unburden himself before he changed his mind. 'It was *new*, that was the thing. She was hungry for it, wanted it all the time. I'd only ever known your mother, and she . . . well, she always acted like it was all an embarrassment, the marital business.'

'Did you tell Mother about it? About *her*?'

He shook his head. 'Didn't have the bottle. But I think she guessed. You sense these things. I couldn't undo anything, so I did my best to make it up to you all. Worked bloomin' hard. Made sure you and Ethne had the very best.'

I stared at him in disbelief. 'So *that's* why you did it? Sent me to the Villa Rosa? I'm surprised you didn't send Mother away somewhere, too, to make it easier for you to sneak back to Italy and see your fancy woman!'

I hadn't meant to say it, but I had been badly hurt – shaken – and I was lashing out.

'It wasn't like that, girl. I admit that I went back to find her. I just couldn't stop thinking about her. Lord knows what I expected to find. I put myself up in this cheap hotel in the town and searched and searched, knocked on doors, asked questions. I even went out to the countryside, to the farm where her parents

226

used to live, but no one seemed to know where she was. And then I found her, in the hotel I was staying at. She'd been there all along, working behind the bar. She'd even served me a drink or two, but I didn't recognise her. Daft, isn't it? I'd gone out there searching for a young girl and I hadn't even noticed this old woman. Well, she's not old, she's only in her thirties, but she'd gone to fat, and everything had just sort of . . . slipped. She'd married and had four kids, and she looked just like any other greasy housewife. And bad-tempered with it. And I just felt bloomin' terrible.' He sighed.

I could see that he was in the grip of a dreadful disillusionment. I actually started feeling sorry for him. 'That's what I was trying to explain to Donald when he hit me. Jeanie's honour, he said. For a revolutionary he's certainly got some old-fashioned ideas.'

Alas, all the most momentous occasions in our lives are hemmed in by mundane events, and at that moment Sam came shuffling into the office to clear away the tea things, grinning and showing his crooked blackened teeth. I had been about to tell Father that I was glad he'd told me, and that I'd grown up more in that half-hour than in the whole of my year in Switzerland.

He sighed and started sorting through the pile of mail on his desk.

'You'd better cut along home now, pet.'

Then, as I reached the door, he caught hold of my hand so I was forced to turn back and look at him. 'Thank you,' he said.

I was still thinking about Father and Mariella that evening as I sat alone with Mother, waiting for Father to get back from Nine Elms. Donald was out at a meeting in Bermondsey, and Ethne was rehearsing for a concert with Ashley Player. I was pretending to be engrossed in *The Moonstone*, but every so often I would glance up at Mother, who had her nose in a gardening book. Had she ever felt lust? I wondered. If it had been she who had gone to Italy, would she have dallied with some swarthy Italian youth? It seemed highly unlikely, if not impossible. Mother, with her tweed skirts and sensible shoes, her talent for coaxing vegetables out of the soil – and yet as I looked at her I couldn't feel pity for her. She was too self-sufficient. She had what she wanted, here in Magnolia Gardens, didn't she? If that was the case, then Father's restless philanderings surely couldn't hurt her much. And yet. . . .

'You should go out more,' she said to me suddenly.

'Go out? Where?'

'A girl of your age, you should be going out more, to dances and so on. Now that you've got such lovely clothes, and such nice manners. It seems a pity to waste them.'

I stared at her in amazement. 'Well, who would I go with?'

'How about all the girls you met at the Villa Rosa? They must be having dances and going to parties.'

'I don't know. . . .' I thought of Juliana and her friends. How could I ever begin to explain to Mother the intricacies of petty social discrimination amongst the upper middle classes?

'Or how about Loveday?' Mother suggested. 'She must be making all sorts of new friends, now she's living in the thick of things. You ought to do what she's doing perhaps, and look for some sort of interesting job.'

'Mmm . . . I'll think about it—'

The door of the sitting room burst open, and Father stumbled in, half carrying, half dragging Donald. There was blood all over Donald's shirt, and from the strange swollen appearance of his face I guessed that his nose was broken.

Mother jumped to her feet. 'Oh dear God, Donald. . . .'

'It's all right, Jeanie love, make a space on the sofa so we can lay him flat . . . that's it.'

'I'll go and get something to clean him up with,' said Mother, heading for the door, calm and practical as ever.

I stared aghast at the half-conscious Donald. 'Father, you haven't. . .?'

'Don't be so bleeding ridiculous!' he snapped. 'D'you think I'd do something like that to my own brother-in-law? Look at him!' Father pointed to a massive bruise on the side of Donald's face. 'They pistol-whipped him, the bleeding cowards!'

'I just thought . . . after what we talked about this morning.' I kept my voice down as Mother had just come back into the room with a bowl of hot water, but I threw a meaningful glance in the direction of his own black eye.

'What happened Frank? Was it the meeting?'

'Yes, they jumped him, the bastards, after he was leaving. Armed blackshirts. He was just walking down the street by himself, and they came after him shouting "Commie bastard!" At least, that's what young Donald here told me when I found him staggering back to the Gardens.' Father took the hot water and a cloth from Mother's hands and started bathing Donald's wounds himself, handling him as tenderly as though he were a baby. He looked visibly shaken. 'If I could get my hands on them, I'd teach them to do something like this to *my* family. . . .'

Donald groaned and tried to speak.

'Is it worth it, eh, Donald? Is it really worth all this bother, when they're going to beat you to within an inch of your life?'

Blood trickled from Donald's mouth as he grinned his crooked grin. 'We can't all sacrifice our principles for the sake of an easy life, Finzel. Someone's got to wage the fight against social inequality, whatever the cost.'

'Oh, I'm all for equality,' said Father. 'It's just that you lot want everyone to be poor, and I want everyone to be rich.'

To atone for his wanderings, Father set about rebuilding our house.

'I've got the money,' he announced to Mother. 'I've got the money, and there's no bloomin' good in hanging on to it; we can't take it with us.'

Mother insisted that she didn't want the upheaval of a move, that she was content and settled where she was, so Father alighted on the compromise of building a bigger and better house where the existing one stood. And, as with everything that Father did, enthusiasm took on the proportions of obsession. Not only must the new house be bigger, but it must also be grander, more ornate, more stylish.

The builders were put to work straight away, and during August, while the house was actually uninhabitable, we repaired to Eastbourne to stay with my Aunt Agnes.

I passed those weeks in a sort of torpor, burying myself in novels, pretending that I was anyone other than Mel Finzel, the over-finished, rather useless product of the Villa Rosa. In those days it was quite acceptable for spinster daughters to be at home with their parents until they married, and they certainly weren't expected to want a career if there was no need for them to earn their own living. And what was I qualified to do? Nothing, except to lay the fish-knife in the correct place. There was little opportunity to exercise my social skills in Eastbourne; in fact there was nothing to do at all but sit in the window-seat and stare out at the lapping waves and the mewling seagulls and listen to Ethne interminably singing scales.

I was shaken out of my apathy when I returned to Magnolia Gardens and saw what Father had done to the house.

'Isn't it a bit . . . self-indulgent?' asked Loveday, when she came down to Magnolia Gardens one day to visit Magdalena and view the progress of Father's campaign of aggrandisement.

We stood on the pavement together and looked at the new edifice of 48 Magnolia Gardens, still surrounded by dust and rubble.

'Poor Father . . . it really is dreadfully ugly,' I sighed, 'but the trouble is that he doesn't really understand about architecture. You're not really supposed to mix up so many different styles.'

'I suppose that's what they taught you at your finishing school,' said Loveday, unable to resist the opportunity to be arch. I turned and looked at her, impossibly beautiful as ever, the surface of her skin as smooth and luminous as that of a screen goddess, her cunningly simple silk dress fluttering around her ankles. She seemed pleased that our friendship had been renewed, yet she remained ever so slightly aloof and could not resist little digs and barbed remarks about the year I had spent in Switzerland, while she had been fetching and carrying for the spoilt ungrateful Clifford family.

'You only have to *look* at the thing,' I said, 'to see what I'm talking about. He thought he'd be Gothic at first, and then he went Elizabethan. . . .' I pointed at the imitation black-and-white boarding that had been clapped on to the original mid-Victorian gable at the front of the house. The front elevation now had red brick, rough cast and stucco, in layers. ('A bit like a birthday cake, really,' observed Loveday.) But the worst thing of all was the first storey, divided into panels with wooden laths painted a chocolate brown and a purple brick diamond in the middle of each panel.

'Perfectly hideous,' pronounced Loveday. 'What on earth does your mother think of it? Surely she can't think it's an improvement.'

'You know Mother,' I replied. 'She likes a quiet life. Besides, he's done it all for her, and that's enough to please her.'

'Well, I don't know about you, but my eyes are aching from looking at this . . . gesture of devotion. What's he going to call it, by the way? The Taj Mahal? Let's go and scrounge a cup of tea from Neville.'

Neville was at home and set about making us tea, but we found him despondent and distracted. He still looked remarkably young, but his moustache was untrimmed and his hair straggly and unkempt. His sad brown eyes had a clouded blankness to them.

'Come on, then, Neville,' said Loveday briskly, making an effort to jolly him along. 'Tell us all the gossip, then. What's new in the Gardens?'

'I did hear,' said Neville, stroking his moustache with one hand and dunking his biscuit in his tea with the other, 'I did hear that the job of rector of St Luke's has gone to Edwin Clifford. He'll be coming back to Magnolia Gardens with his wife.'

'Oh, Neville, what a perfectly sweet pot you've got your geranium in,' said Loveday, jumping up and walking over to the window. 'I've only just noticed it. Do come and look, Mel. I suppose you finishing-school girls would call it a *jardinière*, wouldn't you?'

'I've had it for ages,' said Neville gloomily. 'Which you two would know, if you came slumming it round here more often.'

'I say, Mel,' said Loveday as I walked her back to the bus-stop afterwards. 'I do think Neville was being a bit . . . well, you know.'

'Yes, he was a bit horrid,' I agreed. 'But it must be because he's unhappy.'

'Do you think he's lost his job and he's afraid to tell us?'

'I don't know. Loveday.'

I turned to face her, blocking her way so that she was forced to stop and look at me. 'Are you having an affair with someone? Is that why you're living in an expensive flat and being . . . well, so dreadfully secretive about everything?'

Loveday's pretty mouth twitched slightly before it broke into a smile. 'Really, Mel.' She laughed, and gave my hand a squeeze. 'You're still a romantic, aren't you? What on earth makes you say that?'

'That time I came to the flat – the first time – someone telephoned and you were talking to them so furtively, I thought—'

'Oh, that! That was just someone I work with.'

But when I called in at Dulong's, the salon where Loveday worked, there was no sign of anyone who it might have been.

Apart from Loveday, enthroned like a princess on her powder-blue and gilt chair in the powder-blue showroom, I saw only a few mannequins, a pale asthmatic errand-boy and a white-haired seamstress who sat half-buried in bales of satin, organza and taffeta, dropping cigarette ash on to her ageing bosom as she sewed.

'Father, you can't possibly be serious!'

'Why not?'

'Because you just *can't*.'

'A house has got to have a name, doesn't it? I'm not going and spending all that bloomin' money on a place for it to be called "number forty-eight".'

When the work on the house had been finished and it had been fitted out with smooth velvety carpet, miniature chandeliers and mock-baronial fireplaces, Father announced that it was going to be called 'Camelot'. I was aghast, Mother made quiet noises of protest, and even the diffident Ethne looked dismayed.

'I'm calling it "Camelot",' Father insisted, 'after *King Arthur and the Knights of the Round Table*.'

'But that doesn't make sense,' I wailed. 'You can't call a house after a book.'

'I don't see why not. It was always my favourite book, and I always fancied living at Camelot. So I'm going to.'

I was able to laugh about it with Loveday later.

'That's exactly the sort of thing you'd do, though, Mel,' censured Loveday. 'Choose a name based on something you'd read in a book.'

I ignored this remark. 'And he's throwing a party to celebrate the completion of his brainchild,' I went on. 'He's even invited Mr and Mrs Clifford. Imagine!'

'Which ones?' demanded Loveday. She looked annoyed, and I guessed that she didn't much like the idea of socialising with her former employers.

'The younger. Helena Clifford has pleaded a prior engagement, and I shouldn't think Robert Clifford would come on his own, do you?'

It was several years since Father had first conceived his passion for formal dewy-eyed studio photographs of us all, and on the day of the party he packed me off to a West End studio to have a portrait photograph taken in the dress I was to wear that evening. It was one of my Baden 'finds', a creamy white silk crêpe cut on the bias and draped from the shoulders to give a Grecian look. It was very fragile and terribly easy to smear with dirty stains, and when I climbed out of the taxi in Magnolia Gardens on my return from the studio I did so with great care, straightening up slowly and shaking out the folds of my dress.

It was then that I saw Edwin.

The sun was shining so brightly that I had to shade my eyes to be sure it was him. He stood, tall and graceful, a good head and shoulders above the removal men who were carrying packing cases into number 26, the rectory of St Luke's. And he had seen me, too; I could tell that from the way he was staring. I remembered our times in Paris and I felt the stirring of something within me, a sensation of bursting warmth beneath my ribs and an overpowering longing for the sights and sounds and smells of Paris by night. I called out to him.

'Edwin!'

He smiled at me, and then a tall woman with ash-blonde hair appeared at his side, and he slipped his hand under her elbow to guide her up the steps of their new home.

Mr and Mrs Robert Clifford were absent from the housewarming party, but Mr and Mrs Edwin Clifford attended as part of their new parochial duties.

I disliked Jane Clifford instantly. I felt a little guilty about this, especially as everyone else seemed to think she was so nice, such a *good* rector's wife, so interested in the life of the parish. Everyone except Loveday, of course, who muttered, 'Pious Mrs Goody Two-Shoes', before drifting off looking remote and beautiful in crushed velvet the colour of blood. Perhaps another woman would have worn a red velvet dress, but only Loveday would have thought of decorating it with a corsage of extraordinary flowers that looked like lilies, in shades of glowing orange and pink that clashed wonderfully with the dress and with her russet hair. Very much a product of glamorous Mayfair; ill at ease in the less exotic habitat of Magnolia Gardens. I even noticed a flicker of pride cross the face of the phlegmatic Magdalena Stark, grown vastly fat and tired-looking, who stood chain-smoking in the corner.

I disliked Edwin's wife because she treated the occasion like a children's tea-party, a celebration to be indulged and smiled on from a great height, a source of very private amusement. I saw it there in her eyes as she was offered champagne by one hired footman wearing white gloves, and lobster patties by another.

'This is lovely,' Jane murmured to me. 'Such a sweet idea, christening a house. And your father has just promised a very generous donation for the repairs to the church roof. So kind.' And she gave me a warm smile. But when I crossed the room and glanced back over my shoulder she was staring at me, staring very hard as though she were doing some sort of calculation. I blushed and turned away.

Every time I drifted towards Edwin, to greet him, I was conscious of his wife's presence in the background. Perhaps I only imagined that she was looking at me, but after a while I lost my inclination to go and speak to him. The last time I had seen him he had been carefree and relaxed, a foreigner in a strange city, like myself. We had been friends. And he had scarcely mentioned his fiancée, an omission that now seemed terribly odd. Closer inspection revealed that he had become paler and thinner, and I didn't like seeing him in a dog collar. Confused and disturbed by a series of conflicting images, I retreated. I saw Edwin trying to catch my eye, but I went to talk to Neville.

We were jostled close to one another, and I realised that it was because Father was trying to clear a space at the centre of the room. My heart sank to my shoes. What was he up to now?

'Ladies . . . ladies and gentlemen. . . .' Father pulled himself up to his full height, which was not very great. 'If you will be so good as to listen for a few moments, my daughter Ethne is going to sing to us.'

I had not expected this. Nor, it seemed, had Ethne. She blinked violently and made as if to protest, but Ashley Player egged her on, pushing her forward and seating himself at the piano, in readiness to provide an accompaniment. His own reputation as a tenor was waning, and I guessed that he derived professional satisfaction from pushing his protégée into the limelight. He was a nondescript-looking man with thinning hair, who had a preference for the sort of 'artist's' clothes – velvet smoking jackets and floppy ties – that our drama master Mr Carnie, had favoured.

As his long thin hands began the stately introduction to Handel's 'Ombra mai fu', a strange look came over Ethne's face. She looked at once frightened and self-absorbed as though she was searching for something inside herself. She half-closed her eyes, and there was a tense silence that couldn't have lasted more than a fraction of a second but which seemed to suspend the expectant audience in time and space. Then she opened her mouth, and that first perfect note soared above us, full of warmth, colour, passion even. Passion, from the lips of Ethne. Her dark blonde hair was scraped back from her forehead and knotted at the nape of her neck, her dark green dress was ugly and unflattering, yet for those few brief minutes while she sang the largo Ethne was transformed. She was the most beautiful woman in the room. And I could see the overweening pride on Father's face, the quiet pleasure on Mother's.

Edwin appeared at my elbow, looking visibly shaken. 'Mel . . . I had no idea that your sister. . . .' He smiled, recalling our days in Paris. 'That, if anything, must be the way to get nearer to heaven.'

I glared at him, then turned on my heel and escaped from the crowded drawing room, from the clamour of congratulation.

I leaned against the closed door and listened. They had persuaded her to sing again. At first there were a lot of twiddly bits – arpeggios. Then it came. That pure, clear, soaring sound. It was so beautiful that it made me weep. Or was I weeping to think that it was Ethne? Plain boring Ethne, who never said anything. Who had never *wanted* anything. And she could sing like one of God's own angels. It was a terrible moment.

Father threw himself into the management of Ethne's career with the same energy and enthusiasm that he invested in Camelot. He had staunch allies in the ambitious Ashley Player and the choirmaster, Herbert Williams, who between them managed to coax a range of two octaves from bottom G to top G. Their big chance to push her came when one of the soloists dropped out of a local performance of 'Elijah'. Ethne stood in for the contralto with some reluctance and, to Father's wild delight, received a mention in the newspaper: 'Miss Finzel's performance was pleasing. . . . More will be heard of this young vocalist.'

London, it seemed, was not large enough to contain the talent of Ethne Finzel. In the autumn she travelled to the Carlisle Festival and sang Schubert's 'An die Musik' to a rapturous reception. The critics were more forthcoming this time, and the clipping that Father stuck in his new scrapbook eulogised 'the most glorious contralto voice, and a natural dignity'.

I held my breath and waited for all the fuss to die down, but I should have known that it would not end there.

'Bloomin' marvellous!' cried Father, after the telephone had rung one day and he had taken a message. 'Just think, our little Ethne. . . .'

It had been a BBC producer, who had heard her in Carlisle and wanted her to broadcast some popular songs. According to Ashley Player, this allowed Ethne to start charging a fee when she gave a performance, and he set to work expanding her repertoire, putting her through endless hours of practice until she had mastered Brahms and Purcell songs, Bach's B Minor Mass, 'The Dream of Gerontius'. . . .

Where was Ethne in all this? Where was my serious introverted younger sister? Her personality, always shadowy, seemed to recede and melt into her music until she was no more than a Voice. And where was I? I felt increasingly that I was a useless appendage at the new court of Camelot, beautifully, expensively finished but lacking in real substance.

It would be unfair of me to imply that Father was unconcerned about my future. He found the odd piece of work for me to do at his office in Nine Elms, and I fell into the habit of going in there regularly to help out. My heart wasn't in the work, but it was a way of escaping the interminable talk about Ethne. For the rest of the day I would bury my head in a book and escape to the worlds of my favourite heroines.

And I started to spend a great deal of time in St Luke's Church.

Father had been raised in a strict church-going tradition, and throughout our childhood Ethne and I were taken regularly. Now there was the added appeal of the Reverend Edwin Clifford, and on some days I attended Matins, Sung Eucharist and Evensong, burning with guilt at the impiety of my motives. St Luke's had always been 'high' Anglo-Catholic, and its new minister took it higher still. He wore a caped cassock with a moiré silk band and was preceded down the aisle by a thurifer swinging incense. I could almost see him wearing one of those Roman hats, a biretta. Certainly Edwin would not have been out of place in the Vatican. He looked immensely beautiful and imposing as he stood in front of the altar. His hair was the lovely rich brown of a formerly blond child and seemed to light up when he stood beneath the window of the north transept, and when he stepped up into the pulpit his dark eyes flashed with a fire that had been missing in the aloof controlled Edwin that I had first met. As a preacher, he sparkled, he sought to convert by excitement, he appealed to the heart rather than to the head. And he made a cry for self-denial that I, for one, could never achieve.

'The prophets wore sheepskins and goatskins, John the Baptist ate the food of the wilderness, Christ had nowhere to lay his head. . . . Are we, then, to seek material comfort?'

This was a new Edwin. The look he wore when he prayed was the look I had seen on his face at the top of Notre-Dame when we strove for heaven, but Edwin seemed both unattainable and powerful now. He was speaking for God, and in doing so a little deity seemed to have rubbed off on him.

And always Jane Clifford was there in the front pew, dressed in a neat tweed suit and pearls, smiling slightly. I ignored her.

Uncle Donald had certainly not abandoned me since my return from the Villa Rosa and, indeed, it was he who was most keen that I should not languish at home and do nothing. Shortly after the party to celebrate Camelot's completion, he told me that he had found a job for me. One of his colleagues at Oxford, an elderly lady professor of English literature, needed an assistant to help prepare her work for publication, to proof-read and check references.

'I'd have thought it was just up your street, lass,' said Donald with a grin, 'since you seem to have your nose stuck in a book half the time. And you'd like Oxford. There'd be plenty of young men your own age willing to give you something other than your frocks to think about!'

'Donald!' reproved Mother.

I told him I'd like some time to think about it. What I really wanted was a second opinion. I consulted Loveday, who said: 'Take it, darling. Anything to get away from Magnolia Gardens.' But somehow her answer was unsatisfactory. I decided that I would ask Edwin.

He was in the church, preparing for evensong. He caught me peering about in the vestry. 'Are you here as a tourist?'

'No, I'm here as a member of your flock, seeking guidance.'

'Even so, we have some very fine wall tablets. . . .'

We both laughed; it sounded so silly, and I was thinking that I could no longer remember what he looked like without his cassock, which I privately thought of as his 'dress'. When I told him about Donald's idea, he answered very much as Loveday had done. And then, as I had feared, he changed the subject to the Voice.

'I hear your sister's singing career is starting to blossom. You must all be very—'

'I don't know why everyone expects me to be glad!' I shouted, and suddenly I was giving vent to all the dreadful jealousy that I had been hiding inside me. 'Isn't it enough that she can sing without everyone having to go on about it endlessly? Well, I'm sick of it . . . I'm sick as hell . . . and it's not fair. Why should it be Ethne?' There were shameful tears in my eyes now that I could not control, and my voice was high and tremulous as a child's. '*I* was the one who was going to be famous and have everyone take notice. *I* was! Not Ethne.'

I had somehow expected Edwin's sympathy as my right, but I was to be disappointed. His voice was hard, almost sarcastic.

'And where was it that you were going to be famous? In your head?'

I gave him a cold look.

'Come with me. I want to show you something.'

He led me into the centre of the church and pointed to a large painting that was hanging there. 'It's rather beautiful, don't you think?'

I nodded. I already knew the picture by heart, for I had stared at the chained man and the angel through many a sermon when I was little, inventing a romantic story for them in which they fell in love and lived happily ever after.

'Not everyone could paint something like this. I couldn't. You couldn't. We all have different gifts. Ethne has the gift of an angelic voice. It may be her only gift, but it's hers. Now, for goodness' sake, get out there into the world and find out what your gifts are!'

I left this interview feeling disgruntled; a disciple who has expected praise from his teacher and found criticism instead. And on a simple level I felt that Edwin and I had got on to a bad footing. I went back to see him the next day, to try to make amends.

It was quite late when I came to the church, and I was by no means certain that Edwin would be there. When I saw his silhouetted figure in the dim light of the church I felt an excitement which lingered after my initial relief had passed.

He was kneeling before the altar with his head bowed, praying. From the urgency with which his lips were moving, I sensed he was troubled, and I instinctively hung back in the shadows until he had finished and risen to his feet.

I did not speak. I simply went and knelt before him with my hands folded behind my back, in readiness to receive a blessing as one would at the altar rail. Edwin placed his hands on my head, with the very lightest of touches so that I could barely feel them. I remained motionless for a few seconds, then made as if to rise, but his hands moved. He placed them on my shoulders, more firmly this time, and I could feel their warmth through my thin dress. My heart began to pound so hard that I was sure I would no longer be able to breathe. Then he put one hand on either side of my chin, cupping my face and lifting it so that I could see his expression, not smiling but intent and sombre as though the waves of my longing were reaching him; invisible and inaudible but still managing to shake the cold musty air of St Luke's Church.

Neither of us spoke that evening, nor was any reference made to it afterwards; nevertheless, the situation had changed in some way that I did not understand. And I could not forget the sensation of Edwin's touch or the look on his face. The image returned to me time and time again with a photographic sharpness.

There was great excitement at Camelot that autumn, not only over Ethne's BBC recordings but also over a proposal of Jane Clifford's that there should be a performance of 'The Dream of Gerontius' at St Luke's with Ethne singing the part of the Angel. Naturally. An admission fee would be charged, and the money raised would go towards the fund for a new church roof.

The concert was to be at the end of December, and I witnessed the preparations with mixed feelings. I was still finding it difficult to come to terms with Ethne's fame, but when Uncle Donald and Father pressed me for an answer about the job in Oxford I procrastinated, using the organisation of the concert as an excuse.

The night of the concert came.

It was terrible.

It was wonderful.

It was both of these things.

Ethne, pale and fragile-looking in a dark dress, sang with more depth and passion than ever before. Her voice and those of the choir soared above the mesmerised audience: Uncle Donald with his hands folded in his lap, staring at his feet, Father unable to stop grinning, and Edwin. . . . His eyes were half-closed and there was a look of torment on his face as he listened to the words.

> *O wisest love! that flesh and blood*
> *Which did in Adam fail*
> *Should strive afresh against the foe*
> *Should strive and should prevail.*

Jane was at his side, the omnipresent smile on her lips, but he scarcely seemed aware of her.

After the concert, the audience thronged around Ethne, congratulating her, then moved slowly in a tide towards Camelot where Father was holding a champagne reception. I saw Edwin giving Ethne a kiss of congratulation as she reached the porch of the church, still surrounded by admirers.

'Mel,' he said, and held out his hand.

I brushed past him and returned to Camelot alone.

'Such a credit to you, Mrs Finzel. . . .' Jane Clifford *already was* in the hall when I arrived. 'A God-given gift, indeed – and a real gift to the parish. We now have ample funds for the roof . . . really most gratifying. . . .'

I went up to my room and sat down at the dressing table, and touched the petals of the yellow silk rose I had brought back from Paris, knowing as I looked at it what I had only suspected before; that I was in love with Edwin Clifford. Then I switched off the lights and lay on my bed in the dark, listening to the rain beating against the window and the sighing of the trees in Magnolia Gardens, giving myself up briefly to the terrible, terrible agony of loving someone I could not have.

Inside the church it was dark but still warm, from the battered electric heaters and the closely packed bodies of the recently departed audience. He was waiting for me, as I had known he would be.

'I hoped you'd come back,' he said.

'I'm sure I don't know why you're bothering. All you're interested in is Ethne's singing and the money for your wretched church—'

'Look! Come here!' Edwin seized me by the wrist and led me back to the painting of the Angel and the Sinner. 'Why do you think I showed this picture to you before?' he demanded. 'Because you remind me of the Angel, that's why – or the Angel reminds me of you; I'm not sure which. All I know is that when I saw you the other day – you were getting out of the taxi and you were dressed all in white, floating white. . . .' He tightened his grip on my wrist. 'It was then that I realised.'

'What will you do when you leave here tonight?' I asked.

'I should go and join the others at your father's—'

'No,' I said, my voice urgent. 'No, I mean what do you do normally when you go home at night?'

'What do *you* think I do?' He sounded angry.

'*Make love to your wife.*'

I didn't know how or why I had said it; the words seemed to have spoken themselves.

Edwin looked aghast. Then he shook his head slowly. 'I think of you.'

'Have you forgotten Paris?'

'I haven't forgotten anything.'

'Oh, Edwin. . . .' I stepped towards him. Before I came into the church he had already started unbuttoning the heavy cassock that covered his clothes, and he made as if to remove it completely, but I reached out and stopped him. 'No, don't,' I said softly. 'I want you to keep it on.' I could hardly hear my voice for the sound of my heartbeat drumming in my ears.

Later it vexed me that I could not remember more, but everything was forgotten on that first miraculous contact.

I experienced both disbelief and certainty.

He wants me. He desires me. And he can no longer pretend. Not to me. . . .

Standing there, being kissed by Edwin, feeling the rough musty cloth of his cassock against my cheek – it didn't seem quite real, and was all the more wildly exciting as a result. Edwin the priest, chosen by God, Edwin, down from his pedestal. I had reached out and touched the unattainable, penetrated the taboo. The thought of my desire as a sin filled me with a delicious erotic pleasure, and I pressed myself against him.

Then he broke away from me. I reached towards him again, but he stepped back. 'Someone might come in. . . .'

And then I felt afraid. I saw that I was playing a game in which

I could never control the rules. I might want to kiss him again – at some time, at any time in the future I might want to kiss Edwin and hold him again, but I would never be sure if it would happen. There was no certainty. Even then, as I stood there, I realised with horror that I might just have touched Edwin for the last time. I turned and ran from the church into the dim street, rain mixing with tears on my face.

Thy will be done, Oh Lord. . . .

I went to confess to Loveday.

After the night of the concert I avoided St Luke's Church for several days, turning over all that had happened, examining everything that Edwin had said as though it might give me some clue.

'I think of you. . . .' Yes, but how exactly? And when he said 'someone might come in' was he genuinely reluctant to end our embrace, or was it an excuse? I wrote endless letters and destroyed them all. And I longed, with every atom of my being, to see Edwin again.

In the end I took a bus to Hyde Park Corner and went to see Loveday. She was in the bedroom, drying her hair. I sat on the edge of the bed and watched her as she sat on her dressing stool with her head tipped forward and rubbed vigorously with a towel until the dark soaking mass was transformed in a mass of frothing red-brown curls.

'Loveday—'

'One moment, darling. I've just got to get some face cream. . . .' She disappeared into the bathroom and left me sitting there on her bed. The covers were flung back and the pale satin sheets had a rumpled look to them, as though only recently somebody had been lying on them. As I stared at them, I realised that I would never be able to tell Loveday about Edwin. She wouldn't understand. Whatever she knew of men, it was surely very different.

Then I saw something lying on the sheet, glinting in the pinkish light from the fringed lamp beside the bed. I picked it up and examined it. It was a man's cufflink, made from fine yellow gold and with an engraved family crest. So Loveday's secret lover was not only rich, but also a gentleman. As I handled the cufflink, it was slightly warm to the touch. I imagined it falling from a hurriedly removed shirt and lying unnoticed on the sheet, pressed beneath warm limbs. . . .

Suddenly I had an idea.

'You were about to tell me something?' said Loveday as she returned, smearing cold cream on her face.

'Yes . . . I . . . Loveday, could I possibly . . .? Oh dear, this sounds dreadful, however I put it. . . . Would you mind terribly if I used your flat while you were at work . . .?'

'You mean bring someone here?'

I nodded, blushing slightly.

'Why, Mel! Aren't you the dark horse! Are you going to tell me who it is, this mystery man?'

'No, I—'

'Not even if it means I refuse?'

'Loveday, you wouldn't be so mean!'

She laughed. 'Wouldn't I? . . . Oh, all right. What are friends for, after all?'

It wasn't difficult to persuade Edwin to come to Loveday's flat with me. After Midnight Mass on Christmas Eve I hung back as everyone was leaving, and he murmured: 'Mel, I have to talk to you soon . . . somewhere away from all this. . . .' I smiled back at him, unable to hide my relief and my joy.

I didn't tell him that the flat was Loveday's. I didn't think that he would mind but, on the other hand, her mother still lived in Magnolia Gardens and . . . well, it just seemed simpler to say nothing. Little did I realise the terrible consequences my silence was to have.

We first met there one cold January afternoon, while Loveday was working at the salon. I arrived first and sat waiting at the window, waiting the interminable minutes until Edwin's yellow sports-car roared up outside the apartment block. He wore a dark overcoat and a trilby pulled down low over his face, and my heart missed a beat when I saw him looking so mysterious, glamorous even. At this remove, perched behind a fourth-floor window, I could scarcely believe that he had anything to do with me.

I dare say that both of us had privately rehearsed what we were going to say and do, but the shock of being alone together in a strange flat left us tongue-tied. I made some lame joke about him not wearing his dress, and we kissed for a while. Somehow I managed to manoeuvre him towards Loveday's exotically fringed, draped bedroom. With its gory red walls and heavily

243

shaded lights it was like being in a dark subterranean cavern. Edwin stared around him in disbelief.

'Good God, what a place!' He frowned at the slippery satin sheets. 'I don't think much of your friend's taste in décor. What is she, an actress?'

'Edwin. . . .'

He removed my hands gently. 'Mel . . . please . . . I really must talk to you. . . .' We sat on the edge of the bed, next to one another. 'My dearest Mel. . . .' He took my hand in his. 'It was after I had left Paris; it was then I realised you had become so very dear to me. I had told myself before that I looked on you as a sister, but it was a lie. When we were at the fair and those men pawed at you and I was so angry – you remember? – well, afterwards I found myself analysing why I'd been so angry. It wasn't just that I felt protective. . . . I realised –' he buried his head in his hands and sighed deeply – 'I realised that it was because I . . . too . . . wanted you as a woman.'

I wound my arms around Edwin's neck, smoothing the hair that curled in duck-tails behind his ears, kissing his fine strong neck. 'I want you, too, Edwin. You know that. . . .'

He burst out. 'But how can I, Mel? I've spent most of my life wanting to serve God and I've spent most of my life wanting someone like you . . . but how can I have both? Oh, Mel, you understand these things. At least, that's what I felt in Paris. You understand about the voice that always tells us there must be more to life than what we see around us, and creates a yearning. A yearning that prompts us towards either religion . . . or love. But we have to choose. . . .' Edwin clenched his fists and thumped them down hard on the side of the bed, his face twisted in anguish. 'And I cannot choose! I *will* not choose!'

'But surely with Jane you have—'

'Jane . . . yes, there's Jane . . . she's a good woman, but I can't love her. Or perhaps that's *why* I can't love her, because she's so good. I can't get near her.' He turned to me and stroked my cheek with one finger. 'But that's not the only problem, little Mel. I don't want to hurt you . . . you're so young . . . it would be selfish.'

'Then, why are you here?' I kept my voice as level as I could, and as a result it sounded cold. We stared at one another.

Then the telephone rang in the hall, and I went to answer it. 'Yes?'

'Loveday? Is that you?' A man's voice, well bred, faintly familiar.

'No, I'm afraid—'

There was a click and the line went dead.

I did not press Edwin for an answer to my question when I returned to the bedroom. Instead I suggested that he get into the bed with me for a while, not to make love but just so that I could be held closely. I undressed quickly so that he would not have time to try to change my mind, then I lay in the bed and watched him pick up the clothes I had flung carelessly to the floor, fold them up and put them over a chair. This small poignant gesture moved me.

Then Edwin turned out the lights and undressed to his undershorts.

'Ah, Mel . . .,' he sighed. 'My angel. . . .' Then we lay there silently between Loveday's satin sheets, my priest and I, folded in a warm embrace, both relieved that there was no need to say any more.

As the months went past, I realised where I had made my mistake.

I had imagined that if someone loved you they belonged to you, but this was not so. Edwin remained out of my reach. It was maddening and yet exhilarating, because I was never allowed to stop striving, nor was I prevented from dreaming. We carried on meeting at Loveday's flat, and I relished the furtiveness of these assignations, and their tantalising brevity. I was allowed a glimpse of heaven, but the gates never parted fully. Edwin still refused to make love to me properly. His conscience always took over at the last moment, though as we became more familiar with one another his arousal became more and more difficult for him to conceal. By the summer I sensed that he was teetering on a precipice, and that perhaps something might happen to send him hurtling over the edge. He gave the impression of one whose emotions are well ordered, but beneath whose calm surface turbulent waters churn, only just in check. And if a stone were to be cast into the millpond. . . .

But Edwin was still a priest. And he was still married. Once I saw a pale gold hair glittering on his jacket, and realised with shock that it was *hers*. Had *she* been touching him? I hated the thought of his lips kissing mine after they had touched hers, almost as if *she* was kissing *me*. Yet I couldn't stop thinking about it. It was like a sickness, an obsession. Yes, I was as obsessed with Edwin as my father was with plumbing, and the building of Camelot, and Ethne's career. And to think that I had laughed at him.

As for Edwin, it seemed that as long as our affair remained chaste and its passion confined to the love-letters we exchanged he could devote himself to God with a clear conscience.

'Even to think about doing it would be wrong,' he explained once when I tried to coax him into my arms.

'Then, since you've already thought about it, you might as well do it . . .,' I cajoled.

Edwin just laughed and stroked my hair. 'You would have made a good theologian, Mel.'

Despite Father's bullying, I found excuse after excuse to stay in Magnolia Gardens without gainful employment. But, while I languished there in the early months of 1933, Ethne's career flourished in the hands of Ashley Player. She had achieved a national reputation, and he was now anxious to thrust her on to the international stage. Poor Ethne tried as hard as she could to escape from her fame, burying herself at home and reading lives of the great composers when she wasn't working, but Ashley was relentless. He announced that the time had come for her to sing opera, and proposed *Carmen*, which was one of his own favourites, for a summer season culminating with performances at the Royal Opera House. Ethne refused at first on the grounds that the part was too high for her range, but I was sure that the real reason was her reluctance to flounce around a stage in a gypsy dress with a red rose between her teeth. Ashley Player was persistent, and he had a great deal of power over Ethne: in the end she relented and began to study for the role, working up to fourteen hours a day to improve her technique.

She drew the line at *Lucretia*, however. A copy of the libretto was lying on a footstool in the grand drawing room at Camelot, and one day Mother had picked it up and started to read out loud from it.

'"*Even great love's too frail to bear the weight of shadows/Now I'll be forever chaste, with only death to ravish me.* . . ." Oh, Ethne, are you going to sing this one, too?'

Ethne had shaken her head. 'No, not that,' she replied firmly. She refused to be ravished.

A few weeks later, on a hot June afternoon, I was sitting in a deckchair, composing a tortuous love-letter to Edwin, when I heard Ethne coming back from a practice session with Ashley.

'Like some tea?' I shouted through the french windows Father had installed to look over a vast brick structure which he called a 'patio'.

'It's all right, I'll do it,' she replied, but she sounded distracted. When, after ten minutes, no tea appeared, I went inside the house to find her. She had been reading voraciously in her precious spare time, and I was expecting to find her in what was now her customary attitude: curled up in her favourite chair with her nose in a book, shutting out the world. But the book she was reading, Marcia Davenport's story of a singer, *Of Lena Geyer*, was lying face down on the sofa, and Ethne was standing in the bay window looking out at Magnolia Gardens. My first thought was 'she must be crying', but she was too still for that. She stood there, absolutely without movement, her eyes fixed on some distant point.

'Has something happened?' I said.

'He's asked me,' she replied without turning round.

'Who has? Who's asked you what?'

'Ashley has. He's asked me to marry him.'

'Ethne! What did you say?'

'I refused. Of course.' She turned round to face me, and I saw the streaky marks on her face where tears had dried. 'How could I marry him, Mel? How could I?' The grey-blue eyes blazed out from beneath her broad serious brow.

'But, Ethne—'

'The person he wants to marry doesn't exist!' she burst out, with as much vehemence as I ever heard from her. 'I can't go on with my career and be a wife to him. I just can't. It's like in this book.' She snatched up *Of Lena Geyer* and flicked through the pages until she found what she was looking for. Then she read it out loud to me: "*I am not the great love, dear Louis – for anybody. I cannot be, I am only*' – she made a futile gesture – '*a throat.*'" I'm like Lena, Mel. I'm like that. The only thing I can do is sing.'

Ethne's words haunted me. For the first time I had seen her strong and decisive and I felt a grudging admiration. But I had also seen her commit herself to a sterile life. That thought made me feel frightened for myself. My own position was hardly more promising. She had committed herself to singing, I to a chaste affair with someone else's husband. Which was the emptier? I resolved to push my relationship with Edwin out of its safe little backwater. I owed it to myself at least to try.

In June 1933, as Adolf Hitler was appointed Reich Chancellor, the church of St Luke prepared to celebrate the feast of Corpus Christi. The ceremony, held at dusk, was dangerously papist and all the more wonderfully romantic as a result. The entire congregation processed down the main aisle of the church carrying candles, and every corner was banked high with flowers; with red and pink roses in full bloom. Their heady scent hung in the air, mixing with incense as the thurifer preceded Edwin down the aisle, swinging his golden censer on its long chain. And Edwin looked magnificent as he strode past in a white silk cope, his dark eyes fixed on the altar. I could not take my eyes off him, nor did I dare breathe as the silk hem of his robe brushed over the toe of my shoe and sent the blood rushing to my face.

'You were wonderful,' I said to him when we met for lunch the next day in Loveday's flat. I poured him another glass of chilled Lachryma Christi, 'the tears of Christ'. The name of the wine appealed to my sense of the melodramatic. 'I'd love to see you in a cardinal's red.'

Edwin smiled and squeezed my hand, but his face adopted the remote distant look it wore whenever I mentioned a religious subject. 'I don't think there's much chance of that, Mel.'

'Edwin. . . .' I pressed the cold glass of wine against my mouth, running my tongue round the rim thoughtfully. 'Edwin, you do love me, don't you? I know you do.'

He kissed my hand. 'More . . . much more . . . than you'll ever know.'

'Well, if that's true, will you do something for me if I ask you to? Just one thing?'

'Yes, of course. . . .' He hesitated, as though he was afraid I was going to ask him to leave his wife. 'As long as it's something that's within my power.'

'Edwin, I'd like to. . . . Can we, oh, please Edwin, can we just have one night, one evening together when we can pretend we're just a normal couple – I don't know, just go out somewhere like any other man and woman. . . .'

'Darling Mel . . . I don't know.'

'Perhaps if you stopped being a priest just for one evening and saw what it was like, then it might help you to choose. What was it you said to me about self-knowledge?'

Just as I had once used Uncle Donald's political tenets to bolster my arguments, I was now learning to use Edwin's theology against him, battling with the words that were the only weapon I had.

'Self-knowledge is at the root of all religious knowledge.' He quoted Cardinal Newman at me.

'Yes, that's what I mean. I mean you should look on it as a sort of exploration – a voyage of discovery.'

Edwin stood up and walked from the table to the silk-draped window of Loveday's sitting room, stirring the mandarin chimes to a faint ringing as he passed. The trees of Hyde Park made a brilliant block of colour in the distance. 'You're very clever, Mel,' he said. 'You would have made an excellent politician, in fact. There must be something of your uncle in you. Beneath that unworldly façade there's someone hell-bent on getting her own way, isn't there?'

He swung round to face me, and I caught my breath, afraid that this incisive summary of my character was a prelude to an angry outburst. But he smiled instead. 'However, my Mel, you may be right. Perhaps I need a better understanding of what sin is.'

'So you'll do it?'

He walked slowly towards me, and I was aware of his stunning grace, and of his impressive height as he tapped my cheek gently. 'May God forgive me, but I find I can refuse you nothing. I'll do it. But just once. Only once.'

It was to be the thirtieth of June. The date which I had privately labelled 'The Day of Edwin's Defrocking'.

Everything had been planned with the utmost care. Edwin had invented a diocesan meeting that required his absence from London overnight. I had told my parents I was going to a party with Loveday and staying at her flat afterwards. And, disguising my voice to sound like a mature married woman, I had telephoned a hotel and booked a room for the night in the name of Mr and Mrs Snowe. I didn't tell Edwin about this part. We had avoided discussing how the evening would end, and I sensed that ultimately he would try to shy away from sex.

I was not discouraged as I made my preparations that night. I had insisted not only that we should eat in a fashionable West End restaurant, but also that we should go and dance afterwards in a nightclub, just like any other Normal Young Couple.

At seven o'clock I carried the wireless into the bathroom with me and started to run a bath. Camelot boasted the sort of bathrooms that were appropriate to the house of a sanitary-ware magnate, and in my opinion they were the best thing about the place. There were three, so Ethne and I had one each. Mine was a mini-palace in pink marble, with gold taps in the shape of winged sylphs and huge mirrors on every wall. I dropped my bathrobe on to the floor and sank into the hot perfumed bathwater, disappearing into a cloud of steam through which I could see very little, but hear the wireless crackling its way cheerfully through 'The Teddy Bears' Picnic'. I closed my eyes and sang along with it for a while.

'*If you go down to the woods today, you're sure of a big surprise. . . .*'

My dripping body was bright pink and fragrant with 'Shalimar' when I dragged it from the tub and began to dress. So great was the quantity of steam in the room that I had to rub the mirror with one finger before I could see the finished result. I smiled at what I saw.

I had dressed in black, in a concerted attempt to prove to Edwin that his 'little Mel' was grown-up. The dress was the crowning glory of my wardrobe and, to my mind, dreadfully sophisticated: a Jean Patou with tiers of black organdie and a plunging back which could be covered with a matching evening cape. Above it, my face looked infuriatingly young and fresh. I dragged some powder over it, added crimson lipstick and my diamanté hair-clips, and the overall effect was much improved. I smiled again. The smile was entirely smug and self-satisfied. I was in the throes of a Great Love. Life no longer happened to the characters I read about in books. I was a heroine at last.

I floated down the stairs and into the back of the taxi that was waiting to spirit me off to my assignation. I leaned back on the leather seat with a sigh, my eyes half-closed, the smile still on my lips and my heart beating very hard at the thought that soon, in only a few minutes, I would be touching Edwin. . . .

'Where to, miss?'

'What? Oh, er, Wardour Street, please.'

Then I saw her.

'Oh God, oh God, stop!'

The taxi pulled in sharply to the kerb. Jane Clifford was walking along the pavement towards us, her head held high and a pious smile on her face. Over her arm she carried an empty basket, which had no doubt contained the alms for the poor she had just finished distributing. She stopped at the gate of number 26 and glanced at the taxi. The pious smile disappeared.

'Wot's the matter, miss? You changed your mind or something?'

'Or something . . .,' I muttered weakly. 'No, it's all right, I'm still going. I'm sorry. Please drive on.'

And we sped away from Magnolia Gardens, over the bridge and towards the glittering bauble of the West End.

'Are you all right, darling? You're not cold?'

Edwin and I stood on the pavement outside the restaurant in Wardour Street.

'Not cold, no,' I replied. 'I'm shivering because I'm happy. And a little drunk.' And I lifted my arms and wound them round his neck, moving my lips to and fro over his until he was forced to respond.

'Mel . . . oh, Mel. . . .' Edwin embraced me hard, and I could feel his body straining against mine. 'I'm more than a little drunk myself. I don't know what I'm going to think tomorrow – or feel – but at the moment I think this is the best idea you ever had. Wonderful idea.' He kissed me again.

Edwin was enjoying himself, and his enjoyment was infectious. He was dressed in white tie and tails, and he looked the picture of every woman's dream escort: tall, sophisticated, strikingly handsome. Yet as I looked at him the shadow of Edwin the priest lurked in the background; the image of Edwin in a drab black cassock was faintly superimposed, and I found the duality unbearably exciting, as though I were solely responsible for his 'disguise'. I felt like a smuggler involved in an elaborate plot to spirit a precious piece of merchandise to a foreign shore.

We left the restaurant and took a taxi to the Silver Slipper Club in Regent Street. I had never been inside a nightclub in my life, but I had read about the Silver Slipper, with its fabled glass dance-floor, in the 'Londoner's Log', and it had fired my imagination. Edwin and I descended the steps into the smoky gloom, and I was reminded of the night in Paris when we visited the *maison d'illusion* and saw love being hideously mocked. I suppressed an ominous shiver.

'Oh. . . .' Edwin drew in his breath, and then stood very, very still.

'Yes, isn't it wonderful?' I sighed, grabbing at his hand like an excited child and pointing up at the great silver ball which hung from the ceiling, its faceted surface catching the light like so many winking eyes, bouncing it off the mirrors on the walls as it spun so that the effect created was one of continual movement.

'No,' said Edwin. 'Look. Over there. . . . I. . . . Oh God, please say this isn't happening. . . .'

They were reflected in the mirrors on the walls, and the glass dance-floor, and then the circling silver ball picked up the reflections and divided them into a myriad more, so that we saw them once, twice and then a hundred times.

Loveday and Robert Clifford, leaning over a bottle of champagne in order to kiss one another on the mouth.

Edwin took hold of my wrist and we fled up the stairs and into the street, but they followed us. The four of us stood there staring at one another: two girls, a father and his son.

'Edwin, what in hell's going on?' demanded Robert, and as he spoke I recognised the voice I had heard on the telephone and at last everything fell sickeningly into place. Loveday's job at the Cliffords' house. Loveday's apartment in the West End. Loveday's secret benefactor. I clung to Edwin's arm, not caring now how damning it looked. I don't think it occurred to any of us to try to pretend. Loveday, petite and chic in ice-blue satin, stared at Edwin with a look that was half pity, half contempt. I felt I wanted to kill her.

The events that followed melted into a blur, a sequence that was grotesquely comical. We could hardly have nodded to one another and then passed on, so it was somehow agreed that we should go somewhere and talk. We tried to hail a taxi, but of course none came, so Robert Clifford said he'd fetch his car, then spent ten minutes searching for his car keys while we all looked in diverse directions, avoiding one another's eyes. In the end the doorman of the club, thinking we must be very drunk indeed, hailed a taxi for us, and we sat opposite one another, staring at our hands, or examining our shoes in frosty silence.

We couldn't start the row in the taxi because it might arrive while we were just heating up, and then we'd have to stop in mid-recrimination while we all piled out into the street again. So we made ineffectual remarks about the Silver Slipper Club – the décor, the standard of the service, et cetera – like a vicarage tea-party gone horribly wrong. I found myself wishing irreverently that Edwin was wearing his dog collar to define his role. Until this moment he had looked like a dangerous and beautiful animal in his evening clothes; now the white tie and tailcoat had the same impact as borrowed women's clothing.

That long terrible taxi-ride was acutely uncomfortable to the point of hysteria, and I kept expecting someone to burst out laughing and say how ridiculous the situation was. But no one did. So I concentrated on looking daggers at Loveday. She wore a smirk on her pretty face as though the whole thing was a divine punishment visited on Edwin. I still didn't quite understand why she disliked Edwin so much; I assumed it must be something to do with Robert's influence.

And then there was the dreadful problem of our destination. The taxi-driver demanded to know where we were going, but no one knew. The most obvious place was Loveday's flat, but the idea of the satin sheets that all four of us had unwittingly shared was too sordid. It was Loveday, practical as ever, who decided.

'Magnolia Gardens,' she said to the cabbie, then slid the little window shut with one sharp swift movement. As the taxi trundled over the bridge, I couldn't help but remember my elation as I had travelled in the opposite direction. We could not go to either Robert or Edwin's home, obviously, and Camelot seemed equally out of the question. But Loveday jumped out of the taxi first and walked smartly up to the door of number 47. We followed her like sheep.

'Mother's sleeping,' she said as she unlocked the door, 'so for God's sake be quiet.'

We went into the drawing room. Loveday switched on the lamps and flung her silver-fox stole over the back of the ottoman. Lamplight gleamed on her blue satin gown like sun on a glacier. Robert Clifford sank heavily on to the white ottoman, and it groaned beneath his weight. He reached out and stroked Loveday's fur wrap with one finger, looking at it, but not seeing it. Edwin stood by the open window, and I stayed close at his side.

'If you two are going to stand there, you should at least close the curtains,' said Loveday. It seemed she was the only one of us whose mind could embrace such practical considerations. Indeed, she was the only one of us capable of speech, breaking into a taut unhappy silence.

Robert Clifford looked up. 'Where's Jane?' he asked, addressing Edwin 'I suppose she thinks you're somewhere else?' Then, realising that this invited the question of what Helena thought, he went on 'Well, this is the last thing I expected, I must say.'

He sounded ridiculously like a reproachful schoolmaster expecting an apology.

Edwin straightened himself up, and beneath my fingers I could feel the muscles in his arms grow tense. 'Father . . . I know what you're thinking, but I absolutely must. . . . This is *not* what you think. . . .'

Robert laughed, looking at his shoes and shaking his head. Then his laughter stopped abruptly, and he looked at Edwin again. The expression on his face was ugly. 'Don't lie to me, Edwin! *Don't you bloody lie to me*! We'll draw a veil over your morals for the time being, but don't you dare lie to me about this!'

'I'm not lying to you, Father.' Edwin's voice was cold, but I sensed that inwardly he was coiled like a spring ready to release itself.

Robert stood up and towered in front of us. His heavy handsome face was flushed. '*You're lying!*' he shouted. 'Loveday told me that she was lending her flat to her friend here.' I looked at Loveday, but she avoided my glance. She was sitting in her mother's rocking chair, the satin of her gown rippling over the rockers. 'I'll spare her the embarrassment of asking what for, but it's not exactly hard to guess, is it?'

'Father, I'm telling you, it isn't . . . *wasn't* like that. . . .'

Robert modulated his voice to the low deadly tone reserved for his victims in court. 'Oh, it wasn't like that, was it? I do beg your pardon. So you just sat and discussed world affairs, did you?' There was a split second's silence. '*And you a man of the cloth! I was so bloody proud of you!*' he thundered.

The tension inside Edwin surged and burst. '*You hypocrite!*' he shouted. 'What about the plank in your own eye? A girl . . . this girl . . . young enough to be your daughter . . . and I'm quite sure she wasn't the first, either. Did you do this to my mother as well?' Edwin was wild, raging. He leaped towards Robert. 'While she was ill? *Did you?*' And he flung back his arm and punched out at his father with all his force, catching him on the side of the jaw. Robert raised his own fists.

'Loveday, for goodness' sake, can't you . . .?' I appealed to her, but she merely shrugged helplessly and continued rocking.

But Robert let his arm drop by his side. He looked sad all of a sudden, almost wistful. 'No. . . . No, I promised Lorna I would never strike you and, by God, I'll keep my promise. Even though it's done more harm than good. . . .' He looked into his son's face. Edwin was still tense and shaking with anger, but Robert's expression was almost tender as he said: 'No . . . I think your conscience will punish you enough. I'm sure of it. That and the words of the Bible: "But whoso committeth—" '

'The Bible? What would you know about that?' said Edwin in disgust. He turned on his heel and walked towards the door. I followed him, pausing only to look at Loveday. Her small pointed chin was held up defiantly, but there was an expression in her eyes that I didn't recognise. In fact I didn't recognise her at all.

We went to the church.

Edwin seemed desperate to get in, and actually banged his fists against the locked door before I had the presence of mind to remind him that the spare key was kept inside the porch.

'Edwin, I'm not sure we should, though. . . .'

In our evening clothes we were like a pair of heretics defiling the sanctum. The idea of Edwin even entering the building in his white tie seemed sacrilegious in the extreme. He didn't seem to hear me, or even to be aware of my presence.

Inside we breathed the familiar smell of cold hymn-books and brass polish. The Corpus Christi roses were still on display, but they were fading and their red and pink petals beginning to fall. Edwin walked slowly to the painting of the chained sinner and stared at it. Then he turned to face the altar, his hands in his pockets, his white silk evening scarf slung round his shoulders. He laughed.

'"But whoso committeth adultery with a woman lacketh understanding: he that doeth it destroyeth his own soul." ' He turned to me. 'That's what we're going to do, Mel,' he said fiercely. 'Between the two of us we're going to destroy my soul. It seems the process has already begun, so we might as well finish it off. Here in His house, so He can witness it.' He held out his hand to me. 'Come.'

I was more than a little afraid when I saw the crazed look in those deep dark eyes; yet I also wanted him dreadfully, so I stepped forward willingly into his arms.

The terrible tension was still there in him. I sensed it as he kissed me long and hard on the mouth and then struggled with the hooks and clasps at the back of my dress, swearing as the fragile black organdie tore under his fingers. We were standing, there in the aisle of the church, but as my dress fluttered to the floor I sank back so that I was half sitting, half lying on one of the uncomfortable wooden pews. In the half-light of the church Edwin's face was bright white, and he seemed to hover above me for a few seconds like an angel.

Then he, too, sank down, tearing at his cummerbund and the fly buttons of his trousers, and we were clasped together, our flesh hot against cold hard wood. He was so close now that I was aware only of the devouring touch of his mouth on my breasts, of the solid, strong, compact feel of his body as he balanced his weight on mine, his silky hair against my goose-pimpled skin.

I needed time to separate and assess all these sensations, but Edwin seemed impatient, driven. He lifted my hips and entered me and there was a moment's shock and pain and then from being cold our bodies suddenly seemed to grow hot and slippery with sweat and I plunged towards him in the grip of unimaginable pleasure. The pleasure was in my mind as much as in my body, the idea that *this was actually what I was doing*.

And then he reared up above me with a great shout. 'Oh God . . . it's done now. . . .' He sank back but clung as fiercely as ever, like a drowning man afraid to let go of a life-raft, his chest rising and falling in rapid breaths, his hair damp against my neck. The vase of roses in the alcove above us trembled slightly and dropped a sudden shower of red petals into my hair, and on to Edwin's back where they lay like large drops of blood.

As he moved away from me I reached and touched my own thigh. 'Oh . . . I'm bleeding.'

And he knelt down and licked the blood from my fingers.

I can't remember exactly how long it was before I knew that something was wrong.

Of course, I expected him to come back, and to want more when he did, just as I so desperately wanted more. I had lain in my bed that night at Camelot in my chintzy girly room with the black organdie dress on the floor, unable to sleep or even to lie still. I was terribly conscious of my body, as if it had woken up and now had a life of its own. It felt slightly bruised and tender, but warm and alive. And full of joy.

I wasn't sure what I expected to happen next, but it was probably nothing short of the skies opening and a thunderbolt appearing, or ghostly letters across the sky, spelling 'EDWIN CLIFFORD LOVES MEL FINZEL'.

Instead, nothing happened.

Three days later, a handwritten letter was pushed through the door at Camelot. It was from Edwin requesting a meeting in the church that afternoon.

It was a shock to see him dressed in his cassock, after his semi-nakedness the last time we had been together. But I was joyful and I leaped on him, devouring him with kisses.

'No, Mel.'

As I stepped back from him, I saw the expression on his face. And then I was afraid.

'Jane knows about . . . what's happened.'

I felt as though someone had punched me in the chest.

'Why?' I asked, stupid with shock, then comprehension dawned. '*They* told her, didn't they?'

'They?'

'Robert and . . . her.'

I couldn't bring myself to speak her name. That bitch Loveday.

'You're wrong, Mel. It was my decision. I did speak to my father about it, yes. We had a talk about . . . some of the hard truths. And he made me see that I was wrong . . . to get involved with you.' Edwin spoke in a wooden rehearsed way, but I could tell that the words had no connection with what he really felt inside. 'I couldn't in all conscience continue to be a priest if I were conducting an adulterous affair. And if I abandon my marriage I must leave the Church.'

For the first time I knew the meaning of the expression 'clutching at straws'.

'But we could go on as before . . . just meeting . . . without. . . .'

'No.' Edwin's face was expressionless, as though part of him was dead. He picked up a hymn-book from one of the pews and turned it over in his hands, brushing off a red rose petal from its surface. I watched the petal float to the floor. 'We can't ever see one another again.'

I found myself in my pink marble bathroom in Camelot.

I had been crying for several hours; crying and walking. I had sat on a bench in the Gardens for a while, until the harsh July sunlight hurt my eyes and gave me a headache. Then I walked down Clapham Road and on to the Common, walking, just walking aimlessly. . . .

The wireless was still in the bathroom from the fateful evening when I had prepared to go to meet Edwin. I switched it on.

'. . . In Berlin, the Reich Chancellor has spoken of his hopes for a united Germany. The National Socialist—'

I switched off the authoritative newscaster. I no longer cared about the struggle against fascism. Uncle Donald would have to carry on the fight alone. I looked at my face in the mirror. It was pink from the sun and swollen, my eyes scarcely visible. From far away, I was vaguely aware of Ethne rehearsing *Carmen*.

'*L'amour est enfant de Bohème*. . . .'

The music stopped, and there were footsteps on the stairs. Ethne tapped on the bathroom door. 'Mel, you've been in there an awfully long time. Are you all right?'

Had I? It had only seemed like seconds.

'Mmm,' I said loudly and twisted all four golden sylphs, two on the bath and two on the basin, so that the bathroom filled with gushing water and hissing steam. To compound the impression of ablutions in progress, I switched on the wireless again.

'. . . said that the Oxford Pledge has become a rallying cry for Youth of all ages.

'That was the the BBC news at nine o'clock. And now, on "In Town Tonight", we are proud to present Jack Payne and his orchestra. . . .'

Ethne's footsteps retreated. I opened the glass-fronted cabinet over the pink marble basin and divested it of its contents. A bottle of milk of magnesia, half a dozen painkillers the size of horse pills and a handful of aspirins at the bottom of a jar. I swallowed all the tablets and washed them down with a liberal dose of milk of magnesia.

Lying on my bed and feeling the room swim, I was seized with panic. And then once I accepted that I had done it, and it was too late to go back, I felt an incomparable sense of freedom. I was Ophelia, floating peacefully in the water.

The moment and the nun are come. The crisis and the revelation are passed by. . . .

The quotation from *Villette* floated unbidden into my mind, and I smiled. My last thought as I lapsed into unconsciousness was that there was nothing left to dread any more. I was simply . . . myself.

My body, however, had plans for survival. I woke up several hours later feeling very sick and found that I had wet the bed. So much for Ophelia.

I turned to Neville. There was no one else. Loveday was by now firmly entrenched with 'them' in my mind, in the other camp.

I had only been vaguely aware of Neville's existence over the months of my obsession with Edwin, but somehow he had always been there in the background, as a reassuring presence. I often saw him locking his front door and setting off from his house in the evening, and he would smile and wave at me. He did not look happy, but hurried and distracted.

Neville became my confidant.

I spent many hours sitting at his kitchen table and bemoaning the fate that had befallen me, to be cursed with wanting something I could never have. Neville didn't really understand.

'I don't know, girl . . .,' he said, stroking his moustache thoughtfully as we sat dunking biscuits in our tea. 'You've got to tell yourself this, that there's plenty more pebbles on the beach.'

'Not for you, there weren't,' I reminded him.

'Ah, but that was different. This fella's done you wrong.' I had drawn a discreet veil over the identity of my former lover. 'Men like him aren't worth bothering with.'

Neville didn't understand, but he would at least let me ramble on as much as I liked. And there was no one else. My parents were too engrossed in Ethne's latest concert tour.

'What about old Loveday, then?' asked Neville, when I told him for the umpteenth time how unlucky I was. 'What's she up to these days? Still swanning around up the West End? Only, you two were always such good mates. Never saw one without the other when you were little.'

'Loveday and I aren't speaking to one another,' I divulged.

Whether it was contrived or not, I don't know, but the next day Loveday showed up at Neville's house for a cup of tea after work. 'Someone here wants to talk to you,' said Neville as he led her in, then he tactfully withdrew.

'Go away,' I said. 'Bugger off.'

Loveday stood there looking pretty and chic, with a picture-hat sloping over one eye à la Ginger Rogers. She removed the hat, laid it carefully on the table and poured herself a cup of tea. 'I wondered where you'd been hiding.' She had abandoned the upper-class drawl in favour of the brisk bossy tone of old. 'I telephoned Camelot – eeugh, sounds ridiculous, doesn't it? – a couple of times, but you weren't there. I thought you might want to talk about . . . what happened the other night.'

I pushed my chair back from the table with such force that its wooden legs screeched on the linoleum. 'There's nothing to talk about. Jane Clifford knows all about it now. *Satisfied*, I hope?'

'Look, Mel, it's not the end of the world. Frankly, I'm amazed that Edwin confessed. It would have been much better if he'd lied. God, the very thought of guilty men blundering around making things harder than they already are – it makes me feel irritable. But all you have to do, surely, is let Jane Clifford think the two of you have split up, wait till things die down a bit and then start all over again.'

I stared at Loveday, appalled. 'Is that what you'd do?'

'Of course. It's the only logical thing to do.'

'*Logic!*' I shouted. 'What's logic got to do with it? I expect that sort of advice was Robert Clifford's idea, wasn't it? He's typical of the sort of people who run this country – the Old Guard – and if *that's* the sort of attitude they have, then it's no wonder the system—'

'Uncle Donald's politics won't help you now, Mel.'

I was rambling, lashing out in my anger, and she knew it. But I had to go on. I felt like a clockwork toy that had been wound up to its fullest potential and then set down, to go spinning and hurtling around in circles until all momentum was spent. I wheeled round to face Loveday again. 'What did you have to go and interfere for, anyway? You two must have put Edwin up to this! He wouldn't do something like that. He *loves* me—'

There was a resounding crash as Loveday slammed her teacup

down into her saucer. She stood up and came towards me, putting her hands on my shoulders. With her elegant high heels she was just about as tall as I was. 'You fool!' she hissed. 'You silly bloody romantic fool! Edwin Clifford's never going to make you happy! A man like that . . . yet another one stuffed full of guilt. . . . He doesn't know *what* he wants, Mel, that's his trouble—'

'Get out!' I pushed her away from me roughly. 'Get out! Go on, just get out!'

The end of August. Warm and muggy. And sad. There is something sad about that time of year, almost pitiful. The dying summer on its last legs. With the faintest hint of autumn creeping in around the edges of the jaded flowers. Full-blown flowers, sagging a little beneath their bright petals like middle-aged mistresses.

The shock of my severance from Loveday was greater than I had anticipated. I could no longer flee from the Gardens to her flat and sit and gossip beneath the fringed silk hangings. No Loveday, no Edwin. Just an empty aching void that threatened to bury me alive at Camelot.

'D'you think I should go and work for Uncle Donald's friend in Oxford?' I asked Mother. 'D'you think I could still go?'

Mother was in the garden at Camelot, snipping the dead heads off the roses. She paused to consider my question, shears in one hand, the other raised to the brim of her old straw hat, shading her eyes. 'Yes, yes, I do, dear,' she said eventually. 'I think you should go as soon as possible. It will do you good to get away from here. You've been doing nothing too long.' She bent and snipped at a stalk, and a beheaded rose rolled at my feet.

'You're right,' I said. 'I'll do it.'

Delighted that I had shaken off my apathy, Father set about arranging for me to start work in October at the beginning of the academic year.

The matter was already out of my hands by the time I discovered I wouldn't be able to go.

It was early one morning in September. I was in my bathroom in Camelot. I remember it so well. I don't think I'll ever forget that moment of dreadful fear. Downstairs I could hear the telephone ringing.

'Mel!' Mother called me.

'One minute. . . .'

I was trying to quell the trembling in my legs. Cold sweat was running down my forehead. I splashed my face with water and towelled it dry.

Mother was on the landing, outside the door. 'Mel, that was Uncle Donald's friend, Professor Millward. . . . She's still on the line now. She'd like to know if you can be in Oxford two weeks from now. . . .'

'Tell her yes,' I said, hardly taking in what Mother was saying. Anything to get rid of her. Then I retreated into the bathroom again and sat down on the edge of the bath. Mother could tell Professor Millward what she liked; I knew I wouldn't be going to Oxford. It wasn't that I didn't want the job. But it was too late for me to leave Magnolia Gardens now.

'So, you say you're in trouble?'

I had resorted to Neville, since Loveday was now out of the question. He stroked his moustache and dunked his biscuit in a cup of tea. 'You'd better tell me all about it.'

I did. When I had finished, he gave my hand a sympathetic squeeze. 'Tell you what – why don't you and me go up West tonight and cheer ourselves up? Just the two of us?'

Neville's idea of an evening's entertainment, I discovered, was to sit at a bar and empty one glass after another until he was sliding from the stool. We ended up in a place in Soho called Chez Alvaro's. The title's curious hybrid of French and Italian signified nothing except that the bar's owner was really called Alfred Blackhall and came from somewhere in Middlesex. A setting less likely to cheer one up is hard to imagine. Once one had penetrated a heavy bead curtain, the basement room was dimly lit, with just a dull gleam from the chrome and brass fittings. The walls were smothered liberally with signed photographs of little-known actors and actresses. The rain was leaking in from the ceiling, and there was a bucket standing on the bar to collect it. Alfred Blackhall seemed oblivious to any inconvenience this might cause his customers, moving to and fro to collect glasses and whistling 'O Sole Mio'.

'Neville?'

He was not listening to me, but staring into the back of the room where a singer had just bobbed up behind a huge microphone.

'What? Oh, yes. Here, this singer's pretty good, isn't he?'

I could scarcely see him through the haze of cigarette smoke. Once I had pierced the dreadful gloom, I could see that he was a good-looking young man, dark-skinned and sultry, with a luscious mouth and slightly oily black hair flopping over one eye. We sat and listened to him crooning tunelessly while Neville ordered himself another cocktail.

'Aren't you having one?' he asked.

I shook my head. 'No, thanks. I feel a bit sick.'

'What you need is young Loveday to sort you out. You should go and talk to her.'

'Nothing,' I said firmly, '*nothing* will induce me to do that.'

Neville shrugged. 'Have it your way. I don't see what I can do, though, except see you home safely.' The singer was just finishing his spot, and stepping down from the platform to some half-hearted applause. Neville watched him, then turned back to face me. 'Tell you what – why don't we leave now? You look done in.'

He hailed a cab, but after handing me into it he bent to kiss my cheek.

'Aren't you coming?' I asked.

'No, I've got to go and see a man about a dog. You'll get home safe, won't you?'

I got the taxi-driver to put me down in the Strand. I wasn't ready to go home yet. I wanted just to walk and think. I didn't really look where I was going, staring down at the dark pavements, greasy with rain, relying on other people to steer a course round me. Before long I had gone full circle and was back in Soho, near Chez Alvaro's.

Then I saw Neville. He was walking fast, with his head down and his collar turned up, and there was someone with him, another man. Instinctively I began to follow him, weaving my way through a forest of neon lights and honking taxis, crowds leaving the theatre. They headed up Dean Street and then west, into Peter Street and then to smaller, darker streets that didn't have names. I started to wonder how I would get home, and realised that I might not have enough money. I did an extra spurt to try to catch Neville.

They had stopped on a corner outside a small dingy building whose broken sign read 'THE CAMELOT HOTEL'. I shuddered at the coincidence. The two of them spoke for a while, and the stranger smoked a cigarette. His face was in shadow, so I couldn't see who he was. Then Neville put his hand on the man's arm. He threw his cigarette butt into the gutter, and the two of them moved off into a narrow alley that led from the street. I crossed the street so that I was outside the Camelot Hotel, and peered round the corner.

'Neville?'

The two of them were embracing. Seeing stubbly masculine jaws rubbing against one another as they kissed, I was reminded of the dance-hall of the Montagne St-Geneviève in Paris, and I experienced the same stabbing sensation that was half revulsion, half disappointment. As their movements became more urgent they stepped sideways to where the beam of a street-lamp just penetrated the alley, and the thin yellowish light illuminated the sultry features of the singer from Chez Alvaro's.

He was unbuckling his trousers and his upper thighs gleamed starfish white.

I stared, unable to turn and run away, but unable to watch any further. Giving way to a mad impulse, I lunged between them, sabotaging their coupling, crying: 'No, no, not that!'

'What the—?' Neville stared at me in astonishment while the singer buttoned his trousers and lit a cigarette, looking sulky rather than ashamed or embarrassed.

'What the bloody hell do you think you're doing?' hissed Neville, his eyes narrowed with fury. 'You had no right to follow me like that. Push off, d'you hear me!'

I stared back at him wordlessly.

And then he laughed at my horrified expression. 'Love is sordid. I thought you'd just found that out for yourself!'

I turned and ran through the streets, taking wrong turnings, jumping in front of cars, knocking into astonished pedestrians.

Eventually I found myself on Waterloo Bridge and slowed to a walk, staring at the inky river and snivelling quietly to myself. Behind me were the lights of Soho and a hundred sordid assignations such as those I had just witnessed. Ahead lay Magnolia Gardens, and the unpalatable facts of my own life. Who was I to make moral distinctions?

Hurried footsteps drew level and slowed to my own pace.

'Please,' said Neville, 'I need to talk to you. I'm sorry . . . I shouldn't have spoken to you like that.'

In reply I simply sighed and linked my arm through his.

Neville lit a cigarette and started to explain. It had begun, he said, before the war, when he was working at a place called the Dover Hotel.

'But did you *want* . . .? I mean, did you love men, not women? I was thinking of Rosheen. . . .'

At the mention of her name, Neville's lips moved in response but soundlessly, like a film with no soundtrack. A cloud of cigarette smoke hung around him in the cold night air.

'It's got nothing to do with love, you've got to realise that, Mel.'

'Is it the money, then? Were you . . . meeting this man for money?'

Neville shook his head. 'Not this time. Sometimes. I just fell into my old ways again after Rosheen was gone. A way of comforting myself, I suppose. It's just like a drug really; you can't stop it. You just see someone – you know, looking at you – and that's it. But it's not about love; for me it's not even about pleasure. It's about losing yourself. Does that make sense?'

I nodded my agreement.

'But you hold on to your dreams of love, somehow, girl; don't let go.' Neville sighed, blowing out another cloud of smoke. 'If you do that, you've had it.'

'DEAR MEL, COME ROUND AS SOON AS YOU CAN, YOU'VE GOT TO HELP ME, PLEASE, I'M DESPERATE.'

I stared at the incoherent, scrawled note that had been pushed through the letterbox of Camelot. It was from Neville.

In the week that had passed since our trip to Soho he had shut himself away from me, avoiding me.

'What's all this about, then?' I asked Neville, confronting him in his kitchen with the note. 'Are you in some sort of trouble with men?'

He nodded, opening one of the cupboards and fumbling about in it. 'It's about this.'

He held out an engraved silver goblet. 'I stole it,' he said, and then to my horror he began to cry.

I took the silver cup from his hand and examined it. Even to an ignorant layman like myself, it was obviously very old and very precious. 'Good God, it's not from the church, is it, Neville?'

He shook his head, taking out a handkerchief and blowing his nose. 'It's from my boss; I nicked it from my boss.'

I tried to be brisk, but was hopeless at it. 'You'd better tell me about it, over a nice cup of tea,' I said, but couldn't find the kettle or light the gas-stove. So Neville made the tea and found a plate of cakes, which I ate one by one as he talked.

'The boss had us backroom boys over to his place for drinks – it's a cheap way of avoiding giving us a rise. Anyway, I saw this thing just sitting there in the hall and I slipped it into my overcoat pocket—'

'But *why*, Neville, why? What on earth did you want it for?'

'The money. I was going to sell it and then use the cash. I'm being blackmailed, Mel.'

I put the cake down and stared at him in horror, my sticky fingers poised in mid-air.

'*Blackmail?* Oh, Neville, surely not. What—?'

'It's this fellow at work. He saw me. Oh Christ! I hate having to tell you this. . . .' Neville paced the room, making sure his back was towards me when he said: 'He caught me in the gents' with this other bloke. And he threatened to tell if I didn't pay up – just a bit each week. I've used up all my savings, so when I saw this silver thing I thought I could sell it for a few bob; then at least I'd be able to buy myself some groceries—'

'But, Neville, how *terrible*! Why didn't you ask me?'

'I couldn't. Not with all the troubles you've got already. I just couldn't. And I was idiot enough to think this thing wasn't very valuable, but when he came into work on the Monday – the boss – there was a hell of a shindig about it. Turns out its from eastern Europe and there's only one like it in the world, or something; anyway, if I'd known, I never would have touched it, but it was too late. I couldn't put it back, could I?' Neville's shoulders heaved. 'And then Osborne – the boss – went crazy when we all denied it and said it had to be one of the people who was in his house that day and that the coppers are going to come round and question us all at home and that they'll ask permission to search. . . .' He swung round to face me. 'I've got to get rid of the fucking thing, Mel. Will you help me?'

Finding the right solution proved almost impossible. We couldn't sell or pawn the cup; it was too easily identifiable. I suggested throwing it into someone's dustbin, but this was vetoed on the grounds that we might be seen. Besides, an honest dustman – and we had to assume there were some – would hand it in to the police, and it was covered with Neville's fingerprints. Neville wanted me to take the dreadful object and hide it somewhere at Camelot, but I was worried that it might be found by one of the maids, or even that the police would ask to search other houses in the neighbourhood.

'I think we should bury it,' said Neville. 'Not in my garden, but yours is big enough. . . .'

'Out of the question. . . . Mother spends all her time digging in that garden, and she knows every inch of it by heart.'

In the end I did the only thing I could think of. I telephoned Loveday.

'Very nice,' said Loveday, handling the silver goblet. 'But we really can't have it just sitting around like this, can we?'

We were in my bedroom at Camelot. Loveday wrapped the offending object in a pair of my Parisian silk knickers and replaced it in my underwear drawer. It was odd to be sitting there with her, almost like old times. Except that we weren't friends now. We were temporary allies because we both wanted to help poor Neville. Robert and Edwin hung unmentioned between us. The cross-currents of the past months were still there, dividing the two camps, and we behaved with a dreadful still coldness.

She picked up my battered teddy bear and gave him a playful punch.

'It'll have to be tonight,' she said. 'This is a bloody ridiculous situation,' she went on, with her usual bluntness. 'And I can't help feeling we're only making things worse in the long run, but if that's what Neville wants us to do, then so be it. He's had such a hard time lately, I don't see how we can refuse.'

I had told Loveday about what happened when we went to the bar in Soho.

'We're being accomplices, aren't we, really? In an Agatha Christie book of Mother's—'

'Life isn't like a book, Mel!' snapped Loveday, picking up my hairbrush and pulling it through her abundant red-brown locks. 'But we ought to get it over and done with as soon as possible.'

'What are we going to do?'

'Bury it, of course. In my mother's garden.'

*   *   *

267

My alarm clock went off at three in the morning; its shrill cry bursting into my dream.

I was dreaming that Edwin was dead. The strange thing was that I couldn't grieve or feel any sense of loss. I was at the funeral. I got as far as looking at the coffin – and then I was distracted by the vision of myself dressed in stunning black, looking the picture of bereaved beauty, and the church bells were ringing, ringing. . . .

It took me a few moments to recall why I had set my alarm clock. When I remembered I panicked, afraid that I would be late, blundering around my bedroom looking for clothes, trying to open and shut drawers without making a noise. I dressed myself in a black jersey and slacks like a cat-burglar, anxious to feel the part.

My accomplice was nowhere to be seen, however, when I crept around the side of number 47 and into the back garden.

'Loveday?'

'Shut up, Mel!' she hissed, appearing from the shadows. She had found some reason to stay at Magdalena's for the night, and was still dressed in her nightgown, which shone blue-white in the moonlight. 'Have you got the thing?' she whispered.

I nodded and held out my gloved hand.

'Well, come on, then. . . .'

She led me to the bottom of the garden, to the base of a large chestnut tree which grew near to the garden wall. The only tools she had at her disposal were a kitchen spoon and a fork ('I couldn't find the key to the garden shed'), so digging a deep hole was a laborious business. We crouched in the shadow of the tree, I kneeling and Loveday squatting on her heels to avoid getting mud on her *peau d'Ève* nightdress.

'Couldn't you have worn something else?' I whispered.

'I only had a dress and high heels.'

We dug in stony silence, Loveday picking at the wet earth with her manicured nails while I dug in my fingers in a more earnest attempt to clear away the earth. The garden looked strange and fantastic in the moonlight, an unfamiliar landscape with its silver lawn and blue-grey branches probing an inky sky.

Suddenly what we were doing seemed very funny indeed.

I leaned back on my heels and laughed out loud. 'Whoever would have thought—'

'*Sssh, Mel!*'

'Whoever would have thought', I whispered, 'that on the twenty-ninth of October 1933 you and I would find ourselves at the bottom of a garden, burying stolen goods.' I laughed harder, toppling over and dropping my fork with a clatter on top of the silver goblet, which gleamed on the lawn like pirates' treasure.

'*Mel!*' Loveday looked as though she might become annoyed, but then she changed her mind and joined in my laughter. 'It is utterly ridiculous,' she agreed.

We turned back to the task in hand and our hole, which was so far only about two inches deep, but the tension between us had eased.

'Mel . . . about Edwin.'

I looked up, crushing the wet sticky soil between my fingers.

'You've stopped seeing him, haven't you?'

'Yes.' I uttered the word in as neutral a tone as I could muster.

'Only I want you to know that I wasn't judging you. And I *didn't* interfere over Jane, whatever you think. I just wanted what was best for you.'

I nodded slowly. 'I know. I was getting angry with the wrong person.' I picked up the silver goblet and stroked its cold smooth surface. 'What about you and Robert?'

Loveday shrugged. 'I don't know.'

'I mean, are you in love with him?'

'Not in love, no.'

'Then, why do you do it?'

Loveday lifted her delicate pointed chin; I thought that it was a gesture of stubbornness, but then an extraordinary thing happened.

Her chin trembled and she began to cry. Loveday, who never cried.

'Oh God . . . oh God, Mel . . . !' She flung herself down on the grass, sobbing wildly, her shoulders heaving. I moved over and touched her gently, patting and stroking her, still amazed that it was Loveday who had lost control and I, for the first time, who was the comforter. This was what our friendship needed all these years, I reflected, for our roles to be reversed occasionally, for me to be the giver.

'My life's such a bloody mess, you know!'

Loveday sat up again, unconcerned by the muddy streaks on her nightdress. The tears still glittered on her cheeks. 'Oh, wanting no one was very pleasant in its way, very safe, even rather superior,' she said fiercely, 'but I only did it because I was afraid of letting on. That I cared about anyone. And that I hated not knowing who the hell I am. Whatever sort of coupling went into my making it was very probably sordid!'

'You don't know that, Loveday—'

'That's exactly it!' She forgot that we weren't supposed to be raising our voices. 'I don't know . . . and inside I feel . . . it's so hard to express this, but . . . inside I can't *feel* myself. . . . It's as though I'm grasping for something that's not there. I have no sense of self. No identity. That's why we were always so different, you and I.'

I sat in silence, toying with my fork and musing on the differences between us. 'But that was why I admired you so much, Loveday. You loved things like logic and reason. I feared them. You seemed so . . . *sure*.'

'I had to appear to be sure; I had no choice. I had no one to fall back on. I *am* no one – just a tart really. I'm not important to anybody.'

'You're important to me,' I said gently. 'And to Robert, presumably.'

'Perhaps. But I always feel that he can discard me when he chooses. I'm disposable – like I was to Edwin.'

I stared at her.

'No, I don't suppose he told you, did he? While you were in Switzerland, before he went abroad, he . . . we. . . .'

It came to me in a flash, and suddenly I understood. Why Loveday had changed the subject or turned sour whenever I mentioned Edwin. Instead of feeling angry I took courage from Loveday's vulnerability, and her honesty.

I picked up the silver goblet and laid it tenderly in its bed of earth. Then: 'I'm pregnant, Loveday.'

She leaned back on to the grass with a sigh. 'I see. How long is it since you've had your—?'

'I've missed three.'

Loveday sighed again; a long whistling sound. 'And I really believed the incorruptible Edwin when he said he was innocent.'

'It only happened once.'

'Once?' Loveday laughed. 'I'm sorry, darling, I know it's not funny, but – oh, Mel – it could only happen to you!'

Loveday sorted me out.

'I can't go to Oxford now,' I wailed.

'Why not?' she demanded, brisk and practical as ever. 'It's the perfect alibi. Everyone will think you've gone to Oxford to work for Professor What's-her-name, and only you and I will know that you've really gone to have a baby. And your Uncle Donald. We're going to need his help.'

Between the two of them, Loveday and Donald arranged lodgings for me with the wife of a sympathetic don who had a lot of young children and a large rambling house in Norham Gardens. I was duly packed up and despatched, unable to look my parents in the eye and thanking God that they had Ethne's career to pre-occupy them.

I began to wish I had taken the job after all, because just waiting for the baby was dreadfully dull. I suppose I pretended it wasn't real, that it wasn't really going to happen to *me*. I read everything the Brontës had ever written and wandered around in a Lucy Snowe-like daze.

Then one day I was walking down Cornmarket when I had a terrible shock. I saw a young mother, struggling past me with a pram and two ill-kempt children clinging to its handle. She was pregnant, her stomach bulging hugely.

I stared at her and, as I did so, I was aware that I was becoming horribly upset; I just couldn't escape this feeling of mounting panic, nor could I stop looking at her. Very soon, I would be as fat as her, and then I would have a baby that I didn't know what to do with. And people would pass one in the street and see me looking as wretched as she was.

Cold waves of shock rolled over me, and at last I allowed myself to realise fully that my life was changing, for ever. I blundered amongst the students with their bicycles and baskets full of books, avoiding looking anyone in the face. I was on my way to All Souls to see Donald. I *had* to talk to someone.

There was another shock in store for me that day.

'Your dad's here,' said Donald as he opened the door to me. 'He found out about you not taking the job.'

It's difficult to imagine Father looking grim-faced or acting in a Victorian fashion but, sure enough, he was. He even had his hands clasped behind his back.

'I thought it was something like this,' he said, eyeing my midriff with contempt. As if aware of the scrutiny, the baby chose this moment to make its presence felt for the first time, a strange fluttering.

'I thought I was doing the best for you!' he shouted. 'Sending you away to that bleedin' place in France—'

'Switzerland.'

'Don't you cheek me! You had everything a girl could want. Living in a nice place like Magnolia Gardens—'

'At *Camelot*?' I sneered. 'Father, you can't protect yourself from the world by spending money!'

He sighed, and all the blustering went out of him, leaving him suddenly small and vulnerable.

'You're right.' He hugged me fiercely. 'But . . . oh, Mel, I wanted so much for you! I wanted you to be bleedin' prime minister! I thought I could help you get what you wanted!'

I patted him, comforted him. Taller than him with my shoes on, I pressed his head against my shoulder. 'You were the one who always said you can't buy happiness.'

'I know, sweetheart, I know. I never wanted to buy it for myself. But I would have killed to get it for you!' He took out a large handkerchief and blew his nose loudly. 'What are we going to do about this pickle?'

'Father, there's no need—'

His hand closed over my mouth.

'No arguments. You helped me over that Italian business; you accepted what I did and you didn't moralise. Now it's my turn to do the same. . . . Now, you'll need money, somewhere decent to bring up my grandson—'

'Or grand-daughter.'

'Grandson,' he said firmly, and I wondered how much he'd wanted a son. 'I don't suppose you're going to tell me who knocked you up!'

'No.' I felt myself blush.

'Well, have you told *him* about it yet?'

'No, not yet.' Then I answered before he could ask the next question. 'Not ever.'

I didn't think she would do it, but I had to make sure.

After Father had finished rearranging my life in Oxford – a process which included setting me up with a small house of my own – I telephoned Loveday and asked her to come to Oxford for a weekend. I met her at the station and we went for a walk in the University Parks together.

It was early November and a most perfect autumn day, the air cold and invigorating to the lungs, the colours of the sky and the falling leaves crisp and clean; blue, gold and red. We paused on the little bridge that crosses the Cherwell.

I picked up a stick and dropped it into the still water. 'I'm glad Neville won't have to go to prison. I hope he'll be all right.'

'You let me think about that,' said Loveday, a trifle tartly.

I smiled. I had got my old Loveday back again; bossy, bullying, ordering the affairs of others.

'You'll have enough to worry about over the next few months.'

Burying stolen goods in Magdalena Stark's garden had brought Loveday and I together again but, apart from that, it had been futile. The police had come to question Neville, and he had broken down and confessed to the theft. Of course he never once mentioned our names, claiming that he had sneaked into the garden of number 47 and buried it himself.

'With a knife and a fork, by the look of it,' said the phlegmatic policeman who came to exan and confessed to the theft. Of course he never once mentioned our names, claiming that he had sneaked into the garden of number 47 and buried it himself.

'With a knife and a fork, by the look of it,' said the phlegmatic policeman who came to examine our lumpy untidy cache. 'Not exactly a professional job, is it?'

Although it would be an exaggeration to say the police were amused, they seemed at least prepared to be lenient, and with the help of Robert Clifford an able barrister was found, and Neville escaped with a heavy fine.

We left the bridge and walked on. Undergraduates strolled in groups or couples, and children were playing in the piles of leaves under the watchful eye of a grey-uniformed nanny.

'And what about you, Loveday?' I asked. 'What will you do?'

'I'll go on as before, I suppose. Dulong's seem satisfied with me, and Robert's extended the lease on the flat. . . .' She didn't sound happy. 'And I'll keep an eye on your family, darling,' she said more brightly. 'Especially that sister of yours.'

One subject hovered over us, unmentioned. Edwin.

I had to speak. 'Loveday,' I said, 'I don't want you to tell Edwin . . . what's really happened to me. You and Donald and Father are the only people who know about the baby, and I want it to stay that way. If Edwin found out about it, he might try to "do the decent thing" – whatever that means.' I sighed. 'And I couldn't bear to think that *I* had ruined his career in the Church.'

Loveday raised an eyebrow. 'Are you sure that's the reason, Mel? Are you sure you're not running away from reality again? Afraid that your relationship with Edwin might turn out to be . . . a disappointment?'

I didn't contradict her. I stared up at the golden leaves of a maple tree, their outline hard and spiky against the dazzling blue sky. 'Whatever the reason,' I said slowly, 'I want you to promise that you won't tell him. Not just about the baby, but where I've gone to. I need that peace of mind. Will you promise, Loveday?'

'I promise.'

I turned and looked at her. Wisps of bright hair escaped from her fur-trimmed hat, and the thick fur collar of her coat framed her small pointed face. Her eyes sparkled, and the colour in her cheeks was unusually bright. Dear Loveday. . . .

'I trust you,' I said simply.

And linking my arm through hers, leaning on her, I walked on into the bright autumn sunshine.

47 Magnolia Gardens

Loveday

I FOUND THE LETTER ON MY DOORMAT when I got back from Dulong's.

It was from Mel, announcing the birth of her son on 21 March 1934. I waded through several pages of hyperbole.

'. . . *God, the pain, Loveday; you can't imagine the dreadful pain, I felt as though I was giving birth to an elephant and I was surely going to die. Anyway, after what seemed like two days of this, He arrived. He is Gabriel Finzel and he is wonderful, though I can't imagine why some women want to have more than one child. I'd never willingly go through that again.*

'*After he was born I took one look at him and burst into tears. "Poor little beggar," I said to the nurse. "Take him away."*

'*But now I think he's lovely. He's small and fair and has a sort of lucky look to him. I think he's going to be luckier than I ever was. . . .*'

I heard the door of the lift clanging, and then the sound of a key in the lock.

Robert.

He towered in the doorway, exquisitely dressed as ever, and suddenly my flat seemed small, as it always did when he was there. He made it into a doll's house.

'You look as lovely as ever, darling,' he said, with punctilious charm, and handed me a bunch of roses.

After this overture, the ritual began; a ritual that never varied from one meeting to the next. Robert liked a sense of order, a neatness to his life.

First he took off his expensive cashmere overcoat and put it on a hanger, the same hanger that always hung on the back of the sitting-room door. He removed his bowler hat, and put it with his briefcase, on a carved Turkish chest that stood near the door. Always in the same place.

Then: 'Drink, darling?' He always said that. He went to the

tray and poured a Scotch and soda for himself and a gin for me. That was what we usually had.

The Clifford family's affairs would be next on the agenda. Robert never ceased to amaze me with his fondness for chatting to me about his family, as though I were still Helena's secretary and not his mistress.

'. . . so Zanna's taken up with this Bloomsbury set. . . . Sharing a house with a couple of theatrical types in Gordon Square. And now, apparently, she's publishing a book herself.'

'*Rosanna?* She's written a book? But she's only a child!'

'She's nineteen. What sort of a book can a nineteen-year-old write? Probably not much of one, is the answer. It'll be a load of self-indulgent nonsense, if I know Zanna, but I'm glad she has something to keep her occupied. . . .'

Robert welcomed any news that would lessen his overpowering sense of guilt towards his children. He stood up and drew the curtains, which was the usual preliminary to our lovemaking. It was a symbolic gesture as much as anything, since the bedroom window was too high for prying eyes and we were not going to bed in order to sleep. Robert liked to draw the curtains and retreat into a world of decent standards, Christian worship, feminine modesty and, of course, gross sexual hypocrisy. A mistress was a good thing to have as long as she kept to her allotted place – in bed, behind closed curtains, high up in an apartment block away from the eyes of the Establishment. No doubt many of the other barristers in his practice did exactly the same; but of course they would never, ever talk about it. I kicked against this convention, insisting that Robert take me out and about in town and risk being seen with me. Hence that evening at the Silver Slipper when, by a chance in a million, we bumped into Edwin and Mel. But increasingly Robert shied away from these outings. He was very much a part of the pre-war world of E. M. Forster and H. G. Wells, and he was a fish out of water now that world had been abolished. He was ill at ease with the new political consciousness and the doings of the Bright Young Things.

I looked at him now as he undressed and folded his clothes in the usual neat methodical way, still feeling a shiver go through me as his large naked body loomed towards me. He had a high colour, but his looks had never become florid; his hair still gleamed golden beneath the brilliantine, and his figure was remarkably trim for a fifty-five-year-old man. And he exuded the same sense of power that had awed me so much in Edwin – power that came from snobbery, and financial security and the firm belief that the world has reserved a special place for you.

It was Robert's quality of certainty and self-confidence that was responsible for our affair. He had been the initiator, but I was quick to see what he could offer. After Edwin had left for the Continent he had been there all the time, watching me at my work, instigating numerous small acts of kindness. I was irritated at first, still angry and hurt over his son's rejection, but after a while I began to find myself listening for his step and missing him on the days I didn't see him.

On Christmas Eve 1932, I was given the afternoon off by Helena to do some Christmas shopping. It was a damp sleety afternoon, and I returned from the West End shops on the bus, struggling back from the bus-stop in the dark with my armful of parcels. A car pulled up at the kerb as I picked my way through the slush in my high heels.

'This won't do at all. We can't have this!' said a familiar voice, and Robert Clifford swept me and my parcels into his black Daimler.

'I didn't have far to go . . . only back to Magnolia Gardens. . . .'

'Nonsense, you're soaked through, my dear. What you need inside you is a good stiff drink!' And he whisked me off to a pub on the edge of Clapham Common which boasted a discreet 'saloon' bar, and bought me a couple of brandies. His manners were impeccable, and he didn't lay a finger on me – except, of course, to help me out of the car.

The next morning 47 Magnolia Gardens was awash with hot-house lilies. There was no card with them.

'Did you like the flowers?' asked Robert in a low voice after he had returned from his chambers the next day. He stood over me in the study as I typed my way through Helena's interminable letters.

And I realised then that he was laying siege to me. Discreetly, out of sight of Helena. There were more flowers, more 'chance' meetings which resulted in us spending the evening together drinking, and then: 'My dear Loveday . . . you deserve better than . . . better than a job as Helena's secretary. I think I could help you. . . .'

This was what I had been waiting for. I liked Robert enough to let him make love to me. But I remembered my vow. Only when he had given me what I wanted.

'What I'd really like to do is leave Magnolia Gardens altogether,' I said, over lunch in Robert's favourite oyster bar near the Temple. Helena Clifford believed that I was running about town doing errands for her.

'What would you like to do?' asked Robert, helping himself to rice pudding. He was one of those well-bred Englishmen who had never quite grown up, and given his own way he would have eaten nothing but nursery food. 'Zanna said something once about you being an actress. Is that what you'd like to do?'

I shook my head. 'Not any more,' I said, thinking of my brief foray into the theatrical world. 'That's not the sort of life I want. I'd like to have a turn at ordering other people around; that would be a nice change. . . .'

A few days later Robert came up with the job of manageress at Dulong's. Then came the flat.

'You'll need somewhere to live, my dear. . . . I could arrange something. . . . Perhaps one of these pretty little houses on Clapham Common . . .?'

'No,' I insisted, 'it has to be on the other side of the river.'

We met in Hyde Park in order for him to hand over the keys. We stood on the path, a few feet apart, and he placed them in my hand. I looked down at them for a moment – bright shiny things – before closing my fist around them. Only then did I allow Robert to kiss me, which he did with fervour.

'Oh, Loveday . . . my dear . . . I've been wanting to do that ever since I first set eyes on you. Let's go there now straight away – to your flat.'

'Oh, yes,' I agreed, as enthusiastic as he was. But I was not thinking about making love to Robert. I was thinking about having a home of my own at last.

'Oh, Robert!' I said when we unlocked the front door of the flat.

'Yes, I know, darling, we're alone at last!' He started to kiss my neck.

'The furniture will have to go,' I said. 'This isn't exactly my taste. . . .'

'Mmm.' He was nuzzling my neck.

'. . . and I'll have to redecorate.'

He carried me into the bedroom and laid me on the bed, unbuttoning my blouse. 'God, you're so beautiful. My beautiful little Loveday. . . .'

I was looking over his shoulder at the Regency-stripe wall-paper. That would definitely have to go, I decided.

'Oh, Loveday, oh God. . . .' Robert lifted my hips and pressed me hard against him.

. . . and the hideous little wall-lights.

And so it began. I spent days rooting through junk shops to find old forgotten bits of Art Nouveau and oriental silks to drape over the furniture. I hung mandarin chimes from the ceiling and found curious lampshades that gave a muted light. I failed to find satin sheets in Gamage's but tracked them down in Soho. And finally I painted the walls red.

'What do you think?' I asked Robert when it was finished.

'Lovely, darling,' he said, forcing a smile. It was clearly not to his taste, but he was so anxious to humour me that he was prepared to keep his opinions to himself. 'As long as you're happy with it.'

I was delighted. It was my place and it reflected me. It symbolised my escape. For I had made sure that nothing in it would remind me of Magnolia Gardens. This place would be the antithesis of that dull suburban world.

'What are you thinking about, darling – is it, Rosanna?'

After we had made love I was lying very still and very quiet next to Robert, staring at the tiny patch of grey March sky that was visible through the closed curtains. I was thinking about Mel. Despite the problems of unmarried motherhood, I couldn't help feeling that she had escaped somehow. She had the baby, she had problems, and yet she was managing on her own without a man. She had achieved a sort of independence that I didn't have. I looked around the room at the furnishings I had insisted on. Were they enough for me?

'Robert,' I said, placing my hand on his arm, where it looked very small and very white, 'I've been thinking, darling. . . . There really isn't any need for you to go on forking out all this money on the flat; I earn quite a bit at Dulong's, and I have some savings. I could get a place of my own—'

'No need for that, surely!' Robert sat up and faced me. He was smiling his easy smile, but I could see from his eyes that he was afraid. 'If you're dissatisfied because we don't go out enough, we can change all that, can't we? Easy as blinking. Tell you what, I'll take a day off tomorrow and we can go out into the country somewhere, go to the races. How about that, eh? You'd like that, wouldn't you?'

I smiled back at him, reassuring him as if he was a child. 'It's an utterly wonderful idea, Robert. But not tomorrow. Tomorrow I have to go and see my mother.'

'Bridie's gone,' she said.

Mother was sitting in her rocking chair in the sitting room at number 47. This chair, which she had had since before my birth, was now favoured over the white ottoman. She sat in it for hours, just rocking, rocking. . . .

'Bridie's gone, you know, dead.'

I didn't speak, but she glanced at me and said as if I had: 'Bridie was one of the old crowd. From the old days. At the Dover. . . .'

As a rule, Mother was disinclined to talk about her past. I seized my chance.

'My father was one of the old crowd, too, wasn't he?'

'What?' She hadn't heard me, or at least pretended not to.

'My father. He was one of the "old crowd"?'

Mother passed her hand over her eyes wearily. 'Not now. . . .' She reached past me to the table and took a cigarette out of a packet.

She looked terrible. She had put on even more weight, her hair was coarse and lifeless, and her pale skin had a faintly purple tinge to it. I had been worried about her of late; that was why I had taken time off work to visit her. Mother had never been energetic, and for as long as I could remember she had been a late riser, but she had plenty of friends and an independent lifestyle. Now she seemed to have lost her will to do anything. I watched her in silence as she extinguished one cigarette and lit another.

'Mother, are you all right?'

'All right?' She looked at me balefully, and I glimpsed some of her old spirit. 'Of course I'm all right, you fool!'

And she sent me into the kitchen to make her a cup of tea with some gin in it.

* * *

A few weeks later Robert burst into my flat in a terrible state, his habitual sang-froid gone.

'Look at that, will you! Look at it! What the hell am I going to do?'

He flung a copy of the *Daily Herald* on to the coffee-table. The front-page headline jumped out at me: 'BARRISTER'S DAUGHTER IN OBSCENITY TRIAL.'

'Robert? What the—?'

'Read it!'

I ran my eyes rapidly down the column. According to the journalist, nineteen-year-old Rosanna Clifford, 'only daughter of top society lawyer', had written a semi-fictionalised account of her sexual relations with another woman, and her publishers, a left-wing outfit in Bloomsbury, were being prosecuted under the Obscene Publications Act.

'And no doubt hoping to boost their sales figures as a result,' I said, leaning back on the sofa and toying with the fringe of the Indian-silk shawl that was draped over it.

Robert looked horrified at my cynicism. 'Dear God, girl, have you no idea what this means? Quite apart from the effect of my career, what the hell's it going to do to my family?'

I didn't want to think about the Clifford family. I had been growing increasingly uncomfortable and claustrophobic in my relationship with Robert. My secret knowledge about Mel's child, his grandson, nagged away at me, and frequently made me tense when Robert talked about his children. He did so now.

'I can't understand what I've done wrong,' he said, unfastening his tie and groping around in the cabinet for a bottle of brandy. 'Rosanna . . . Rosanna's a *lesbian*.' He paused over the word, rubbing salt in his own wound. 'Hughie's a spoilt brat, and Edwin . . . well' – he drained the brandy from his glass – 'I suppose Edwin's done better than the rest of them, but even he went off the rails, didn't he? Abandoning his vestments and cavorting around in nightclubs while his wife runs the parish. . . .'

I let him ramble on in this vein for a while. But when I suggested that there might be something wrong with his marriage he was wildly defensive, insisting that Helena was 'all right'.

'But how do you know she's all right?' I demanded. 'What does "all right" mean?'

'Oh, you know. . . . She has her lunches and her cocktail-parties and her accounts in the right shops—'

'And in return you have me?'

'Something like that. She knows there is . . . someone. She doesn't know who, of course, but she knows. And she accepts it. It's part of the arrangement that we've . . . evolved over the years. Other couples do the same. As long as it doesn't intrude. . . .'

I think it was then that I decided that I couldn't go on seeing Robert any more, that I didn't want to be part of his 'arrangement' with the glacial Helena.

'But I really came to talk to you about the trial. It starts at the Old Bailey tomorrow. I want to be there. If the press are going to make mincemeat of us, I want a chance to make a statement, at least. Otherwise they'll be camping on our doorstep.'

'Have you seen the book?'

'I've got hold of a copy, yes.'

He fumbled inside his black leather briefcase and took it out. *A Tender Rose* was the title, in Gothic script, and beneath it a badly drawn picture of a rosebud being attacked by a phallic-looking worm.

'Oh dear . . .,' I said. I flicked through the pages, trying to glean the gist of the story. In essence the heroine (who sometimes, confusingly, took on a male ego and referred to herself as 'he') had a lonely and repressive childhood and subsequently fell in love with an older, married woman, whom she seduced by the assault of her forceful personality. The two characters repaired frequently to bed, where their lovemaking was punctuated by much angst.

'Absolute filth, of course,' said Robert.

I reread a paragraph.

She lay in mysterious stillness. I kissed her breast softly and felt it rouse. She sighed, and her sigh warmed me like a tropic breeze. 'Ah, my love,' she said, as I rubbed my cheek against her belly and touched the secret skin of her thighs, 'come! Come inside me, and I'll make a man of maid. . . .'

'Oh, I don't know . . .,' I said. 'It depends how you look at it. It's self-indulgent certainly, but it's also something that she wanted to say. *Something* must have . . . must have driven her—'

'Yes! Driven her into a torrent of . . . of *filth* . . . and abuse. . . . Will you come to the court with me, Loveday, please! I feel I must be there, but I'm afraid of being there alone.'

'What about Helena?'

'She won't come, of course. She doesn't want anything to do with the whole business. She's more or less disowned Rosanna. You know Helena – it's her way.'

'But if I go with you we might be photographed – everyone will see us. It'll all be open.'

'I don't care about that any more. They can think what they like. I *need* you to be there, Loveday!'

I went to the Old Bailey with Robert the next day, though I knew that my motives were all wrong. I was fired by curiosity more than by a wish to help Robert. Walking up the steep steps to the imposing door of the court, with Robert a discreet yard ahead of me, I felt rather as though I was attending a society wedding. I was dressed in my best clothes and, although my suit and hat were dark, I had the same feeling of being groomed for a ritual. There was that same sense of adrenalin-filled expectancy in the air. Journalists were scattered in our wake as we walked smartly down the corridor to the courtroom, my heels making a defiant ringing sound on the highly polished parquet floors.

'Mr Clifford, over here, over here, please!' There was a wheeze and a pop from a camera flash-gun, and Robert and I narrowly avoided being photographed together.

The trial would have been quite amusing if it hadn't been for the presence of Rosanna in the front row, dressed in a man's suit, her hair raggedly cropped. She sat on the very edge of her seat, her back slightly bowed, and her eyes wore the watchful look of a hunted animal.

The portly prosecuting barrister, sporting his silly wig (I wondered what Robert looked like in his), stood up and read a passage from *A Tender Rose* in a Sunday-school voice, pausing with an actor's delivery over words like 'buttock' and 'climax', so that the jury squirmed visibly in their seats and an excited ripple ran through the press gallery. He must have had fun combing the book for the most sensational passage he could find, I thought with contempt.

The jury were to decide, first, whether the book would deprave and corrupt, and second, whether the publishers had it in their possession for gain. After an hour they returned a unanimous verdict: Guilty. *A Tender Rose* would be banned.

A great cry went up from the press, and they raced for the door to begin their pursuit. Robert took my arm and hurried me along the corridor, but we ran straight into another crowd of trilby-clad reporters, who rushed towards us like a flock of crows alighting on a few small crumbs of bread. Rosanna was the centre of their attention, but then someone shouted, 'Get the father and his girlfriend!' and we were mobbed. I was squeezed and jostled from side to side, unable to see their faces, only to smell them: wet raincoats, beer and tobacco. My hair came loose from its chignon and caught on someone's coat button; I stumbled, twisting my ankle. Robert caught me in his arms and at that moment a flash-gun went off. A triumphant photographer had his picture.

But not for long. Letting go of me, Robert pushed forward into the crowd with a cry of rage and snatched the camera from the culprit. He threw it to the ground and smashed it with his foot, grinding the toe of his highly polished Lobb shoe into the splintered glass of the lens. Then he pushed me, alone, towards a waiting taxi.

I turned to look back at him, and it was then that I saw Rosanna. She was standing on the steps, her gaunt face with its thick brows just visible as a white blob amongst the dark suits of the scandal-hungry reporters.

She did not seem aware of them, however. Her face was turned towards Robert and me, and her eyes wore the look of bitter betrayal.

The summer of 1934 was a summer of great change.

It began one day in July when I went to Magnolia Gardens to see Mother. It was a hot day, and I thought she would probably be in the garden sunning herself, so instead of knocking on the front door I went around the side of the house and straight into the garden. There, in the corner, was the messy patch of turf where Mel and I had buried the silver cup, and in the centre of the sun-bleached lawn was an empty deckchair. Apart from that there was a terrible stillness. The door of the french windows had blown open, and the curtains flapped in the open doorway, moved by the breeze.

I went into the house.

'Mother?'

She was sitting in the rocking chair. Her body was motionless, but the chair rocked slightly, creaking back and forth. Her face was an angry purply red.

'My God . . . Mother!'

At first I was sure that she was dead. But when I bent closer I realised that she was still warm, and there was a bubble of spittle moving to and fro on her lower lips as she breathed.

I was remarkably calm, moving slowly, severed from all feelings, thinking of practical things. I fetched an eiderdown from the bedroom and covered her before I went to the telephone. It was only when the operator came on to the line and I had to ask for the hospital that I realised I was crying.

There was one last thing I had to do before the ambulance arrived. I knelt beside the rocking chair. 'Mother? Mother? Can you hear me?'

She moaned slightly. I was panicking; seeing my only link with my past fading away before my eyes.

'Can you tell me who my father is, Mother? Please, I need—'

'I don't know,' she whispered. 'Don't know. . . .'

But I wasn't even sure if she had heard me. I stood over her and watched her, as though aware of her for the first time. My mother. It was a little like looking at a photograph, long after an event has happened. I noticed tiny details: a whisker growing out of a mole on her cheek, a stain on the faded pink and white Regency-stripe wallpaper, a darn on the cover of the eiderdown. It was very, very quiet.

She died then as I stood watching, before the ambulance came, though I wasn't really aware of the end coming. It wasn't how it is in books. They told me at the hospital that she'd had heart disease, but that she hadn't bothered to go to the doctor. I almost laughed when they said that; it was so typical of Mother. She didn't have a very high opinion of the medical profession. My chief feeling was that I would rather she were dead than lonely and suffering. How much of that feeling was selfish, and how much for Mother's sake, I couldn't tell.

Far worse than the funeral, to which none of Mother's family came, was going back to the empty house afterwards. I stood in the drawing room and looked at the rocking chair, and I was suddenly afraid. I was completely alone, and always would be, and all my old insecurities came rushing in like a flood, bearing down on me. I threw myself on to the ottoman and gave way to my first crying fit in years.

'You'll have to decide what to do about the house,' people had said to me. I was afraid that the decision would be made for me. The house had been rented for my mother by someone – my father? – but now that she was dead I faced the possibility that I would lose the only home I had ever had. (I discounted the flat near Hyde Park.) As I sat down at the desk to try to find the title deeds or the lease agreement, my heart began to thump with excitement. It was possible that somewhere amongst the paperwork I might find some clue to my father's identity. The very thought made me faint with dread and apprehension. Of course, I could have found the opportunity to go through these papers before, but I realised now that I had wanted to hear his name from Mother's own lips. That was what I had been battling for all these years. To get her to confess.

After a prolonged search I found a manila envelope that contained the papers about the house. I ran my eyes down the page, skipping the legal jargon, until I came to what I was looking for: 'Name and address of lease holder.' I squeezed my eyes tight shut and took a deep breath. Then I opened them and there it was.

'Lord Justice Desmond Hallet, c/o The Dover Hotel, London W.'

'Can I help you, madam?'

The receptionist at the Dover was a drab young woman in a floral print dress, who wore her hair plaited and coiled behind her ears. She didn't look quite right in the faded colonial grandeur of the hotel, among the vast potted ferns and the moth-eaten heads of East African game that were mounted on the walls.

'I'm looking for a Lord Desmond Hallet,' I said. 'It's rather a long shot, I know, but he used this address some years ago.'

'I could look it up in the records for you,' she said, 'but you'd have to give me a rough idea when it was.'

That was easy. 'About twenty-two years ago.'

The receptionist frowned. 'I'm not sure our records go back that far, but if you'd like to take a seat I'll have a look for you. . . .' A wall had been knocked through from the reception area to create a bar, and I wandered in there to find a seat amongst the battered cane furniture, whose cushions sagged sideways at drunken angles.

Not having anything to read, and wishing to appear occupied, I took my ivory cigarette-holder out of my handbag and lit a Balkan Sobranie. I didn't really like cigarettes very much, but smoking was an integral part of my West End persona, and it gave me something to do with my hands. There was a man watching me as I lit up. His black hair was greying at the temples and I guessed that he was about forty. A real lounge lizard, I thought as I took in the details: the Ronald Colman moustache, the monogrammed cigarette-case, the matching cufflinks, collar-studs and tie-pin, the pigskin shoes. . . .

'Excuse me staring at you,' he said, leaning forward, 'but you remind me of someone I used to know. Buy you a drink?' He twirled his empty Martini-glass.

I shook my head. 'No, thank you.'

He sauntered over to the bar, which was unattended, and poured a large measure of gin into his glass. Warm afternoon sunlight streamed in through the slats in the venetian blinds, making a rainbow of colours in the clear liquid and picking out the dust on the surface of the bar. 'It goes on my slate,' he explained when he realised that I was watching him help himself. 'I've had one here for years. Of course it's quite different from the old days now. Lost its style. I remember the hotel before the war, in Bridie's heyday. The Roaring Twenties rather took it out of the old place – too much fast living. But good old Bridie gave it all its character. She used to own the Dover, but she's dead now.'

I remembered Mother mentioning her name, and I was about to say so, but something stopped me. Mother's death was still too fresh in my mind for me to want to discuss it with a stranger.

The man walked back from the bar, his drink in one hand, the other extended. 'Really ought to introduce myself. Name's Monty Devereux.' He clicked his heels; an affected gesture. 'At your service, ma'am.'

He hadn't once taken his eyes off my face, and I was so unnerved that I said, 'Excuse me, please,' and went back to the receptionist. 'Any luck?' I asked her.

'No, I'm afraid not, madam. I can't help you.'

I stared at her in desperation. She had been my only chance of finding my father, though of course she couldn't know that.

'Is there a problem?' Monty Devereux strolled towards us, drink in hand. 'Can I help?'

'I came here looking for someone,' I said, 'but it appears this lady can't help me.'

'If he was one of the regulars, I might know something. Try me,' he coaxed.

'His name's Lord Hallet. I don't—'

'Desmond Hallet? Old Desmond? Course I know him. Great friend of my father's. Friend of yours, is he?'

'A relative actually.'

'Oh dear. Thing is, you see, I'd heard that old Desmond wasn't too well. Tell you what, there's a private nursing home just round the corner that his family use. Why don't you go and ask there?'

I thanked him and set off, unable to rid myself of the feeling that Monty Devereux's eyes were boring into my back.

I found the place easily: a smart white-painted townhouse with a shiny black door and a brass plaque with the legend 'IVY LODGE NURSING HOME'.

'Yes, we have a Lord Hallet here,' said a starchy nurse in a low voice, 'but I'm afraid he's a terminal case.'

'But can I see him?' I pleaded.

'I don't know. . . .' The nurse looked doubtful. 'Well, you can *look* at him, I suppose. . . .'

She led me upstairs. Before the door was opened I tried very hard to empty my mind, so that I would *expect* nothing. But it was difficult. In a sense, I had been waiting for this moment for years.

He was lying on a bed in the centre of the sterile white room. Just an old man. Lying on his back, breathing noisily. With a few tufts of white hair visible at the open neck of his pyjamas.

My father. . . .

'He's sleeping,' explained the nurse.

'It's all right,' I said, stepping backwards, groping for the door. 'I didn't want to stay.' I felt no warmth, not even pity. Just crushing disappointment.

But I could not leave my search there. I had to find out what was going to happen to 47 Magnolia Gardens. I persuaded the reluctant nurse to give me the address of his wife, soon to be his widow by all accounts.

Lady Felice Hallet was 'at home' to callers, according to the maid who answered the door of the elegant house in Kensington Square. She was sitting straight-backed in a tobacco-coloured velvet chair, in front of a tall first-floor window which opened on to a balcony with colourful window boxes. She wore an ankle-length skirt, and her white hair was piled high on her head, rather like Queen Mary's. Something in the pose implied an indomitable will, but the smile was friendly enough.

'Do come in, Miss. . . ?'

'Stark,' I said.

288

'Come and sit next to me here' – she patted a chair next to her – 'and we'll have a cosy little chat. Enid said you wished to speak to me about poor dear Desmond?'

'Yes, I. . . .' I groped around for a suitable overture but found none. In a situation like this, directness was the only way. I preferred it to diplomacy anyway. 'I'm his daughter,' I said.

I expected either a steely frown or tears into a lavender-scented handkerchief, but I got neither. Lady Hallet just smiled, and picked up the lorgnette that dangled on her bosom, in order to inspect me more closely. 'Really, my dear, are you *sure*?'

I told her about Mother's death and my subsequent discovery. Lady Hallet's face lit up in recognition. 'Of course, you're Magdalena's daughter! I was so sorry to hear about her death from my solicitors. . . .'

'You know about her, then?'

'Desmond told me many years ago. Oh, now don't look so shocked! We'd been married for forty years. A husband and wife don't keep that sort of secret. Don't think I'm belittling your dear mother, please, Miss Stark. From what Desmond said, she was a lovely girl. . . .'

'Didn't you mind?' I asked bluntly.

The smile again, but a little more hesitant this time. 'It wasn't a question of minding. Marriage isn't like that. As a wife, one is expected to tolerate certain things . . . for the sake of domestic harmony.' She tilted her head up, but I saw the pain in her eyes. Lady Hallet belonged to Robert's pre-war world in which the men drew up the rules, and women faced the consequences. Lady Hallet had obviously done so with great courage, and I respected her for it.

Not only was I welcomed like a special guest, but my hostess was also eager to reassure me about my future. Long before he had fallen ill, she explained, Lord Hallet had arranged for the tenancy to be passed on to me on Mother's death, and for the small allowance she had received to be transferred to me. In fact what was to be a confrontation turned into a pleasant conversation over a trolley of tea and cakes and translucent sandwiches. I suspected that Lady Hallet was rather lonely.

'And here, there's something very special I must show you,' she said, tripping across the room with small precise steps, very much the Edwardian. 'Your brothers.' She handed me a large framed photograph of two rather portly middle-aged men. They looked secure, prosperous. My brothers? The idea was strange; they were each old enough to be my father.

'Cecil and Everard,' said Lady Hallet proudly. 'I have their picture taken every year. And they have seven children between them!'

Another photograph, of my assorted nephews and nieces, most of them older than me.

'I've so enjoyed meeting you, my dear, and I know the boys would like it, too, if you wished it. . . .'

'It's a nice idea,' I said politely, but I left Kensington Square making a mental note *not* to contact my half-brothers, or any member of the Hallet family. Lady Hallet had earned her peace of mind.

Robert. What was I to do about Robert?

As the summer wore on, so did the problem. The obscenity trial had destroyed him, and his family were no help. In fact, they were falling apart at the seams. Helena washed her hands of the whole situation and withdrew into a round of bridge-parties and charity dances, no doubt being congratulated by her friends for putting on such a brave face. Rosanna, whose hostility to her family had been brought to the surface, broke contact with them completely. And Edwin, who had been forced to keep a safe distance from the trial because of his position in the Church, did the polite minimum when it came to supporting his father.

For a while, Robert's work suffered. He took on few cases and spent most of his time at my flat, ranting about his children. 'My little Zanna . . .,' he would lament. 'How can this have happened?'

But his favourite topic was Edwin. It was as if all the guilt that had been building up over the years began seeping out. He was guilty that he survived his first wife, guilty that he married again so soon after her death, that he had foisted a stepmother on Edwin, that he hadn't spent more time with his son. . . . Poor Robert; his attitude to unpleasantness or irregularity was to pretend that it wasn't happening. Until it was too late, and a crisis had arisen; like Edwin's adultery or Rosanna's lesbianism. Like it or not, I was seeing another side to the debonair worldly Robert Clifford; and, like it or not, he needed me.

The trouble was that I no longer felt I needed him. I had the house in Magnolia Gardens sitting there empty, waiting for me to do what I wanted with. I had independence, and I also had an identity though I hadn't completely accepted it. I no longer wanted to be tidied away behind closed curtains.

And there was another reason for wanting to break away from Robert. I had discovered what lay behind my mother's aversion for the Cliffords. It happened one day just before I went to the Dover Hotel. Robert was sitting with me in my flat, stroking my hair, when he suddenly said: 'You've always had such pretty hair, Loveday, even when you were a tiny girl.'

I sat up. 'What do you mean, "when I was a tiny girl"?'

Robert stared at his fingernails. 'Oh . . . I sometimes used to go round and . . . see your mother when she first moved to Magnolia Gardens. She had one or two legal problems she needed help with—'

'Did you sleep with her?' I demanded.

He nodded.

I felt the colour drain from my face. I whispered: 'You're not my father, are you?'

'Good God, no! You were a couple of years old when I—' He broke off, realising how sordid it sounded.

After that I did my best to avoid making love to him. It was impossible for me to break away while he was in such a state over the trial, even I couldn't be that heartless. So I waited. I waited until all the publicity had died down and he had started taking an interest in his work again. Then I told him.

'I don't want us to meet any more, Robert.' We were sitting on the silk-draped sofa of my flat for the last time.

He stared at me. 'Loveday . . . my dear . . . what do you mean?'

'I mean it's over, Robert.' I stood up and reached for my ivory cigarette-holder, but in my agitation I squeezed it too hard and it broke, snapped in two. I looked down at the pieces. 'I can't be the person you wanted me to be. I thought I could play the role of mistress and be happy, but I can't.'

There was the strangest silence – what I can only describe as a loud silence. I went and sat next to Robert again, and he sort of slumped over me. A weeping Robert, overcome by emotion, a Robert I didn't recognise – covering my hands with kisses, his tears falling on them. I was alarmed. He kissed me fiercely, despairingly.

'. . . All I ever loved. . . . Look at you, Loveday; you're so beautiful. If you had only *known* how I loved you. . . .'

I was shocked. It had never occurred to me that Robert was actually in love with me. But now I could see that he was simply too repressed to have the means of showing it. And this made my task even harder. I eventually persuaded him to go, telling him that I would leave the flat the next day and return the keys to him, but on reflection I could see that the sooner I left, the better. He might come back later that evening and try to persuade me to change my mind. I considered all this while I finished up the remains of the bottle of wine we had been drinking.

I walked slowly round the flat, the place that I created. I took down the mandarin chimes and put them back in the box. I pulled the oriental silk shawls from the furniture they draped and folded them up. I stripped the satin sheets from the bed and put them in a suitcase with my clothes.

Then I ordered a taxi to take me back to Magnolia Gardens.

As the taxi rumbled round the curve of the crescent and pulled up at number 47 I closed my eyes and sighed with relief. The empty house was no longer threatening but a symbol of escape, a sanctuary. Now, at least, I could be free of the Clifford family.

Or so I thought. But, as the taxi-driver carried my cases up the steps, blinking in the dusk I made out another figure standing by my front door. A tall man.

It was Edwin.

'Loveday, I wondered if I could have a word with you. I need to talk to you about Mel. . . .'

'This really isn't very convenient,' I said as I unlocked the door and Edwin carried my cases into the hall.

This was true, but it was not the only reason for my bad temper. According to my hasty calculations, this was the first time that Edwin and I had been alone together since I had risen from his bed, sticky and dishevelled, nearly three years ago. I just hoped that he felt as uncomfortable as I did about it.

'You're moving back?' he asked.

'Yes.'

'You've . . . left my father?'

'Yes.'

We stood there in the dusty neglected hallway, staring at one another.

'Well, we can't just stand here like this,' I said briskly, unpinning my hat and hanging it on the hat-stand, along with my coat. 'There's some gin upstairs, or we could have some tea. . . .'

'Nothing for me, thank you.'

I went into the kitchen and started crashing about with the kettle and the tea-pot. Edwin leaned on the mantelpiece, resting one foot on the fire-dog. His extraordinary grace still had the power to move me and, although his hair had started to recede, there was a quality of youthful beauty about his face, his complexion as clear and unsullied as if he had lived in the countryside all his life. He wore a clerical collar underneath an expensive-looking suit of herringbone tweed.

'I wondered if you knew how Mel was.'

'What makes you think I would know?' I asked, as I scooped the tea from the caddy into the pot and slammed down the lid.

'You *do* know, don't you?'

I didn't deny it, but my patience was running out. I wanted him to leave. He reminded me too painfully of my failed attempt to change my life by seducing him. I disliked failure. 'What *are* you doing here, Edwin?' I put the tea-pot down and rounded on him. 'I mean, we're not exactly friends, are we?'

'I thought we were, once,' Edwin said in a low voice.

I ignored this. 'Damn you, Edwin Clifford! You should have put Mel out of your mind,' I said angrily. 'You made your choice! You had to choose between Mel and the Church, and you chose Mel. And you hurt her terribly in the process. You . . . you . . . *played* with her, like—'

'Loveday!' Edwin stepped forward and placed his hands on my shoulders. He was so much taller than I that I was eclipsed by his shadow, and I felt some of the simple awe that he had inspired when we danced together in the mock-Tudor roadhouse. 'I *love* Mel. I know that you and my father find something absurd in that, but nevertheless it's true. *It is the truth*, God knows. . . .' He paused, correcting himself. 'Believe me, I've had ample time to think about all this. I've struggled with my conscience for months now, asking myself what I really wanted from the Church in the first place. Was it just the warmth and the security that many people find from their chosen partner?' He released his grip on my shoulders and turned away to stare into the fireplace again. 'Loveday, I think I'm losing my faith.' He spoke with the sincerity of old, but with such humility that even I could not fail to be moved. 'You can't be a Christian except by living a truly

Christian life. If I covet a woman other than the one who is my wife, I'm hardly living a Christian life. Therefore, I'm not a Christian any more.'

'And what does Jane think about all this?'

'I haven't been able to discuss the matter of faith with her. Since she found out . . . I don't think her feelings for me are strong enough to tolerate this new crisis. I don't think she loves me now, if she ever did. I'm certain she doesn't respect me. I'm not the sort of churchman that she would have wanted me to be. So . . . if I could only talk to Mel—'

'Edwin, I'm not able to tell you where Mel is.'

He stared at me in disbelief, and at once I felt resentful of the natural Clifford arrogance that had led him to believe I would tell him whatever he wanted to know. 'Why ever not?'

'Because I told her I wouldn't. That's why.' And I turned and walked back into the kitchen to indicate that the subject was closed.

'Please, Loveday, it's so important. . . .'

'No. I can't.' I'm afraid it gave me pleasure to say those words, as he had once said them to me.

'*Please!*'

'I can't, Edwin.' I saw the wretchedness on his face and I tried to be more gentle. 'I promised Mel I wouldn't tell you. Whatever else I do, I must keep that promise.'

After my encounter with Edwin, there followed a lull which was first peaceful, and then boring.

Edwin didn't pester me again. I used to glimpse him in the distance in the Gardens, and sometimes Jane would be at his side, wearing a forced smile and a look of pity for those less fortunate than herself. How she must despise poor Mel, I thought.

Robert kept out of my way, too, although the proximity of our houses made it difficult for us to avoid one another. One day we both arrived home from work at the same time. I watched him walk up the steps of number 50 and unlock the front door. His shoulders were hunched, and he looked tired. I turned away, feeling a stab of guilt.

I worked at Dulong's salon until the spring of 1935. My position there had been due to Robert's influence, but he was not a spiteful person, and did not use that influence against me once we had parted. Besides, I liked to think that Dulong's would have retained me anyway, for my efficiency. But I grew tired of the commuting between south London and the West End, and the work was not challenging, so I handed in my notice. I still had a small allowance from Lord Hallet's estate (he had died at Christmas), so it was just a question of waiting for something to turn up.

Before long, it did.

One day in May, I found Ethne Finzel on my doorstep. By then she was a household name. She travelled thousands of miles each month, gave scores of performances and had made several of the new disc recordings. Yet it never ceased to amaze me that it was plain boring Ethne Finzel who was famous, while the charismatic Mel. . . .

'Loveday, I was wondering. . . . I've just had a dress made up, only it's not quite right. Could you come and take a look at it? You always had such good taste. . . .'

I went with her to Camelot and waited in the drawing room while Ethne changed into her dress. It was a fussy pretentious room with scrolls and flounces everywhere, velveteen furniture and pink-shaded candelabra borne on the backs of gilt cherubs. Jeanie Finzel gave me a quiet smile, and then returned to the gardening almanac she was reading.

What an extraordinary woman she was. Queen of Camelot, sitting quietly in that hideous monument to her marriage, dressed in tweed and thinking about runner beans while her husband roamed the world in search of the perfect lavatory.

'You see, Loveday, there's something not quite right about it.'

'Stand up here, then.' I motioned Ethne towards a pink velveteen footstool and she hopped on to it like an obedient dog.

'What do you think?' she queried nervously.

'H'm. . . .' The truth was that when it came to her professional wardrobe Ethne had never done well. Her clothes were unbecoming and over-complicated, so that they distracted the audience. This dress was just as disastrous: a lumpy brocade with a low neckline. I don't know who her dressmaker was, but she must have been blind as well as clumsy.

I made Ethne turn a full circle. 'If you want my advice, I'd scrap it. Completely.'

Jeanie made tut-tutting noises, and Ethne stared in consternation.

'But I've got a big concert coming up, in Oxford. Uncle Donald arranged it. . . .'

'Leave it to me,' I said briskly. 'I'll get you the right dress.'

'But will you have the time?'

I explained about having left my job at the salon.

'Oh, that would be very kind of you, dear,' murmured Jeanie. 'It's such a worry for poor Ethne.'

I took Ethne's measurements and called in at Dulong's. Antoinette, the old French seamstress, had become friendly with me while I worked there, and she was only too glad to take a private commission from the famous Mam'selle Finzel ('Mon dieu, qu'elle chante comme un rossignol!'). Three days later I returned proudly to Camelot bearing a large cardboard box.

Ethne sighed with pleasure as she folded back the layers of tissue paper and lifted out the gown of blue-grey crêpe. It was cut on severe Grecian lines.

'Oh, Loveday! This is wonderful! You really are so clever, you know. So sensible . . . and practical.'

. This was fulsome praise indeed from the diffident Ethne. She went on: 'Mother and I have been talking, and we . . . we wondered whether you would like to work for me full time, as a personal assistant. Oh dear, that sounds rather condescending, doesn't it? Only, I'm booked up a year in advance now and I need someone to help with my clothes and take care of all the other arrangements. Would you be interested? I think . . . I think you and I could get along.'

I smiled at her. 'Yes, Ethne. I think you and I will get along very well.'

Oxford.

Ethne's concert was to be held at the Sheldonian Theatre, a domed building like an oversized pepper-pot at the centre of the city. It was May, and Oxford was looking at its best, bursting with fruit blossom and new leaves, the golden stone of the spires standing out cleanly against a bright blue sky.

I could appreciate its charm, but my natural scepticism prevented me from falling in love with the city. There was something in the combination of the gracious beauty of the surroundings and the careless confidence of the students who strolled and cycled through its narrow streets that brought out all my old insecurities. Oxford meant a world to which I didn't belong.

And, of course, Oxford meant Mel.

The night that we arrived in Oxford and settled ourselves into our palatial accommodation at the Randolph Hotel, I went to Ethne's room. She was sitting in the window-seat with a score in her hand, her eyes closed, humming.

'I do hope the Voice is going to be all right tomorrow night,' she said. 'My throat is a little sore.'

'Well, rest it, then.' I went and felt her forehead. 'You don't seem to be feverish. But no more singing. Promise me.'

I think Ethne quite enjoyed being bossed around. There was relief in her smile. And I enjoyed having someone to boss around. It made me feel that I had a defined place in life.

'Ethne, I'm going to see Mel. She's only about a mile from here. Do you want to come with me?'

Ethne looked startled, and coloured slightly. 'Oh, I don't know, Loveday. . . . No. I think I'd better not.' She hesitated. 'I just think it would be easier if you went alone.'

'It's not much, but it's home. Dreadful mess, I'm afraid. Don't look too closely!'

Mel didn't sound apologetic, but happy. I went to see her during the afternoon before the concert, while Ethne was in rehearsal. The house that Frank Finzel had bought for her was solid red-brick Victorian, compromised only by pointed Gothic turrets and a magnificent wrought-iron weather-vane.

Mel greeted me at the front door, and as soon as I saw her face I was swamped by a sense of how very, very good it was to see her. So good in fact, that tears sprang to my eyes before I had a chance to tell myself to stop being so bloody sentimental. Mel was dressed in a simple grey dress with a white collar. Once upon a time I would have advised her that such severity didn't flatter her rather gaunt looks; but the dress suited her, and I was forced to look more closely to see how she had changed. Her figure had filled out a little, her skin had a wonderful sheen to it and her hair was glossy. In short, she looked very well.

She led me out through the cluttered untidy house that seemed to overflow with books, to a lawn studded with daisies. And in the middle of it, on a rug, was the most adorable little child I had ever seen. The sun made his blond fluff of hair glow like a white halo. He was engrossed in stuffing daisies into his mouth, and did not look up.

'This is Gabriel,' said Mel simply, kneeling down and extricating the wet daisies.

'Wonderful,' I murmured, and I reached out and touched the small downy skull with one gloved finger. It was a tentative gesture, and an experiment, but all of a sudden I felt hard and overdressed in my feather-trimmed hat and my narrow skirt with the elegant little slit in it – grotesque even.

'Loveday, I do feel so dreadfully shabby and lumpy now you're here. . . .'

I laughed, and kicked off my shoes, settling myself on the rug next to the angel Gabriel. 'Is that better?'

'The hat, too, I think.'

I took it off, and Gabriel grabbed at the red feather. Removing it from the hatband, I tickled his face with it, and he sneezed and then laughed, a delighted baby chuckle.

'Loveday, my God, your *hat*! You've ruined it!'

'Doesn't matter.' I spied a Fortnum & Mason catalogue lying on the grass and flicked through it.

'Yes, I've been ogling those gorgeous things, but it's no use. . . . You might be interested in borrowing it, though. You always cared so much about clothes.'

'Too much,' I mused. 'Listen to this, though.' I adopted the sing-song voice we used to use when we were reading 'Londoner's Log' out loud, trying to make one another laugh. '"*Tremendously becoming new beach frocks have been designed for this year . . . worn by Miss Diana Gould, one of our leading young dancers, who is making a big success in Atalanta and the Ballet Club. The dress is backless and the flared skirt is amusingly slit up to show your proudly tanned legs.*" *Your proudly tanned legs!* What a load of old nonsense.'

Mel laughed. 'I'm sure mine will be proudly sporting varicose veins. Or dropsy. The weight I'm gaining. . . .'

I flung the magazine away, as far as I could throw it, and Gabriel pulled himself to his feet and started to stagger after it.

'Tell me what you're up to. Apart from baby-minding.'

Mel fixed me with her amazing eloquent golden eyes. 'There's no need to patronise, Loveday! As a matter of fact . . . I have a job!'

'Tell me about it.'

'There's a relief centre for the unemployed in the east of Oxford, near Cowley. Uncle Donald helped found it. And I go along and help. I do everything from doling out soup to helping with form-filling – the Means Test, Welfare, that sort of thing.

Most of them can't read. And I take Gabriel along with me. He plays with the other children.'

'I'm impressed,' I said, meaning it.

'Oh, Loveday!' Mel's eyes were glowing with enthusiasm. 'You've no idea what it means to be doing something *real* for once. All that time I wasted doing nothing! And those years spent paying lip-service to Uncle Donald's socialism but never actually doing anything to help anyone. At least I'm not a hypocrite any more – a "drawing-room pink"!'

I plucked a daisy and pressed it against my lips. 'And Edwin? Do you think about him?'

Mel turned away and looked towards Gabriel, shading her eyes with her hands. 'I think about him, of course. . . .' She sighed. 'And I sometimes wish he could see Gabriel. But I'm not at all sure that I want him to be here. I've changed, and I don't think I can *believe* any more . . . in all the things I used to believe in. I suppose that's rather sad.' But she did not sound sad. 'That's why I don't want Edwin to know where I am; it would upset the balance. I know that I could never go back to being his mistress. You see Loveday' – she turned and took my hand in hers – 'I feel as though I'm just on the verge of a great discovery.' Gabriel turned and staggered towards her, and she held out her arms to him. 'I'm thinking of people other than myself for a change. I feel as though I'm just about to discover what love *really* is.'

She smiled at me, anticipating my reply, but I did not speak. I was lost for words.

Many years later, I was to look on the night of Ethne's Oxford concert as a turning point in my life. Or perhaps it was that whole day. Perhaps witnessing the changes in Mel changed me, too.

The concert was a glittering occasion, attended by the Vice-Chancellor of the University and his wife, resplendent in a diamond tiara and long white gloves. The cream of Oxford society was packed into the small auditorium – eminent academics, well-connected undergraduates and the gentry from the surrounding county. I was afraid that this sophisticated and critical audience would make poor Ethne too nervous, but she rose to the occasion magnificently. Ethne would never be a star of the stage. Acting in operas presented a problem. The Voice could sing the music, but Ethne could not portray the part. No, she was at her best like this, standing alone on a makeshift platform with only a piano for accompaniment, singing the simplest and loveliest music in her repertoire. I saw the plump Vice-Chancellor's wife brush away a tear during 'O Death, How Bitter Thou Art'.

It was gratifying to hear the tumultuous applause, and I couldn't help a thrill of pride when I overheard people murmuring 'What a *divine* dress', 'Doesn't she look wonderful tonight? So elegant.'

After the concert there was a reception at the Oxford Union, with Donald McDowell as its host. He picked me out amongst the throng. 'So, Miss Loveday Stark!' he said, his face breaking into its wolfish grin. 'A starmaker now, are you, eh?' He waved away a glass of champagne, asking the waiter to bring him Scotch instead. 'Ashley Player fell out of favour and, hey presto! another manipulator on the scene, ready to mould our uncertain young star!'

I remembered this tactic of old. Donald liked to needle people; make them rise to his offensive. But I knew just how to deflate him. I smiled my best smile. 'You know, Dr McDowell, someone just told me that the money you've raised with this concert is going to the socialist party funds. I put paid to the rumour right away. After all, I said, that would be tantamount to manipulating Miss Finzel – and a member of her own family, too.'

Donald threw back his head and laughed loudly. 'Ach, I love a woman that can give as good as she gets! I knew you wouldn't fail me, little Miss Loveday. And I think you can take at least some of the credit for this evening's performance, which is more than I can claim. She really looked bonny.'

'Thank you.' My smile was genuine this time. I had always liked Donald McDowell. He was stimulating company, but there was also something in his piercing directness which made me feel . . . myself. I wasn't quite so sure how I felt about his attractions as a man. His looks were so unusual. He was tall and sinewy and still wore his hair rather long, although it was almost completely silver. He sported a trim little beard, too, and I decided that if his baggy suit were replaced with a ruff and doublet he would be perfect as an Elizabethan courtier, or perhaps a Spanish don. While I was thinking these things, I was staring at Donald quite brazenly. But of course Donald was not one to balk at staring, either. He was gazing hungrily at my hair, which I had twisted into a long rope and wound with a string of pearls.

'You look like a Shakespearian heroine,' he said, and I jumped, so apt was this parallel with my own thoughts. 'Will you join me for dinner after this cursed jamboree is over?'

'I'd love to,' I said. 'I'll just go and tell Ethne.'

She was surrounded by so many admirers that it was difficult to get close. As I pushed my way through the throng, someone tapped me on the shoulder.

'May I introduce myself to the most beautiful lady in the room?'

A tall young man stood in front of me, with glittering dark eyes and black hair smoothed back with brilliantine. He clicked his heels and gave a formal bow. 'Count Victor Kranski, at your service.'

The gesture was more than a touch theatrical, and I felt inclined to laugh. He bent to kiss my hand, and I raised my glass to my lips to hide my smile. But when he raised his head and looked at me . . . there was something entirely hypnotic about those eyes. I did not withdraw my hand immediately.

Having sought me out, Count Kranski was eager to engage me in conversation. He was a *real* count, he assured me, an émigré from Bohemia. And while his family's political opponents plundered their estates he was reading English at Magdalen College.

'You're an undergraduate,' I murmured, feeling a twinge of disappointment. 'How interesting.'

He shook his head. 'No, not interesting. It is exciting and fun and . . . *radical.*' He rolled his *r*'s. 'Come with me and I'll show you. There is a bottle-party in my college tonight. Please.'

He held out his hand with a slight bow.

I looked at him, immaculate and distinctly foreign in his tails and starched white collar and gleaming black hair. A decoration engraved with a coat of arms sparkled on his chest. I was over-come with curiosity.

'Give me five minutes, please,' I said, and went to break my dinner engagement with Donald.

He minded, but did his best not to show it, bless him.

'A real Bohemian, eh?' he said with a slight curl of his lip. 'That should be quite something.'

Victor spirited me along the High Street and into Magdalen College. To get to the party we had to thread our way along an

301

ancient colonnade and up a spiralling stone staircase – a difficult exercise in my long narrow skirt. I tried not to feel too disappointed when I saw how tiny the room was and how impossibly crowded. It had yellow walls covered with Aubrey Beardsley prints, and an ancient horsehair sofa leaking both springs and stuffing. From the gramophone in the corner came the strains of Josephine Baker singing 'Si j'étais blanche . . .'. There weren't many girls amongst the revellers, and those there were had dressed in sober skirts and blouses. They all stared at me.

Victor introduced me to everyone, but I quickly forgot the names. I felt rather like a spy or an eavesdropper; much more interested in listening to the conversations than in joining in.

'Turn that racist music off, will you? Let's have some Hungarian songs, so *romantisch*.'

'Freud says that neurosis is born of the repression of instincts. Denying yourself all the sex you want makes your health suffer.'

It was obvious that Victor and his friends considered themselves affiliated with Oxford's left-wing intelligentsia, disciples and hangers-on in a clique that had once included Auden, Spender and MacNeice, but had now lost its way and clung desperately to the doctrine that being alcoholic and paranoid was less boring than belonging to the dreaded Old Gang. I spotted a pile of required reading from Victor Gollancz's Left Book Club, easily discernible by their bright yellow jackets, and a copy of Edward Upward's *The Mind in Chains*. There was even a copy of Rosanna Clifford's *A Tender Rose*. But the way they were arranged was too deliberate. I had the feeling that they were mere props.

Nevertheless, I enjoyed the party. Victor's friends wore their adopted beliefs like an ill-fitting suit of clothes, and I found this rather charming. Their affected world-weariness couldn't quite conceal a fresh-faced optimism that made me feel very old. Victor himself treated me with rather heavy-handed Continental charm. I wasn't sure quite how much of his attentiveness stemmed from the cachet of being seen with an older woman. He gave me potted biographies of his friends, and their all too predictable ambitions.

'He's in the middle of his first novel,' he said, pointing to one of them.

And then he added, quite seriously: 'It is a hatchet job on middle-class cant.'

* * *

I laughed about this with Donald McDowell the next day.

To make up for my truancy at dinner I arranged to go and take tea in his rooms in All Souls. I told him about the bottle-party, and it came as a relief to be able to laugh about the whole thing.

'Promiscuous little buggers!' snorted Donald. 'Sex on doctor's orders, that's why they love Freud so much. Because he tells them that if their slightest sexual itch is not immediately gratified they'll end up in the loony-bin!'

I smiled. 'I think they're worse on politics than on sex. I couldn't believe it when I heard a boy who looked as though he'd never shaved saying he dreamed of "the flowering of social justice in the Soviet Union".'

Donald drained his glass of Scotch and laughed contemptuously. 'That lot make me sick! They're so busy being committed that they don't even bother to get their facts right. Most of them have never met anyone outside their own social class.'

I could tell that Donald felt a certain discomfiture about his own lifestyle. His study was beautiful: large and airy with a domed ceiling and windows looking out over the crenellated golden spires of All Souls. There were handsome carved book-cases and a grand leather-topped desk. But Donald insisted on stressing the discomforts of his lifestyle – that the bedroom was monastic, the study damp and impossible to heat in winter. As he listed these hardships there was a knock on the door and a white-jacketed college servant carried in a steaming tray of tea.

I took one look at Donald's face and laughed outright.

Having known Donald since I was a child, it was easy for me to relax in his company. But he also had an uncanny ability to see through me.

'I would say it's a very useful arrangement, you working with Ethne,' he remarked as he poured me a cup of tea and lit a pipe for himself.

'Yes, I think so. What Ethne needs—'

'I wasn't referring to Ethne's needs,' he said abruptly. 'Ethne has her music, after all, and that will always sustain her. But you *need* her, don't you?'

I didn't reply.

'I reckon so,' he went on. 'I've thought that ever since I first set eyes on you – that what you needed was a good dose of security. And security can come from having someone else to take care of.

303

Ach, what a little waif you were!'

I felt myself blushing. Annoyed, I tried to change the subject. Donald just laughed his wild laugh. 'Why waste time avoiding the things about yourself that you can't change, little Miss Loveday? Why not just come to terms with them?'

'Just as you've come to terms with the fact that you enjoy a comfortable middle-class lifestyle while others starve?'

'Touché!' cried Donald, quite delighted with this defence, and we were friends once more.

'But tell me,' he said in a pensive tone, 'this cardboard count . . . what does he want from you?'

'Prestige,' I said bluntly.

'So he's asked to see you again.'

'Yes.' I didn't dare mention the roomful of hothouse flowers that had arrived at the Randolph that morning.

'Ach, no, you're never going to get involved with a mere boy, are you. . .?'

I wasn't.

Not a younger man, I kept telling myself as I accompanied Ethne on a round of recording sessions in London and then a series of concerts in northern cities. But I kept on thinking about Victor, and I wasn't really surprised when the telephone rang on my first night back in Magnolia Gardens.

'Where have you been?' he demanded, like a petulant child.

'In Hull,' I replied. I was sure that Victor had never even heard of Hull.

'Well, now you can come up to Oxford. Come up at once!'

I went.

When I looked back on it, my desire to humour Victor was like a sort of madness that seized me, a madness born of despairing of ever belonging to anyone. I even dressed to please him when I set off to Oxford that day, in my most sophisticated and elegant polka-dot dress and a jaunty veiled hat. I knew that on no account should I try to look like a female undergraduate, in tweed skirt and flat shoes. Victor wanted to be seen with a grown woman in the hope that the intellectuals would take him more seriously.

When I saw him standing on the platform of Oxford station, beaming and waving, I felt that my efforts were worthwhile. He was, after all, an extremely handsome and engaging young man.

It was late by the time we got into town, and I murmured something about needing to find a hotel for me to stay in before they all closed, but Victor turned a deaf ear and hurried me back to his rooms in Magdalen. They were full of people. Once again I was introduced to everyone, including extraordinary twins called Orlando and Benedict Warner. One was a painter and the other a writer, though I couldn't remember which was which. They looked identical, except that one of them was much bigger than the other. When I suggested that this discrepancy in size must give rise to all sorts of nicknames they looked horrified, as though the use of nicknames smacked of fascism or something equally undesirable.

They were all in a state of great excitement because the next day a friend of theirs was addressing a political meeting in the Union on the subject of Mussolini's dangerous effect on European politics. Their excitement was inflamed by an expectation that the meeting would be 'interfered with' by the diehard members of the Socialist Workers' Club in Cowley. My heart sank to my boots when I realised that Victor expected me to join his friends. The Socialist Workers' Club was the place where Mel worked, founded by Donald McDowell.

I pressed Benedict Warner to tell me what sort of interference they expected, but Victor decided abruptly that the evening's entertainment was over.

'Come on now, it's time to leave!' he said, and ejected his friend in mid-sentence. The others followed, as if by some prearranged signal. I gathered up my coat and hat.

'Please,' said Victor, putting his hand on my arm. 'I did not mean for you to leave.' He was so young and so eager I couldn't bear it.

I removed his hand. 'Really,' I said, 'I must.'

The next day Victor sulked about my premature departure. But by the evening he was so excited about the rally at the Union that he had forgotten about the game of courtship.

It appeared that it was more important to see and be seen at these meetings than to have any deep political commitment. The ugly Victorian debating hall at the Union was packed with students who all looked very like Victor and his friends. They greeted the speaker enthusiastically, though I found it difficult to see why: Walter Drayton was a pale callow youth, with thinning hair, a cut-glass accent and little grasp of rhetoric.

'Gentlemen, the time has come when all eyes are on Europe, and the menace of fascism in Europe. . . .'

And so on, through a string of predictable clichés and quotes from Lenin. The students muttered 'hear, hear' at first, then clapped, and had just begun to cheer when the voting doors at the side of the hall, marked 'AYES' and 'NOES' burst open and a crowd of cloth-capped workers streamed in through them. There was an unnatural silence for a few seconds, and Mr Drayton's attack on Mussolini petered out.

And then there was uproar as the newcomers began to press forward into an already crowded debating chamber. I recognised Donald's silvery locks amongst the cloth caps, but there was no sign of Mel with him. I was disappointed, for she would have shared my refusal to take the speaker seriously ('Walter falters' was the sort of observation she would have made).

The Real Socialists, as I privately termed them, began by heckling the unfortunate Walter.

'Bloody public-school nancy boy!'

'Forget about Italy – what about bread for the poor?'

'You lot don't give a bugger about unemployment!'

They started to stamp their feet, quietly at first, but with increasing insistence until Walter could no longer be heard. The students shouted at them to keep quiet, and scuffles broke out then full-blooded fights, with Donald's mob leaping on Victor's.

I tried to do the sensible thing and stay out of the way, but I was pushed roughly from side to side, and there was no chance at all of my escaping – the space between me and the doors was ten deep in angry shouting men. Inevitably, I lost my balance and fell to the floor, clinging to jackets . . . to trouser-legs . . . but still going under. I screamed, but no one could hear me above the din. And then came the feet, kicking and crushing me on all sides, and the terrible sour smell of sweating human bodies packed together. A steel toe-cap caught me on the face and I felt my lip torn open and blood filling my mouth.

Oh my God, I'm going to be trampled to death.

I closed my eyes, because I could not bear to see the feet and legs any more, and I shouted: '*Victor! Victor!*'

Strong arms closed around me, and I was pulled from above, lifted like a doll and carried up . . . and into the air, gasping as we broke through the rank sea of bodies as though I were emerging from underwater.

'Get out of my way, you bastard! Can't you see the girl's hurt?'

I didn't have to open my eyes to know who had saved me; I recognised the voice.

Donald McDowell.

He took me back to All Souls and sorted me out; giving me a tumbler of whisky and bathing my cut lip – in that order.

'Don't worry, lass, your beauty won't be impaired. Not for long, at any rate,' he said, sponging the dried blood off my cheek. 'So where was our young hero? Why wasn't he coming to your rescue?' He sounded pleased.

'I don't know.'

'Ach, men, eh? Never there when you need 'em!'

On 2 October 1935, Mussolini invaded Abyssinia, thereby elevating Walter Drayton to the status of prophet amongst his peers.

Victor and his friends spent the Michaelmas term campaigning for his election as president of the Oxford Union, while I toured the country with Ethne on a gruelling round of performances of 'Elijah' and the 'St Matthew Passion'. The demanding schedule ended with a special performance of 'Messiah' at the Albert Hall. More and more work flooded in, more than Ethne could possibly have undertaken, even though she worked a fourteen-hour day. It was a full-time job for me just turning down engagements.

After Christmas there was a lull for a time while Ethne rested, and I was rather glad when Victor telephoned and asked me if I would visit Oxford on the first weekend after the January term had begun.

I shall never forget that evening. The train journey was terrible. The heating had broken down, and I sat shivering as we rattled through the darkness with wind and sleet finding their way in through the frames of the windows and doors. We seemed to stop at every signal halt, and by the time we ground into Oxford I was stiff from hugging my coat around me.

Victor met me at the station and took me to dinner at the Victoria Arms where I kept my coat on through the meal and drank port and brandy in an attempt to keep warm, but only ended up cold and tipsy.

Poor Victor, he was trying to be entertaining, but I was exhausted and not at all in the mood for his overblown charm.

'All I'd like right now', I mumbled as we left the restaurant with me leaning on his arm, 'is a nice warm bed.'

'Of course,' said Victor, and took me back to his rooms in Magdalen, which was not what I had intended at all.

Victor wound up the gramophone. 'Come, we can dance,' he said. I swayed sleepily to the strains of Cole Porter, but my heart wasn't in it.

'Victor . . .,' I murmured, 'I ought to go—'

He stopped dancing abruptly and stared at me with a strange expression in his eyes. Through my rather drunken haze I could just discern anger. Then suddenly he kissed me, hard, on the mouth. I could feel his teeth against my lower lip.

'Victor—'

'What's the matter? It's what you want, isn't it?' He was snarling, quite unrecognisable without the mantle of aristocratic charm. That was the only side of Victor I knew, and it had disappeared into thin air. I was frightened. 'You shouldn't come here . . . you shouldn't behave like that if you don't want it.' He was unbuckling his trousers.

'Victor, I know I've flirted with you, and maybe I shouldn't—'

He pushed me back on to the sofa, kissing me with an ugly gnawing motion, squeezing my breasts so that I winced with pain.

'You like it like this, hey? You like it a little rough?'

I twisted my head violently from side to side.

'I think you do. . . .'

He was pressing against my naked thigh, trying to enter me, but I could no longer feel him. In the shock and outrage of the moment, I was above it all, floating. A succession of pictures flashed before my eyes. My four-year-old self sitting on the floor with my book and screaming to my mother for a Daddy Rabbit. The smelly, badly lit cloakroom at Stone Hill High and Margaret Collins's lip curling as she called me a bastard. And Lord Desmond Hallet – my father, perhaps – lying on his back in a hospital bed, breathing through his mouth. Breathing his life away, unaware of my presence. . . .

Victor groaned and said something unintelligible in German. And then before I had a chance to move he ejaculated over my oyster silk lingerie and collapsed sobbing on my chest.

'I'm sorry, oh my God, I'm so sorry. . . .'

'Come in, come in, whoever you are!'

Donald McDowell was sitting in front of the fire with his pipe, listening to the wireless. At the sight of the roaring, crackling flames, I shivered. I had just run all the way down the High Street. My fur collar was beaded with moisture, and sleet had collected in my eyelashes, dissolving my mascara into black circles around my eyes.

'Our little waif, eh? This is a strange time to come calling.'

I looked at the clock on the mantelpiece. It was after eleven o'clock.

'Well, I'll ask you why you're here in a minute. First, you'd better sit yourself down and get warm. Wait a moment – what's this?'

He turned up the wireless, and we heard the calm eloquent voice of Stuart Hibberd. 'The king's life is moving peacefully towards its close. . . .'

Donald switched off the wireless. 'So that's it, then. We're to have a playboy king on the throne. . . .'

I sighed and reached out my hands to the blaze.

'So what about *your* wee playboy, then? I take it he's not been treating you too well?'

I shrugged, trying to be nonchalant. 'Nothing I can't handle.'

At that, Donald became angry. 'Don't try it on with me!' he shouted. 'You don't know what the hell you're doing!'

I stared at him, stunned.

'When are you going to stop playing the hard bitch, eh? Just look at you!'

He reached out and touched the bruises on my lips, gently, very gently. Then he stroked my damp hair. 'You've been playing some mighty dangerous games, Miss Stark.'

'I know,' I said, 'but it's the last time, I swear it.'

'PEER'S DAUGHTER ELOPES TO SPAIN WITH YOUNG EMIGRE.'

Donald showed me the headlines in the summer of 1936, along with the photograph of Victor and some fresh-faced chit waving from the deck of a ship.

'Good riddance, eh?' said Donald. 'To the lot of them – young idiots!'

He was referring to the stampede of undergraduates to join the International Brigade and fight in the Spanish Civil War, imagining that their guilty, socially self-conscious little personalities would fall away and they'd be reborn as men and brothers.

'What a bloody mess, eh?' As ever, Donald was free with his opinions when I called to see him after a visit to Mel. 'The middle class jumping in regardless, as usual. If only they'd realise that the feelings that are inspiring the Spaniards to massacre one another have got little or nothing to do with middle-class bloody idealism! Eighty-five per cent of them are illiterate peasants and only *they* know what they're fighting about. Ach, the whole vindictive bloody mess has nothing at all to do with social justice. . . .'

I felt nothing as I stared at the photograph of Victor, nor when I saw him in the newspaper again in 1937 with the other volunteers who had returned, giving a clenched-fist salute for the press. I felt nothing but a terrible emptiness.

So when Ethne asked if I would consider accompanying her on a three-month concert tour of America in the New Year of 1938, I said yes. I would have said yes anyway. Ethne would have been quite incapable of crossing the Atlantic alone.

We sailed from Southampton in the Cunard liner RMS *Mauretania*. I tried not to mind that Ethne was treated like a diva, with a cabin stuffed full of flowers and telegrams, while I was just a minion. It probably helped that Ethne didn't behave like a diva. She was an unlikely international star, when all was considered. Before her career began she had attended no opera and very few concerts. She knew little of the history of music, her foreign languages were limited, she had little physical strength and an introverted character. As Mel had once said, she was just a Voice. But Mel had been wrong when she claimed that Ethne had no strong feelings about anything. She cared desperately about singing well.

On board ship, Ethne seemed more interested in the food than in anything else; lobster, and blueberries and other things that we had never eaten before. Of course, we were seated in the best position at the captain's table. Captain Gates was a suave handsome man in his forties, with thickly brilliantined hair and a dark sun-tan. On the little finger of his left hand he wore a large signet ring studded with a diamond.

He opened the conversation by asking me what I thought about our ex-king and Mrs Simpson. 'You'll find the papers over there are full of it, I'm afraid.'

'I think she sounds perfectly ghastly,' I said. 'She should have had the decency to leave him alone.'

'I quite agree, Miss Stark,' said Captain Gates with his sleepy heavy-lidded smile. 'His Majesty should choose someone more suitable. Someone . . . more like you. As a British subject I would consider it a blessing to have a queen as beautiful as you.' This elaborate compliment was accompanied by a courtly kiss on the hand. I smiled, then laughed, and allowed him to continue in this vein for the rest of the evening, for I could see no harm in it.

'Thank you, Captain, for a most enjoyable evening,' I said as he pulled my chair back for me. 'You've been very kind.' And I turned to smile at him over my shoulder as I walked out of the dining room and back to my cabin.

An hour later, just as I was smothering my face with cold cream, there was a knock on my door. Pulling on my négligé, I went to answer it.

'Captain Gates! What on earth . . .? Is something wrong?'

The professional smile faded. 'Surely you were expecting me?'

'Expecting you? No. Why?'

He looked almost angry. 'But this evening . . . I thought . . . damn it, you most certainly gave *me* the impression that you wanted—' He started to use his weight to force the door.

I remembered Victor and slammed it in his face.

'Goodnight, Captain!'

My first sight of New York was as breathtaking as everyone had said it would be. The combination of the bright blue sky and the light reflected from the snow was quite dazzling. Even the buildings seemed to sparkle.

Once again Ethne was greeted with armfuls of flowers, both on the docks and in her hotel room, and I told myself that I had better accept that that was the way things were going to be. But she was quiet when we said goodnight, and the next morning she summoned me to her room in tears.

'Loveday,' she croaked, 'I can't sing!'

The doctors diagnosed it as a common cold brought on by the atmospheric changes; namely the contrast between the fierce American heating and the sub-zero temperatures outside. For three days she was forced to rest while the best specialists we could find douched her nose and painted her throat. By the end of this time the Voice had recovered and was as clear as a bell, but Ethne had not. She complained that she still did not feel well, and I sensed her struggling with herself for the rest of the trip, somehow 'lagging behind' the Voice.

'You needn't worry about Chicago, Ethne, if the reviews there are anything like these.' It was the day after her concert at New York's Carnegie Hall, and I carried a pile of papers into Ethne's room and threw them triumphantly on to the bed. 'I know you feel you didn't do your best job because you were under the weather, but this lot don't agree. According to the *New York Times*, you've taken the town by storm and your voice is "warm and vibrant, full and beautiful". Now, that's not bad, is it?'

'Let me see.' Ethne reached for the paper.

'And this man at the *New York Tribune* claims to have been moved to tears by "O, Death, How Bitter".'

And so on to dizzying, exciting Chicago, and the vast frozen expanse of Lake Michigan. It was the same story there, too. The Voice went from strength to strength, enrapturing audiences with a velvety texture and a suppleness it had never had before – while Ethne seemed to grow weaker and weaker. By the time we had made an overnight train journey to Canada, to give a series of concerts in Ottawa, she was obviously ill again, feverish and shaking. On the first night, even my cosmetic skills could not hide her pallor.

'It's no good, Ethne,' I said briskly, sweeping into her dressing room as she changed out of her evening gown. 'This has got to stop.'

'Yes . . . you're right. . . . I'm sure to feel better after a few days' rest.'

'No. That's not what I meant. I mean it's got to stop – all of it. The whole tour.'

Ethne sank down on her dressing stool. The face that stared back from under the bright make-up lights was white and drawn, the eyes staring. 'Loveday . . . I can't. . . . Think of the people we'll disappoint . . . and Mr Dumeau will be *furious*.' Dumeau was the organiser of the Canadian tour.

'I agree that it's a shame to disappoint people, but if you're too ill they'll just have to be disappointed. And as for Dumeau – I'll deal with him.'

I knew that I was going to have to fly in the face of the authorities, and that I would not be popular. 'But, Mam'selle,' blustered Dumeau, a pompous little French Canadian, 'it is impossible, quite impossible, at this stage, to cancel the tour. . . . Quite apart from the fact that the sponsors will look ridiculous, there is the money . . . there are financial commitments—'

'Money is *not* my prime consideration,' I blazed, 'and it should not be yours, either! We should all be concerned with the health of Miss Finzel, first and foremost.'

'Quite so. But perhaps if she could manage one more concert – just one more night. Preceded by a notice in the press with news of her illness. Now, that would be a *coup de foudre – hein?* We would have all the publicity we could ever need . . . a packed house. . . .'

I wavered for a while. Dumeau was very persuasive, and Ethne insisted that she could manage one more performance. In the end I put a call through to Donald in Oxford. I didn't want to worry Frank and Jeanie Finzel, but Donald could be relied on for sound advice.

Besides, I found that I had missed him while I was away and wanted to hear his voice.

'Sweet Jesus Christ!' he stormed. 'God, if I could get my hands on. . . . Don't let those bastards get another note out of her, d'you hear? Poor wee Ethne, what is all this doing to her? If she's ill, she must come home at once! At once!'

I immediately cancelled the special farewell performance. Instinct had already told me that it was the right thing to do.

The most agonising time in my life was during those months in 1938, when I knew that something was wrong but was unable to do anything.

Ethne continued on a punishing round of concerts, and the Voice reached new heights, but she suffered from cold after cold, fever after fever. I confided my fears to Jeanie, and she agreed that Ethne needed more rest. But she wouldn't rest.

The storm finally broke one day in June. I ran into the music room at Camelot, where Ethne was rehearsing, waving a letter aloft.

'Ethne! Ethne! Look at this. You've finally reached the top!' It was a letter from Buckingham Palace, inviting 'our most distinguished contralto, Miss Ethne Finzel', to go and sing before members of the royal family: the king and queen, old Queen Mary, the Duke and Duchess of Kent. . . .

'I wonder if "that woman" will be mentioned. Ethne? What's wrong?'

She was sitting staring at the letter, crying as though her heart would break.

'Ethne, darling!' I threw my arms around her, but she continued to weep. I knew why. 'You're ill, aren't you?' I asked in a low voice.

She nodded.

'Ethne, you must see a doctor.'

'I have.'

I felt my heartbeat quicken. I barely trusted my voice. 'And . . . oh God, what did he say? Why didn't you—?'

'I've got cancer.'

I stared at her. For a long while I simply could not believe it. Not Ethne, I kept saying inside my head, not this shining natural talent. Cut down at the height of her career – the sort of thing that happens in books.

Out loud I said: 'I wish to God you'd told me, Ethne!'

'I wanted to, Loveday,' she said through her sobs. 'But I didn't think I should. You've done so much for me already . . . worried about everything for me. . . .'

'Oh, Ethne . . .' I said, putting my arms around her and pressing her head against my chest. 'You silly old fool!'

Ethne never did sing at Buckingham Palace.

The doctors admitted her straight away to a private London clinic, where they carried out an operation to remove a tumour. Her work, of course, had to be cancelled. But a fortnight after the operation she was looking well, sitting up in bed and smiling serenely.

'I *shall* sing again, Loveday,' she said. 'I shall. The doctors say they have a new deep-ray therapy that can help me get better.'

'We'll see,' I said patting her hand. 'Take it slowly.'

'Of course she'll bloomin' well get better!' cried Frank Finzel. 'That's what I'm paying these doctors a fortune for, to make my little girl well again!'

Superficially, he had enormous confidence in Harley Street, and gave the impression of believing that the more money he paid, the better chance there was of a cure. But I knew that he was simply covering his own inability to come to terms with the severity of Ethne's condition.

After she left the clinic, Frank and Jeanie whisked her off to

Eastbourne to stay with her aunt, during which time, according to the postcards I received, Ethne was 'in great form', taking long walks on the beach and breathing the good sea-air. Once back at Camelot at the beginning of the autumn, she began to rehearse again, for Elgar's 'Dream of Gerontius'. The winter brought her new difficulties. Ethne's condition made her particularly sensitive to cold and draughts, causing rheumaticky pains in her legs, and I had to make sure that the room she was using to rehearse was heated by several fires.

Ethne was right. She *did* sing again. To tumultuous applause she stepped on to the stage in the Royal Albert Hall to sing her best-known role – the part of the Angel in 'Gerontius'. The pale sick Ethne seemed to recede as the warm rich notes floated into the auditorium. The Voice did not let her down. There was not even the slightest tremor. At the end of her last aria, she acknowledged the standing ovation and walked slowly and with great dignity off the stage. The ecstatic audience continued to cheer, unaware that anything untoward was happening.

I knew better.

I hurried backstage to her dressing room, and found a calm smiling Ethne accepting congratulations. 'Ethne, is there anything I can do for you, darling?'

'Yes. Take me to the hospital.'

She died on a cold November day three weeks later, with her parents at her bedside.

I had summoned Mel and Donald from Oxford, and took them straight from Paddington to the hospital. But after Mel had been with her for only a few minutes she came out into the corridor again.

'It's you she wants to see, Loveday.' There was disappointment on Mel's face, but she spoke without rancour.

'Loveday. . . .' Ethne took my hand. 'I know I've never said much . . . I'm not very good with words . . . but I do so want to thank you. . . . You've been so very kind to me. Like family really. I don't know what I would have done without you these last three years. . . .'

I watched my tears splash down on to her thin hand.

'Don't cry, Loveday!' This hardly sounded like the timid Ethne, so firm were the words. 'You're the bravest of all of them.'

Then she seemed to lose strength, and sank back on her pillows. 'I always knew this would happen . . . it was like a sad tune at the back of my mind. And it was the sadness that made me want to sing.'

Ethne's parents found it impossible to come to terms with her death.

Especially Frank. I went to Camelot to discuss the funeral arrangements with them and found him sitting in an armchair listening to his favourite recording of 'An die Musik', with tears streaming down his face. He didn't speak, but just lifted the gramophone needle and put it back to the beginning of the song, over and over again. . . .

You see, the Voice was still with us. Ethne was gone, but the Voice could still be conjured up, to fill the air with its vibrant beauty. I found it quite eerie. Jane Clifford suggested that perhaps we might like a recording to be played at the funeral, but I vetoed the idea completely. The funeral would be bad enough without that.

It was held in St Luke's. The church was packed to the rafters and, outside, the Gardens were filled with crowds of wellwishers clutching white flowers, so many people that a policeman had to help clear our path into the church. The choir sang a favourite anthem of Ethne's, and then Edwin gave an address about the joy that she had brought to the whole world with her music.

As I listened, it struck me suddenly that this was the first time Edwin and Mel had been under the same roof for several years. And during those years Mel had raised a son that Edwin didn't even know about. The more I thought about this, the more extraordinary it seemed, until I was not able to think about anything else, not even poor Ethne. I looked at Mel. She was wearing a hat without a veil, and her face looked sallow and drawn. Her black-gloved hands were clenched tightly together. I recognised that she was in a special kind of shock; the shock that comes from the death of someone to whom you were not as close as you ought to have been. Her relationship with Ethne had always been difficult. It wasn't just simple jealousy. Mel seemed to think that their roles within the family had become confused; transposed or inverted. She had assumed that she would be famous while the silent Ethne. . . . If she was jealous, it was of the adoration that Frank showered on Ethne. She wouldn't have admitted it, but she wanted her father's approval. Perhaps she was thinking about that during Edwin's speech of thanksgiving. She scarcely seemed aware of his presence.

Edwin, on the other hand, seemed painfully aware of Mel. His eyes kept straying in her direction.

After the burial in a graveyard that had become a sea of white flowers, Edwin moved amongst the mourners, offering professional words of comfort. Frank and Jeanie Finzel, Ashley Player, Neville. . . . I watched him; watched his dark eyes flicker as he talked, away from the face of the person he was addressing. He ensured that his progress took him ever nearer to Mel, who was standing with her feet planted slightly apart, staring at the flower-massed grave.

'Mel. . . .'

He kept his voice so low that from where I was standing I couldn't really hear it, only see his lips frame the single urgent syllable. And his hand, moving out to touch the sleeve of her black coat. . . .

'No!' Mel jumped back as though she had been scalded. Shocked faces turned in her direction.

'Keep away from me!'

And she started to run, pushing past people, scattering the black-clad mourners in her path as she fled from St Luke's and into Magnolia Gardens.

'You haven't told him . . . anything, have you, Loveday?'

'No. As I promised.'

'Oh, thank God for that. . . .' Mel sank down wearily into Mother's rocking chair and peeled off her black gloves. I had guessed correctly that she would go and take sanctuary in my house and had followed her there. Meanwhile the stunned mourners would be convening at Camelot for the funeral baked meats and the drier-than-dust sherry.

'Pour me some gin, there's a darling,' said Mel. 'Mother's ruin,' she said as I handed her the glass, and grinned at the irony. 'This mother's ruined, eh, running and hiding, unable to appear in public with her son – the *vicar's* son, of all things. . . .' She took a gulp of the gin and fell silent. I watched her face closely. 'I know what you're going to say, Loveday. You're going to say that today I shouldn't be thinking about myself, I should be thinking about Ethne.'

317

'I wasn't going to say that.'

'Well, it's true, isn't it? You know, years ago I had this fantasy that *I* was the one who was going to die young. I plotted all sorts of grand deaths for myself – wasting away to an early grave like the heroine of a Victorian novel. If *this* had happened then, I think I would have felt that Ethne had stolen "my" death, that it should have been me in that coffin. . . .'

'But you don't feel that way now?' I poured myself an inch of gin and went to sit on the white ottoman.

Mel shook her head, running her fingers through her dark hair in that same restless gesture of old. 'I think I'd just about managed to come to terms with . . . what Ethne was. Anyway, I like life too much now I've got Gabriel. But walking behind the coffin today when they played that dreadful dreary music . . . it was strange.' Mel's face was set, tearless. 'I was trying to imagine Ethne lying inside that wooden casing, but the imagination just can't do it, can it? There's a gap there that it can't bridge. I'm rambling now. It's the gin. Give me some more, Loveday, there's a dear.'

I handed her the bottle, glancing at my watch. They would be wondering about us at the wake, and I didn't want Frank and Jeanie getting more upset. Somehow I would have to persuade Mel to come with me. 'And you won't speak to Edwin, even now?'

She shook her head. 'I've spent five years putting up defences; I'm not going to have them broken down now, whatever I might feel for Edwin.' Anyone with less experience of Mel would have missed the note of longing in her voice. I did not. 'What I said earlier about having to run and hide . . . it's true. Oxford isn't far enough. I've decided that I'm going to take Gabriel to live in Paris.'

'Paris! Oh, Mel, do be sensible. With the political situation as it is—'

'Now who's been listening to Uncle Donald!'

'And what will you *do* there?'

'I don't know. But I'll find something. I lived there alone before, remember, and I was happy there. And you, Loveday, what will you do now?'

'I don't know.' It was true. I hadn't thought about it, not even for a moment. I had been so emotionally involved in Ethne's death that I hadn't thought of it in terms of the loss of a job.

'Has Uncle Donald spoken to you?'

'Spoken to me? What about?'

Mel smiled, tipping the chair forward so that her feet were on the ground and the rocking stopped. 'You do realise that he's in love with you, don't you? I think he always has been, ever since you were a little girl.'

'Nonsense! A diehard Marxist like Donald doesn't believe in romantic love!'

'Romantic love. . . .' Mel sighed and looked far into the distance. 'But you're evading the issue, aren't you, dear Loveday? Just because a man's not supposed to believe in something doesn't mean it can't happen to him. It just prevents him from admitting it, that's all.'

I stood up, and pinned my hat on again, pulling the veil down over my face so that Mel was viewed through a haze of black polka-dots. 'Mel, we really must go over to Camelot now. People will be offended—'

'No. You go. I've paid my respects to Ethne, and that's what I wanted to do. Please tell Mother and Father that I've had to get back to Gabriel. . . .' She came towards me and kissed me, lifting my veil first; a curiously nuptial gesture. 'And now, like Cinderella, I'm going to disappear. You won't tell, Loveday, will you?'

I didn't want Mel to go to Paris.

An irrational person probably would have claimed to have a 'bad feeling about it'. My own reaction was to look at the facts. In March, Hitler had invaded Austria, and there were rumours that Czechoslovakia was next on the list. At home in England air-raid precautions were being instigated, buildings were sand-bagged and new official organisations were springing up, known only by their absurd initials and putting those who worked for them in a position to order everyone about. Uniforms started popping up everywhere, and I must admit to looking at the ones I saw on women with more than a passing interest. Those severely cut suits and pert little hats. . . .

But Mel packed up and went to Paris anyway, as ever flying in the face of reason. She sent a card promising to keep in touch and to send an address as soon as she had one.

When I saw this card I knew at once what was going to happen. And a few days after Ethne's funeral it did. I saw Edwin Clifford walking up the steps towards my front door.

I had just been to see Ronald Colman in *The Prisoner of Zenda*, and I was still dressed in my coat and hat. I had the absurd idea of going through the french windows and into the garden, and slipping round the side of the house without being seen. I dismissed this as a ridiculous Mel-like scheme, but I did resort to standing back out of sight of the window and pressing myself against the wall, so that it would appear there was no one in.

Damn you, Clifford, leave me alone. . . .

The doorbell rang again. And again. I flung the front door open. 'Edwin, I'm afraid I was just going out. . . .'

He burst past me and into the house, his enormous frame almost knocking me over. 'I'm sorry, Loveday, I simply have to talk to you.'

It always made me angry when people said they were sorry when they weren't at all. I was very cold. 'Edwin, if this is about Mel again, I have nothing further to say. I'd be grateful if you would go.'

He was already up the stairs and into the sitting room.

'Edwin!'

'Something's happened to her, hasn't it? I can just tell. Something – I don't know – why else would she run away from me like that?'

I didn't answer.

To my surprise and horror, Edwin gave a cry of rage and swooped on me, crushing me against the wall.

'*Aaahh!*' I could only make a gasping sound.

He towered over me, his large hands pressing on my shoulderblades, his dark eyes flashing. I thought for a moment he might strike me . . . or kiss me.

Then his muscles went limp, slackening his hold, and he hung his head. 'Ah, Loveday . . . pretty little Loveday. I could never hurt *you*. Always managing things for other people – what do you ever take for yourself?' He looked around the room in a distracted way, at the pile of glossy magazines, the arrangements of fresh flowers. 'You were always so smart, so independent. If only you could have been more like Mel – or she more like you.'

'Mel's more independent than you know,' I said, almost without thinking.

'So I was right. You *do* know what I'm talking about. And you still won't tell me where she is?'

'I promised her.'

'Loveday, do you still not understand why I have to know? Nothing can be good or beautiful or worthy any more. My duties as a priest are a charade, my marriage. . . .' He sighed.

I noticed for the first time how pale and gaunt he had become. 'Edwin, please—'

'No, I'm being unfair to you, asking you to break your word. I'll leave you in peace. There must be other people I can ask.'

And he went.

Edwin's visit left me troubled.

It was only too clear how desperate he had become, and that made the situation dangerous. It seemed entirely possible that he could go and pester Frank and Jeanie Finzel, and if they told Edwin that Mel had a four-year-old son he might well reveal his identity as the father – which would make life difficult for everyone.

The only person whose advice would be valid was Donald McDowell.

It was an easy decision to make, for the emptiness that followed Ethne's death had made me long for the self-absorbed bustle of Oxford. A few weeks before Christmas I took an evening train from Paddington. Dr McDowell had had to pop out, the porter at All Souls informed me, but he had asked if I would kindly wait in his study. He delivered the message with a sniff, eyeing my gauntlet gloves with their chinchilla cuffs as though I had stolen them. There was open disapproval at all times of female callers in that exclusively male bastion, and particularly late at night.

In Donald's book-lined study a fire was blazing. His papers were spread out all over the desk, and he had clearly been working before he went out. I succumbed to temptation and read what he had just written.

Donald's post involved his publishing sarcastic reviews of the work of postgraduate scholars and other academics who had the poor sense to stray into his field. The name of the unfortunate author in this case was, I noted, Walter Drayton, Esquire.

'*It is a pity*', Donald wrote, '*that the author did not take the trouble to inform himself of some of the elementary facts underlying the mores of the British working class. We would then be less likely to find such howlers as "the universal brotherhood of the oppressed*".' (He had given the words heavy, scornful quotation marks.) '*It is also a pity that the money spent on the education of these fine young minds did not result in them mastering spelling of vernacular terms in everyday use. These errors are bound to make the reader question whether public-school fees might have been more effectively spent on correcting some of the social ills of which the author purports to inform us. . . .*'

The last sentence had been deleted, and Donald had simply ended the review: '*Scholarly rubbish; the work of people living in an ivory tower with no more grasp of the issues than Herod had of child welfare.*'

I laughed out loud when I read this last statement, delivered with the thick black strokes of Donald's cavalier handwriting.

And as I laughed I realised two things. That Donald McDowell was an extraordinary man. And that I was very, very fond of him.

After I had spoken to Donald, I returned to London . . . and waited.

He had sworn and blustered at first about 'other people's dirty linen', but I had succeeded in talking him round. Edwin should know about his son, he decided. 'Damn it, whatever creed or class we are, we should all have respect for the truth. A man isn't alive if he is forced to hide from Truth!'

But I was not to be the one to tell him, and thus I would be exonerated from breaking my word to Mel. Donald would tell Edwin, that Mel had borne him a child, but not where she was. It was an awkward compromise, but it was the best we could think of. And we decided that Donald should write to Edwin, rather than meet him face to face.

'My brawling days are over, lass!' he said, with his crooked grin. 'And that Clifford fellow is bigger than me. I fancy he might lay a punch on me if I lost my temper with him. . . .'

And so I waited. I waited for Edwin to come hammering on my door again, but he didn't. He conducted the Christmas services as usual, and if he and Jane Clifford were seen about in the parish less than usual it was not considered worthy of comment.

I had far too much time on my hands to be able to forget the matter. I was without work, and with no financial pressure driving me. Ethne's will had stipulated that the earnings from her career (and she had spent very little) were to be divided equally between Mel and myself, and so were any future revenues from her recordings. I was hardly rich, but I had a measure of financial security, and I was grateful to Ethne for that. I began to plan a holiday. Europe was out of the question, but I thought I would like to return to America and visit some of the friends I had made during the tour in 1938. Mel's reaction to the news about the money was less straightforward. 'I feel I don't deserve it,' she wrote from Paris, 'and that in turn makes me dreadfully guilty. I shall assuage the guilt by making sure Gabriel reaps the benefits. Paris is gay and defiant in the face of Hitler, normal life prevails. . . .' She had given an address, in the Val de Grâce quarter on the Left Bank, but predictably there was no mention of Edwin.

In the end my curiosity got the better of me. After New Year festivities had died down, and the ostentatious Christmas tree had disappeared from the window of number 26, I went to call on Edwin. I wanted to see him alone, so I watched out of the window until I saw Jane Clifford, in tweed coat and felt hat, closing the gate of the rectory behind her and marching off on some philanthropic errand with her basket over her arm.

I had never been inside 26 Magnolia Gardens before. It was furnished in quiet good taste, with deep carpets that muffled all sound and dark oil-paintings of aged clerics in their robes. There was no dirt or dust or untidiness anywhere, but there was the same dead atmosphere that I had hated so much in number 50.

I knew as soon as I saw Edwin's face that he had heard from Donald. He wore his dog-collar, but beneath his angry grimace it looked like a theatrical prop or, worse still, some sort of macabre joke.

'Does Jane know?' I asked, once we had seated ourselves in the drawing room.

'Not yet.'

'I think she really should.'

'I know.' Edwin stared down at his hands. His body was hunched, tense, dispelling the easy grace that had once been its most striking characteristic. He laughed a mirthless laugh. 'Jane and I are at the end of a very short rope. This will be the wrench that breaks it. She demands all or nothing. I know that Jane looks to the world like a very pious lady but, believe me, beneath the piety she's tough, ruthless . . . almost vicious. She insists that if I do not carry out my duties as she thinks I should, if I do not *appear* to be happy, then she will drum me out of the Church—'

'But can she?'

'Oh, yes. She has the power to do that.' He laughed again. 'That's why I married her, for her father's influence. What a wonderful piece of irony.'

'Leave the Church, Edwin,' I said, falling back on directness. 'Just leave it, get out.'

'Oh, I'd like to, I assure you. But without Mel and . . . and the child . . . what will I be doing it for? It's not a question of "all or nothing", is it? It's nothing or nothing. If I were to stay with the Church, I tell myself, I might at least be doing other people some good. Otherwise, I might as well end it all.'

He buried his head in his hands. I stared at him, appalled.

Then an unmistakable sound intruded. The sound of a key turning in the lock.

'That'll be Jane. She said she wouldn't be gone long.'

'I should leave—'

'No, don't.'

Jane came into the drawing room, her fine English gentle-woman's complexion slightly flushed from the cold January air. I had only ever seen her in her 'professional' role of rector's wife, but here in private her expression remained exactly the same. She didn't scowl or sneer, but wore the eternal bemused smile.

'You're *entertaining*, Edwin. . . .' The smile was still there, but the inference was obvious. Edwin was not to be trusted on his own.

'We were discussing Mel Finzel,' I said boldly, fixing her with a stare but not bothering to smile back.

'Mel Finzel . . .,' said Jane slowly as she began to peel off her kid gloves. 'That poor child. That wretched deluded creature – we should all feel sorry for her. However, that's in the past. Edwin, have you prepared the text for Evensong? I left the marker in the Bible for you . . . here . . . .' She pointed to the large Bible that had a conspicuous place on the table in the centre of the room.

'Tell her,' said Edwin without looking up. 'Tell Jane about Mel.'

I gazed steadily at Jane. 'Edwin has recently discovered', I said, 'that after the end of his . . . friendship with Mel she gave birth to his child. A boy.'

There was no sound in that sterile pin-neat room. Jane's face had turned an ugly colour. 'How dare you!' she said to Edwin.

She did not raise her well-modulated voice, but its tone was deadly. '*How dare you call yourself a man of God!*'

Edwin did not reply. He did not even look up, but I could see his chest rising and falling as though he were struggling to contain some miscreant force, and his hands were clenched tightly together.

'People like you abuse the good name of the Church of England,' Jane went on. 'How would your congregation feel if they knew the truth of what lay behind your tawdry high-church rituals and your pathetic romanticism! You disgust me! You're incapable of distinguishing devotion from self-love.'

'*You bitch!*' Edwin flung back his arms as though he were breaking invisible bands around his chest, leaping to his feet. '*I've had enough, d'you hear me, enough!*'

And he picked up the Bible and hurled it at Jane's head.

It struck her shoulder and fell on to an elegant Hepplewhite chest, sending a bowl of pot-pourri smashing to the floor. The dried brown petals spilled out of the broken glass and on to the carpet where they lay like discoloured confetti. Like a symbol of a marriage that had long since ended.

'What do *you* know of devotion?' Edwin was shouting. 'You and your "practical Christianity". Those good deeds are just a sham! You've no love in your heart! They're all carefully stage-managed to reflect the worth of St Jane! You're so strong on pity, well, it's not Mel you should pity, but yourself. For your coldness and your barrenness!'

Jane stood quite still, but her eyes were narrowed in anger. 'Have you finished, Edwin?'

But he had not. 'I don't want the sort of God you worship. I'm going to leave your precious Church – *and my God will still love me!*'

There was a stunned silence.

Jane turned on her heel and stormed from the room. We heard the front door slam, and Edwin stood up and went into the kitchen. He was distracted, silent.

I followed him.

'Edwin, I think I ought to go now.'

'No,' he said. 'No, I don't want you to!'

I was reaching for the doorknob when Edwin's hand appeared from nowhere, locked the kitchen door and pulled out the key. It all happened very slowly; in slow motion.

'Edwin, don't be ridiculous; there's nothing I can do for you.'

He ignored me, veering clumsily around the room, opening drawers and cupboards, looking for something.

'Edwin! If you don't open this door at once, I'm going to start screaming!'

He glanced at me and continued his search.

I rattled the doorknob furiously. When I turned round again, Edwin had found what he was looking for. He opened a drawer and pulled out a long knife. Its blade was smooth and cool-looking, and glinted beneath the light.

My God, he's finally lost his mind . . . he's going to kill me. . . .

I pressed my back against the door.

And Edwin lifted the blade, examined it dispassionately, then laid it against his own wrist.

I dialled Mel's number in Paris with trembling fingers.

'Hello.' Mel's voice was very faint and far away. 'Heavens, it's you, Loveday! Something wrong?'

'Mel, it's Edwin. He's coming to see you. I told him where to go. Please forgive me.'

There was a silence, either of shock or of anger – I couldn't tell. Then she said something that I couldn't hear through the crackling.

'Mel, please forgive me – I had no choice.' My own voice was high, hysterical.

'. . . Forgive me.'

FINALE

Mel

HE FOUND ME WAITING FOR HIM outside Le Sélect.

I would always remember that beautiful day in March, when the gentlest of breezes ruffled the brand-new leaves on the trees that lined the boulevards. As he walked towards me I felt that old rush of longing.

My beautiful Edwin.

His dazzling smile was the same, but he looked stiff in his immaculate 'civilian' suit and tie, and he was dreadfully formal with me. 'Thank you for agreeing to see me.'

'I'll get you a drink.' I flagged down a waiter and ordered in French. 'I'm still horribly addicted to these cream cakes,' I said, with my mouthful of *tarte aux fraises*, 'as you can see!'

Edwin laughed, and after that things were a bit more like old times. Except, of course, for one thing.

Gabriel Finzel.

'I just want to see him,' said Edwin in a low voice, after he had finished his *café calva*. 'I won't stay long. You needn't tell him who I am—'

'It's all right.' I patted Edwin's hand, reassuring him. 'I said I'd take you to see him and I won't go back on my word.'

We walked back through the Jardin des Tuileries and over the Pont du Carrousel as it was going dark. 'What do you do during the day?' Edwin asked. 'Don't you ever get lonely?'

'Heavens, no! I work at an orphanage three days a week; it's part of a charitable foundation. And the Left Bank is teeming with the most fascinating people – writers, journalists, émigrés. I've got to know a lot of my neighbours, and some of them are now friends.'

'This is Colette,' I said, as the smiling nursemaid opened the door of my small apartment in the rue Paul Nicole, 'and *this*' – I brought forward my beloved son, who had been clinging behind Colette's skirt with his thumb in his mouth – 'is Gabriel.'

He was a few weeks short of his fifth birthday. His blond hair had darkened to the colour of ripe corn, and I guessed that it would eventually be a rich brown like Edwin's. His eyes were like mine – grey with a funny yellowish ring round the pupils.

'What a beautiful child,' murmured Edwin, and as he gazed at his son's face for the first time I saw the painful recognition in his eyes. But his behaviour was completely natural, and I felt a grateful rush of love for him. He didn't pick Gabriel up, or do anything that would have seemed possessive. Instead he fished in his pocket. 'Here, I've got something to show you.' He took out a shiny red fire engine, and the two of them played with it together.

'Thank you' was all he said after Colette had put Gabriel to bed. 'It would please me very much if I could take you out to dinner – a token of my gratitude.' The intensity of emotion in that small room had made us very stiff and formal again. 'I hear Maurice Chevalier is at the Casino de Paris. Or we could go to the Cirque Médrano. . . .'

'No,' I said. 'Nothing like that. Let's just walk.'

And as soon as we were out in the Parisian night, with the lamplight winking on the Seine, and reflecting in the 'ox-eye' windows of the mansard roofs, we were the old Edwin and Mel again, or as near to them as we could ever be.

'We're quite near to St Séverin,' I said. 'Shall we go there again?'

We gazed up at the spire of the church, and then across the river at the floodlit steeple of Notre-Dame. 'Did we *really* climb up there?' asked Edwin.

And we both knew that we would not be trying to reach heaven this time.

'Surely it will be dangerous if you stay in Paris much longer?'

We had walked along the rue de Saints-Pères and across the Boulevard St-Germain to the Brasserie Lipp where we had eaten a delicious dinner and were now drinking ice-cold Slavia.

I considered this question carefully. 'The French are not consistent,' I said. 'At first their attitude was to dance the night away, and pretend they didn't care. I even saw a travel agent offering "Voyages de la Paix", five-day trips to Germany. Can you *imagine*, Edwin! Then they feigned indifference, claiming to be dreadfully *tired* after losing a million and a half men in the Great War – no tanks and aeroplanes to fight with, so what was it

330

to do with them. That sort of thing.' I chewed thoughtfully on my cocktail olive. A group of soldiers came into the restaurant, dressed in the traditional French *bleu horizon* and carrying manganese steel helmets. 'When Chamberlain came away empty-handed, and then the Jewish pogroms started in Germany, people started to worry rather more. A lot of Americans started to leave. Now . . . I'm not sure.'

'My dear Mel—'

'Don't worry, Edwin, I won't let the Huns get the better of me!' I grinned at him, and he smiled back, but I could tell that I had not allayed his fears.

Before he returned to his hotel we walked some more, to the centre of the city. We saw more and more people, and finally the streets became blocked altogether.

'Dear God, there are thousands of them!' said Edwin, as we approached the Châtelet. 'We ought to turn back.'

'It's another protest meeting, I expect. About the treatment of the Jews. They'll have come to hand in a petition to the Chambre des Députés. . . .'

We retraced our steps with difficulty, because scuffles had already broken out and rage and anger seemed to spread through the protesters like fire through paper, until we were watching, horrified, from the safety of a doorway as they tore down railings, ripped up paving stones, set cars alight. . . .

'Look, Mel. Good God, what on earth are the policemen doing?' The *gendarmes* had taken off their swirling blue capes and were using them to beat the protesters.

'Those capes have hems lined with lead,' I told Edwin. A few feet away from us a Jewish girl stumbled and fell on to the cobblestones, her head bleeding.

'Mel, I'm taking you away from Paris. You can't stay here. It's just too dangerous.' Edwin put his hands on my shoulders and turned me around to face him. I shivered at his touch. We stood facing one another in the narrow doorway. 'I wasn't going to say this to you yet, but Mel, my dearest Mel, I've come to Paris to offer myself to you, heart, body and soul. I've left the Church. I've left Jane. After a little while she and I can be divorced, and we can marry.'

I stared at him. 'Edwin, I can't—'

'Well, at least think about the other thing. About letting me take you away from Paris.'

'I like it here.' It was a silly thing to say, but it was the first thing that came into my head.

'I know that. I understand. But if not for your sake, then for the sake of . . . our son.' He faltered over the words. 'For Gabriel. You want him to be safe, don't you?'

I could not argue with that.

The next day, 15 March, Hitler invaded Czechoslovakia.

Panic in the city reached new heights, and rich Parisians fled in their large cars. Edwin decided that we should leave at once, and managed to book us a night passage from Calais in a passenger boat called *Athenia*. We almost missed the crossing because the time we allowed to get to Calais was pathetically inadequate in the end; the roads were blocked by vehicles full of people with the same idea. It was the same when we reached the quayside. Hundreds of people were thronging up the gangplank, pushing and shoving. Gabriel took one look at them and started to bawl, a sentiment which I shared.

I simply wouldn't have managed without Edwin. His sheer height made it possible for him to push his way up the gangplank, holding Gabriel above his head, while I held on to his coat. There were over a thousand people on the *Athenia*, mostly Americans and Canadians who hoped to get a passage home from England, and only twenty-six lifeboats. A hasty long division in my head confirmed my fears: if anything happened to the boat, we couldn't all be saved. And in the dark waters lurked German submarines. . . . My over-active imagination was fuelled by the pictures I had seen of their ugly black silhouettes with a large 'U' on the side.

Edwin found us a cabin. It was small, with four berths and no toilet facilities, but at least we could have some privacy for the few hours that we were aboard. He played with Gabriel, running up and down the deck with him until he was exhausted and fell asleep as soon as I laid him down in his bunk.

'We'd better turn out the lights,' I whispered to Edwin, perching myself on the edge of the bunk opposite my son's sleeping form.

Edwin went to the switch by the cabin door and then stood over me in the darkness. He cupped my chin in his hand and lifted my face. 'Mel . . . oh, Mel . . . I love you so much. . . .'

I took him into my arms, drowning in the remembered longing

of the past five years. Our bodies seemed to know one another so well that it seemed impossible to believe that this was truly only the second time that we had ever done this, made love. I could not count the times that I had wanted to.

And as it grew light we woke Gabriel and went on deck together to watch the magnificent cliffs of Dover sliding into view, grey rather than white in the early-morning mist. It was a lovely sight. I hadn't anticipated this – feeling glad to be home.

We stood there, the two of us, with Gabriel in between. Like a family.

I turned and smiled at Edwin as the wind whipped my hair about my face.

'Well,' he said, 'have you decided?'

Loveday

ON THE DAY BEFORE MEL'S LETTER ARRIVED in Magnolia Gardens, I had been to Oxford to tell Donald of my decision.

I found him sitting in the armchair in his study, trying on his gas-mask.

'How do I look?' The question was muffled by the rubber breathing-apparatus. 'Damned if I'm ever going to wear the bastard!' he said as he struggled out of it and pushed his unruly silver locks back from his forehead. He put the gas-mask upside down on the hearth. 'I'll use it to keep my tobacco in.'

'I've been given one, too,' I said, sitting down in my usual chair, facing him. 'I suppose that means it's definite.'

'Ay. I reckon the warmongers'll have their way before the end of the summer.'

Donald sighed, and I remembered that in the last war he had chosen to go to prison rather than fight, and that the slight bump in his nose was from the break inflicted by a blackshirt's pistol-butt. Outside, a chapel bell was sounding and gentle April drizzle misted the windows. I could see a crowd of students in Catte Street using their books to keep the water off their heads, laughing as though things like wars were no concern of theirs.

'So . . . you came to tell me how it went in London?'

I smiled at him. 'I had my interview yesterday, at Princeton House in High Holborn, and . . . I'm now the proud possessor of a railway warrant to take me to the WRNS headquarters in Chatham. The First Officer – the lady who interviewed me – said I'd have to do three months in the ranks, and then there was a good chance I'd get a commission. I'll be an officer – think of that!'

'You little vixen! You just want one of those fancy white uniforms.'

'Those are only worn on overseas duty. For the moment it's three pairs of hose (black), nine stiff collars and hideous regulation bloomers.' I shuddered. 'According to the clothing list I've been given. No glamour, I'm afraid.'

'And yet it's something you want to do. I can tell that.' There was a long pause, during which Donald examined his fingernails: an uncharacteristically self-conscious gesture, I thought. 'And, if you had decided against joining up, I was going to offer you marriage. . . .'

'Go on,' I prompted.

'Well, we're good friends, The Waif and I, even though I'm old enough to be her father. We share the same, largely cynical view of the world. Now, you know I don't have much use for marriage, but I can offer you security, the respectability of a name. Things you've never had. You could have a good life as the wife of a don. . . .'

I felt my heart pound, and tears prick at my eyes.

'I know you, Miss Loveday; I've always known that these things matter to you. I can offer them, and in return you can give me companionship. We could come to an arrangement. . . .'

I was still reeling from the curious sensation of having my soul laid bare. For old times' sake, I now turned the tables on Donald. 'And you do love me a bit – more than a bit – don't you?'

'Ay, I do,' he said gruffly, avoiding my eye as he reached for his tobacco. 'But, if you've set your heart on a career in the forces, there's not much point my whining on about it.'

'Donald. . . .' I took his hand for the first time since I was a little child, stroking it. 'Donald, I would very much like to be your wife. But I have to do this thing first. My last fling with independence, if you like. Then, when the war's over, or I'm tired of it – whichever happens first – I'll come back. Will you wait for me?'

Donald pretended to consider my request. 'Ay, I reckon I'll do that. Reckon I'll still be here sitting by this fire when you get back from your warmongering!'

The next morning I walked slowly down the stairs of number 47 Magnolia Gardens and picked up the letter from the mat. Yawning, I carried it into the morning room and propped it against the toast-rack. I had slept badly, lying awake and staring at the unfamiliar gas-mask on the table beside my bed. I had been thinking about Donald. And about a promise I had once made, and broken.

I picked up the letter and looked at it. It was from Mel. I hadn't heard from her since I had telephoned Paris, and part of me had been afraid that I would never hear from her again.

I unsealed the envelope and took out the letter. It was post-marked Wales.

'*Darling Loveday, This will come as a surprise, I know, but I am renting a house in north Wales, in Portmeirion. It's a mock-Mediterranean village by the sea; very charming with pink and blue and yellow villas, and statues all about in odd corners. It's run as a sort of artists' colony, so there are lots of terribly interesting people about. More important, it will be safe here for Gabriel when you-know-what comes.*

'*Edwin is with me.*

'*He came to France, as you probably know. Oh, Loveday, you asked for my forgiveness, but can you ever forgive me? I placed such a burden on you, making you keep my secret all those years. It was more than I had a right to expect.*

'*Edwin has asked me to marry him and I've given him my answer. The answer is that I don't know. We seem to be happy together for now, but one thing I've learned is that one's feelings constantly change. And the war brings so much uncertainty. Will you and I ever be back in Magnolia Gardens again? I wonder.*

'*I've told Edwin to ask me again in a few years' time. But by then, Loveday. . . .*

'*. . . Well, who knows what might have happened to us?*'